CONSUMER LAW AND PRACTICE

AUSTRALIA

LBC Information Services

Sydney

CANADA and the USA

Carswell

NEW ZEALAND

Brooker's

Auckland

SINGAPORE and MALAYSIA

Sweet & Maxwell Asia

Singapore and Kuala Lumpur

CONSUMER LAW AND PRACTICE

Fifth Edition

ROBERT LOWE, LL.B.
Solicitor

and

GEOFFREY WOODROFFE, M.A. (Cantab.)
Solicitor, Professor and Director of the
Centre for Consumer and Commercial Law Research,
Brunel University

with Precedents by

District Judge Stephen Gerlis

LONDON
SWEET & MAXWELL
1999

First Edition 1980
Second Edition 1985
Third Edition 1991
Reprinted 1993
Fourth Edition 1995
Reprinted 1996
Fifth Edition 1999

Published in 1999 by
Sweet & Maxwell Limited of
100 Avenue Road, Swiss Cottage,
London NW3 3PF
Phototypeset by MFK Information Services Ltd,
Hitchin, Herts.
Printed in England by
Clays Ltd, St Ives plc.

No natural forests were destroyed to make this product; only
farmed timber was used and replanted

A CIP catalogue record for this book is available from the
British Library

ISBN 0421 67170X

PREFACE

The Fourth Edition of this book was published in 1995 and this new Edition is designed to bring the text right up to date, and to widen its appeal. We can look at the changes under three main headings—past, present and future.

The major development in the past five years has been the activity of the Office of Fair Trading (OFT) in controlling unfair contract terms under the 1994 Regulations—almost entirely by persuasion (some might say coercion) rather than litigation. We examine this activity fully—with a number of "before and after" examples—in Chapter Nine. As foreshadowed in paragraph 9.03, the DTI announced on July 22, 1999 that regulations had been laid before Parliament that very day enabling action to be taken against unfair terms by the Consumers' Association, trading standards authorities, the Data Protection Registrar and the regulators for gas, electricity, water, rail and telecommunications.

Turning to the present, we have the fundamental changes to legal aid and civil litigation that will start to bite as we go to press—notably the extension of the small claims jurisdiction to £5000 in most cases. A new Chapter (Chapter Eleven) is devoted to this topic and we hope that this will help to make the book particularly useful to litigation advisers (and perhaps even litigants in person).

Finally, the future. Chapter Twenty-Seven foreshadows a number of changes to consumer credit in the light of various announcements by the DTI. Chapters Ten and Twenty-Eight deal with E.C. Directives on distance selling and consumer guarantees which are almost certain to become part of English law in the next two or three years. In addition, the Government has announced that it will place consumers at the heart of policy making; this will include (1) empowering trading standards officers to close down businesses that are trading fraudulently and (2) strengthening the enforcement powers of the OFT. We must wait and see how and when the White Paper, published as we go to press, will become law (for a summary of the proposals and a number of horror stories see *The Times*, July 23, 1999 at page 4).

The philosophy of the litigation reforms "use the courts as a last resort" has led to an expansion of the sections on Ombudsmen and Alternative Dispute Resolution in Chapter Ten, and we have added a brief section on the proposed new Consumer Councils in the major utility services. There is, of course, a limit to what a book of this size can include and we have not therefore dealt in any detail with the benefits which consumers will derive under the Competition Act 1998.

We would like to thank Alan Wilson (University of East London) who revised the chapter dealing with the E.C. Dimension; District Judge Gerlis who revised the county court precedents in light of the Civil Procedure Rules; and Professor Malcolm Leder who read some of the proofs and made a number of valuable suggestions.

As always we would like to hear from our readers with any comments or suggestions they may have.

We have managed to include a number of last minute changes in the final proofs; subject to this, we have tried to state the law as at July 1, 1999.

Robert Lowe
Geoffrey Woodroffe

PREFACE TO THE FIRST EDITION

There are many ways of writing a book on consumer protection. One can trace the historical development; one can analyse the economic and social effects; one can deal with the subject from a comparative point of view. In this book we have decided to concentrate on practical problems and remedies. The book is written primarily for law students and for those who are called upon to advise on consumer problems, whether legal or para-legal practitioners. We hope that it will also be useful to persons in industry and their legal advisers as an indication of the growing battery of controls—civil, criminal and administrative—which the law now imposes on business activity. With this aim in mind we have tried to adopt a very practical approach.

A further problem for writers on this subject is that of selection. The term "consumer protection" has no precise definition and it could quite properly be given an immensely wide meaning. Thus every citizen of this country is a consumer, or potential consumer, of welfare benefits, public utilities, health services, educational services and so on. Then again it can be argued that the term "consumer protection" should include the law relating to the supply of housing. Another relevant area is the law of competition which has an underlying consumer protection philosophy. Finally, we have had Government regulation of business activity and in particular we have had price control. In view of our basic approach outlined above we have decided not to deal in any detail with these wide areas. Indeed, we shall concentrate on the types of problem most likely to arise where an individual consumer orders goods or services from a supplier who then proceeds to render defective performance or no performance at all.

Our remedies-based approach has influenced the structure of this book. Part I is entitled "The Consumer and the Civil Law" and deals with such matters as defective performance of contracts to supply goods or services, product liability, the remedies available to the consumer, attempts to exclude them and finally the all-important question of how the remedies can be enforced. Special attention is given to the methods of extra-legal enforcement provided by the growing number of voluntary Codes of Practice. Part II of the book is entitled "The Consumer and the Criminal Law"; special consideration is given to the Trade Descriptions Act 1968 and there is also a chapter dealing with compensation orders. Part III of the book describes the most significant development of consumer protection—administrative control under the Fair Trading Act 1973. Part IV contains nine chapters dealing with "Consumer Protection in Credit Transactions". The book ends with a chapter entitled "The EEC Dimension".

This is a new venture and we would welcome suggestions for improvement. In the meantime we would like to thank the many people who took the trouble to read parts of the typescript and to answer our questions. Special thanks are due to a number of individuals at the Office of Fair Trading, Department of Trade, National Consumer Council, Society of Motor Manufacturers and Traders, Motor Agents Association and the Manchester Arbitration Scheme. The views which they expressed are necessarily personal ones but nevertheless we have found them of great value. We would also like to thank Bill Thomas (solicitor), Valerie Chiswell (consumer adviser), Malcolm Leder (Senior Lecturer at Middlesex Polytechnic), and Peter Chiswell, Peter Hawkins, Tony King, and Chris Whitehouse (all at the College of Law). All of them made very helpful suggestions and assisted in the tiresome task of proof reading.

At the time of going to press there is a Bill before Parliament entitled the Sale of Goods Bill. This is a pure consolidation measure which does not make any changes in the law. The future of the London Small Claims Court, which is discussed in Chapter 9, is still in the balance; we understand that a grant of £5,000 will enable it to survive.

We have tried to state the law as at October 1, 1979.

Robert Lowe
Geoffrey Woodroffe

CONTENTS

PART II: THE CONSUMER AND THE CRIMINAL LAW

PART III: ADMINISTRATIVE CONTROL

PART IV: SPECIAL PROTECTION IN CREDIT
   TRANSACTIONS

TABLE OF CASES

(References are to paragraph numbers)

TABLE OF STATUTES

(References are to paragraph numbers)

TABLE OF STATUTORY INSTRUMENTS

(References are to paragraph numbers)

Chapter One

INTRODUCTION

"The coffee at McDonalds was too hot" said the scalded customer
"The central heating isn't working"
"The holiday was ruined"
"The car has been off the road for a month"
"The salesman wouldn't go away until I signed"
"There were worms in the pork chops"

This book is concerned with complaints which consumers may have against a **1.01** supplier of goods or services and with the remedies available to them. It is a vast subject and, as indicated in the preface to the First Edition,[1] it is necessary to curtail it.

In the words of the Molony Committee on Consumer Protection (1961) "the consumer, unlike some classes with claims on public bounty, is everybody all the time". In the present book, however, the word "consumer" will be used to describe a customer who buys for personal use and not for business purposes.[2]

A number of learned writers, *e.g.* Borrie and Diamond in their excellent book *The Consumer, Society and the Law*, have traced the history of the subject and have shown that, although the subject is comparatively new, its roots are old. Thus the law has imposed duties on persons exercising certain callings for many centuries, *e.g.* inn-keepers and carriers. Nevertheless, the explosion of interest in consumer matters is very much a creature of the second half of the twentieth century. We can see this simply by looking at the dates of some of the principal reforming legislation:

Hire-Purchase Acts 1954 and 1964
Misrepresentation Act 1967
Trade Descriptions Act 1968
Unsolicited Goods and Services Act 1971
Fair Trading Act 1973
Supply of Goods (Implied Terms) Act 1973
Consumer Credit Act 1974
Unfair Contract Terms Act 1977

---

[1] Above, p. vii.
[2] Note, however, the extended meaning of "consumer" in the Consumer Credit Act 1974, below, para. 18.02.

Consumer Safety Act 1978
Supply of Goods and Services Act 1982
Consumer Protection Act 1987
Consumer Arbitration Agreements Act 1988
Sale and Supply of Goods Act 1994
Sale of Goods (Amendment) Act 1995

What is the reason for this tremendous upsurge of activity? The answer is two-fold—a combination of new business methods and changing social attitudes. The key factors on business methods are to be found in the complexity of the goods themselves and in the changing forms of advertising and distribution. To quote again from the Molony Report (p. 31):

> "[The last half century] has seen a growing tendency for manufacturers ... to appeal directly to the public by forceful national advertising and other promotional methods ... a further influence during the same period has been the development of a mass market for extremely complex mechanical and electrical goods. ... Their performance cannot in some cases be accurately established by a short trial; shortcomings of design are not apparent to the inexpert eye; inherent faults may only come to light when the article breaks down after a period of use."

In other words, the need for what is called consumer protection has become far greater because the consumer is no longer in a position to rely on his own judgment when buying a complex article.

The second motivating force is the general move from individualism to collectivism. The twentieth century has seen not only consumer protection but also the Rent Acts, Financial Services Act, the large volume of legislation protecting employees and, of course, the welfare state. The extent to which some of these measures hamper business activity is, of course, a matter of keen political debate.

The international dimension

1.02   It is clear that the judiciary of the United States has been a long way ahead of this country in recognising and dealing with consumer problems. In particular, the American courts have increased the manufacturer's liability in two respects (1) by moving from negligence liability to strict liability, and (2) by breaking the shackles of the privity of contract rule. In this country these changes have been left to Parliament.[3]

The subject of consumer protection is also very much alive in the European Union. The Third Edition of this book dealt with the implementation of Euro-Directives in three areas—product liability, doorstep sales and misleading advertisements. It also foreshadowed major legislation in the field of unfair terms. Some two years later, the Council of Ministers gave final approval to the Unfair Contract Terms Directive and this was brought into

---

[3] See paras 4.05 and 5.10 below.

English law by statutory instrument on July 1, 1995. The far-reaching importance of this Directive is fully considered in Chapter 9. The final Chapter of this book describes the consumer functions of the E.U. and foreshadows further developments in two key areas—distance selling and consumer remedies.

Consumer protection agencies

There are a very large number of bodies concerned with consumer protection matters and they can be divided into Government departments, Government-sponsored bodies, local authorities and voluntary bodies.   **1.03**

(a) *Government departments*

The Department of Trade and Industry now has a Minister for Competition and Consumer Affairs. The name is appropriate. In a recent speech to the Yorkshire Fiscal Group Dr Howells said this: **1.04**

> "To prosper, companies need satisfied customers, but the expectations of customers are growing. Well-informed consumers able to make discerning choices put pressure on businesses to provide better goods and services, tailored to the needs of their customers and sold at competitive prices ... The revolution in shopping via the Internet and digital highways will enable consumers to compare prices and product quality not only against those available in the other Member States of the European Union but elsewhere in the world including the U.S. I have no doubt that this will change forever the ways in which we judge whether or if we are getting a good deal ... we are also working on proposals to ensure that consumer law is consistently enforced and that traders who cheat consumers are quickly stopped."

He also referred to the new Competition Act 1998 which will give the OFT wide powers to take action against "firms and cartels which try to restrict competition or rig prices ripping off the consumer."

Among its principal duties are the making of regulations under the Consumer Credit Act 1974 and the Consumer Protection Act 1987, Pt. II.[4] It also issues a large number of Press Releases and provides a great deal of business and consumer information on its website www.dti.co.uk. The Home Office has responsibilities in certain areas, including firearms and explosives, and the Ministry of Agriculture, Fisheries and Food has a number of duties under the Food Safety Act 1990.

Closely linked with the Department of Trade and Industry (DTI) is the Office of Fair Trading (OFT) which was set up as a result of the Fair Trading Act 1973. The extensive powers and duties of the Director General will be discussed later in this book. The bulk of the provisions in the Act are concerned with restrictive practices, monopolies and mergers but the Director General of Fair Trading is also given very extensive powers in relation to consumer protection matters. His duties include:

---

[4] Below, paras 18.01 and 17.06.

   (i) keeping under review the commercial supply of goods and services to consumers in the United Kingdom;

  (ii) making recommendations to the Department of Trade and Industry—either if asked to do so or on his own initiative;

 (iii) taking action against individual traders who have persisted in a course of conduct which is unfair to consumers[5];

 (iv) providing information to the public;[5a]

  (v) encouraging trade associations to prepare codes of practice for their members.[6]

In other words he is a statutory watchdog who can take action if undesirable trade practices come to his notice. He has also been given very extensive powers to supervise and control the consumer credit industry under the Consumer Credit Act 1974. His principal weapon of control lies in the operation of the licensing system; every trader who carries on a consumer credit or consumer hire business needs a licence[7] and the Director General is responsible for the grant, renewal, suspension and revocation of licences. He is also responsible, along with trading standards inspectors, for the enforcement of the Act by criminal proceedings. The Consumer Credit Act is examined in Part IV of this book. The most recent addition to his powers is to be found in the Unfair Terms in Consumer Contracts Regulations 1994 which will be fully discussed in Chapter Nine. Like the Minister for Competition and Consumer Affairs (see above) he warmly welcomes the consumer protection impact of the new Competition Act for which he and his predecessors have been campaigning for many years. He has recently pointed out that "safeguarding the consumer interest is, and always has been, the OFT's top priority" (News Release IV March 1999). Advice for persons shopping on the Internet can be found on the OFT website www.oft.gov.uk.

(b) *Government-sponsored bodies*

1.05   The Consumer Council, set up as a result of the Molony Committee recommendations, was abolished by the Conservative Government in 1971, but a new body—named the National Consumer Council—was set up by the Labour Government in 1974. It is an independent, publicly-funded body which acts as a watchdog and pressure group to protect the consumer interest; in 1993–1994 it responded to more than 60 Government consultations. Two bulletins (July and November 1994) illustrate the broad sweep of its activities. Topics covered include (1) the price of electricity and water and the disconnection problem; (2) the NHS complaints procedure; (3) the secrecy of drug-testing; (4) the new Personal Investment Authority; (5) access to

---

[5] Fair Trading Act 1973, Pt. III, below, para. 17.20.

[5a] See for example News Release 53/98 warning consumers against "you have won a prize" scams from abroad.

[6] Below, para. 10.04.

[7] Below, para. 20.02.

justice; (6) the effect of competition between schools; and (7) proposals to change the joint liability of creditor and supplier under the Consumer Credit Act.[8] The 1994 Report states that "our role is to raise the awkward questions that would otherwise go unasked". It publishes a large number of reports. A report of the Council "Service Please" by Lantin and Woodroffe led directly to the passing of the Supply of Goods and Services Act 1982. A recent publication "A–Z of Ombudsmen" provides a valuable guide to the 27 schemes currently in operation and describing what each Ombudsman can and cannot do. This topic is dealt with in Chapter Ten.

The Department of Trade and Industry (DTI) also makes a grant to the British Standards Institute (BSI). This voluntary body has been in existence for more than 75 years, and one of its functions is to lay down uniform specifications for certain products. If a product bears a BSI "kite mark" this means that it has been tested by BSI. Regular spot checks will follow and the mark will be withdrawn if these prove unsatisfactory.

(c) *Local authorities*

The county councils and the London boroughs make two major **1.06** contributions to consumer protection. First they employ trading standards inspectors (their former name was weights and measures inspectors) who have extensive responsibilities in the enforcement of the Trade Descriptions Act 1968, the Consumer Credit Act 1974 and Part II of the Fair Trading Act 1973. In all these cases they must give the Director General of Fair Trading notice of an intended prosecution[9] and they will also keep him informed of undesirable trade practices which come to their notice. They currently have no formal powers under the Unfair Terms in Consumer Contracts Regulations 1994 (as to which see Chapter Nine) but in practice they work closely with the OFT. If we look at the OFT Bulletin No. 4 on Unfair Contract Terms we find (on p. 7) the following passage:

> We recognise that local expertise and being close at hand may make it entirely appropriate for traders' home authority TSDs to guide and influence them in the drafting of their consumer contracts; clearly, this may remove the need for the OFT to invoke the threat of proceedings in the High Courts. Such informal local action can represent a speedy, cheap and informal way of achieving improvements in consumer contracts, particularly those used by small traders.

The second major field of local authority involvement lies in the field of consumer advice. Consumer Advice Centres have been set up in many parts of the country under the Local Government Act 1972. They give pre-shopping advice and they also give advice on complaints. Sometimes they take up individual complaints with the object of achieving a satisfactory settlement but they do not normally assist in litigation if a settlement proves impossible.

[8] Below, para. 23.05.
[9] See, *e.g.* Fair Trading Act 1973, s.130.

(d) *Voluntary bodies*

1.07   The Consumers' Association is widely known for its comparative testing of goods and services. The results are published in *Which?* and are clearly of great value to prospective consumers. The Association is very active in promoting legislation dealing with consumer affairs (including consumer awareness of legal remedies). Thus it played a large part in seeing the Unfair Contract Terms Act 1977 on to the statute book and improving the buyer's right to reject under the Sale and Supply of Goods Act 1994 (below, para. 7.21).

There are also a number of consumer groups at local level; their main function is to carry out research into the quality of local services and to publish the results of these surveys to their members. There is a central co-ordinating body known as the National Federation of Consumer Groups and it is believed that total membership of the groups is in the region of 2,000. Another body working in a closely related field is the Money Advice Trust which is an umbrella organisation formed in 1991 to bring together a large number of money advice bodies. The Chairman Robert Colville recently stated that "over a million people every year seek help from money advisers and demand for their services is exceeding supply" (See DTI press notice P/99/58.)

Finally we should mention trade and professional associations (*e.g.* the Retail Motor Industry Federation or the Association of British Travel Agents). These are in no sense consumer protection agencies but many of them operate voluntary conciliation and arbitration procedures. A consumer with a complaint may well find that an approach to the relevant association may produce a more satisfactory outcome than embarking on the hazards of litigation. The codes of practice and arbitration procedures operated by a number of associations are examined in Chapter Ten of this book.[10]

One important aspect of the voluntary procedures referred to above has been the creation of an "Ombudsman" for particular business activities. The Insurance Ombudsman's Bureau was set up, on a voluntary basis, in 1981. Similar bodies now exist in relation to other sectors such as banking, building societies, funerals, pensions and unit trusts. These schemes are discussed in Chapter Ten.[11]

---

[10] Below, para. 10.04.
[11] Below, para. 10.53.

Part I

THE CONSUMER AND THE CIVIL LAW

The civil law assists the consumer by imposing certain obligations on manu-   **1.08**
facturers and suppliers of goods and services and by restricting attempts to
exclude or cut down these obligations or the remedies available on breach.

It must be said at once that in many key areas the law is in a very uncertain
state and the case law is very sparse. This is particularly so in relation to
(1) the meaning of "satisfactory quality",[1] and (2) the circumstances in which
the buyer loses his right to reject goods by "accepting" them.[2] There is also
the question of "reasonableness" under section 3 of the Unfair Contract
Terms Act where, for example, a builder seeks to avoid liability for delay or
non-performance.[3] When one thinks of the many millions of consumer contracts concluded each day this absence of authority may seem surprising. A
charitable view would be that traders, for reasons of commercial goodwill,
settle all genuine complaints without litigation. A more realistic view is that
consumers are deterred from bringing proceedings by a variety of factors
including ignorance, lethargy and cost.

In Chapters Two to Four we shall consider the consumer's rights against
his *immediate supplier* of goods for failure to pass title, to deliver the goods
contracted for or to deliver goods of the right quality and fitness. Then in
Chapter Five we shall discuss his rights against the *manufacturer (and other
suppliers in the distribution chain)* both under the general law and under Part
I of the Consumer Protection Act 1987. Chapter Six deals with a number of
common consumer problems including defective performance, late delivery
and disputes about the price. In Chapter Seven we shall analyse and explain
the remedies available to the consumer and to members of his family. This
will be followed in Chapter Eight by an examination of exemption clauses
and in Chapter Nine we shall consider the Unfair Contract Terms Directive
and the regulations which incorporate the Directive into English law.

The last two Chapters in this Part deal with questions of enforcement. In

---

[1] See the Sale and Supply of Goods Act 1994 in para. 4.18 below.
[2] See now s.2 of this Act which deals with some of the problems.
[3] The Unfair Contract Terms Act 1977 and the emerging case law is examined in Chap. Eight,
para. 8.01 below.

Chapter Ten we shall describe ways in which the consumer can seek redress without going to court—including arbitration schemes under codes of practice, the use of the new consumer councils for public utilities and alternative dispute resolution. Finally a new Chapter Eleven is entitled "What happens if I go to court?"; it describes the availability of legal aid, the new "no win, no fee" schemes to finance litigation and the conduct of cases under the radically new Civil Procedure Rules.

CHAPTER TWO

"THEY SAY IT ISN'T MINE"

(1) A owns a diamond ring. B steals it and sells it to C who sells it to D. The **2.01**
police have now traced the ring and have seized it from D's home.
(2) E takes his car to F, a car dealer, and says "Find me a buyer but don't sell
for less than £1,000." F sells to G for £600 and disappears.
(3) H, a finance house, supply a car to I on hire-purchase. Before completing
her payments I sells the car to J, a motor dealer, who lets the car out to K on a
fresh hire-purchase agreement. H now claim from K the unpaid balance due
on the original agreement.

In unravelling this type of problem three closely connected principles must
be distinguished:

1. Does any buyer acquire title to the goods?
2. What are the rights as between each buyer and seller? This question will
   usually only be relevant in advising a buyer who has not acquired title.
3. What are the rights of a buyer who has spent money on improving the
   goods?

In this chapter it is proposed to deal separately with these three questions.
Before doing so, it may be helpful to define the term "sale of goods" which
occurs throughout this book. By section 2(1) of the Sale of Goods Act 1979:

> A contract of sale of goods is a contract by which the seller transfers or agrees to
> transfer the property in goods to a buyer for a money consideration called the
> price.

A contract of sale must be distinguished from other supply contracts—hire,
hire-purchase, work aid materials, exchange—although the law is similar in
many key areas. The extent to which computer software can be regarded as
"goods" is debatable (see para. 4.22 below).

1. DOES THE BUYER GET TITLE?

Where goods are sold by a non-owner the law is faced with a clear policy **2.02**
choice. Lord Denning M.R. has described it as follows[1]:

---

[1] *Bishopsgate Motor Finance Corp. Ltd v. Transport Brakes Ltd* [1949] 1 K.B. 322 at 336–337.

"In the development of our law two principles have striven for mastery. The first is for the protection of property; no one can give a better title than he himself possesses.[2] The second is for the protection of commercial transactions; the person who takes in good faith and for value without notice should get a good title."

Faced with this choice the law has developed in a piecemeal and haphazard way with a basic rule protecting property and a number of exceptions protecting commercial transactions. The Crowther Committee on Consumer Credit described the rules as "arbitrary and capricious" and pointed out that their application depended "not on principles of equity or justice but on fine technicalities which have little rhyme and less reason".[3]

There has been only one small step to bring this area of the law into line with modern commercial life. The rules of "market overt", dating back to the sixteenth century, enabled a buyer in certain types of market to acquire a good title from a non-owner (*e.g.* a thief). This ancient rule was enshrined in section 22(1) of the Sale of Goods Act 1979 but, following a DTI consultation paper published in January 1994,[3a] it was finally abolished by the Sale of Goods (Amendment) Act 1994 which applies to all sales concluded after January 3, 1995.

The nemo dat rule

2.03   With this warning we can examine the relevant provisions. The cornerstone is to be found in section 21(1) of the Sale of Goods Act 1979. It reads:

> Subject to this Act, where the goods are sold[4] by a person who is not their owner, and who does not sell them under the authority or with the consent of the owner, the buyer acquires no better title to the goods than the seller had, unless the owner of the goods is by his conduct precluded from denying the seller's authority to sell.

If we revert to our three examples, the effect of section 21(1) is that the goods will still belong to A, E and H unless someone along the line acquired title under one of the exceptions to the basic rule. We must now consider the scope and extent of these exceptions.

Does an exception apply?

2.04   Let us first list the principal exceptions:

(i) Sale under order of court
(ii) Sale under a common law or statutory power

---

[2] This is commonly referred to as the "*nemo dat*" rule, *i.e. nemo dat quod non habet.*
[3] Report, p. 178.
[3a] *Transfer of Title: Sections 21 to 26 of the Sale of Goods Act 1979*; other reforms are proposed too, broadly to extend protection to innocent purchasers.
[4] "Sold" does not cover an agreement to sell by the intermediate seller: *Shaw v. Commissioner of Police of the Metropolis* [1987] 1 W.L.R. 1332, CA.

   (iii) Sale with the owner's consent
   (iv) Sale where the owner is precluded from denying the seller's right to sell ("estoppel")
   (v) Disposition by a mercantile agent
  (vi) Sale under a voidable title
 (vii) Disposition by a seller in possession
(viii) Disposition by a buyer in possession
  (ix) Disposition of a motor vehicle under Part III of the Hire-Purchase Act 1964 (as re-worded by the Consumer Credit Act 1974)

It is now proposed to examine some of the more important of these exceptions. Nearly all of the examples chosen relate to cars; this is clearly the area where the consumer is most likely to buy goods which turn out to have been stolen. There is substantial overlap between these provisions and it is often advisable to plead more than one.

(i) *Is the owner estopped?*

Section 21 itself displaces the basic *nemo dat* rule where the owner, by his **2.05** conduct, is precluded from denying the seller's right to sell. The courts have construed this provision in a fairly narrow way. In the words of Lord Wilberforce:

> "English law has generally taken the robust line that the man who owns property is not under a general duty to safeguard it and that he may sue for its recovery any person into whose hands it has come."[5]

In *Central Newbury Car Auctions Ltd v. Unity Finance Ltd*[6]:

> A distinguished looking swindler wished to acquire a car from Central Newbury Car Auctions on hire-purchase terms and intimated that he was prepared to leave his own car in part exchange. He filled in an application form for a hire-purchase agreement. If the deal went through the dealer would sell to a finance company who would let the car to him on hire-purchase. Central Newbury allowed him to take the new car and its registration book away. Within a very short time it was discovered that (i) he had given a false name, address and employer; (ii) the car which he had left in part exchange did not belong to him; and (iii) he had sold the new car to Unity Finance. Central Newbury sued Unity Finance for the return of the car.

It was the classic situation; which of two innocent parties should suffer for the fraud of a third? Many people would agree with Lord Denning that the loss should fall on Central Newbury in view of their carelessness in parting with the car. Nevertheless this was a minority view; the majority in the Court of Appeal applied what Lord Wilberforce has described as the "robust"

---

[5] *Moorgate Mercantile Co. v. Twitchings* [1977] A.C. 890 at 902.
[6] [1957] 1 Q.B. 371.

view.[7] All that Central Newbury had done was to hand over physical possession; that was not conduct which precluded them from setting up their ownership; the car was still theirs. The only right of Unity Finance would be an action against the swindler under section 12 of the Sale of Goods Act[8] and this would almost certainly be worthless.

In the more recent case of *Moorgate Mercantile Co. v. Twitchings*[9]:

> Finance companies set up a company called HPI and 98 per cent of all finance companies belonged to it. The object was to register subsisting hire-purchase agreements—some four-and-a-half million—and to pass on information to motor dealers who were associated members. Any dealer who was considering buying a car could contact HPI to find out whether a hire-purchase agreement relating to that car was registered. Several thousand inquiries were made each day. The M. Finance Co. entered into a hire-purchase agreement, but for some unexplained reason they failed to register it with HPI. The hirer offered to sell the car to T, a dealer. T contacted HPI and was told that nothing had been registered. He then bought the car from the hirer. M. Finance Co. claimed that the car was still theirs. The House of Lords, by a majority, upheld this claim.

The case was fought on two grounds—estoppel and negligence. As to estoppel the question was twofold: (i) were HPI the agents of the finance companies? (ii) did their answers amount to a representation that no finance company had an interest in the car? By a majority of four to one (Lord Salmon dissenting) the House of Lords gave a negative answer to both of these questions. The other argument was negligence—the M. Finance Company owed a legal duty of care to dealers and were in breach of that duty. This argument was accepted by the Court of Appeal and by Lords Salmon and Wilberforce but the majority of the House of Lords rejected it. One of the main reasons which influenced the majority was the fact that (i) membership of HPI was voluntary and (ii) there was no duty to register agreements. Neither of these arguments appears totally convincing but they indicate that the owner of goods will seldom lose his ownership by reason of carelessness, even though this causes serious loss to an innocent buyer. We shall see later that HPI can also be used by a prospective private buyer.[10]

The only type of case where the owner may be estopped is where he makes a positive representation that the seller owns the goods[11] or where he signs a document which clearly conveys that impression.[12]

(ii) *Was there a disposition by a mercantile agent?*

2.06   We have seen that the mere delivery of possession does not preclude the

---

[7] See above.
[8] Below, para. 2.12.
[9] [1977] A.C. 890.
[10] Below, para. 2.10.
[11] See *Henderson v. Williams* [1895] 1 Q.B. 521.
[12] See *Eastern Distributors v. Goldring* [1957] 2 Q.B. 600.

owner from setting up his ownership. There is, however, one statutory exception. The basic effect of section 2 of the Factors Act 1889 is that if the owner transfers possession to a "mercantile agent", this may amount to a representation that the agent has authority to sell. If the agent then sells in the ordinary course of business, the owner may lose his ownership even though the agent went beyond his instructions.

The Act of 1889 starts by defining a mercantile agent. By section 1:

> "Mercantile agent" shall mean a mercantile agent having in the customary course of his business as such agent authority to sell goods, or to consign goods for the purpose of sale, or to buy goods, or to raise money on the security of goods.

Then comes the key provision. By section 2(1):

> Where a mercantile agent is, with the consent of the owner, in the possession of goods ... any sale, pledge or other disposition of the goods, made by him when acting in the ordinary course of business of a mercantile agent, shall ... be as valid as if he were expressly authorised by the owner of the goods to make the same; provided that the person taking under the disposition acts in good faith, and has not at the time of the disposition notice that the person making the disposition has not authority to make the same.

This section could apply to the second example at the beginning of this chapter.[13] If the agent receives instructions not to sell for less than £1,000 or if he is merely instructed to take offers, the buyer will usually not be aware of these restrictions and will get a good title under section 2 even though the agent exceeded his authority.

The sale by the agent must be in the ordinary course of business and the buyer must have no notice of the restrictions on the agent's authority. In practice these points are unlikely to give rise to difficulty. There are, however, two other points which could defeat the buyer's claim. Thus:

(a) The section will only apply if the agent was in possession *in his capacity of mercantile agent*. It would not apply if, for example, a garage which happened to be a mercantile agent received a car for servicing or repair and then sold it.[14]

(b) The agent must have received possession of the goods with the owner's consent. The mere fact that consent was obtained by fraud[15] or that consent has ended[16] does not affect the buyer unless he knows of

---

[13] Above, para. 2.01.
[14] See, *e.g. Belvoir Finance Co. Ltd v. Harold G. Cole & Co. Ltd* [1969] 1 W.L.R. 1877.
[15] *Folkes v. King* [1923] 1 K.B. 282; but perhaps the position would be different if the owner was under a fundamental mistake as to the agent's identity. See *Benjamin on Sale of Goods* (3rd ed.), para. 526.
[16] Act of 1889, s.2(2).

this—an obviously sensible rule. On the other hand, the owner may
decide to keep the registration document and/or the ignition key.
What happens if he accidentally leaves them with the dealer or in the
car? In *Pearson v. Rose and Young*[17]:

> The owner of a car instructed a dealer to obtain offers. He never intended to hand
> over the registration book but by mistake he left it in the dealer's showroom. The
> dealer sold the car with its registration book to a buyer. The Court of Appeal held
> that (i) in the case of a second-hand car the words "goods" included the regis-
> tration book and the consent of the owner must extend to the registration book as
> well as to the car itself; (ii) there had been no consent to the handing over of the
> book; (iii) the dealer must therefore be treated as if he had sold the car without the
> book; (iv) such a sale would not be in the ordinary course of business; (v) conse-
> quently the buyer obtained no title under section 2.[18]

(iii) *Did the seller have a voidable title?*

2.07   Where a contract is voidable (*e.g.* for misrepresentation) it is a valid contract until the innocent party takes steps to set it aside, *i.e.* rescinds the contract. The remedy of rescission is an equitable one and in certain cases it will
not be possible to rescind. One such case is concerned with third party
rights—once a third party has acquired rights under the voidable contract it
will be too late to rescind it. This principle now appears in section 23 of the
1979 Act as follows:

> When the seller of goods has a voidable title to them, but his title has not been
> avoided at the time of the sale, the buyer acquires a good title to the goods,
> provided that he buys them in good faith and without notice of the seller's defect
> of title.

In virtually all the reported cases under this section the goods were
obtained as a result of a fraudulent misrepresentation. The position of the
ultimate buyer depends on a highly technical rule—was the title to the fraudulent buyer *voidable* for misrepresentation or *void* for mistake? In the well-
known case of *Ingram v. Little*[19]:

> Three ladies agreed to sell a car to a man who called himself "Hutchinson". They
> were reluctant to take a cheque from him but he gave them the initials and
> address of a real Hutchinson. After checking in the telephone directory they let
> him take the car away in return for a cheque. He sold the car to a buyer; the
> cheque was dishonoured. The Court of Appeal held that (i) the offer to sell was
> made to Hutchinson and could not be accepted by anyone else; (ii) consequently
> the contract with the rogue was void; (iii) consequently section 23 did not apply
> and the buyer acquired no title.

Some years ago, the Law Reform Committee recommended that the fraudu-

---

[17] [1951] 1 K.B. 275.
[18] See also *Stadium Finance Ltd v. Robbins* [1962] 2 Q.B. 664, CA (book accidentally left in car;
    key not handed over at all; buyer from agent not protected).
[19] [1961] 1 Q.B. 31.

lent person should always be treated as having a *voidable* title, so that the ultimate buyer would be protected. No such legislation has been enacted but the courts have, in effect, achieved this result. In the more recent case of *Lewis v. Averay*[20] the facts were somewhat similar to those in *Ingram v. Little* but the decision went the other way. In that case:

> A rogue calling himself Green—a well-known television actor—induced the owner of a car to sell it to him in return for a cheque. He resold the car to a buyer. The cheque was dishonoured.

The Court of Appeal held that the rogue had a voidable title, with the result that section 23 protected the buyer. They treated *Ingram v. Little* as a case turning on very special facts and they laid down the broad principle that where the parties were face-to-face, the seller would normally be treated as intending to deal with the actual person in front of him. If this intention was brought about by fraud or by a trick this would make the transaction voidable but not void.

Section 23 does not apply if the owner has avoided the contract *before* the resale takes place. In general the innocent party must give notice of rescission and this can raise a practical problem, since not all fraudulent buyers supply their sellers with an address. In *Car and Universal Finance Co. v. Caldwell*[21] the Court of Appeal held that avoidance was possible in this type of case without notifying the fraudulent buyer. In that case the seller reported the matter to the police and the AA as soon as the cheque was dishonoured and asked them to trace the car. It was held that his conduct did amount to an avoidance of contract. The practical effect of this case has however been largely undermined by the later case of *Newtons of Wembley Ltd v. Williams* which is considered later in this chapter.[22]

(iv) *Did the seller remain in possession after a previous sale?*

We have seen that the owner of goods may lose his ownership if he trans- **2.08** fers possession to a mercantile agent who disposes of them in the ordinary course of business.[23] We now meet two further cases where ownership and possession are split. The first concerns a sale where the buyer becomes the owner but the seller retains possession. Let us assume that X, an antique dealer, agrees to sell to Y an antique vase. Y agrees to collect it on the following day. By mistake the dealer sells the same vase to Z who pays for it and takes it away. On these facts the first sale may have initially passed the ownership to Y[24] but nevertheless the second sale, coupled with delivery, may have then passed the ownership to Z. The authority for this is section 24 of the Sale of Goods Act 1979 which reads as follows:

[20] [1973] 1 Q.B. 198.
[21] [1965] 1 Q.B. 525.
[22] Below, para. 2.09.
[23] Above, para. 2.06.
[24] s.18, r.1, below, para. 6.18.

> Where a person having sold goods continues or is in possession of the goods ... the delivery or transfer by that person or by a mercantile agent acting for him of the goods ... under any sale, pledge or other disposition thereof to any person receiving the same in good faith and without notice of the previous sale, has the same effect as if the person making the delivery or transfer were expressly authorised by the owner of the goods to make the same.

Thus in advising Z one would start by claiming that X was still the owner at the time of the sale to him. If this is not so (see above) Z may acquire title under section 24, provided that the sale to him was coupled with delivery. After earlier doubts it now seems clear that the nature of X's possession is immaterial—he may be in possession as seller, as repairer, as warehouseman or in any other capacity.

As already stated[25] these rules are highly technical. Consider the following problem:

> X sells a car to Y as a result of a fraudulent misrepresentation made by Y. Y pays by cheque. Y sells to Z and retains possession. When Y's cheque is dishonoured X comes to Y's premises. Y allows X to take the car back in return for a promise by X not to enforce the cheque.

The sale from Y to Z gave Z a title under section 23.[26] After that sale Y became a "seller in possession". The return of the car to X amounts to a delivery under a "sale, pledge *or other disposition*" within section 24. Consequently title is re-transferred to X.[27]

(v) *Was the sale by a buyer in possession?*

2.09   Section 25(1) is the exact converse of section 24. It is again concerned with a split between ownership and possession but this time it is the seller who retains ownership and the buyer who obtains possession. There is, in fact, a very substantial overlap with section 23. Let us assume that A buys a car from B and pays by cheque. The contract provides that no property shall pass to A until the cheque is cleared. A obtains possession of the car with B's consent, and sells and delivers the car to C. A's cheque is dishonoured. Although C bought from a non-owner he may acquire title under section 25(1). The section reads as follows:

> Where a person having bought or agreed to buy goods obtains, with the consent of the seller, possession of the goods ... the delivery or transfer by that person, or by a mercantile agent acting for him, of the goods ... under any sale, pledge or other disposition thereof, to any person receiving the same in good faith and without notice of any lien or other right of the original seller in respect of the goods, shall have the same effect as if the person making the delivery or transfer were a mercantile agent in possession of the goods ... with the consent of the owner.

---

[25] Above, para. 2.02.
[26] Above, para. 2.07.
[27] See *Worcester Works Finance Ltd v. Cooden Engineering Co. Ltd* [1972] 1 Q.B. 210, CA.

This provision has been before the courts on a number of occasions and the following points emerge:

(a) The section only applies where a person has *bought or agreed to buy* goods. It does not apply where, for example, the goods have been let out on hire-purchase[28] or stolen.[29] Similarly, a buyer under a conditional sale agreement within the Consumer Credit Act 1974 is *not* (for this purpose) a person who has "agreed to buy" so that a transfer by him will not enjoy the protection of the section.[30]

(b) The first buyer must obtain possession with the *consent* of the seller; this includes consent obtained by fraud.[31]

(c) The section can apply even where the first buyer has obtained a voidable title and even if the disposition by him takes place *after* his title has been avoided (see below).

(d) What is the meaning of the obscure words "shall have the same effect as if the person making the delivery or transfer were a mercantile agent in possession ... with the consent of the owner"? In *Newtons of Wembley Ltd v. Williams*[32] the Court of Appeal reached the astonishing conclusion that the disposition by the first buyer must be in the ordinary course of business of a mercantile agent—even though that buyer is not such an agent! In that case:

> A agreed to buy a Sunbeam Rapier car from Newtons of Wembley. The contract provided that no property should pass to the buyer until his cheque was cleared. When the cheque was dishonoured Newtons took steps to trace the car and recover it. A then sold it to B in an open-air market in Warren Street. B resold it to Williams. A pleaded guilty to obtaining the car by false pretences and Newtons of Wembley sued Williams for the return of the car. The claim was unsuccessful.

The Court of Appeal held that A was a buyer in possession; even though he was not a mercantile agent the sale to B was in the ordinary course of business of a mercantile agent; B took in good faith; accordingly B acquired a good title which he could pass on to Williams.

It will be appreciated that the first transferee from the original buyer must take "in good faith". This condition was satisfied in this case but not in the earlier case of *Car and Universal Finance Co. Ltd v. Caldwell*.[33] The effect of the *Newton* decision is to severely restrict the practical consequences of the

---

[28] *Helby v. Matthews* [1895] A.C. 471. Note however that the label used by the parties is not conclusive. If therefore a "hire purchase" agreement contains a binding obligation to pay all future instalments (and a provision that the property will pass when the final instalment is paid) the section will apply: *Forthright Finance Ltd v. Carlyle Finance Ltd* [1997] C.C.L.R. 84.

[29] *National Employers' Mutual General Insurance Association v. Jones* [1990] 1 A.C. 24, HL. Lord Goff's judgment contains a clear, historical analysis of this and related statutory exceptions.

[30] See Consumer Credit Act 1974, Sched. 4.

[31] *Du Jardin v. Beadman Bros* [1952] 2 Q.B. 712.

[32] [1965] 1 Q.B. 560.

[33] Above, para. 2.07.

original seller avoiding a voidable title acquired by the fraudulent buyer. The original seller may, however, recover his goods from the sub-buyer if (a) the original sale and sub-sale both reserved ownership until payment, and (b) payment has not been made.[33a]

(vi) *Was there a disposition of a motor vehicle held on hire-purchase or conditional sale?*

2.10   The final rule which may protect the consumer was introduced by Part III of the Hire-Purchase Act 1964 and verbal amendments were made to it by the Consumer Credit Act 1974. The provision was introduced after an earlier proposal had been rejected, for administrative reasons, by the finance companies. This would have provided for the retention of the registration books by the companies and the issue of cards to the hirers. One of the real problems in this area of law is that many people ignore the warning in the registration document that "The Registered Keeper is not necessarily the legal owner."

Part III applies if the following conditions are satisfied:

(a) a motor vehicle is let out on hire-purchase or agreed to be sold under a conditional sale agreement; and
(b) the hirer or buyer ("the debtor") disposes of it before the property has passed to him.[33b]

The Act then makes a distinction between:

(a) a disposition to a *private purchaser*; and
(b) a disposition to a *trade or finance purchaser*.

In the former case the purchaser may get a good title. In the words of section 27 of the 1964 Act (in its amended form):

> Where the disposition ... is to a private purchaser, and he is a purchaser of the motor vehicle in good faith without notice of the hire-purchase or conditional sale agreement (the "relevant agreement") that disposition shall have effect as if the creditor's title to the vehicle had been vested in the debtor immediately before that disposition.

Two points should be noted. First, the private purchaser must have no actual notice of a subsisting hire-purchase or conditional sale agreement.[34]

[33a] See *Re Highway Foods International*, *The Times*, November 1, 1994.
[33b] Where a finance company lets out goods to two or more hirers, each of them can be reported as a "debtor"; consequently a disposition by one of them can confer title under Part III; *Keeble v. Combined Lease Finance Plc* [1996] C.C.L.R. 63, CA.
[34] *Barker v. Bell* [1971] 1 W.L.R. 983, CA.

Secondly, the "creditor's title" means the title of the person who was described as the creditor in the hire-purchase or conditional sale agreement (*i.e.* the person who made the relevant agreement as owner or seller).

> Suppose that X, a thief, sells a car to Y who lets it on hire-purchase to Z and Z sells it to A. Even if A takes in good faith he will only get the title which was vested in Y. Since Y had no title, the section does not protect A.

If we now assume that the hirer or buyer disposes of the vehicle to a trade or finance purchaser, that purchaser has no Part III protection (presumably because he will be able to use the HPI facilities[35]) but if further dispositions take place the Act protects the *first private purchaser* if he takes in good faith and without notice. It, therefore, becomes crucial to find out whether the original transferee was a trade or finance purchaser. A trade purchaser is defined as a person who at the time of the disposition carries on a business of buying motor vehicles for sale,[36] while a finance purchaser is one who provides finance by buying motor vehicles and letting them out under hire-purchase or conditional sale agreements. Any other purchaser is a private purchaser. The following points can be important:

(i) "Private purchaser" is much wider than "private person"; thus many large public companies will enjoy the "private purchaser" protection of the Act.

(ii) If the purchaser is a trade or finance purchaser, he will not have Part III protection even if he buys for his private use.

(iii) The term "disposition" can include a fresh hire-purchase agreement. Thus in the third example at the beginning of this chapter[37] the ultimate hirer will be entitled to remain in possession under Part III even though he finds out about the original agreement before completing his payments.[38]

Conversely (and controversially) the private purchaser can rescind the agreement and recover all his payments—on the basis of total failure of consideration—if he does so before he has acquired little. In other words, it seems that he can have his Part III cake and eat it![38a]

Two final points can be made. First, there are bound to be serious practical problems in proving that the vehicle was transferred by the hirer or buyer to a private purchaser. The purchaser's job is made somewhat easier by a series of

---

[35] Above, para. 2.05.

[36] This may be a part-time business: *Stevenson v. Beverley Bentinck Ltd* [1976] 1 W.L.R. 483, CA.

[37] Above, para. 2.01.

[38] See also *Dodds v. Yorkshire Bank Finance Ltd* [1992] Consumer Credit Law Reports 92, CA (car held on hire-purchase; hirer sold it as part of a loan agreement; only to take effect if he defaulted (which he did); buyer got Pt. III title).

[38a] *Barber v. NWS Bank Plc* [1996] C.C.L.R. 30, CA.

rebuttable presumptions which are to be found in section 28 of the 1964 Act. Secondly, one must always bear in mind that prevention is better than cure. A member of the public who is considering buying a car can always check with HPI.[39] HPI make their information available to the AA, RAC and Citizens Advice Bureaux.

Hire-purchase generally

2.11   X lets out goods to Y on hire-purchase and it then transpires that X is not the owner of the goods. A number of the provisions discussed in this chapter refer to a "disposition" and this is clearly wide enough to cover a hire-purchase agreement. Thus Y could, in appropriate cases, claim the protection of section 2 of the Factors Act,[40] section 24 or 25(1) of the Sale of Goods Act[41] or Part III of the Hire-Purchase Act. He would also be protected if X had a voidable title, since it will be too late for the original owner to rescind the agreement once third party rights have been acquired.[42]

2. BUYER'S RIGHTS AGAINST SELLER

2.12   We have dealt at some length with the *nemo dat* rules because it is likely that the real battle in practice is likely to be fought between the original owner and the buyer. We must now consider the position as between buyer and seller. The general principle is clear enough; under a contract of sale the transfer of ownership from seller to buyer is a fundamental term around which the whole contract revolves. Section 12(1) (as amended by the Sale and Supply of Goods Act 1994) spells out the seller's basic obligation:

> In a contract of sale, other than one to which subsection (3) below applies, there is an implied [condition] on the part of the seller that in the case of a sale, he has a right to sell the goods, and in the case of an agreement to sell, he will have a right to sell the goods at the time when the property is to pass.

In addition, section 12(2) implies warranties that:

> (a) the goods are free, and will remain free until the time when the property is to pass, from any charge or encumbrance not disclosed or known to the buyer before the contract is made, and
> (b) the buyer will enjoy quiet possession of the goods except so far as it may be disturbed by the owner or other person entitled to the benefit of any charge or encumbrance so disclosed or known.

These provisions have been before the courts on a number of occasions and the following points emerge from the cases:

---

[39] Above, para. 2.05.
[40] Above, para. 2.06.
[41] Above, paras 2.08–2.09.
[42] Above, para. 2.07.

(1) If the goods are delivered in such a form that any sale can be stopped by an injunction there is no "right to sell".

(2) If the seller is in breach of this essential condition, the buyer can recover the price even though he has used the goods for a considerable time.[43] The basis of his claim is a "total failure of consideration". If he asks for the return of the price his right will crystallise and will not be affected by anything done *after* this to cure the defect. If the principle of "total failure" were applied literally it would enable a buyer of stolen wine to have the best of both worlds—consume the wine and get his money back on discovering the theft![44]

(3) If the buyer has incurred other expenses, *e.g.* the cost of necessary repairs, these can also be claimed from the seller.[45]

An unsettled question is the precise relationship between section 12 and the *nemo dat* exceptions considered earlier in this chapter. If the seller had no title he would technically have no *right* to sell, even though the effect of the sale would be to pass title to the buyer. Nevertheless, it is inconceivable that a court would allow a claim based on "total failure of consideration" if the buyer got exactly what he paid for, *i.e.* the property in the goods. If, however, he was put to trouble and expense in proving his title he might well have a claim.

Can sections 12(1) and 12(2) be excluded?

There may be cases where the seller of goods is uncertain as to whether or not he has a right to sell and he may wish the buyer to bear this risk. Section 12(3) allows the seller to give a more limited undertaking in a case where there appears from the contract or is to be inferred from its circumstances an intention that the seller should transfer only such title as he or a third person may have. In this type of case the basic title obligations referred to above are replaced by two implied warranties,[45a] *i.e.*:

2.13

(4) ... that all charges and encumbrances known to the seller and not known to the buyer have been disclosed to the buyer before the contract is made.

(5) ... that none of the following will disturb the buyer's quiet possession of the goods, namely—

(a) the seller;

(b) in a case where the parties to the contract intend that the seller should transfer only such title as a third person may have, that person;

---

[43] *Rowland v. Divall* [1923] 2 K.B. 500, CA.
[44] If the true owner re-appeared he could, of course, sue the buyer for conversion.
[45] *Mason v. Burningham* [1949] 2 K.B. 545.
[45a] See the 1994 Act, Sched. 2, para. 5(3).

(c) anyone claiming through or under the seller or that third person otherwise than under a charge or encumbrance disclosed or known to the buyer before the contract is made.

Subject to this, section 12 cannot be excluded.

Hire-purchase

2.14   The Supply of Goods (Implied Terms) Act 1973 implies title provisions into hire-purchase agreements.[46] These are similar to those implied in a sale of goods and only one point calls for brief mention. Under the 1973 Act the condition of "right to sell" is a condition that the owner will have a right to sell when the property is to pass (this usually occurs when the hirer has completed his payments). It seems, however, that the hirer may be in an even stronger position under a term implied at common law, *i.e.* that the owner has the right to sell at the time of delivery to the hirer.[47] A breach of the condition gives the hirer the right to recover all his payments with no set-off for user.[48]

Other contracts

2.15   There may be other cases where a contract is made involving the transfer of ownership of goods to the buyer. Examples include contracts for work and materials (installation of central heating, double glazing, etc.) and contracts of exchange. The obligations as to the right to sell, quiet possession and freedom from encumbrances are similar to those implied in a sale of goods (see s.2 of the Supply of Goods and Services Act 1982). In contrast, the contract of hire does not involve the transfer of ownership at all and consequently the only "title" terms are (a) a condition that the owner has the right to transfer possession, and (b) a warranty for quiet possession (s.7 of the 1982 Act).

3. IMPROVEMENTS AND REPAIRS

2.16   S sells goods to B who spends £200 on repairs and improvements. It then transpires that the goods belong to C who claims them, or their value, from B. It has been well established for many years that, in assessing damages for conversion, credit must be given for improvements made by the defendant.[49] In *Greenwood v. Bennett*[50] this principle was applied in interpleader proceedings between the owner and the improver. This seems fair enough but one point is unclear; if the owner seizes the goods from the improver, does the improver have a cause of action to recover the cost of the improvements from

---

[46] s.8.
[47] *Karflex Ltd. v. Poole* [1933] 2 K.B. 251 and more recently (and controversially) *Barber v. NWS Bank Plc*, para. 2.10 above.
[48] *Warman v. Southern Counties Finance Corporation* [1949] 2 K.B. 576, CA.
[49] *Munro v. Willmott* [1949] 1 K.B. 295.
[50] [1973] 1 Q.B. 195.

the owner? No English authority supports such a claim, although Lord Denning M.R. suggested (*obiter*) that such a claim would be allowed on the basis of unjust enrichment.[51]

The principle of *Greenwood v. Bennett* now appears in statutory form in section 6(1) of the Torts (Interference with Goods) Act 1977. It reads:

> If in proceedings for wrongful interference against a person (the "improver") who has improved the goods, it is shown that the improver acted in the mistaken but honest belief that he had a good title to them, an allowance shall be made for the extent to which, at the time as at which the goods fall to be valued in assessing damages, the value of the goods is attributable to the improvement.

The section goes on to give a similar right to a subsequent buyer who acted in good faith.[52] If the buyer then sues his seller under section 12 of the Sale of Goods Act[53] the seller can claim a similar reduction provided that he acted in good faith.[54]

> O owns a car which is stolen by T who sells it to A. It is worth £200 but A increases its value to £900. He then sells it to B for £900. O claims the car from B.

If we assume that O has been the owner at all material times, the court may well order O to pay B the sum of £700 (the improvement figure reflected in the price paid by B to A) as a condition of getting the car back. In the result, B is out of pocket to the tune of £200. If he then sues A for the return of the £900 it seems only right that his claim should be limited to £200 and (assuming that A acted in good faith) section 6(3) allows such a reduction.

Two final points may be made. It will be seen that the section uses the words "if in proceedings ... against a person". In other words it does not create a new cause of action. If the owner seizes the goods from the improver, there is nothing in the Act to give the improver a claim against the owner.[55] Secondly, the right to claim compensation for improvements will only be relevant where the improver or his successor in title is liable to the owner and it will not be relevant where the improver or his successor in title has himself become the owner under one of the *nemo dat* exceptions discussed at the beginning of this chapter.

---

[51] For further discussion, see (1973) 36 M.L.R. 89.
[52] s.6(2).
[53] Above, para. 2.12.
[54] s.6(3).
[55] He may of course have a claim against the seller—see *Mason v. Burningham*, n. 45, above.

CHAPTER THREE

"IT'S A GOOD LITTLE BUS"

(1) During negotiations for the sale of a car the dealer says to the consumer **3.01** "it's a good little bus—I'd stake my life on it." The consumer then takes the car on hire-purchase from a finance company. The steering is defective and the consumer is injured.

(2) The vendor of a site of a petrol filling station tells the prospective purchaser that it should have a throughput of 200,000 gallons per year. This is far too high and the purchaser suffers severe financial loss.

(3) A prospective hirer of barges asks the owner how much they could carry and the owner replies "1,600 tonnes". The hirer makes the contract but the statement is wrong and the hirer refuses to pay the hire charges.

The supplier of goods is likely to make extravagant claims about them before or during negotiations. What are the remedies of the consumer if, as in the three cases cited, the statement turns out to be wrong? The position depends on how the statement is classified. There are at least five possibilities:

(a) The statement may be nothing more than "trader's puff". In this case the consumer has no remedy.

(b) The statement may be an actionable misrepresentation; in this case the consumer may have (i) a right to rescind the contract unless it is too late to do so; (ii) a right to damages at common law if the supplier was fraudulent; (iii) a right to damages under section 2(1) of the Misrepresentation Act 1967 unless the supplier can prove that he had reasonable grounds for believing, and did believe, the statement to be true.

(c) It may be a negligent misstatement giving rise to an action for damages in tort. This branch of the law of negligence is based on the House of Lords decision in *Hedley Byrne & Co. Ltd v. Heller & Partners Ltd*,[1] but the law has been developing slowly and the precise scope of liability has still to be determined.

(d) It may be a contractual term. In this case the consumer can claim damages; whether he can also treat the contract as discharged depends upon the importance of the term and upon the seriousness and the consequences of the breach.

---

[1] [1964] A.C. 465.

(e) It may form part of the description of the goods (this overlaps with (d) above). If this is so, a breach will be a breach of condition and the consumer can choose between (i) treating the contract as repudiated and claiming damages, and (ii) affirming the contract and claiming damages.[2] Until recently the term "description" has been given a very wide meaning but it seems that the pendulum is now swinging the other way.[3]

It remains to add that the supplier may be in breach of the Trade Descriptions Act 1968[4] and a criminal conviction could lead to an award of compensation under the Powers of Criminal Courts Act 1973.[5] Further, if the statement is a credit advertisement within the Consumer Credit Act 1974 the provisions of sections 46 and 167(2) of that Act must be borne in mind. These matters are considered in later parts of this book.

1. MERE PUFF

3.02   The praising of goods by a prospective supplier is a universal fact of commercial life and the lifeblood of the advertising industry. The following phrases are typical:

> "the most popular bike in Britain"
> "clean, healthy and alive"
> "super value for money"
> "the bathroom bargain of the year."

This is typical sales patter; it is not intended to give rise to legal liability and it does not do so. The difficulty is to know where to draw the line between (a) mere puff and (b) a representation or a term. In the above examples the statements were vague and not specific; as soon as the supplier makes an inaccurate specific statement, for example, as to measurements or ingredients, the consumer should have little difficulty in proving an actionable misrepresentation or breach of a contractual term. In an early case a seller of port who described it as "superior old port" was held liable as the maker of a contractual promise. More recently in *Andrews v. Hopkinson*,[6] the facts of which appear in example 1,[7] the dealer who described the car as a "good little bus" was liable for breach of a collateral contract (and also in tort under the rule in *Donoghue v. Stevenson*).[8]

---

[2] Sale of Goods Act 1979, ss.11, 13.
[3] See below, para. 3.10.
[4] Below, para. 13.03.
[5] Below, para. 16.02.
[6] [1957] 1 Q.B. 229.
[7] Above, para. 3.01.
[8] [1932] A.C. 562, below, para. 5.24.

2. Misrepresentation

A misrepresentation can broadly be described as a half-way house between   **3.03**
mere puff and a contractual term. The essence of a misrepresentation is that it
is a statement made *before* the making of the contract which *induces* the other
party to enter into the contract. There can, of course, be an overlap between a
misrepresentation and a contractual term; a dealer may represent a car as
being a 1997 model and this may later be incorporated into the contract.
Subject to this, a mere pre-contractual inducement is less potent than a term
of the contract itself.

Until the 1960s it was often vital for the injured party to prove that the
statement was something more than a misrepresentation; the reason was that
the only remedy for misrepresentation was the equitable remedy of
rescission, with no right to damages unless there was fraud. If it was too late
to rescind the innocent party might find himself with no remedy at all. This is
what happened in *Oscar Chess Ltd v. Williams*[9] where the following facts
arose:

> A consumer who was buying a car was asked by the dealer to state the age of the
> car which he was giving in part-exchange. He said that it was a 1948 model, as
> appeared from the registration book. In fact it was a 1939 model and the dealer
> suffered loss in that the part-exchange allowance was too high. He sued the
> buyer for damages.

The Court of Appeal held that the statement made by Mr Williams was a mere
representation and not a contractual warranty. Accordingly, as the law then
stood, no damages could be awarded. In the words of Lord Denning M.R.:

> "If, however, the seller, when he states a fact, makes it clear that he has no knowl-
> edge of his own but has got his information elsewhere and is merely passing it on
> it is not so easy to infer a warranty."

On these particular facts the result of this case might be the same today even
after the changes made by section 2 of the Misrepresentation Act 1967 (as the
consumer could prove reasonable grounds for his belief) and even after
Hedley Byrne v. Heller.[10]

If the parties are on an equal bargaining footing the courts may again be
reluctant to find a contractual promise. Thus in *Howard Marine and Dredging Co. Ltd v. Ogden & Sons (Excavation) Ltd*,[11] the facts of which appear in
Example 3 at the beginning of this chapter,[12] the statement about the barge
capacity was held to be non-contractual; in this case, however, the hirers
recovered damages under section 2(1) of the Misrepresentation Act.[13]

[9] [1957] 1 W.L.R. 370.
[10] Below, paras 3.05 and 3.06.
[11] [1978] Q.B. 574.
[12] Above, para. 3.01.
[13] Below, para. 7.04.

If, however, we turn to the normal dealer-consumer situation a statement made by the dealer will frequently be classified as a contractual promise because of the dealer's special knowledge. In *Dick Bentley v. Harold Smith Ltd*[14]:

> A dealer told a prospective buyer that the engine of a second-hand car had done 20,000 miles. It was later discovered that the engine had done 100,000 miles. The buyer claimed damages.

The Court of Appeal gave judgment for the buyer. Here was a statement about a matter within the special knowledge of the seller. It was a contractual warranty and the seller was liable for breach of it.

In this type of case, therefore, the plaintiff should allege in the alternative (i) a contractual term, (ii) a misrepresentation, and (iii) a negligent statement.[15] The advantage of (i) is that the consumer will be entitled to damages for *any* breach of the term, even though the maker had reasonable grounds for believing the statement to be true.

The various remedies available for misrepresentation will be further considered[16] but before leaving misrepresentation three further points can be made:

(a) It may be necessary to distinguish a representation of *fact* from a mere statement of *opinion*—a problem which can cause particular difficulty on a sale of a painting which is attributed to an old master.

(b) Whether a person relies on the statement is a question of fact. The maker of a statement cannot avoid liability simply by saying "the accuracy of this statement is not guaranteed and the buyer should make his own enquiries". If, in such a case, the buyer *does* rely on the statement he will have the usual remedies for misrepresentation if the statement is incorrect.[17]

(c) The action for damages for misrepresentation is only available where the statement was made by the other party to the contract. Thus it would not be available if, for example, a consumer bought from a retailer in reliance on a statement made by the manufacturer. There may, however, be a claim against the manufacturer if a collateral contract can be established or if he is liable in negligence under the rules discussed below.

3. Liability in Tort for Negligence

3.04   The history of the law of tort is one of gradual and cautious development.

---

[14] [1965] 1 W.L.R. 623.
[15] Below, para. 3.05.
[16] Below, para. 7.02.
[17] *Cremdean Properties Ltd v. Nash* (1977) 244 E.G. 547, CA. As to exclusion of remedies see para. 8.33.

Although the industrial revolution started in the eighteenth century, it was not until 1932 that the modern law of negligence was born. Until then it was widely accepted that where A negligently performed a contract with B and thereby caused loss to C, A was not liable to C. It was not until *Donoghue v. Stevenson*[18] that the House of Lords, by a bare majority, came down in favour of a more realistic approach. In that case the House decided that in certain circumstances the manufacturer of a product owed a duty of care to the ultimate consumer. The case is also a landmark because Lord Atkin laid down his famous "neighbour" test as the basis of liability in negligence. He said:

> "The liability for negligence . . . is no doubt placed upon a general public sentiment of moral wrongdoing for which the offender must pay. But acts or omissions which any moral code would censure cannot in a practical world be treated so as to give a right to every person injured by them to demand relief. In this way rules of law arise which limit the range of complainants and the extent of their remedy. The rule that you are to love your neighbour becomes in law—you must not injure your neighbour; and the lawyer's question, Who is my neighbour? receives a restricted reply. You must take reasonable care to avoid acts or omissions which you can reasonably foresee would be likely to injure your neighbour. Who, then, in law, is my neighbour? The answer seems to be—persons who are so closely and directly affected by my act that I ought reasonably to have them in contemplation as being so affected when I am directing my mind to the acts or omissions which are called in question."

Despite *Donoghue v. Stevenson* there were, and still are, important areas of non-liability. In particular the courts were (and still are) very reluctant to hold that negligence resulting in purely economic loss gives rise to legal liability; the plaintiff could not succeed merely by proving that he was a "neighbour" of the defendant within Lord Atkin's test.[18a] The reason for this refusal to apply *Donoghue v. Stevenson* to statements was their potentially lethal effect. A distinguished American judge referred to the "three indeterminates"—a careless statement might make the maker liable "in an indeterminate amount for an indeterminate time to an indeterminate class".[19] The refusal of the law to provide a remedy was not without its critics. In *Candler v. Crane Christmas*[20] Lord Denning adopted a statement from an earlier case that:

> "A country whose administration of justice did not afford redress in a case of the present description would not be in a state of civilization."

It was not until 1964 that the House of Lords altered the law. The case of **3.05** *Hedley Byrne & Co. Ltd v. Heller and Partners Ltd*[21] shows a cautious

---

[18] [1932] A.C. 562.
[18a] *Hamble Fisheries Ltd v. L. Gardner & Sons Ltd, The Times*, January 5, 1999, CA and see the building cases discussed in para. 5.24 below.
[19] Cardozo C.J. in *Ultramares Corporation v. Touche* (1931) 255 N.Y. Rep. 170, cited in *Candler v. Crane Christmas*, below.
[20] [1951] K.B. 164 at 176 (a powerful dissenting judgment).
[21] [1964] A.C. 465.

approach and it is difficult to extract one really clear-cut principle from the five speeches. In one sense all the pronouncements in the *Hedley Byrne* case were *obiter* because the actual decision was that the defendants were absolved from liability because of a disclaimer. The facts were as follows:

> The plaintiffs were advertising agents. They placed orders on behalf of E. Ltd with various newspapers and television. They were personally liable to the sellers of the advertising space and they were anxious to make sure that E. Ltd were financially sound. The plaintiffs' bankers got in touch with the defendants who were the bankers of E. Ltd. The defendants gave favourable references "without responsibility". The plaintiffs thereupon made the contracts. The references turned out to be unjustified and the plaintiffs lost £17,000 on the contracts. They sued the defendants on the references. The House of Lords gave judgment for the defendants.

Lord Reid pointed out that a duty of care existed if there was a "special relationship"; he considered that this could be proved:

> "where it is plain that the party seeking information or advice was trusting the other to exercise such a degree of care as the circumstances required, where it was reasonable for him to do that, and where the other gave the information or advice when he knew or ought to know that the enquirer was relying on him."

It is clear from a careful reading of the speeches that the key factor was an assumption of responsibility. In the words of Lord Morris:

> "My Lords, it seems to me that if A assumes a responsibility to B to tender him deliberate advice, there could be a liability if the advice is negligently given."

The case was decided in favour of the bank because (a) the disclaimer made it clear that no responsibility was being assumed and (b) even without such disclaimer it could well be argued that the only duty expected in this type of case was a duty to be honest.

In all the decided cases since 1964 the defendants supplied information in answer to an inquiry or in the course of professional duties and the most recent cases[22] indicate that a private consumer (especially at the lower end of the market) is more likely to succeed than a businessman or professional investor; the "reliance" factor mentioned above will often be crucial.[22a] The cases of *Smith v. Bush* and *Harris v. Wyre Forest D.C.*[23] were heard together because similar issues arose. The facts were as follows:

---

[22] Five of them related to auditors. The leading case on non-liability of auditors is undoubtedly *Caparo Industries plc v. Dickman* [1990] 2 A.C. 605, HL.

[22a] For a recent (and rather special) case where the plaintiff succeeded *without* reliance, see *White v. Jones* [1995] 2 W.L.R. 187 (solicitors' delay in drawing will; testator died before will was ready; solicitor liable in negligence to two daughters who were due to benefit under that will). Similarly a solicitor was liable to a disappointed beneficiary when he failed to advise a testator to sever a joint tenancy: *Carr-Glynn v. Frearsons* [1998] All E.R. 225, CA.

[23] [1990] 1 A.C. 831. The "disclaimer" aspect of the case is considered in para. 8.38 below.

Mrs Smith and Mr and Mrs Harris applied for mortgages for house purchase. In both cases they paid to the lenders a non-returnable fee for a valuation. In one case the valuer was an independent surveyor and in the other he was an in-house surveyor employed by the lender. In both cases they negligently overvalued the property by failing to discover defects and the buyers suffered loss. Mrs Smith was shown a copy of the valuer's report; the Harrises were not.

In both cases the lenders were under a statutory duty to cause a valuation to be made but the House of Lords held that this was irrelevant. They unanimously held that the negligent surveyor was liable to Mrs Smith[24] and that the council who made the advance to the Harrises were liable for the negligence of their surveyor. What emerges from the case is that the "assumption of responsibility" test is not the true one—or rather the question should be "in what circumstances will a negligent party be *deemed* to have assumed responsibility?" The language of the three substantive speeches is cautious. Lord Templeman said (at p. 800):

> "In general, I am of the opinion that in the absence of a disclaimer of liability the valuer who values a house for the purposes of a mortgage, knowing that the mortgagee will rely and the mortgagor will probably rely on the valuation, knowing that the purchaser mortgagor has in effect paid for the valuation, is under a duty to exercise reasonable skill and care and that duty is owed to both parties to the mortgage for which the valuation was made."

The speech of Lord Griffiths shows a typical judicial reluctance to extend the scope of liability. He said (at pp. 815–816):

> "I therefore return to the question in what circumstances should the law deem those who give advice to have assumed responsibility to the person who acts upon the advice? I would answer—only if it is foreseeable that if the advice is negligent the recipient is likely to suffer damage, that there is a sufficiently proximate relationship between the parties *and that it is just and reasonable to impose the liability*" (italics supplied).

Finally, Lord Jauncey of Tullichettle stressed the reliance factor in the following passage (at p. 822):

> "The four critical facts [in the Smith case] are that the appellants knew from the outset:
> (1) that the report would be shown to Mrs Smith;
> (2) that Mrs Smith would probably rely on the valuation contained therein in deciding whether to buy the house without obtaining an independent valuation;
> (3) that if in these circumstances the valuation was, having regard to the actual condition of the house, excessive, Mrs Smith would be likely to suffer loss; and
> (4) that she had paid to the building society a sum to defray the appellants' fee."

---

[24] The lender too can be sued if he "adopts" the negligent valuation. *Beresford v. Chesterfield B.C. and Woolwich Equitable Building Society* (1990) 10 Tr.L.R. 6, CA.

After stating that these facts gave rise to a duty of care both to the building society and to Mrs Smith he added:

> "It is critical to this conclusion that the appellants knew that Mrs Smith would be likely to rely on the valuation without obtaining independent advice."

3.06   In a more recent case[25] (involving a company take-over by a person who had relied on statements made by the company's financial advisers) Hoffmann J. was asked to apply the principles set out above so as to impose negligence liability on the advisers. He declined to do so and in an illuminating passage he stressed the "consumer" aspect of the *Smith* and *Harris* cases. He distinguished *Smith* from the case before him as follows (at p. 335):

> "First, Mr Smith [*sic*] had paid for the survey; although he had no contract with the surveyor, the relationship was, as Lord Templeman said, 'akin to contract.' [The take-over bidder], on the other hand, had not paid for the audit.
> Second, the typical plaintiff in a *Smith v. Bush* type case is a person of modest means and making the most expensive purchase of his or her life. He was very unlikely to be insured against the manifestation of inherent defects. The surveyor can protect himself relatively easily by insurance. The take-over bidder, on the other hand, is an entrepreneur taking high risks for high rewards and while some accountants may be able to take out sufficient insurance, others may not.
> Third, the imposition of liability on surveyors would probably not greatly increase their insurance costs and push up the cost of surveys because the typical buyer who relies on a building survey is buying a relatively modest house. Take-overs on the Stock Exchange involve huge amounts and the effects on accountants' insurance and fees are unpredictable."

This "economic" distinction is not an absolute one. Thus an auditor who prepares and certifies the accounts of a company does not thereby owe a legal duty of care to individual shareholders[26] and there is no distinction for this purpose between a private and a commercial investor.

What is the relevance of all this to supplies of goods? If the statement is made by the supplier it may be useful to plead *Hedley Byrne* as an alternative to other forms of liability. It is unlikely, however, to add a great deal to consumers' chances of success, as the facts will usually disclose a *Bentley v. Smith* contractual term[27] or an actionable misrepresentation under section 2(1) of the Misrepresentation Act 1967[28] as well as a *Hedley Byrne* duty situation. Apart from the inherent uncertainty of establishing such a duty, the plaintiff is on stronger ground under the Misrepresentation Act because under that Act the burden is on the defendant to prove that he had reasonable grounds for believing the statement to be true. There is, however, a possi-

---

[25] *Morgan Crucible Co. v. Hill Samuel Bank Ltd* [1990] 3 All E.R. 330. The Court of Appeal subsequently held that, on the case as pleaded, a duty of care *might* arise—see [1991] 1 All E.R. 148.

[26] *Caparo Industries plc v. Dickman* [1990] 2 A.C. 605, HL.

[27] Above, para. 3.03.

[28] Above, para. 3.03 and below, para. 7.04.

bility that a *Hedley Byrne* claim could be pursued where the consumer has relied on a statement made by the manufacturer (for example, in sales literature or in a leaflet giving instructions for use). There is no doubt, however, that this would represent a major extension of the *Hedley Byrne* rule and in the only modern case in which the matter was raised the claim was rejected.[29]

4. Contractual Terms

We have already seen that a statement made during negotiations may sometimes be classified as a contractual term.[30] When will this occur? The leading case is *Heilbut, Symons & Co. v. Buckleton*[31] where Lord Moulton said:

> "An affirmation at the time of the sale is a warranty, provided it appears on evidence to be so intended."

3.07

The key word here is the word "intended" and the courts apply an objective test; they do not look into the minds of the parties but at their conduct. In the words of Lord Denning M.R.:

> "If an intelligent bystander would reasonably infer that a warranty was intended, that will suffice."[32]

To avoid confusion it must be stressed that the word "warranty" has at least two meanings. In the above examples it is used in its normal sense to mean "a term" or "a contractual promise". There is, however, a second meaning which is used in the Sale of Goods Act 1979. By section 61:

> warranty ... means an agreement with reference to goods which are the subject of a contract of sale, but collateral to the main purpose of such contract, the breach of which gives rise to a claim to damages, but not to a right to reject the goods and treat the contract as repudiated.

In other words it means a minor term.

If an express statement is classified as a contractual term we have seen that the innocent party can claim damages. Can he also treat the contract as repudiated and reject the goods? The answer is that he may be able to do so, provided that he has been substantially deprived of what he bargained for. Under the Sale of Goods Act 1979 terms are classified as conditions or warranties but the Court of Appeal has held that this rigid classification is not exhaustive.[33] The court held that there were intermediate stipulations (some-

---

[29] *Lambert v. Lewis* [1980] 2 W.L.R. 299 at 328, CA (the claim was actually brought by an intermediate dealer). In the House of Lords the case was decided on a different point. See also below, para. 4.15.
[30] Above, para. 3.03.
[31] [1913] A.C. 30.
[32] *Dick Bentley v. Harold Smith* [1965] 1 W.L.R. 623 at 627.
[33] *Cehave N.V. v. Bremer Handelsgesellschaft GmbH* [1976] Q.B. 44.

times called "innominate terms") where the right to reject depended on the consequences of the breach. This decision helps to bring the law of sale of goods more into line with the rest of the law of contract and with the reasonable expectations of the parties.

5. DESCRIPTION

3.08 The final possibility is that the statement formed part of the description of the goods. By section 13 of the Sale of Goods Act 1979:

> (1) Where there is a contract for the sale of goods by description, there is an implied term[33a] that the goods will correspond with the description.
> (2) If the sale is by sample, as well as by description, it is not sufficient that the bulk of the goods corresponds with the sample if the goods do not also correspond with the description.
> (3) A sale of goods is not prevented from being a sale by description by reason only that, being exposed for sale or hire, they are selected by the buyer.

The section is largely self-explanatory. Thus if a handbag is described as "leather" there will be a breach of section 13 if it is plastic; if a car is described as a 1999 model there is a breach of section 13 if it is a 1996 model; if the seller agrees to sell "woollen underpants" he will be in breach if the material is cotton, rayon or linen. In this type of case the section adds nothing to the general law. It is a central obligation of the seller to supply the goods contracted for and he is guilty of non-performance if he fails to do so.

We now have to consider two problems, namely:

(1) What is a sale by description?
(2) What stipulations form part of the contract description?

What is a sale by description?

3.09 The courts have given a wide meaning to this term—in the words of the Law Commission "It [is] to all intents and purposes comprehensive." The following examples show how wide it is.

> (a) Sales of purely generic goods, *e.g.* "50 rolls of hand-blocked wallpaper".
> (b) Sales of specific goods which the buyer has not seen where he is relying on the description, *e.g.* "my 1988 wooden skis, ideal for Alpine downhill skiing".
> (c) Sales of specific goods which the buyer has seen if they are sold as goods answering a description, *e.g.* "Canadian salmon".[34]

[33a] The "term" is a "condition": Sale and Supply of Goods Act 1994, Sched. 2, para. 5(4).
[34] The relationship between s.13 and "bought as seen" has recently been considered by the Divisional Court, below, para. 17.13.

(d) Goods selected by the buyer at a self-service store or supermarket. This is the effect of section 13(3).[35] Thus if a tin on a supermarket shelf is labelled "Scotch salmon" and it contains Canadian salmon there will be a breach of section 13—so also if a label wrongly states the ingredients or quantity.

The principle that goods can describe themselves was affirmed by the courts in the remarkable case of *Beale v. Taylor*[36] where the following facts occurred:

> The plaintiff saw an advertisement "Herald convertible white 1961". He went to see it and saw a "1200" disc on the rear of the car. He agreed to buy it for £190 in the belief that he was buying a 1961 Triumph Herald model. Unfortunately, he was only half right; the front part consisted of an earlier model which had been welded on to the rear end of a 1961 Herald 1200. He claimed damages from the seller, but the county court judge dismissed the claim. The Court of Appeal allowed his appeal.

The court held that the combined effect of the advertisement and the disc was that the seller was offering to sell a 1961 Herald. This was, therefore, a sale by description and the seller was in breach of section 13. Damages were agreed at £125 (the price less the scrap value to the buyer).

It is not clear from the judgments whether the buyer would have succeeded on the strength of the disc alone. It is clear, however, that if a seller says to the buyer "I am offering to sell this to you—I am making no representations and you must exercise your own judgment," there would not be a sale by description. It was presumably on this ground that the county court judge had given judgment for the seller.

This principle was recently applied and extended in *Harlingdon and Leinster Enterprises Ltd v. Christopher Hull Fine Art Ltd*[37] where the seller started by telling the buyer that he had come to sell two paintings by one Gabrielle Munter and then went on to say that he was not an expert in these matters and knew nothing about that particular artist. In holding that this was *not* a sale by description, Nourse L.J. in the Court of Appeal said (at p. 18):

> "Authority apart, those words [*i.e.* s.13(1)] would suggest that the description must be influential in the sale, not necessarily alone, but so as to become an essential term, *i.e.* a condition, of the contract. Without such influence a description cannot be said to be one *by* which the contract for the sale of goods is made."

Accordingly, the buyer will fail if, viewed objectively, the court is satisfied that he did not rely on the description.

---

[35] This "supermarket" rule was first introduced in 1973 as an amendment to the original Sale of Goods Act 1893 to reflect the changing pattern of retail trading.

[36] [1967] 1 W.L.R. 1193.

[37] [1991] 1 Q.B. 564. The legal effect of attribution may depend on whether the buyer was (as here) a dealer or a private buyer (*ibid.*). Note the strong and convincing dissenting judgment by Stuart-Smith L.J.

What statements form part of the description?

3.10   Until recently the courts have given an extremely wide meaning to the term "description". The term has been held to include such matters as the quantity, the measurements, the manner of packing and even the date of shipment. The practical result of this can be very serious from the seller's point of view and unduly favourable to the buyer. We have seen that if the goods do not comply with their description there is a breach of "condition"; this means that the buyer can reject the goods, even though he has suffered no loss. In the leading case of *Arcos Ltd v. Ronaasen*[38]:

> Sellers sold a quantity of wooden staves to the buyers. The thickness was given as half an inch. When the goods were delivered the arbitrator found that (i) only 5 per cent were half an inch thick; (ii) a large proportion were between half-an-inch and nine-sixteenths of an inch; (iii) some were between nine-sixteenths and five-eighths of an inch; (iv) a very small proportion were more than five-eighths of an inch; (v) the staves were fit for the buyer's purpose and commercially within, and merchantable under, the contract specification. Despite the finding in (v) the buyer claimed that he was entitled to reject them. The High Court, the Court of Appeal and the House of Lords upheld the buyer's claim.

The judgments in the House of Lords are brief but they emphasize the need for strict compliance. In the words of Lord Buckmaster[39]:

> "If the article they have purchased is not in fact the article that has been delivered, they are entitled to reject it, even though it is the commercial equivalent of that which they have bought."

Lord Atkin, in a well-known passage, commented that:

> "If the written contract specifies conditions of weight, measurement and the like, these conditions must be complied with. A ton does not mean about a ton, or a yard about a yard. Still less, when you descend to minute measurements does half an inch mean about half an inch. If the seller wants a margin he must and in my experience does stipulate for it."

He did, however, go on to add that:

> "No doubt there may be microscopic deviations which businessmen, and therefore lawyers will ignore."

Another well-known illustration of the doctrine of strict compliance is *Re Moore & Co. and Landauer & Co.*[40] which, like the previous case, reached the courts via an arbitrator.

> Sellers agreed to sell tinned fruit in boxes containing 30 tins. When delivered

---

[38] [1933] A.C. 470.
[39] *ibid.* at p. 474.
[40] [1921] 2 K.B. 519.

some contained only 24 tins. The arbitrator found that there was no difference in the market value of the goods whether they were packed 24 tins or 30 tins in a case. The Court of Appeal upheld a claim by the buyer that he was entitled to reject the entire consignment.

It may be, however, that the position is changing. In a passage which can be equally relevant to consumer cases Lord Wilberforce said this:

> "Some of these cases ... I find to be excessively technical and due for fresh examination in this House. Even if a strict and technical view must be taken as regards the description of unascertained future goods (*e.g.* commodities) as to which each detail of the description may be assumed to be vital, it may be, and in my opinion is, right to treat other contracts of sale of goods in a similar manner to other contracts generally so as to ask *whether a particular item in a description constituted a substantial ingredient of the 'identity' of the thing sold, and only if it does to treat it as a condition."* (italics supplied).[41]

Finally, it should be noted that a non-consumer will no longer be able to reject for minor breaches (see below, para. 7.18).

Special meaning

If words have acquired a special trade meaning there will be no breach of   **3.11**
section 13 if they answer that meaning. Thus in the case of *Grenfell v. E.B. Meyrowitz Ltd*[42] it was proved that the words "safety glass" had acquired a special meaning and that this was known to the buyer. It was held that the sellers were not in breach of section 13 when they supplied "safety glass" goggles which corresponded to the special trade meaning.

Relationship between description and fitness

A final question which can be important for the consumer relates to the   **3.12**
distinction between description and fitness for purpose. If goods are unfit for the buyer's particular purpose, can he allege that there is a breach of section 13 or must he rely on the condition of fitness for purpose under section 14 (considered in Chap. 4)? This is yet another problem where the law is uncertain; the practical importance lies in the sphere of private sales.

> Suppose that the seller of a house agrees to sell to the buyer his furniture, lawnmower and television set. Both the lawnmower and the television set break down almost immediately and a cocktail cabinet collapses shortly afterwards.

As the law stands at the moment it is very unlikely that the buyer would have any remedy against the seller. Section 14 only applies to a sale "in the course of a business". There is nothing to suggest that any of the goods have been misdescribed.

---

[41] *Reardon Smith v. Hansen-Tangen* [1976] 1 W.L.R. 989 at 998, HL.
[42] [1936] 2 All E.R. 1313.

One point which is clear is that unfitness for one particular use does not amount to a breach of section 13. Thus "herring-meal" is still "herring-meal" even if it has defects making it lethal when fed to mink.[43] If, however, the goods have only one use (*e.g.* "touring skis") it might be arguable that fitness for purpose forms an intrinsic part of the description. Perhaps the courts might adopt the words spoken by Birkett L.J. in another context that "a car which will not go is not a car at all".[44]

6. OTHER SUPPLY CONTRACTS

3.13   Where goods are let out on hire-purchase the condition as to description is identical to that for sale of goods.[45] An identical condition also applies in other cases where the property in goods is transferred to the customer (notably contracts of exchange and contracts for work and materials)[46] and in cases of hire.[47]

---

[43] *Ashington Piggeries v. Christopher Hill* [1972] A.C. 441. Such goods might, however, fail to satisfy the new (and expanded) test of "satisfactory quality" as to which see below, para. 4.18.
[44] *Karsales (Harrow) Ltd. v. Wallis* [1956] 1 W.L.R. 936 at 942.
[45] Supply of Goods (Implied Terms) Act 1973, s.9.
[46] Supply of Goods and Services Act 1982, s.3.
[47] *ibid.* s.8.

Chapter Four

"IT DOESN'T WORK"

1. The Problem

(1) A buys a dishwasher. It fails to work. The seller calls on numerous **4.01** occasions to try to put it right. It invariably breaks down again after a few days.
(2) B orders central heating which is installed by X. The radiators leak and damage the carpet.
(3) C takes his suit to the cleaners. It comes back in a ruined condition.
(4) D buys a pair of new patent leather shoes for a party. The soles come away from the uppers almost immediately and·D is unable to wear them.
(5) E takes his car to a garage for repair. The garage puts in faulty brake linings and E is injured when the brakes fail.

By far the most common consumer complaint is that the goods or services were not up to the expected standard. How does the law protect the consumer? There are four sets of provisions which may give him rights against the supplier:

(a) Section 14 of the Sale of Goods Act 1979 (as amended) is vitally important if the contract was a contract of sale.
(b) Section 10 of the Supply of Goods (Implied Terms) Act 1973 contains virtually identical provisions relating to hire-purchase agreements.
(c) Sections 4 and 9 of the Supply of Goods and Services Act 1982 contain virtually identical provisions in relation to other contracts for the transfer of goods (exchange, work and materials, etc.) and contracts of hire.
(d) At common law, an analogous condition of fitness for purpose may be implied in relation to computer software (see para. 4.30, below).

Until the passing of the 1982 Act it used to be important to distinguish clearly between a contract for the sale of goods on the one hand and a contract for work and materials (central heating, double glazing, loft conversion, etc.) on the other. The need for a clear distinction has been reduced considerably in relation to quality and fitness but it can still be important for other purposes— including the *nemo dat* rules discussed in Chapter 2.

2. SALE OF GOODS

The general position

4.02   If a contract is for the sale of goods the obligations of the seller in relation to quality and fitness are governed by section 14 of the Sale of Goods Act 1979 which is one of the most important provisions of the Act.[1] The Act is a consolidating Act and many of the key provisions (*e.g.* "merchantable quality") were originally to be found in the Sale of Goods Act 1893; that Act was passed before the consumer explosion of the present century and much of its terminology is more appropriate to a contract between two businessmen rather than between a businessman and a consumer.

The "business-to-business" flavour can be seen not only in the terminology (see above) but also in relation to remedies. The two remedies which the consumer most wants (namely, to have the goods repaired or replaced) are not provided for in the Act. The Law Commission have commented that:

> "one reason for the longevity of the provisions of the original 1893 Act may be that in many instances the Act is in practice not relied upon. For example, there are shops which will always allow customers to return recently purchased goods whether defective or not."[2]

In relation to "merchantable quality" four dates are significant, namely:

1973—The Supply of Goods (Implied Terms) Act 1973 made minor changes and introduced a statutory definition.

1979—The Acts of 1893 and 1973 were consolidated.

1987—The Law Commission Report[3] made proposals for certain changes (including changes to the rules governing the buyer's right to reject, as to which see below, paras 4.18–4.19 and paras 7.18–7.26).

1994—The Sale and Supply of Goods Act 1994 gave effect to most of these proposed changes. It introduced the term "satisfactory quality" although the Law Commission had recommended "acceptable quality".[4]

Let the buyer beware

4.03   In the light of what has been said above, the early law developed on the basis that it was for the parties to make their own bargain—it was up to the buyer to decide whether the goods were merchantable and fit before he agreed to buy them. The principle ("*caveat emptor*" or "let the buyer beware") has been severely eroded but is not entirely extinct. By section 14(1):

---

[1] See Law Com. No. 24, p. 9.
[2] Law Com. No. 160, Scot. Law Com. No. 104, para. 1.9. The popularity of manufacturers' guarantees is a further example of the by-passing of the Act.
[3] Law Com. No. 24.
[4] See Report cited in n.2 above, at paras. 319–322.

Except as provided by this section . . . there is no implied condition or warranty about the quality or fitness for any particular purpose of goods supplied under a contract of sale.

We shall see that the Act protects the consumer if the seller sells in the course of a business. If, however, the seller is a private seller the principle of *caveat emptor* may still apply.

Suppose that A, a private individual, sells a hedgecutter to B. It is in poor condition and breaks down after a few days. In the absence of any express promise or representation B has no claim against A.

The distinction then is between a sale "in the course of a business" and a sale **4.04** which is not in the course of a business. After earlier doubts, and after referring to Hansard debates on the 1973 Act (which amended the original Sale of Goods Act 1893), the Court of Appeal has recently held that the seller does not have to deal in the particular class of goods. Thus the conditions would apply to, *e.g.* the sale of surplus computer equipment by a solicitor or (as in the present case) the sale of a fisherman's boat. The words "in the course of a business" must be construed broadly and purposively, the mere fact that they have been construed differently in other contexts is immaterial.[4a] There is one hybrid situation; what about a dealer who sells in the course of a business as agent for a private seller? Section 14(5) makes it clear that the seller must endeavour to bring this fact to the buyer's notice. It provides that:

[The conditions of quality and fitness] apply to a sale by a person who in the course of business is acting as agent for another as they apply to a sale by a principal in the course of a business except where that other is not selling in the course of a business and either the buyer knows that fact or reasonable steps are taken to bring it to the notice of the buyer before the contract is made.

A recent Scottish case illustrates that a buyer can take advantage of section 14(5) if he buys from a dealer without knowing that the dealer is acting for a non-business seller.[4b]

Section 14(5) is concerned with the case where a private seller appears to be selling in the course of a business. What about the converse case—trade sellers masquerading as private sellers? An inquiry under Part II of the Fair Trading Act 1973 disclosed that some motor traders were guilty of this practice—they advertised their cars for sale in newspapers and gave only their private addresses. Such practices are now a criminal offence under the Business Advertisements (Disclosure) Order 1977 (below, 313).

Privity of contract—new law on the way

The conditions of quality and fitness are implied *as between seller and* **4.05**

[4a] *Stevenson v. Rogers* (1999) 149 N.L.J. 16, CA.
[4b] *Boyter v. Thomson, The Times,* June 16, 1995, HL.

buyer. If, for example, a mother buys a defective washing machine and gives it to her daughter as a present, the daughter currently has no claim against the supplier if it breaks down. The mother would have a claim but she might find it difficult to prove damage flowing from the breach (although she might have a claim if she paid for the cost of repairs).[5] The question of "who made the contract?" may also be relevant if, for example, a group of people go to a restaurant for a meal. It seems that the restaurant makes a contract with each of them, so that each of them would be entitled to claim damages if the supplier was in breach of the implied term.[6]

The mother-and-daughter example given above will soon have to be modified under the Contracts (Rights of Third Parties) Bill if the mother deals with the matter when she makes the contract. The Bill provides that a non-party can enforce a contractual term if (a) the contract so provides or (b) the contract purports to confer a benefit on the third party—but this will not be so if, on a proper construction of the contract, it appears that the parties did not intend the third party to have enforcement rights.

Questions of agency must also be borne in mind in this connection. A woman who does the shopping may do so as agent for her husband or cohabitee, so that *he* would have a claim in contract if the goods turn out to be defective. There is no agency case (so far) the other way round. Thus if a man buys typhoid-infected milk which injures his wife, it was held in *Frost v. Aylesbury Dairy Co.*[7] that only the husband has a claim in contract. In modern social conditions it might well be possible for the courts to hold that the husband was buying for himself and as agent for his wife. An argument on these lines should certainly be tried in appropriate cases; if it were accepted it could help to loosen the shackles of the privity rule.

Strict liability

4.06   The practical importance of the point just mentioned lies in the concept of strict liability. Section 14(2) says that the goods "are of satisfactory quality". It is clear from the case of *Frost v. Aylesbury Dairy Co.*, above, that the absence of negligence is no defence; the seller will not be able to avoid liability by proving that he neither knew, nor ought to have known, of the defect.

If, however, the privity rules bar a claim in contract an injured plaintiff will have to bring proceedings in *tort*. This used to mean having to prove negligence—by no means an easy task. However, since the arrival of the Consumer Protection Act 1987 and the imposition of strict (or at least semi-strict) liability on producers and some distributors, the plaintiff's position has improved significantly.[8]

---

[5] See *Jackson v. Horizon Holidays* [1975] 1 W.L.R. 1468 where the Court of Appeal allowed a contracting party to recover damages for a third party's loss (the facts are given below, para. 7.39). But see the comments of Lord Wilberforce in *Woodar Investment Development v. Wimpey Construction U.K.* [1980] 1 W.L.R. 277 HL.

[6] *Lockett v. A.M. Charles Ltd* [1938] 4 All E.R. 170.

[7] [1905] 1 K.B. 608.

[8] Below, paras 5.10 and 5.23.

The law before the 1994 Act

Section 14(2) of the 1979 Act dealt with "merchantable quality" in the   **4.07**
following way:

> where the seller sells goods in the course of a business, there is an implied con-
> dition that the goods supplied under the contract are of merchantable quality,
> except that there is no such condition—
> (a) as regards defects specifically drawn to the buyer's attention before the
>   contract is made; or
> (b) if the buyer examines the goods before the contract is made, as regards
>   defects which that examination ought to reveal.

This definition gave rise to four problems and three of them (numbers (1), (2)
and (4) below) are unaffected by the 1994 Act changes. The problems are:

(1) Was the sale in the course of a business?
(2) What is the meaning of "goods supplied"?
(3) Are the goods "merchantable"? ˙
(4) Do either of the exceptions apply?

Even the one area where the law has been changed (namely (3) above) will
continue to be relevant for some years, because the 1994 Act applies only to
contracts made on or after January 3, 1995.

(1) *Are the goods supplied "in the course of a business"?*

We have already considered the purposive interpretation of these words   **4.08**
(see para. 4.04, above).
Some borderline cases can be imagined. What about goods sold at a charity, tennis club bazaar or jumble sale? It could be argued that such a "one-off"
activity is not a business sale. Again, if a dentist or an accountant sells his
private car, the mere fact that he sometimes used it for business would not, it
is believed, make it a sale "in the course of a business". The Act itself merely
provides that the term "trade" includes a profession and the activities of a
local authority, government department or statutory undertaker. The concept
of "business" is also central to the Unfair Contract Terms Act 1977[9-12] and to
the Consumer Credit Act 1974[13] and both of these Acts merely give a limited
definition similar to the one referred to above.

(2) *What is the meaning of "goods supplied"?*

The courts have given a sensible answer to this question by giving the   **4.09**
words their normal meaning. Thus the condition of merchantable quality can
apply not only to the *contents* of a bottle or tin but also to the *container, i.e.*

[9-12] Below, para. 8.21.
[13] Below, para. 20.03.

the bottle or tin itself, even if it has to be returned—it is still "supplied" under the contract.[14] Similarly, if the goods actually supplied contain a foreign body (for example, a worm, a snail, a piece of glass or a detonator) the totality of the goods supplied may be unmerchantable.[15]

(3) *When are goods unmerchantable?*

4.10   As already stated (above, para. 4.02) the first statutory definition was introduced in 1973. This became section 14(6) of the 1979 Act which read as follows:

> "Goods of any kind are of merchantable quality ... if they are as fit for the purpose or purposes for which goods of that kind are commonly bought as it is reasonable to expect having regard to any description applied to them, the price (if relevant) and all the other relevant circumstances."

The basic thrust of this definition is clear enough, but three matters have given cause for concern—namely minor and cosmetic defects, second-hand goods and durability.[16] Before considering them various points can be made. First, if the goods are unfit for their only proper use they will not be "merchantable". If a thermos flask breaks when it is filled, if a piece of a jigsaw puzzle is missing, if wallpaper cannot be stuck to the wall, the seller is liable. In the words of Lord Ellenborough in an early case[17]:

> "The purchaser cannot be expected to buy the goods to lay them on the dunghill."

Again in the well-known "sulphite in the pants" case of *Grant v. Australian Knitting Mills Ltd*[18] Lord Wright commented that:

> "it [merchantable quality] does mean that the article sold, if only meant for one particular use, is fit for that use."[19]

Before considering the three problems mentioned above various other points can be made. First, the definition uses the word "are". This confirms the ruling in *Jackson v. Rotax Motor Co. Ltd*[20] that if goods are unmerchantable, the mere fact that they can be made merchantable by a simple process is immaterial and it is very doubtful whether the seller can legally rectify the defect after the buyer's rejection of the goods. Secondly, the reference to price supports what Lord Reid said in *Brown & Son Ltd v. Craiks*,[21] namely

---

[14] *Geddling v. Marsh* [1920] 1 K.B. 668.
[15] See the interesting case of *Wilson v. Rickett Cockerell & Co. Ltd* [1954] 1 Q.B. 598 where a detonator was mistakenly included in a bag of coalite.
[16] s.14(6).
[17] *Gardiner v. Gray* (1815) 4 Camp. 144.
[18] [1936] A.C. 85.
[19] *ibid.* at p. 100.
[20] [1910] 2 K.B. 937.
[21] [1970] 1 W.L.R. 752, HL. If, however, the buyer relies entirely on his own judgment, the mere fact that he makes a bad bargain will not give rise to a claim: *Harlingdon Enterprises Ltd v. Christopher Hull Fine Art Ltd*, above, para. 3.09.

that if a particular description covers different qualities of goods, a buyer who pays a price appropriate to a *superior* quality can reasonably expect to receive that quality, and can regard the goods as unmerchantable if he receives an inferior quality. Thirdly, what about goods bought at a "sale" at reduced prices? There is no reported case on this point but a buyer should have no difficulty in satisfying a court that the "sale" aspect is irrelevant; it results from a commercial decision to dispose of surplus stock and it cannot in any way be relied on by the seller to justify the supply of inferior goods.

Finally, what is the meaning of "fit for the purpose or purposes" in section 14(6)? Does it mean that multi-purpose goods will be unmerchantable if they have defects rendering them unfit for some (but not all) of their normal purposes? Such an interpretation would involve a major change in the law and the Court of Appeal has recently confirmed that the statutory wording introduced in 1973 has not had this effect; in other words multi-purpose goods will only be unmerchantable if they are unfit for *all* their normal purposes.[22] However, such a change has now been effected by the 1994 Act (see below, para. 4.18).

Minor and cosmetic defects. In a report[23] published by the Consumers' Association in 1979 it was pointed out that the statutory definition was unsatisfactory in two respects. In the first place, it concentrates excessively on the fitness of the goods for their purpose and ignores aesthetic considerations and appearance (dents, scratches, etc.). Secondly, the reference to the standard which a buyer might reasonably expect could open the door to an argument that a buyer could not complain if his new car had "teething troubles" since it was widely known that all new cars had them. The Law Commission Report[24] refers to a number of cases which lend some support to these fears[25] but in two recent cases these fears have been largely laid to rest. The leading modern case on the point is *Rogers v. Parish (Scarborough) Ltd.*[26]   **4.11**

> Mr Rogers bought a Range Rover for £16,000 under a conditional sale agreement. It was sold as new but it had defects in the engine, gearbox and bodywork and the oilseals were unsound at vital junctions. In the six months following delivery Mr Rogers drove the car some 5,500 miles while unsuccessful efforts were made to rectify the defects. At the end of that period he rejected the car and claimed the return of his payments and damages on the basis that the car was unmerchantable.

Counsel for the sellers argued that since the car was roadworthy, the defects

[22] *Aswan Engineering Establishment Co. v. Lupdine Ltd* [1987] 1 W.L.R. 1, CA.
[23] *Merchantable Quality—What does it mean?*
[24] See n. 2 above, at para. 4.03.
[25] *Millars of Falkirk Ltd v. Turpie* (1976) S.L.T. (Notes) 66; *Spencer v. Claude Rye (Vehicles) Ltd, The Guardian*, December 19, 1972; *Leaves v. Wadham Stringer (Cliftons) Ltd* [1980] R.T.R. 308.
[26] [1987] Q.B. 933. The other case is *Bernstein v. Pamson Motors (Golders Green) Ltd* [1987] 2 All E.R. 220.

did not make it unmerchantable. The judge at first instance accepted this view but the Court of Appeal rejected it and found in favour of Mr Rogers. In a passage which lies at the heart of the 1994 amendment (see below) Mustill L.J. said (at p. 359):

> "Starting with the purpose for which 'goods of that kind' are commonly bought, one would include in respect of any passenger vehicle not merely the buyer's purpose of driving the car from one place to another *but of doing so with the appropriate degree of comfort, ease of handling and reliability and, one might add, of pride in the vehicle's outward and interior appearance* [italics supplied]. What is the appropriate degree and what relative weight is to be attached to one characteristic of the car rather than another will depend on the market at which the car is aimed.
>
> "To identify the relevant expectation one must look at the factors listed in the subsection. First, the description applied to the goods. In the present case the vehicle was sold as new. Deficiencies which might be acceptable in a second-hand vehicle were not to be expected in one purchased as new. Next, the description 'Range Rover' would conjure up a particular set of expectations, not the same as those relating to an ordinary saloon car, as to the balance between performance, handling, comfort and resilience. The factor of price was also significant. At more than £16,000 this vehicle was, if not at the top end of the scale, well above the level of the ordinary family saloon. The buyer was entitled to value for his money."

Even if the car is in the middle or lower end of the market it will still be unmerchantable if (1) the defects have a knock-on effect so that the car can never be restored to its previous condition, or (2) the defects (*e.g.* oil leak) render it dangerous to drive the car.[27]

4.12   Effect of guarantee.   In the *Rogers* case (above) counsel for the sellers raised a further point—namely that a car was not rendered unmerchantable by defects which the buyer was entitled to have rectified free of charge under the manufacturer's guarantee (or warranty). Mustill L.J. was unimpressed. He said (at p. 360):

> "Can it really be right to say that the reasonable buyer would expect less of his new Range Rover with a warranty than without one? Surely the warranty is an addition to the buyer's rights, not a subtraction from them, and, it may be noted, only a circumscribed addition since it lasts for a limited period and does not compensate the buyer for consequential loss and inconvenience.
>
> "If the defendants are right a buyer would be well advised to leave his guarantee behind in the showroom. This cannot be what the manufacturers and dealers intend or what their customers reasonably understand."

4.13   Second-hand goods.   There have been four fairly recent cases dealing with "merchantability" of second-hand cars (and they would have been decided in the same way after the 1994 amendments, below, para. 4.18). The first was *Bartlett v. Sidney Marcus*[28] where the following facts arose:

---

[27] See the judgment of Rougier J. in the *Bernstein* case cited in n. 26.
[28] [1965] 1 W.L.R. 1013.

The plaintiff bought a second-hand Jaguar car for £950. It was pointed out that the clutch was in need of repair, but the defect was believed to be a small one and the price was reduced accordingly. After driving for 300 miles the plaintiff took the car to a garage who found that the defect was more serious than the plaintiff expected. The cost of repairs came to £84 and the plaintiff claimed this amount from the seller.

The county court judge gave judgment for the buyer but the Court of Appeal allowed the seller's appeal. On the question of merchantability Lord Denning M.R. pointed out that:

"on the sale of a second-hand car, it is merchantable if it is in usable condition, even if not perfect. ... A buyer should realise that when he buys a second-hand car defects may appear sooner or later and, in the absence of an express warranty, he has no redress."

In *Crowther v. Shannon Motor Co.*,[29] which was also concerned with a second-hand Jaguar, the buyer was more successful.

The car was eight years old; the engine had done 82,165 miles; the buyer paid a price of £390. He drove the car for another 2,300 miles in three weeks. Then the engine expired. The evidence showed that (a) the engine was in a "clapped out" state when the car was sold to the buyer; (b) the buyer of a Jaguar car could reasonably expect the engine to do 100,000 miles. On these facts the Court of Appeal held that the seller was liable.

In the third case the buyer scored a somewhat Pyrrhic victory. The case was *Lee v. York Coach and Marine*[30] and the facts were as follows:

Mrs Lee bought a second-hand Morris 1100 for £355. Almost immediately it developed defects and it was off the road for a considerable time when the sellers sought unsuccessfully to mend the defects. After seven weeks her solicitors wrote to the sellers saying "we must ask you please to remedy all these defects without delay or to refund £355 to Mrs Lee". The sellers then offered to do some further work on the car; a Department of Environment examiner found very serious defects, and two weeks later a further letter was written by the solicitors. "Mrs Lee would have been justified in rescinding the contract on that basis—that is on the basis that the car was unroadworthy—in our opinion she may still be entitled to do so." Four months later the buyer brought an action claiming the return of the price. The evidence showed (*inter alia*) that the brakes were so poor that they could not have survived an attempt to test them.

The Court of Appeal held that the car, being unsafe to be driven, was clearly unmerchantable. They also held, however, that neither of the solicitor's letters amounted to a rejection of the car. By the time that the buyer finally sought to reject (the start of the proceedings) it was too late to reject.[31]

[29] [1975] 1 W.L.R. 30.
[30] [1977] R.T.R. 35.
[31] See below, para. 7.27.

Accordingly, she was only entitled to damages and the figure of £100 was not disputed. Presumably Mrs Lee would have seen none of the £100 since the court made no order for costs in the Court of Appeal.

Finally, in the most recent case[32] the Court of Appeal have applied the *Rogers* ruling (above) that roadworthiness was not the correct test. Each case would turn on the application of the statutory definition to the particular facts and on the extent to which the actual condition of the vehicle matched the buyer's reasonable expectations.

4.14   **Acts to be done before use.**   If both parties contemplate that some act will be done to the goods before use, they must be merchantable *after* this has been done but not necessarily before. Thus in *Heil v. Hedges*[33] the buyer of pork chops failed to cook them properly and became ill as the result of the chops becoming infected by worms. Had she cooked them properly the infection would not have occurred. Her claim for damages failed. On the other hand in the underpants case[34] the pants were sold for immediate use. Therefore the fact that the sulphite might have been removed by washing was held to be irrelevant.

4.15   **Durability.**   It is clear from commercial cases involving the sale of rabbits and potatoes that if defects appear soon after purchase this may show that the goods were unmerchantable at the time of the contract.[35] What does that mean in the consumer context? A vacuum cleaner breaks down after one month, a freezer after two months, a carpet starts to wear away after three months and a dishwasher ceases to operate after 18 months. The consumer *may* be able to show that the goods were not merchantable right at the beginning but it will not be easy. If the seller wishes to resist a claim, he will point out that all sorts of things could have caused the breakdown and that it is up to the buyer to produce evidence linking the breakdown to the condition of the goods when he bought them. The buyer will argue, "I used the goods in the normal way—a freezer should not break down after only two months." The Act does not spell out any obligation of durability but a recent case lends support to the consumer's argument of unmerchantability. In *Lambert v. Lewis*[36]—a case concerning a tow bar on a Land Rover—Lord Diplock said:

> "The implied warranty [*sic*] of fitness for a particular purpose . . . is a continuing warranty that the goods will continue to be fit for that purpose for a reasonable time after delivery. . . . What is a reasonable time will depend on the nature of the goods but I would accept that in the case of the coupling the warranty was still continuing up to the date, some three to six months before the accident, when it

---

[32] *Business Application Specialists v. Nationwide Credit Corporation* [1988] R.T.R. 332.
[33] [1951] 1 T.L.R. 512.
[34] *Grant v. Australian Knitting Mills* [1936] A.C. 85.
[35] See *Beer v. Walker* (1877) 46 L.J.Q.B. 677; *Mash & Murrell v. Joseph I. Emanuel Ltd* [1961] 1 All E.R. 485.
[36] [1982] A.C. 225.

first became known to the farmer that the handle of the locking mechanism was missing."[37]

Nevertheless there is considerable uncertainty in this area (especially at the level of consumer complaints) and the Law Commission have recommended[38] an express reference to durability in the Act. This has been done (see below, para. 4.18).

Spare parts.   A consumer may find that his goods become useless because, for example, the retailer does not have a supply of spare parts and the manufacturer has discontinued that particular product or has gone out of business altogether. There is no legal obligation on the seller to carry spare parts[39]— although some trade associations have adopted Codes of Practice which require their members to do so.[40]   **4.16**

(4) *Do either of the exceptions apply?*

The first exception in section 14(2)(a) applies where defects are *specifically* drawn to the buyer's attention before the contract is made. This could apply if, for example, a defective clutch or a dent or scratch or other defect was pointed out to the buyer—perhaps with an abatement in price. This is quite common where stores sell shop-soiled showroom models at a discount with labels drawing attention to the particular damage. There could, of course, be room for argument—the buyer might say "the seller told me that the clutch was rather worn but I had no idea I would have to spend £250 on it a week after buying the car."   **4.17**

The second exception in section 14(2)(b) relates to examination where the buyer has examined the goods *before* the making of the contract. The condition does not apply as regards defects which that examination ought to reveal. Two points can be made with regard to this exception. First, it only applies to a buyer who has *actually* examined the goods—not to a buyer who has declined an opportunity to do so. Secondly, what is the meaning of "defects which that examination ought to reveal?" This wording was first introduced in 1973 and differs slightly from the wording of the original 1893 Act, *i.e.* "defects which such examination ought to have revealed". In either case the words appear to refer solely to the examination actually made. If, for example, the buyer of a handbag only examines the outside, he will still be able to complain if on arriving home he finds that the inside has numerous defects including a broken zip (but he could not claim for an external defect which he should have seen, *e.g.* a broken handle). There is a Court of Appeal case which appears to confirm this view.[41] However, in *Thornett & Fehr v.*

---

[37] At p. 276.
[38] *Op. cit.* at pp. 10, 31–33.
[39] See Law Com. No. 160, p. 34.
[40] See below, para. 10.27.
[41] *Bristol Tramways v. Fiat Motors* [1910] 2 K.B. 831.

Beers & Son[42] Bray J. at first instance appeared to treat the words "such examination" as if they read "a reasonable examination". He held that (a) the buyers had examined the goods; (b) an examination would "in the ordinary way" have revealed the defect; (c) accordingly, the condition was not implied.

It is possible that this decision is wrong on the wording of the Act and it appears to be inconsistent with the *Bristol Tramways* case (which was not cited). It can also be argued that if the case was wrong on the original wording of the Act, it may well be even more incorrect on the amended wording. Thus, the courts may well refuse to follow it.

The Law Commission Report and the 1994 Act

4.18   The Law Commission have acknowledged that there is no magic formula to cover all cases[43] because:

> "Sale transactions may take an almost infinite variety of forms. A sale may be of a new jet aircraft from the manufacturers to an international carrier, of a washing machine still in its packing from a department store to a young married couple, of a catapult to a child, of an old motor car by a back-street garage to a student, of a breeding ewe from one farmer to another, of thousands of tons of a primary product (such as wheat) from one trader to another (neither of whom will ever see the goods), of a newspaper or box of matches from a street-vendor to a passer-by."[44]

In the Third Edition of this book we forecast that the Law Commission's proposals were likely to be given statutory force before the next decade was much older. That was written in 1990 and four years later the Sale and Supply of Goods Act 1994 was passed. Section 1 is identical to clause 1 of the Law Commission draft Bill except that "satisfactory quality" replaces "acceptable quality". The section replaces section 14(2) (above, para. 4.07) with the following four subsections:

> (2) Where the seller sells goods in the course of a business there is an implied term that the goods supplied under the contract are of satisfactory quality.
>
> (2A) For the purposes of this Act goods are of satisfactory quality if they meet the standard that a reasonable person would regard as satisfactory, taking account of any description of the goods, the price (if relevant) and all the other relevant circumstances.
>
> (2B) For the purposes of this Act the quality of the goods includes their state or condition and the following (among others) are in appropriate cases aspects of the quality of goods—
>
> > (a) fitness for all the purposes for which goods of the kind in question are commonly supplied,
> >
> > (b) appearance and finish,
> >
> > (c) freedom from minor defects,

---

[42] [1919] 1 K.B. 486.
[43] *Op. cit.*, p. 24.
[44] *ibid.* at p. 23.

(d) safety, and
(e) durability.
(2C) The term implied by subsection (2) above does not extend to any matter making the quality of the goods unsatisfactory—
(a) which is specifically drawn to the buyer's attention before the contract is made,
(b) where the buyer examines the goods before the contract is made, which that examination ought to reveal, or
(c) in the case of a contract for sale by sample, which would have been apparent on a reasonable examination of the sample.

Section 14(6) (which used to contain the 1973 definition of merchantable quality) is replaced by a provision that in England and Wales and in Northern Ireland the "term" in section 14(2) is a "condition" (see Sched. 2, para. 5(5) and below, paras 7.05–7.06).

Effect of the changes

The changes (which are not great) can be summarised as follows: **4.19**

(1) "Satisfactory quality" is more appropriate to a consumer transaction than "merchantable quality".
(2) The new Act gives statutory force to the *Rogers* decision (above, para. 4.11) that the "quality" test is not confined to fitness for purpose and covers cosmetic defects too.
(3) The new Act clarifies the position on durability.
(4) The new Act makes one change of substance relating to multi-purpose goods. Cases before the 1973 Act had decided that where the goods had several purposes, and were suitable for some of those purposes, there was no breach of the condition (in effect "unmerchantable" meant "useless").[45] Then came the 1973 definition which required the goods to be fit for "the purpose or purposes" for which goods of that type were commonly used. Had the definition inadvertently changed the law, so that the goods now had to be suitable for *all* their purposes? In *Aswan Engineering Co. v. Lupdine Ltd*[46] the Court of Appeal decided that the law had not been changed but the new Act does change the law (see s.14(2B)(a), above, para. 4.18) by requiring the goods to be fit for *all* their common purposes.

Fitness for particular purpose

Section 14 of the Sale of Goods Act implies a condition of reasonable **4.20**

---

[45] *Kendall v. Lillico* [1969] 2 A.C. 31, HL.
[46] See n. 22 above, para. 4.10.

fitness as well as the condition of satisfactory quality which has just been considered. Section 14(3) reads as follows:

> Where the seller sells goods in the course of a business and the buyer, expressly or by implication, makes known
>   (a) to the seller, or
>   (b) where the purchase price or part of it is payable by instalments and the goods were previously sold by a credit-broker to the seller, to that credit-broker
> any particular purpose for which the goods are being bought, there is an implied [condition][47] that the goods supplied under the contract are reasonably fit for that purpose, whether or not that is a purpose for which such goods are commonly supplied, except where the circumstances show that the buyer does not rely, or that it is unreasonable for him to rely, on the skill or judgment of the seller or credit-broker.

A number of rules are common to both subsections. Thus (a) in both cases liability is strict[48]; (b) in both cases the seller is only liable if he supplied the goods "in the course of a business"; (c) both conditions apply to all goods "supplied" under the contract; (d) in both cases the condition only applies as between seller and buyer; and (e) in both cases the seller may be relieved from liability if the buyer fails to do something to the goods before use.[49]

What is the need for section 14(3)? The key is to be found in the words "any *particular* purpose . . . whether or not that is a purpose for which such goods are commonly supplied".

> Suppose that a law student goes to a bookseller and says "I want to buy some books which are suitable for the Solicitors examinations." The seller supplies books which are only suitable for the Bar or University examinations.

On these facts the seller would clearly be liable under section 14(3); but there might well be no breach of section 14(2).

The subsection applies where the purpose is made known expressly or by implication. In the case of single purpose goods such as weedkiller, a bun or a hot water bottle, the buyer does not have to go through the ritual of spelling out his purpose—this will be implied because it is self-evident.[50] In this type of case the courts would not give much weight to a clause in a standard form contract (even if signed by the buyer) stating that "the buyer has not made known the purpose for which the goods are required." This type of clause was used in the hire-purchase case of *Lowe v. Lombank*,[51] a case involving a car with numerous defects. The Court of Appeal found no difficulty in holding

[47] The amended section uses the neutral word "term" but in England and Wales and in Northern Ireland that term is a "condition": 1994 Act, Sched. 2, para. 5(5).
[48] Above, para. 4.06.
[49] See above, para. 4.14.
[50] See *Preist v. Last* [1903] 2 K.B. 148—the well-known case of a bursting hot water bottle. The seller would also be liable under s.14(2), above.
[51] [1960] 1 W.L.R. 196.

that the supplier (the finance company) was liable under the implied condition of fitness. The purpose was obvious and the clause was inconsistent with the facts. If, however, the purpose is a special one (for example, a textbook suitable for a particular course) then the seller will be liable only if that purpose was *expressly* made known. In *Griffiths v. Peter Conway Ltd*[52]:

> A lady bought a Harris tweed coat. She had an abnormally sensitive skin and contracted dermatitis from wearing the coat. The evidence showed that the coat would not have caused problems apart from this one special fact. It was held that as this fact had not been disclosed to the seller he was not liable.

Reliance

The condition of fitness is not implied if the seller can prove that the buyer **4.21** did not rely on the seller's skill or judgment. Thus, suppose that John, an amateur jeweller, goes to a general hardware store and asks for glue suitable for jewellery-making. The seller might say "I have no idea whether this brand is suitable—you must decide for yourself and not rely on me." In such a case he might escape liability under section 14(3) (and perhaps also under section 14(2) since the circumstances surrounding the purchase would be one of the "circumstances" in section 14(2A)). The buyer's reliance on the seller's skill or judgment may well be partial. If the goods turn out to be unfit for the buyer's particular purpose, the seller will be liable unless he can prove that the defect fell outside the area of reliance.[53]

Computer software

In the recent case of *St. Albans DC v. ICL*[53a] the Council ordered software **4.22** from ICL in order to calculate the size of the local population so that they could set the appropriate community charge. Owing to an error in the software, the population figure was overstated and the Council suffered a substantial and irrecoverable loss. The judge and the Court of Appeal decided the case in favour of St. Albans on the basis that ICL were in breach of an express term. In the Court of Appeal, and in a double *obiter*, Sir Ian Glidewell considered that (1) where a disk containing software is supplied by one person to another, the disk is "goods" for the purposes of section 14 and (2) if the software on the disk is defective, the transferee will have the benefit of the implied condition of reasonable fitness. The second of these views is highly debateable; if a book contains inaccurate information, liability will be based on negligence—why should software be any different? The exemption clause aspects of the case are considered in Chapter Eight, see para. 8.39 below.

---

[52] [1939] 1 All E.R. 685. See also *Aswan Engineering Establishment Co. v. Lupdine Ltd* [1987] 1 W.L.R. 1.
[53] *Ashington Piggeries Ltd v. Christopher Hill Ltd* [1972] A.C. 441.
[53a] *St. Albans City and District Council v. International Computers Ltd* [1996] 4 All E.R. 481. ICL had inserted the software into the St. Albans computer without supplying a disk.

Warnings and instructions

4.23   If the instructions supplied with the goods are wrong or misleading this can make the goods unfit for their purpose. If, however, there is a clear warning (*e.g.* "Do not use after July 1") a buyer who ignores this cannot complain merely because the damage which he suffers is different from that mentioned in the warning.[54]

Credit-broker

4.24   The term "credit-broker" is taken from the Consumer Credit Act 1974 which is considered in Part IV of this book (below, para. 18.01). The type of case contemplated by section 14(3) is that of a consumer who goes to a dealer and tells the dealer the purpose for which he wants the goods. The dealer then sells the goods on to a finance house which in turn sells the goods to the consumer on instalment terms. Although the consumer has bought the goods from the finance company (which he has probably never heard of until they write to him demanding payment) he will enjoy the protection of section 14(3) if he makes his purpose known to the dealer (credit-broker) unless he did not rely, or if it was not reasonable for him to rely, on the credit-broker's skill or judgment.

The Law Commission

4.25   In their Report No. 160, which has been discussed earlier in this chapter in relation to merchantable quality, the Law Commission do not make any proposals for the amendment of the fitness condition in section 14(3). There are, however, a number of proposals in relation to remedies and these will be dealt with in Chapter 7.

3. CONDITIONAL SALES AND CREDIT SALES

4.26   These transactions (as to which see below, para. 18.05) are treated in the same way as any other sales.

4. HIRE-PURCHASE

4.27   The implied terms as to fitness and quality are virtually the same as in sale of goods.[55] The hire-purchaser will usually conduct the negotiations with a "credit-broker" (see above) and once again it is sufficient if he notifies his purpose to that credit-broker.[56]

---

[54] *Wormell v. RHM Agriculture (East)* [1987] 1 W.L.R. 1091 (herbicide failed to kill farmer's wild oats because it was used too late in the season).

[55] See Supply of Goods (Implied Terms) Act 1973, s.10, as redrafted in Schedule 4 to the Consumer Credit Act 1974.

[56] s.10(3).

5. Work and Materials

We have seen earlier in this chapter that certain contracts may be classified as   **4.28**
contracts for "work and materials" rather than "sale of goods". Contracts to
repair a house or car, or to insulate a loft, are obvious examples. In the words
of Stable J. in a case where a hairdresser applied a hair dye to the head of a
customer:

> "[It] is really half the rendering of services and, in a sense, half the supply of
> goods."[57]

The law applies different standards to the two halves of the contractual obligation. On the first half (*i.e.* the provision of work) there is an implied duty to
take reasonable care[58]; on the second half (*i.e.* the provision of materials)
there is strict liability under section 4 of the Supply of Goods and Services
Act 1982 in respect of quality[58a] and fitness for purpose.

The Act confirms the common law position; thus in *Samuels v. Davis*[59] the
defendant was liable when the denture which he had made did not fit the
mouth of the plaintiff's wife. The Court of Appeal found it unnecessary to
decide whether it was a sale of goods or work and materials contract. The
important point is that the dentist was liable even though the county court
judge had found that he was not negligent. The court approved the reasoning
in the earlier Divisional Court case of *GH Myers & Co. v. Brent Cross Service
Co.*[60] In that case:

> The plaintiff asked the defendant to "knock-in" the engine of his car and to renew
> any parts which required replacement. In the course of the work the defendant
> bought six connecting rods and fitted them. Owing to a latent defect one of the
> rods broke and damage of nearly £70 was caused. When the plaintiff claimed
> damages, the defendant argued that he was not liable because the defect could
> not have been discovered by the exercise of reasonable care and skill. The
> defence was rejected.

The Divisional Court made it clear that if the consumer relied on the
repairers' skill and judgment then liability was strict. In the words of du Parcq
J.:

> "I think that the true view is that a person contracting to do work and supply
> materials warrants that the materials which he uses will be of good quality and
> reasonably fit for the purpose for which he is using them, unless the circum-
> stances of the contract are such as to exclude any such warranty. There may be

---

[57] *Watson v. Buckley Osborne & Co.* [1940] 1 All E.R. 174, 180.
[58] Supply of Goods and Services Act 1982, s.13. Below, para. 6.27.
[58a] But see s.18(3).
[59] [1943] K.B. 526.
[60] [1934] 1 K.B. 46. The principles set out in this judgment are now statutory—see Supply of
Goods and Services Act 1982, s.4. A detailed discussion can be found in Woodroffe, *Goods
and Services—the New Law*, Chap. 3.

circumstances which would clearly exclude it. A man goes to a repairer and says 'repair my car; get the parts from the makers and fit them.' In such a case it is made plain that the person ordering the repairs is not relying upon any warranty, except that the parts used will be parts ordered and obtained from the makers. On the other hand if he says 'do the work—fit any necessary parts' he is in no way limiting the person doing the repair work, and the person doing the repair work is in my view liable if there is any defect in the materials supplied, even if it was one which reasonable care would not have discovered."

Thus, for example, the repairer will be liable where the defect was due to the faulty work of a sub-contractor—unless this was a person selected by the customer.[61]

6. HIRE

4.29 Until fairly recently the rules relating to the quality or fitness of goods let out on hire were somewhat uncertain but the matter is now governed by section 9 of the Supply of Goods and Services Act 1982. Once again the rules are virtually identical to those which apply to sale, hire-purchase and the "materials" element of work and materials contracts.[62]

7. SOFTWARE

4.30 In the St Albans case (para. 4.22 above) Sir Ian Glidewell considered (*obiter*) that the insertion of software into a customer's computer was subject to an implied condition of reasonable fitness analogous to that set out above. The comment was *obiter* because the Court found that the installers (ICL) were in a breach of an express term. This is clearly a developing area of law— especially with the millennium bug just around the corner.

---

[61] *Stewart v. Reavell's Garage* [1952] 2 Q.B. 545.
[62] See Woodroffe, *ante*, n. 60.

Chapter Five

"IT WILL COST £1,000 TO MAKE THEM SAFE"

Scheme of this chapter

In the previous chapter we examined the consumer's rights against his **5.01**
immediate supplier where the goods were faulty. In this chapter we move
further afield to consider the consumer's rights against other persons in the
distribution chain—including in particular the manufacturer. Such rights can
be important for at least three reasons:

(1) A buyer may find that his rights under a manufacturer's guarantee are
    easier to enforce than his Sale of Goods Act rights against his supplier
    where he may have considerable difficulty in proving that the goods
    were of unsatisfactory quality.
(2) A supplier may be unable to meet the claim—perhaps because he has
    gone out of business.
(3) The injured party may not have a contract at all; thus a badly con-
    structed car may cause death or injury to passengers and pedestrians
    while a child may suffer pre-natal injuries caused by a drug supplied
    to the mother.

This chapter will deal first with *poor quality* goods and then with *dangerous*
goods. The distinction is crucial.

Example 1

> A buys goods from B. They are of very poor quality and useless to A unless he
> spends money on repairing them. The goods are *not* dangerous.

Example 2

> The goods in the previous example cause death or personal injury or damage to
> other property. The goods are *dangerous*.

A. POOR QUALITY GOODS

1. Introduction

It is clear from the decided cases that the law of negligence will not help the **5.02**
consumer in this situation (*i.e.* where the goods are safe but shoddy) and it is

equally clear that Part I of the Consumer Protection Act 1987 (below, para. 5.10) will not help either. That leaves just two rights which exist side by side—a claim under the contract of supply[1] (which we have considered in Chap. 4) and a claim under a manufacturer's guarantee.

2. MANUFACTURERS' GUARANTEES[2]

The nature of a guarantee

5.03 A guarantee is familiar to millions of consumers and it has become an integral part of the purchase of durable goods. The manufacturer usually agrees to replace defective parts within a specified time (for example, 12 months). The attraction of this for the consumer may be cut down by further clauses requiring the consumer to pay the cost of carriage and sometimes even the cost of labour. Subject to this, a guarantee can have very real commercial advantages for both parties. For the manufacturer it helps to promote his product and the card which the customer signs and returns may be valuable for the purposes of market research. For the customer, the guarantee may be a valuable way of sidestepping the hazards of litigation, especially as the remedy which he *really* wants—repair or replacement—is not available against the retailer.[3]

There have been very few cases on guarantees and their precise legal status is uncertain.[4] As a matter of strict legal analysis the problem is one of offer, acceptance and consideration. Is there a contract if the consumer is unaware that the guarantee exists when he buys the goods? What is the consideration to support the manufacturer's promise? In practical terms, it is highly unlikely that these matters will ever be litigated; it is difficult to imagine a manufacturer giving a guarantee and then refusing to honour it. The legal points might one day be taken by a liquidator of the guarantee-giving manufacturer. If the points ever did come to court it is likely that the courts would uphold the guarantee as a collateral contract, the consideration being the customer's purchase of the goods from the retailer. The onus will be on the buyer to prove that he knew of the guarantee when he bought the goods; in practice it should not be difficult for him to prove this, especially as the guarantee often forms part of the advertising and promotional material.

The legal liability of the manufacturer can also be established in another way. The consumer is sometimes asked to complete and return a card containing market research questions, *e.g.* "how did you learn of this product?",

---

[1] Or possibly under a collateral contract: consider Example 1 on p. 25 and *Andrews v. Hopkinson* [1957] 1 Q.B. 229.

[2] In practice guarantees are sometimes also given by retailers and by suppliers of services (see, *e.g.* the Codes of Practice relating to motor vehicles and electrical appliances, below, paras 10.15 and 10.27).

[3] Below, para. 7.12. For the interrelationship between guarantees and the condition of satisfactory quality see, above, para. 4.12.

[4] See the OFT Discussion Paper *Consumer Guarantees* published in August 1984, pp. 21–23.

"what persuaded you to buy it?" or "did you compare this unit with other models?" The act of the consumer in completing and returning the card may itself be consideration to support the manufacturer's promise.

The value of the guarantee to the consumer depends on its terms. The most generous ones provide that:

> If owing to a defect in workmanship or material your appliance breaks down within 6 [or 12] months of purchase we will repair or replace it free of charge.

We have seen, however, that the consumer may sometimes be required to pay the cost of transporting the goods; occasionally he even has to pay the cost of labour which can render the guarantee virtually useless. There is also the possibility that the manufacturer may say "there is nothing wrong with this appliance—you have mishandled it". (A similar argument is sometimes advanced by a seller when a buyer complains that the goods are unsatisfactory.) In such a case the consumer might have to negotiate an independent examination of the goods, with the manufacturer paying the whole or part of the cost. The provisions of the various Codes of Practice (*e.g.* for electrical goods) should also be borne in mind.

Statutory provisions relating to guarantees

There is still widespread misunderstanding about who is legally respon- **5.04**
sible for defective products. Perhaps this ignorance may be lessened as the result of an Order made in 1976 whereby a supplier commits a criminal offence if a document setting out his obligations (*e.g.* the guarantee) fails to draw the consumer's attention to his rights against the retailer.[5]

Another feature of guarantees aroused fierce criticism in the past; many guarantees were used not to extend the customer's rights (as he not unreasonably expected) but to cut them down. The Unfair Contract Terms Act 1977 now makes void such exemption clauses in consumer guarantees.[6]

Further reforms?

A discussion paper published by the OFT in August 1984 highlights some **5.05**
of the main problem areas. Attention is drawn in particular to the following matters:

(1) The consumer may buy an "extended guarantee"[6a] or "extended warranty" which may become worthless if the "guarantor" goes out of business during the extended period.

(2) Guarantors delay in dealing with complaints and in carrying out or authorising repairs.

---

[5] Below, para. 17.14.
[6] Below, para. 8.32.
[6a] See generally the OFT Report *Extended Warranties on Electrical Goods* (December 1994).

(3) Consumers take guarantees at their face value (with bland assurances as to "peace of mind") only to find later, when they seek to enforce them, that the small print makes them far narrower than expected; the guarantee may, for example, exclude liability for consequential loss and a warranty for a second-hand car will almost certainly not extend to the clutch.

(4) A consumer wishing to sell a house or car with the benefit of a long-term guarantee may find, to his horror, that it is not transferable.

The paper contains proposals to strengthen the consumer's position in all these areas and to make him more aware of what his rights are and against whom. In the case of extended warranties and long-term guarantees it is pro-posed that the consumer should have a direct contractual relationship with a duly authorised insurer. These proposals have been incorporated in the Code of Practice for Mechanical Breakdown Insurance Schemes, but this covers motor vehicles only.[7]

Consumer Guarantees Bill

5.06   In 1990 the National Consumer Council initiated an attempt to encourage the provision of guarantees by obtaining sponsors for a Private Member's Bill. The Consumer Guarantees Bill would have compelled manufacturers of specified consumer products (*e.g.* cars, cookers and televisions) to inform the public whether or not their products were covered by a "consumer guarantee" lasting for at least a year. The Bill also contained the Law Commission's proposed reforms set out in their Report, *Sale and Supply of Goods.*[8] The Bill was entirely killed off by the Government's opposition to the guarantee clauses.

1992 Green Paper

5.07   In an attempt to bring some order into this complex area the DTI published a consultation document, *Consumer Guarantees*, in 1992. It contains three proposals. First, the manufacturer should be legally liable under its own guarantee. This would overcome the theoretical consideration problems discussed above.

The second proposal is that the retailer too should be liable for the manufacturer's guarantee, so that the consumer could enforce the guarantee against the retailer as well as against the manufacturer. Whether this would be helpful is questionable, since often an after-sales repair service is offered only by the manufacturer.

The third proposal—the most important—is that the manufacturer will also be responsible for the quality of goods under the Sale of Goods Act 1979.

---

[7] Below, para. 10.17.

[8] See Chap. 4 (above, paras 4.18–4.19) for a discussion of these proposed reforms and their enactment in the Sale and Supply of Goods Act 1994.

Where, for example, a washing machine develops a major defect after a couple of years, the consumer will be able to demand that the manufacturer pays the cost of repair even if the guarantee has expired.

The general effect of these proposals, if implemented, will be that any contractual rights which the consumer has against the manufacturer or the retailer will be enforceable against both.

Not surprisingly the last two proposals were not supported by industry. In any case, the chances of early U.K. legislation on this topic are slender, since the DTI paper was overtaken in 1993 by an E.C. Commission Green Paper, *Guarantees for Consumer Goods and After-Sales Services.* This contains a useful, comparative survey of the position in the various Member States on "consumer guarantees" and also what it confusingly calls "commercial guarantees", *i.e.* the buyer's contractual rights against the retailer, *e.g.* under the Sale of Goods Act 1979. A brief note on this important topic will be found in the final Chapter of this book.

Conclusion

It cannot be stressed too strongly that any rights which the consumer may **5.08** have under a manufacturer's guarantee do *not* cut down his rights against the supplier. In virtually all cases retailers seek to create the false impression in the minds of their customers that the legal responsibility is that of the manufacturer. The consumer must be on his guard against this and must be prepared to say (in a loud voice if necessary) "it's *your* responsibility under the Sale of Goods Act". The question of remedy enforcement is considered in greater detail in Chapters Ten and Eleven and the enforceability problem will become a thing of the past when the Directive on the Sale of Goods and Associated Guarantees becomes part of English Law (see para. 28.12 below).

B. DANGEROUS GOODS

1. INTRODUCTION

In the Second Edition of this book it was pointed out that proposals to alter **5.09** manufacturer's liability from negligence to strict liability had been made by no less than four different bodies—the Law Commission, the Pearson Commission, the Council of Europe and the E.C. At the time of publication (March 1, 1985) some seven years had gone by without any progress; negotiations on the E.C. draft directive were stalled over the so-called "development risks" defence. It was, however, only a matter of months before a workable compromise emerged and on July 25, 1985 the E.C. Council of Ministers adopted the Product Liability Directive whereby Member States were required to pass the appropriate legislation by July 30, 1988 (but with the option of excluding the development risks defence). The United Kingdom responded before the deadline by passing the Consumer Protection Act

1987. Part I is designed to implement the Directive and came into force on March 1, 1988.

It is important to appreciate that Part I exists side by side with the general law of contract and negligence. In a contract case the consumer will have his (largely non-excludable) rights under the Sale of Goods Act, etc., and in this situation the 1987 Act is virtually irrelevant. As regards non-contractual claims the basic rule is that the consumer will be in a stronger position under the Act because the need to prove negligence has disappeared. The provisions of Part I will be examined in detail in the next section of this chapter. It will be seen that there are some situations where the Act does not apply and in these cases the non-contractual consumer will have to fall back on the general law of negligence, which will be briefly considered in the final part of this chapter.

2. Part I of the Consumer Protection Act 1987 ("The Act")

5.10 We have seen that Part I is designed to give effect to the E.C. Product Liability Directive and section 1(1) expressly so provides. These Directives generally start off with a large number of recitals and the second recital of this one states that:

> Whereas liability without fault on the part of the producer is the sole means of adequately solving the problem, peculiar to our age of increasing technicality, of a fair apportionment of the risks inherent in modern technological production.

In the light of the provision of section 1(1) above the adviser must refer to the Directive if the drafting of the Act is in any way ambiguous.

The basic rule

5.11 By section 2(1):

> Subject to the following provisions of this Part, where any damage is caused wholly or partly by a defect in a product, every person to whom subsection (2) applies shall be liable for the damage.

Thus in advising the consumer a number of questions must be asked:

(1) Has a *product* been *supplied*?
(2) If yes, did it contain a *defect*?
(3) If yes, did the defect cause *damage*?
(4) If yes, is it the *type* of damage to which the Act applies?
(5) If yes, *who* is liable to the consumer?
(6) Are there any *defences* which may cut down the consumer's rights?
(7) Are there any special *time-limits* for bringing a claim?
(8) Was the product first supplied on or after March 1, 1988?

Burden of proof

The Act is silent on this but on general principle the burden will fall on the **5.12** plaintiff. This is reinforced by Article 4 of the Directive which states that:

> The injured person shall be required to prove the damage, the defect and the causal relationship between defect and damage.

In practical terms the abolition of the need to prove negligence may be of limited value because the task of proving causation (which still exists) can be equally difficult—especially in medical and pharmaceutical cases.[9]

It will be appreciated from the wording of section 2(1) that partial causation is sufficient.

Example 3

Goods manufactured by M injure C; this is due partly to the goods being defective and partly to C not following M's instructions. C can recover damages from M under the Act—but subject to a reduction for contributory negligence under section 6(4).

What damage is covered by the Act?

Section 5, which is based on Article 9, makes it clear that only three types **5.13** of damage are covered, namely death, personal injury and damage to "private" (as opposed to business) property, *i.e.* property is excluded if at the time of the loss or damage it is not—

(a) of a description of property ordinarily intended for private use, occupation or consumption; and
(b) intended by the person suffering the loss or damage mainly for his own private use, occupation or consumption.

Example 4

A defective heater explodes and damages X's office premises. He cannot recover under the Act.

Two other restrictions must be noted. First (and this is an echo of the distinction between defective and dangerous goods)[10] the Act does not cover loss of or damage "to the product itself" or to "the whole or any part of any product which has been supplied with the [defective product] comprised in it."[11]

Example 5

C buys a defective car. It crashes and injures C. The car is a write-off. C can recover for his injuries but not for the cost of replacing the car.

---

[9] See, *e.g. Kay v. Ayrshire and Arran Health Board* [1987] 2 All E.R. 417, HL (penicillin given to child; child became deaf; causal link not proved).
[10] Above, para. 5.01 and below, para. 5.29.
[11] s.5(2).

Example 6

> Suppose in the above example the accident is caused by a defective tyre. If the tyre formed part of the car as originally supplied, the answer is the same as in Example 5. If, on the other hand, the tyre was fitted at a later date, the car replacement cost will be "damage to any property" and recoverable under the Act.

The second restriction (designed to exclude small claims) is set out in section 5(4); the Act will not apply where the total damages awarded, exclusive of interest, in respect of *property* do not exceed £275. What if the damages are, say, £1,000? The wording of the Act is unambiguous—no deduction is made and £1,000 would be awarded. However, Article 9(b) talks of "a lower threshold of 500 ECU". It could be argued—and the French version of the E.C. Directive and the E.C. Commission support this view—that a deduction should be made from *every* award in respect of property. It will be interesting to see how the courts interpret this provision.

It is clear from the wording that any reduction for contributory negligence must be made first.

Example 7

> C's damages in respect of private property are assessed at £500 but this figure falls to be reduced by 50 per cent for contributory negligence so that the final figure is £250. The Act does not apply.

Was the damage caused by a defective product?

5.14 In order to answer this question we must start by asking two questions, namely:

> (a) What is a product?
> (b) When is a product defective?

What is a product?

5.15 Section 1(2) provides that the term "product" means any goods or electricity and it is clear that components are included.

Example 8

> CM supplies a defective component to M who incorporates it into a product which he then supplies to D. Both CM and M have supplied a "product" and, if the component makes M's product defective, both CM and M are liable under the Act.

The term "goods" is defined in section 45 to include "substances,[12] growing crops and things comprised in land by virtue of being attached to it and any ship, aircraft or vehicle". What about houses and land? The effect of

---

[12] This is not itself defined in the Act.

section 46 is that the seller of a house built with defective bricks does not supply "goods", but if the house collapses and causes "damage",[13] the brick manufacturer can be liable to the injured party under the Act.

Agricultural products

Although the definition of "goods" includes crops (see above), section 2(4) creates an important (and politically sensitive) exception from liability. It excludes liability under the Act "in respect of any defect in any game or agricultural produce if the only supply ... by that person to another was at a time when it had not undergone an industrial process."[14]   **5.16**

Example 9

Farmer F grows and supplies defective peas to P who processes them and sells them to a restaurant. C, a customer, eats them and becomes ill. P is liable to C under the Act (even though the defect is unconnected with the processing). F is not liable.

The Act does not define "industrial process" directly but its meaning can be gleaned from the definition of "producer" which includes:

(c) in the case of a product which has not been manufactured, won or abstracted but essential characteristics of which are attributable to an industrial or other process having been carried out (for example, in relation to agricultural produce) the person who carried out that process.

Thus a court may decide that the key factor is whether the alleged "processing" is something which alters the essential characteristics of the product so that washing and packing might not qualify (with the result that the statutory immunity would be preserved). It may also be significant that the word "industrial" does not appear in the Directive which uses the wider term "initial processing" in Article 2. Finally, the Government has expressed the view that the "process" must be something applied to the product *after* it has become a product so that, for example, spraying growing crops or injecting hormones into live animals would not qualify. It is by no means certain that a court would uphold this view.

Is the product defective?

Section 3 rephrases Article 6 of the Directive in the following words: **5.17**

(1) Subject to the following provisions of this section, there is a defect in a product for the purposes of this Part if the safety of the product is not such as persons generally are entitled to expect; and for these purposes "safety," in

---

[13] Above, para. 5.13.
[14] This is one of the cases where the injured party must fall back on his rights under the general law of negligence—below, para. 5.24.

relation to a product, shall include safety in respect to [components] and safety in the context of risks of damage to property, as well as in the context of risks of death or personal injury.

(2) In determining ... what persons generally are entitled to expect ... all the circumstances shall be taken into account, including—

    (a) the manner in which, and purposes for which, the product has been marketed, its get-up, the use of any mark in relation to the product, any instructions for, or warnings with respect to, doing or refraining from doing anything with or in relation to the product;

    (b) what might reasonably be expected to be done with or in relation to the product; and

    (c) the time when the product was supplied by its producer to another;

and nothing in this section shall require a defect to be inferred from the fact alone that the safety of a product which is supplied after that time is greater than the safety of the product in question.

The above definition of "defective goods" is broadly similar to the definition of "satisfactory quality" in section 14(2A) of the Sale of Goods Act 1979 (as amended)[15] with the key word "safe" substituted for "fit". However, one major distinction must be reiterated. Whereas satisfactory quality covers both unsafe and shoddy, poor quality products, "defective" goods in the 1987 Act mean only unsafe or dangerous products; so "defective" is used in an unusually narrow sense. The following points can be made:

(1) "Persons generally" can be contrasted with "a person" in Article 6 of the Directive; the expectation standard will be an objective one in the light of the matters mentioned in the section—notably any safety representations in advertising material.

(2) A warning can make a product safe—provided that it is sufficiently clear; conversely the absence of a warning can make it unsafe. The massive cigarette litigation in the United States has largely turned on the warning factor—and, in a recent class action on behalf of 500,000 Florida smokers a U.S. jury has found a large number of leading tobacco companies liable for deception (see *The Times*, July 8, 1999).

(3) The question of what safety persons are entitled to expect brings in what is known as the "cost-benefit" analysis. In relation to medicines a DTI explanatory note contains the following passage:

> "Establishing the existence of a defect in a medicine administered to a patient is complicated by the fact that not only is the human body a highly complex organism, but at the time of treatment it is already subject to an adverse pathological condition. ...
>
> The more active the medicine, and the greater its beneficial potential, the more extensive its effects are likely to be, and therefore the greater the chances of an adverse effect. A medicine used to treat a life-threatening condition is likely to be much more powerful than a medicine used in

---

[15] Above, para. 4.18.

the treatment of a less serious condition, and the safety that one is reasonably entitled to expect of such a medicine may therefore become correspondingly lower."

(4) The relevant time for assessing the safety factor (and this is important for two reasons) is the time when the product was supplied by its *producer*—not by the retailer. This is often called "the state of the art" factor.

Example 10

In April 1996 M sells to D a car manufactured by him. In August 1996 D sells it to R who sells it to C in 1998. While C is driving the car in 1998 it veers out of control and P is injured. In considering the safety aspects two questions arise, namely (1) what degree of safety could reasonably be expected of a four-year-old car? and (2) what were the relevant safety standards in April 1996? The fact that safer models have been introduced since that time is irrelevant.

Whom can the consumer sue under the Act?

Section 2(2) imposes liability on: **5.18**

(1) The "producer" (see below).
(2) Any person who, by putting his name on the product or using a trade mark or other distinguishing mark in relation to the product, has held himself out as the producer of the product.

Example 11

S, a supermarket, puts its own brand mark on a bottle of wine which it sells to B. Unknown to the seller the wine has been mixed with antifreeze. C becomes violently ill when drinking the "wine" at B's house. C can sue S under the Act. But if S makes it clear that a third party is the producer, *e.g.* with a label stating "produced for S by M", S is not caught—there is no "holding out".

(3) Any person who imported the goods into a Member State of the EC from a place outside the Member States in order, in the course of a business, to supply it to another.

Example 12

F, a French company, imports lethal toys from Taiwan which it then exports to England where one is sold by R to C. C's child is injured.
    The English importer is *not* liable under the Act because he imported the toys from another Member State (*i.e.* France). F, however, *is* liable under the Act and he can be sued in England.[16]

---

[16] Under the E.C. Jurisdiction and Judgments Convention (see Sched. 1 to the Civil Jurisdiction and Judgments Act 1982) a defendant domiciled in a Contracting State can be sued in tort in another Contracting State where the damage is suffered (see Art. 5). A claim under Pt. I of the Act is a claim in tort—see s.6(7). The Act gives the injured consumer a wide choice of where to sue (this is known as "forum shopping"); this can be important because the development risks defence (below, para. 5.21) applies in some E.C. countries but not all.

(4) A person to whom section 2(3) applies—see below.

Returning to paragraph (1) above, section 1(2) defines a "producer" in relation to a product as—

(a) the person who manufactured it;
(b) in the case of a substance which has not been manufactured but has been won or abstracted, the person who won or abstracted it (this covers mining and quarrying);
(c) in any other case, a person who has applied an industrial or other process affecting the essential characteristics of the product.[17]

The section 2(3) defendant

5.19   There may well be cases where the injured party will have great difficulty in identifying the "producer" or the person importing the product into a Member State. To deal with this situation section 2(3) allows him to seek information from another supplier in the chain and makes that other supplier liable if the information is not supplied. Such liability will arise if the following conditions are satisfied:

(1) the injured party asks the supplier to identify one or more of the persons listed in section 2(2) (above, para. 5.18)—whether still in existence or not; and
(2) the request is made within a reasonable time after the damage and at a time when it is not reasonably practicable for the person making the request to identify all those persons; and
(3) the supplier fails within a reasonable time after receiving the request either to comply with the request or to identify the person who supplied the product to him.

Example 4

> The facts are as in Example 12 except that the only person known to the injured party is the retail supplier R. The injured party can ask R to identify the manufacturer and/or the E.C. importer. R can supply this information or alternatively he can say "I bought from X Ltd" (whereupon the injured party can approach X Ltd with a similar request). If R does neither of these things within a reasonable time he will be liable under the Act.

Conclusion

5.20   It will be apparent that the injured consumer has a large number of persons to sue—especially bearing in mind the co-extensive liability of a component supplier and an end-product supplier. He can sue them alone or together and their liability is joint and several; each of them is liable to him for the full amount of his "damage" (see s.2(5)).

---

[17] Above, para. 5.16.

What defences are available?

Section 4(1) lists six possible defences, namely: **5.21**

(a) That the defect is attributable to compliance with any statutory or E.C. *requirement.*

(b) That the person proceeded against did not at any time supply the product to another.

Example 14

> M manufactures a crane. While it is being tested on M's premises it collapses and P is killed. P's estate has no claim under the Act.

The term "supply" is widely defined in section 46. In a hire-purchase case involving dealer—hire-purchaser—finance company the section provides that the *dealer* (and not the finance company) is to be treated as supplying the product to the hire-purchaser—which is what happens in practice (although not in law).

(c) That the only supply was not in the course of the supplier's business *and* that either section 2(2) does not apply to that person or does so only as the result of things done otherwise than with view to profit.

Example 15

> Mrs Jones makes jam for a private function. The jam is defective and a guest is taken ill. There is no liability under the Act.

(d) That the defect did not exist in the product at the relevant time.[18]

Example 16

> M supplies perishable goods to C, a carrier. The goods deteriorate solely because the ventilation in C's lorry breaks down. They were not defective when they left M. M is not liable under the Act.

Example 17

> M manufactures a car and sells it to D. D sells it to C. C has it serviced by S. C crashes because S left the wheel nuts loose. M is not liable.

(e) That the state of scientific and technical knowledge at the relevant time was not such that a producer of products of the same description as the product in question might be expected to have discovered the defect if it had existed in his products while they were under his control.

---

[18] "Relevant time" means the time when the "producer" supplied it to another: s.4(2).

It will be recalled[19] that the dispute over this *"development risks"* defence was the prime reason why the E.C. draft Directive took nearly 10 years to become a Directive. There was strong lobbying from United Kingdom industries (especially pharmaceuticals) on the basis that without such a defence research and development would be severely hampered. The argument on the other side is equally compelling—such a defence would leave victims of a future Thalidomide-type tragedy without a remedy. In the event the Council adopted a compromise—the defence was introduced by Article 7(e) but individual Member States were left free to exclude it (Art. 15(1)(b)) and a few of them have exercised their right to do so, *e.g.* Luxembourg.

The drafting of this provision was hotly debated in Parliament and the Government forced through the present wording in the dying days of the 1986–1987 session just before the 1987 General Election. It is widely felt that the wording is less strict than Article 7(e) of the Directive which reads:

> "that the state of scientific and technical knowledge at the time when he put the product into circulation was not such as to enable the existence of the defect to be discovered."

There is an immense gap between what a producer might be *"expected"* to discover in a particular sector of industry and what he *could* ("enable") discover with all the technical resources available. Nevertheless the ECJ has ruled that the two provisions are not inconsistent.[20]

(f) That the defect:
   (i)   constituted a defect in a subsequent product in which the product in question (*i.e.* a component) was comprised; and
   (ii) was wholly attributable to the design of the subsequent product or to compliance with instructions given by the producer of the subsequent product.

Example 18

> CM supplies a component to M. The component makes the end product faulty but only because M's design is faulty. CM is not liable.

When must the claim be brought?

5.22   There are two rules—a consumer rule and an overriding supplier rule. For the *injured party* the basic limitation period is three years from (1) the date on which the cause of action accrued, or (2) (if later) the date on which he first discovered (or should have discovered) the relevant facts.[21] There is no distinction between injury and property damage—the period is the same in both cases.

---

[19] See above, para. 5.09.
[20] *E.C. v. U.K.* [1997] All E.R. (E.C.) 481.
[21] Sched. 1, para. 1, amending Limitation Act 1980, s.11.

As regards the *supplier* there is a 10-year cut-off period for each supplier.[22] This "period of repose", as it is called in the United States, relates to the particular product, not to the product line; so producers must keep precise records (showing the exact date when each item was sold) to enable them to rely on this provision.

Example 19

> CM supplies a component to M in April 1988. M sells the end product to R in April 1989.
> The 10-year period expires in April 1998 as regards CM and in April 1999 as regards M. The fact that no injury has occurred by the cut-off date is immaterial.

Commencement of Part I

As previously mentioned Part I came into force on March 1, 1988 and by section 50(7) it does not apply to any product which was supplied by its producer before that date.   **5.23**

Example 20

> Yen, a Japanese manufacturer, sells a product to its United States distributor in February 1988. In April 1988 it is exported to the United Kingdom. The Act does not apply.

3. NEGLIGENCE

It will be appreciated that there will be a limited number of cases where the regime introduced by the Act will not apply and in these cases the injured party must fall back on the general law of negligence. This will be so where, for example: **5.24**

(1) the product was first supplied before March 1, 1988;
(2) the "primary agricultural produce" exemption applies;
(3) the damage sustained by the plaintiff (*e.g.* to business property) is not covered by the Act;
(4) the damage to property is £275 or less;
(5) the claim is out of time.

In considering negligence we must stress once again what we said at the beginning of this chapter—namely the crucial distinction between defective or shoddy goods and dangerous goods. The courts have always been very cautious to extend the boundaries of liability and one weapon which they have used has been the weapon of "economic loss". They have held that

---

[22] *ibid.*

where the only damage is to the product itself, this loss is "economic" and not recoverable in the tort of negligence.[23]

In relation to dangerous goods the starting point must be the so-called "narrow rule" in *Donoghue v. Stevenson*.[24] The principle of law was stated by Lord Atkin in the following well-known passage:

> "A manufacturer of products, which he sells in such a form as to show that he intends them to reach the ultimate consumer in the form in which they left him with no reasonable possibility of intermediate examination, and with the knowledge that the absence of reasonable care in the preparation or putting up of the products will result in an injury to the consumer's life or property, owes a duty to the consumer to take that reasonable care."

Lord Atkin added that this was a self-evident proposition which no one who was not a lawyer would for one moment doubt.

The duty outlined above is merely one particular type of "duty situation" in the context of the general law of negligence. The cases decided since 1932 show a gradual extension of liability. Thus:

(1) There is no limit to the type of goods covered by the rule. Examples include hair dye, underpants, cars, lifts and even a tombstone.

(2) Liability has been extended beyond manufacturers to cover, for example, repairers and assemblers. In one case even a car dealer was held liable.[25]

(3) The word "consumer" is not confined to the ultimate buyer; it means anyone likely to be injured by the lack of reasonable care. Perhaps the best illustration is provided by *Stennett v. Hancock and Peters*[26] where part of the wheel of a lorry came off and struck a pedestrian on the pavement. She recovered damages from the second defendant who had negligently repaired the wheel shortly before the accident.

(4) The "possibility of an intermediate examination" will only defeat the claim if there was a real likelihood of a type of examination which would (or should) reveal the defect. Thus in *Evans v. Triplex Safety Glass Co.*[27] the buyer of a Vauxhall car was injured when the windscreen shattered. His action against the manufacturers of the windscreen failed for various reasons; one reason was the likelihood of an intermediate examination by Vauxhall before it was fitted into the car; another reason was a failure to prove that the windscreen was defective when it left the manufacturer.

---

[23] The first of three recent House of Lords cases on this point (all concerned with defective construction of buildings) is *D. & F. Estates Ltd v. Church Commissioners* [1989] A.C. 177. Note the similar exclusion under the Act: s.5, above, para. 5.13. A similar result was reached in the other two cases that are cited in n. 45 to para. 5.29 below.

[24] [1932] A.C. 562.

[25] *Andrews v. Hopkinson* [1957] 1 Q.B. 229.

[26] [1939] 2 All E.R. 578.

[27] [1936] 1 All E.R. 283.

This case can be contrasted with the sale of goods case of *Wren v. Holt*[28] where beer containing arsenic was sold by a publican to a customer. The case was fought on section 14(2) of the Sale of Goods Act[29] and the publican was liable even though the customer had examined the beer before drinking it; the defect was not discoverable by any normal examination. Presumably the same reasoning would have applied if the buyer had sued the brewer, *i.e.* the manufacturer would have been liable if negligence could have been proved.

Proof of negligence and causation

As the law stands at present the task facing the injured consumer is not an easy one. He must prove (a) that the product was defective when it left the manufacturer; (b) that this was due to negligence and (c) that this was the cause of his injury. If the article is completely destroyed in the accident, the plaintiff's task may well be insuperable unless the court is prepared to make a dangerous use of circumstantial evidence.   **5.25**

Was the product defective?

In many cases this should present no problem; a bun containing a stone, a loaf of bread containing a cigarette butt or a car with faulty brakes—these are obvious examples. There may, however, be other cases which are less obvious. Thus in *Evans v. Triplex Safety Glass Co.*, the facts of which have already been given,[30] the plaintiff failed to prove that the windscreen was dangerous when it left the manufacturer.   **5.26**

In the examples previously given (for example, arsenic in the beer)[31] the product was out of line with the general run of goods produced by the manufacturers. Alternatively, it may be possible to argue that there is a fault in manufacture or design affecting all goods of a particular type. The cost of such a finding could be potentially astronomic for the manufacturer and for intermediate suppliers; they could be faced with a very large number of claims when the decision became known, or they might have to call in all the defective goods for repair. In view of this the courts (both here and in the United States) have been cautious to base a negligence finding on this ground. There have however been cases in which the injured party has been successful. Thus in *Lambert v. Lewis*[32] the manufacturer of a defective towing hitch which broke and caused a serious accident was held liable to the victims because its design was negligent.

---

[28] [1903] 1 K.B. 610.
[29] Above, para. 4.07.
[30] Above, para. 5.24.
[31] *ibid.*
[32] [1982] A.C. 225. See above, paras 3.06 and 4.15.

Has the manufacturer been negligent?

5.27   This question and the previous one are closely linked. Thus in *Vacwell Engineering Co. Ltd v. B.D.H. Chemicals Ltd*[33] the defendants, who manufactured a chemical, were liable in negligence for failing to appreciate, and to warn prospective users, that contact with water could lead to an explosion. Similarly, in *Wright v. Dunlop Rubber Co. Ltd and ICI*[34] the Court of Appeal held that ICI were liable in negligence for continuing to market a product with knowledge that it constituted a serious health hazard. Finally in *Fisher v. Harrods Ltd*[35] Mrs Fisher recovered damages from Harrods when they sold an untested bottle of cleaning fluid to her husband. She suffered personal injury when it came into contact with her eyes.

The duty owed by the manufacturer does not involve him in strict liability—it is merely a duty to take reasonable care. This is particularly relevant where a manufacturer of (say) a car buys brake linings or wheel bearings[36] which prove to be defective and cause injury to the ultimate consumer. A case from another branch of the law of negligence (employer's liability) is highly relevant here. In *Davie v. New Merton Board Mills*[37] an employer supplied his employee with a tool which the employer had bought from a reputable supplier. The tool had a latent defect which the employer had no means of discovering. The employee was injured when the tool broke and he sued the employer for damages for negligence. The House of Lords dismissed the claim on the ground that the employer had not been negligent. In the employment field the principle underlying this case has been reversed by statute[38] but in the product liability field the principle still stands. If the manufacturer has an adequate inspection system and an adequate system for checking faults this may well be sufficient.

As already stated, the onus of proving negligence is on the injured party and it can be immensely difficult, especially in the case of a highly complex piece of equipment or a chemical or drug. Evidence of previous accidents caused by the same product is highly relevant and should be sought. Sometimes the facts themselves point to negligence; if a consumer loses a tooth through eating a bun containing a stone this suggests that the manufacturer had been negligent and, under the doctrine of *res ipsa loquitur*, the manufacturer will have to adduce evidence from which the inference of negligence can be rebutted.[39] He may say "the defect was in a component and I myself took all reasonable care" or even "I have no idea how the acid got into the lemonade bottle but I had a foolproof system of inspection" (this latter argu-

[33] [1971] 1 Q.B. 88.
[34] (1972) Vol. XIII, Knights Industrial Reports 255.
[35] [1966] Lloyds L.R. 500.
[36] But in *Walton v. British Leyland* (unreported) the defendants were liable in negligence for failure to recall cars when they discovered unexpected defects in wheel bearings.
[37] [1959] A.C. 604.
[38] Employers' Liability (Defective Equipment) Act 1969.
[39] *Moore v. R. Fox & Son* [1956] 1 Q.B. 596.

ment was successfully raised in *Daniels v. White Ltd and Tarbard*[40] but the decision has been criticised and is unlikely to be followed).[41]

When studying all the vast number of reported cases on negligence (perhaps far too many are reported) one point must never be forgotten; whether a defendant has performed his duty of care is a pure question of fact and a decision on this point is not a binding precedent for any future case.[42]

Did the defendant's negligence cause the plaintiff's injury?

The injured plaintiff must be able to prove a causal link between the defect,   **5.28**
the negligence and his injury. This again can be a difficult matter in practice and the result of the case may turn on the inferences which the court is willing to draw from the facts. In the leading case of *Grant v. Australian Knitting Mills*[43] where the plaintiff, a doctor, contracted dermatitis, the Privy Council accepted his argument that it was caused by an excess of sulphite in underpants manufactured by the defendants. The court reached this decision even though the evidence showed that more than four million of these pants had been sold without complaint. On the other hand, the plaintiff will fail if the injury would have occurred in any event. Thus, to borrow again from employment law, an employer is generally not liable for failing to provide safety equipment if he can show that the employee would not have worn it.[44] Similarly, a manufacturer of a car will not be liable for faulty brakes if the plaintiff was driving so fast that the accident would have occurred even if the brakes had been in perfect working order. A "class action" brought by smokers against Gallaghers has recently been dismissed.[44a]

For what damage can the plaintiff recover?

Reverting once again to the poor quality/dangerous dichotomy, the final   **5.29**
question relates to *potentially* dangerous goods. On which side of the line do they fall? Can the buyer of a car claim in negligence for the cost of repairing brakes in order to avert a serious accident? In the Second Edition of this book we expressed the view that such a claim should be allowed but in two recent cases, concerning potentially dangerous buildings, the House of Lords have classified such repair costs as irrecoverable economic loss.[45]

---

[40] [1938] 4 All E.R. 258.
[41] For a recent case where the court refused to follow the *Daniels* decision see *Hill v. James Crowe (Cases) Ltd* [1978] 1 All E.R. 812.
[42] *Qualcast (Wolverhampton) Ltd v. Haynes* [1959] A.C. 743.
[43] Above, para. 4.10.
[44] *Qualcast (Wolverhampton) Ltd v. Haynes* [1959] A.C. 743; *McWilliams v. Arrol* [1962] 1 W.L.R. 295, HL.
[44a] *Hodgson v. Imperial Tobacco Ltd* (1999) N.L.D. March 8, Q.B.D. For another non-liability case see *Hamble Fisheries Ltd v. L. Gardner & Sons Ltd, The Times*, January 5, 1999, CA.
[45] *Murphy v. Brentwood D.C.* [1990] 3 W.L.R. 415; *Department of the Environment v. Thomas Bates & Son Ltd* [1990] 3 W.L.R. 457.

CHAPTER SIX

"DO I HAVE TO PAY?"

If the supplier of goods or services is guilty of a misrepresentation or a serious **6.01** breach of contract the consumer may be able to rescind the contract or treat it as repudiated. In either case this will relieve him of his obligation to pay the price. Some examples of this were examined in Chapters 2 to 4 and the matter will be considered again in Chapter 7. This chapter is concerned with a group of six unrelated but important topics on which the consumer may seek legal advice. The topics are:

(1) Delivery of unordered goods.
(2) Cancellation of contracts made away from business premises.
(3) Loss or damage of goods after contract but before delivery.
(4) Unsatisfactory performance of services.
(5) Late performance.
(6) A dispute about the price.

1. I Never Ordered these Goods

An aggressive salesman may try to boost his sales by delivering goods which **6.02** the customer has never ordered, followed by an invoice demanding payment. He clearly hopes that the consumer will be induced, by a combination of ignorance, lethargy and fear, to pay the price. Some years ago there was a considerable outcry at these and similar practices, and there was a growing demand for legislation to curtail them. Eventually a Bill was introduced into Parliament and this passed into law as the Unsolicited Goods and Services Act 1971.

Before considering this Act it may be useful to dispose of one problem which has arisen under the general law: is the consumer legally liable if the goods are lost or damaged while they are in his possession? Under the tort of negligence the plaintiff must prove that the defendant owed him a legal duty of care.[1] A person receiving unordered goods is known as an "involuntary bailee" and does not owe a duty of care. Therefore he will generally not be liable for accidental loss or damage.[2] On the other hand he may be liable for the tort of conversion if he deliberately destroys the goods or converts them to

[1] *Bourhill v. Young* [1943] A.C. 92.
[2] See *Howard v. Harris* (1884) C. & E. 253.

his own use. Where is the line to be drawn? Thus, if a tradesman delivers an unordered 10-volume encyclopedia the consumer might well be liable if he puts them outside his house and allows them to disintegrate. The editors of a leading textbook[3] have suggested that the consumer might be entitled to destroy the goods in an emergency.

The Act of 1971

6.03   The sanctions provided by this Act are both civil and criminal. The *civil* sanction is that, as between himself and the sender, the recipient can:

> use, deal with or dispose of [the goods] as if they were an unconditional gift to him, and any right of the sender to the goods shall be extinguished.[4]

The recipient will have these rights if the following conditions are satisfied:

(1) the goods were sent to him without any prior request made by him or on his behalf[5];

(2) they were delivered or sent to him with a view to his acquiring them;

(3) he had no reasonable cause to believe that they were sent with a view to their being acquired for the purposes of a trade or business;

(4) the recipient has neither agreed to acquire the goods nor agreed to return them;

(5) (a) during the period of six months beginning with the date of receipt the sender did not take possession and the recipient did not unreasonably refuse to permit him to do so; or

    (b) the recipient served a notice in writing on the sender, stating that the goods were unsolicited and giving the address where they could be collected, and during a period of 30 days from the giving of the notice the sender did not take possession and the recipient did not unreasonably refuse to permit him to do so.

Thus if the recipient serves a notice on April 2 saying, "I didn't order these goods—take them away" and the sender ignores the notice, the goods will become the property of the recipient on May 3.

The *criminal* sanction is provided in section 2 which is confined to persons acting in the course of a trade or business. The section deals with a trader who makes a demand for payment for goods where (a) the goods are unsolicited goods, and (b) he has no reasonable cause to believe that there is a right to payment. An offence is also committed where a person, in such a case, (i) asserts a right to payment, (ii) threatens to bring legal proceedings, (iii) places, or threatens to place, the name of any person on a defaulters' list, or (iv) invokes, or threatens to invoke, any other collection procedure.

---

[3] *Winfield and Jolowicz on Tort* (15th ed., 1998) at p. 591.
[4] s.1(1).
[5] See 1971 Act, s.6.

2. I HAVE CHANGED MY MIND

In the Second Edition of this book we referred to an E.C. draft Directive **6.04** which conferred cancellation rights for contracts "which have been negotiated away from business premises". We commented then on this somewhat surprising approach and in the event a number of changes were made before it was adopted as Council Directive 85/577 on December 20, 1985. It was incorporated into English law by the Consumer Protection (Cancellation of Contracts Concluded away from Business Premises) Regulations 1987.[6]

In June 1998 the DTI undertook a three-month consultation (105 responses) which showed a number of serious abuses affecting elderly and other vulnerable people. The fourth example on page 1 of this book is based on the experience of a 63 year-old Preston man who signed a double-glazing contract after four hours of high-pressure selling. In another case, a salesman persuaded a woman to sign a contract for a £3,000 burglar alarm after telling her that her dog could be blinded or even poisoned by intruders. "Thank goodness I checked up on them" she said "but I hate to think how many old people they manage to con." The regulations have now been amended (S.I. 1998 No. 3050). Consumers can obtain an information leaflet by telephoning 0845-601-0540; information is also available on www.dti.gov.uk/doorstep. The regulations in their amended form are summarised below.

Relationship with Consumer Credit Act

Since May 17, 1985 a consumer has had the right to cancel a regulated **6.05** consumer credit or consumer hire agreement (subject to minor exceptions) where oral representations were made in his presence and the prospective agreement is signed by the debtor or hirer away from business premises (as defined). This right is conferred by section 67 of the Consumer Credit Act 1974.[7] It is clear from the Regulations that section 67 and the new cancellation right conferred by the Regulations are intended to be mutually exclusive (see reg. 4).

What agreements are caught?

Subject to what has been said above, and subject also to the exceptions set **6.06** out below, the Regulations (which are aimed at cold callers and high-pressure doorstep salesmen) apply to a contract for the supply by a trader of goods or services to a consumer where the *contract* is made in any of the following cases:

(a) During an "unsolicited visit" by a trader to the consumer's home or the home of another person or to the consumer's place of work.

---

[6] S.I. 1987 No. 2117 (as amended).
[7] Below, para. 22.04.

(b) During a visit to such premises by the trader at the express request of the consumer where the contract relates to goods or services not comprised in the request and the consumer at the time of the request did not know, and could not reasonably have known, that those other goods or services formed part of the trader's business activities.

Example 1

Albert invites Bert (a central heating specialist) to his home to discuss the installation of central heating. Unknown to Albert, Bert also sells double glazing and Albert signs (at his home) a double glazing contract. The Regulations will apply unless Albert should have known this.

(c) After an *offer* by the consumer was made at such premises or under (d) below.

Example 2

Following a "cold call" by Charles to David's place of work, David offers to acquire a personal computer on hire-purchase terms. The contract itself is concluded a week later at Charles' shop. The Regulations apply.

(d) During an excursion organised by the trader away from his business premises.

Example 3

A timeshare company organises a visit to one of its sites. While relaxing in a restaurant after the visit a customer is induced to sign a timeshare contract. The Regulations apply.

Business "consumers"

6.07 Even if the consumer carries on a business, the Regulations will still apply if in making the contract he is acting for purposes which can be regarded as outside his business.

Unsolicited

6.08 In general a contract is not caught by the Regulations if the consumer takes the initiative by inviting the trader to his home. If, however, an unsolicited telephone call from the trader ("I can come to see you") provokes the invitation, then the Regulations can apply.[8] They will also apply where the trader indicates that he, or another trader for whom he acts, is willing to make a subsequent visit to the consumer.

Excepted contracts

6.09 Regulation 3(2) contains a long list of contracts to which the Regulations do not apply. They include:

---

[8] reg. 3(3).

(1) contracts for the sale of an interest in land, leases and land mortgages;
(2) a bridging loan linked to land purchase;
(3) building contracts (but contracts for the supply of building materials *are* caught);
(4) food, drink and other goods intending for current consumption in the household and supplied by regular roundsmen;
(5) contracts of insurance;
(6) investment agreements under the Financial Services Act 1986 and deposit agreements under the Banking Act 1987.

The cancellation notice

Any agreement to which the Regulations apply is unenforceable against **6.10** the consumer unless the trader has delivered to him a notice in writing, informing him of his right to cancel and containing the information (including a cancellation form) set out in the Schedule to the Regulations. This notice must be given at the time of the contract or, in offer cases,[9] at the time of the offer.

Under the amended regulations, a trader who enters into a contract without delivering this notice commits an offence. The trader has the usual "due diligence" defence in appropriate cases (see para. 13.48 below) and the regulations "lift the corporate veil" by providing that, where an offence is committed by a body corporate; the directors and other officers will also be guilty if the offence took place with their connivance, consent or neglect. The trading standards departments of local authorities are given the task of enforcement.

Time for cancellation

The consumer can cancel by serving a notice in writing (not necessarily in **6.11** the form set out in the Schedule) within seven days following the making of the contract.[10] It is important to note that a posted notice takes effect at the time of posting—even though it never reaches the trader (see reg. 4(7)).

Example 4

Fred (the representative of a local store) visits George at his home and persuades George to sign an agreement for a charge card (this being outside the Consumer Credit Act). The contract is made on April 1. The last day for cancellation is April 8.

Effect of cancellation

The rules are very similar to those under the Consumer Credit Act.[11] Thus: **6.12**

---

[9] See (c) above.
[10] *cf.* the five-day period in relation to consumer credit: below, para. 22.07.
[11] Below, para. 22.09.

(a) the cancelled contract is treated as if it had never been made and any security is extinguished;
(b) sums paid by the consumer are repayable to him and he can refuse to hand over the goods (in legal terminology he has a "lien" over them) until those sums have been repaid;
(c) subject to exceptions, he must have the goods available for collection by the dealer;
(d) where the consumer has already had the benefit of a loan or overdraft, then cancellation will not extinguish his repayment obligation. Regulation 6 contains special rules for computation of interest similar to those in Consumer Credit Act cancellation cases.

3. When I Opened the Box the Plates were Broken

6.13 We have already seen that where goods are supplied in the course of a business, they must be of satisfactory quality. What happens if they were clearly satisfactory at the time of the contract but are accidentally damaged or destroyed at a later date? The basic rules in the Sale of Goods Act 1979 are straightforward but their application in practice is far from easy.

The basic rule as to risk

6.14 Section 20(1) of the Act provides as follows:

> Unless otherwise agreed, the goods remain at the seller's risk until the property in them is transferred to the buyer, but when the property therein is transferred to the buyer, the goods are at the buyer's risk whether delivery has been made or not.

So the key question for the consumer is—had the property passed to him when the loss or damage occurred? If the answer is "yes", then (unless otherwise agreed) the risk will also have passed to him and he must bear the loss; this means that, for example, he will remain liable to pay the contract price. Most consumers would be very surprised to learn that the property (*i.e.* ownership) had passed to them before delivery, but in many cases this will in fact be so.

When does property pass?

6.15 The rules as to the passing of property are to be found in sections 16 to 18 of the Act. The essential distinction is between specific and unascertained goods. All goods fall into one or other of these two categories at the contract moment and it will be convenient to deal with these matters first.

6.16 (a) **Specific goods.** These are defined by section 61 "as goods identified and agreed on at the time a contract of sale is made". For goods to be "specific" it must be possible to identify the precise subject matter of the sale

immediately the contract comes into existence, *i.e.* the very items to be transferred to the buyer. The obvious example is goods selected by the buyer in a
shop, showroom or store.

(b) **Unascertained goods.**   This term is not defined in the Act but it is clear   **6.17**
that the terms "specific" and "unascertained" are mutually exclusive. Thus,
goods are "unascertained" if they are purely generic, as where a buyer gives
an order for "two tons of coal" or for a car or a freezer like the one on display
in the showroom. Goods are also unascertained if they form part of a larger
consignment or come from a source which is specified in the contract, as
where a buyer agrees to buy "10 bottles of wine from the case in the seller's
warehouse".

Passing of property—specific goods

The basic rule of section 17 is that property passes when the parties intend   **6.18**
it to pass. There is nothing in the Sale of Goods Act to prevent an agreement
that "no property in the goods shall pass until the buyer has paid the price".
Such a "retention of title" clause, or an extension of it,[12] is frequently inserted
into commercial contracts and this can give rise to many legal, financial and
accounting problems.[13]

Then again if the price is payable by instalments, there may be a clause that
ownership shall remain with the seller until the final instalment has been paid.
Such agreement is known as a "conditional sale agreement".[14] Apart from
these cases, it is unusual to have an express passing of property clause in a
consumer sale agreement and we must therefore examine the first four rules
of section 18. These rules govern the passing of property in specific goods
where no contrary intention appears. The courts have held that a "contrary
intention" will only oust the statutory rules if present at the time of the contract.[15] The four rules can be summarised as follows:

Rule 1.   This reads: **6.19**

> Where there is an unconditional contract for the sale of specific goods in a deliv-
> erable state, the property passes to the buyer when the contract is made, and it is
> immaterial whether the time of payment or the time of delivery, or both, be
> postponed.

This rule applies to the vast majority of retail sales. Thus if a consumer

---

[12] *e.g.* "the property in the goods shall remain in the seller until all sums due from the buyer to the
seller under this or any other contract shall have been paid." See now *Armour v. Thyssen AG*
[1990] 3 All E.R. 481, HL where an extended clause of this type was upheld. The OFT consider
that such clauses in consumer contracts may be "unfair"—see Chap. Nine.

[13] See *Aluminium Industrie Vaassen BV v. Romalpa Aluminium Ltd* [1976] 1 W.L.R. 676 and,
more recently, *Clough Mill Ltd v. Martin* [1984] 3 All E.R. 982, CA.

[14] Below, para. 18.05.

[15] *Dennant v. Skinner* [1948] 2 K.B. 164.

goes to a store, selects a suite of furniture and agrees to have it delivered in a week's time, the property and risk will pass to the buyer as soon as the contract has been made. If, therefore, the contents of the showroom are destroyed by fire, or damaged by vandals, at any time after the contract the buyer must bear the loss and must pay the agreed price for the lost or damaged goods. In other words, the insurable risk was on him as from the making of the contract. It has, however, been suggested that the courts will be very ready to infer an intention (ousting the statutory rule) that property is not to pass until delivery or payment.[16]

A well-advised consumer of a domestic appliance should try to insert a clause that the risk shall not pass to the buyer until the goods have been installed in his home; in the case of a car he should try to agree that the risk should remain with the seller until delivery by which time the buyer should have insured it.

6.20   **Rule 2.**   This provides that:

> Where there is a contract for the sale of specific goods and the seller is bound to do something to the goods for the purpose of putting them into a deliverable state,[17] the property does not pass until the thing is done and the buyer has notice that it has been done.

If we turn to section 61(5) we will find that goods are in "a deliverable state" when they are in such a state that the buyer would under the contract be bound to take delivery of them. Thus if the seller agreed to enlarge a watch-strap or ring, or to install a sunroof in a car, the risk would remain on the seller until the buyer had received notice that this work had been done.

It will be observed that the Act uses the clear and positive words "the buyer has notice thereof". Thus, if the seller sends off a letter saying that the work has been done this would not, of itself, pass the property and risk.

6.21   **Rule 3.**   This deals with the rather less common case where the seller has to do something to ascertain the price. It reads:

> Where there is a contract for the sale of specific goods in a deliverable state but the seller is bound to weigh, measure, test, or do some other act or thing with reference to the goods for the purpose of ascertaining the price, the property does not pass until the act or thing is done and the buyer has notice that it has been done.

6.22   **Rule 4.**   It is not uncommon that a consumer orders goods (usually from a catalogue or other advertisement) on approval or on sale or return. This is governed by Rule 4 which reads

---

[16] *Per* Diplock L.J. in *R.V. Ward Ltd v. Bignall* [1967] 1 Q.B. 534 at 545.
[17] See *Underwood v. Burgh Castle Brick Syndicate* [1992] 1 K.B. 343.

Where goods are delivered to the buyer on approval or on sale or return or other similar terms the property in the goods passes to the buyer:
  (a) when he signifies his approval or acceptance to the seller or does any other act adopting the transaction;
  (b) if he does not signify his approval or acceptance to the seller but retains the goods without giving notice of rejection, then, if a time has been fixed for the return of the goods, on the expiration of that time, and, if no time has been fixed, on the expiration of a reasonable time.

An extreme example of the risk rules can be seen from the early case of *Elphick v. Barnes*[18] where a horse, which was delivered on sale or return, died during the approval period without the buyer's fault. It was held that the buyer was not bound to pay the price.

It should be added that all these rules as to risk pre-suppose that the loss or damage was purely accidental. The principle is underlined by the two further subsections of section 20 which read as follows:

  (2) But where delivery has been delayed through the fault of either buyer or seller the goods are at the risk of the party at fault as regards any loss which might not have occurred but for such fault.
  (3) Nothing in this section shall affect the duties and liabilities of either seller or buyer as a bailee of the goods for the other party.

A bailment would arise if, for example, the seller of goods agreed to store them for the buyer. If the goods were lost or damaged, the onus would be on the seller (as bailee) to disprove negligence.[19]

Passing of property—unascertained goods

If a buyer agrees to buy "20 square metres of carpet" or "ten bottles of wine   **6.23**
from the crate in your warehouse", this would be a contract for the sale of unascertained goods. Bearing in mind the basic rule that risk passes with property[20] we must start with section 16 which applies to unascertained goods only. It provides that:

Where there is a contract for the sale of unascertained goods no property in the goods is transferred to the buyer unless and until the goods are ascertained.

Thus, if in the above example the manufacturer of carpet sends a large roll to the seller, no property can pass to the buyer until a piece measuring twenty square metres has been cut and set aside for the buyer's contract, *i.e.* until the goods are "*ascertained*".[21] It is important to observe, however, that this is

---

[18] (1880) 5 C.P.D. 321.
[19] See, *e.g. Houghland v. Low (Luxury Coaches) Ltd* [1962] 1 Q.B. 694.
[20] Above, para. 6.14.
[21] For a recent case see *Bryan Noreys Kensington v. Liggett* (1994) 13 T.L.R. 434 (sale of bullion to various buyers—no appropriation, seller became insolvent; buyers had no proprietary claim. This has now been modified by statute (see para. 6.23 below)).

only the first of two hurdles to be surmounted. First, the goods must become ascertained after the contract has been made. Secondly, appropriation must occur; this is discussed next.

We can now turn to section 18, **Rule 5**, which applies where no contrary intention appears. It reads as follows:

> (1) Where there is a contract for the sale of unascertained or future goods by description, and goods of that description and in a deliverable state[22] are uncon-ditionally appropriated to the contract, either by the seller with the assent of the buyer, or by the buyer with the assent of the seller, the property in the goods then passes to the buyer and the assent may be express or implied and may be given either before or after the appropriation is made.
>
> (2) Whether, in pursuance of the contract, the seller delivers the goods to the buyer or to a carrier or other bailee ... for the purpose of transmission to the buyer, and does not reserve the right of disposal, he is to be taken to have uncon-ditionally appropriated the goods to the contract.

Four points call for comment. First, rule 5(2) refers to delivery of "the goods" to the carrier. Thus, if the seller merely delivers a larger consignment (of which the buyer's goods form an unascertained part) section 16[23] will apply. The result is that the property and risk remain with the seller; if therefore they are lost or damaged before becoming ascertained the buyer can reject them.[24]

Secondly, there must be an unconditional "*appropriation*". The mere fact that the seller sets them aside is not enough because he may change his mind. To constitute appropriation:

> the parties must have had, or be reasonably supposed to have had an intention *to attach the contract irrevocably to those goods* so that those goods and no others are the subject of the sale and become the property of the buyer[25] (italics supplied).

Thirdly, there is the question of consent. If the buyer orders goods by post, does he automatically consent in advance to the seller's appropriation? If this is so, then the risk will be on the buyer before he ever sees the goods—a clearly unreasonable result since he will usually not be in a position to insure them. Even here, however, the buyer is not entirely without a remedy. He might, for example, be able to prove that the seller has failed to make a reasonable contract of carriage.[26] In such a case the buyer can refuse delivery or he can claim damages from the seller—even if the loss or damage was not causally connected with the seller's default. Secondly, the buyer may have rights under section 14(2)[27] if the condition of the goods at the time of deliv-

---

[22] *Philip Head v. Showfronts Ltd* [1970] 1 Lloyd's Rep. 140.
[23] Above.
[24] *Healy v. Howlett* [1917] 1 K.B. 337.
[25] *per* Pearson J. (as he then was) in *Carlos Federspiel & Co. S.A. v. Twigg (Charles) Ltd* [1957] 1 Lloyd's Rep. 240 at 255 where the authorities are fully reviewed. See also *Wardar's (Import and Export) Ltd v. Norwood (W.) & Sons Ltd* [1968] 2 Q.B. 663.
[26] s.32(2).
[27] Above, para. 4.07.

ery suggests that they were not of satisfactory quality at the time of the contract and so were not fit to travel.[28]

The question of when property and risk pass where a consumer orders goods from a mail order house has never been expressly decided. In one case a commercial buyer ordered goods from a Swiss seller and it was held by the House of Lords that property passed to the buyer as soon as the goods were posted by the seller.[29] This case, if applied to the consumer mail order purchase, would produce a result which is out of line with the reasonable expectation of most consumers[30] and, as already stated, it can be most unfair to the consumer.[31] The *Badische Anilin* case was not a risk case at all and it turned on a point of patent law. The courts could always side-step this decision by finding an implied "contrary intention" under section 17 which would oust section 18 altogether.

Fourthly, the rules set out above can cause hardship where, for example the buyer buys, and pays for, goods forming part of a larger consignment and then finds himself unable to collect them because the seller has become insolvent.[31a] To meet this situation the Law Commission published a Report which led to the passing of the Sale of Goods (Amendment) Act 1995. The Act only applies where the bulk is *identified* in the contract or by subsequent agreement. Subject to this, there are two basic rules:

(1) If the contract is for a specified quantity of goods in a deliverable state, and if the identified bulk is reduced to (or below) the amount then due to the sole buyer, the bulk will be treated as appropriated to the buyer and the property then passes to him.
(2) If the buyer has paid for some or all of the goods forming part of the bulk then (a) the property in an "undivided share" passes to him and (b) he becomes owner in common of the bulk. The "undivided share" is such share as the quantity paid for and due to the buyer bears to the total bulk. This will give him an enforceable proprietary claim against the seller's liquidator or trustee in bankruptcy.

Effect of risk rules

The Act, the cases and the textbooks are remarkably silent on the precise **6.24** operation of the risk rules in the case of damage. A distinction can be drawn between (a) total destruction, and (b) damage.

(a) *Total destruction*

If the goods are totally destroyed either physically or commercially, they **6.25**

---

[28] See, *e.g.* the pre-Act case of *Beer v. Walker* (1877) 46 L.J.Q.B. 677 (rabbits go putrid on the Brighton train; condition of merchantable quality broken).
[29] See *Badische Anilin und Soda Fabrik v. Basle Chemical Works* [1898] A.C. 200.
[30] See *Which?*, May 1978, p. 316.
[31] See above.
[31a] *Goldcorp Exchange* [1994] 2 All E.R. 806.

can be said to "perish". In advising the consumer in a case where the goods have perished after the making of the contract we must again distinguish between specific and unascertained goods.

(i) If specific goods perish, without the fault of either party, *after*[32] contract but before the risk has passed to the buyer, the contract is avoided.[33] Thus if, in the example cited above,[34] the jeweller's entire stock is destroyed by an accidental fire before he has given notice that the enlarged ring is ready, the provisions of section 7 will apply. Further, the perishing of specific goods is not a case to which the Law Reform (Frustrated Contracts) Act 1943 applies so that the effects of frustration will be governed by the common law rules. Accordingly, since the contract is avoided by section 7, the buyer will not have to pay the price; if he has paid it or some of it, he can recover it because the consideration has failed[35]; he cannot claim damages for non-delivery. The unfortunate seller cannot sue for the price, nor can he claim any payment for work done by him on the goods before the fire broke out.

(ii) When we turn to unascertained goods we must draw yet another distinction. In the case of purely generic goods (*e.g.* "20 square metres of Wilton carpet") no question of perishing can arise. If the goods which the seller intends to supply cease to be available, the seller must find the goods from another source or pay damages for non-delivery, unless he has covered himself by an effective exemption clause.[36] If, however, the source of the goods is specified in the contract (*e.g.* "10 bottles of wine from the case in my warehouse") the destruction of the source after contract but before the risk has passed to the buyer will frustrate the contract. The position of the parties is similar to that under section 7 [37] except that the Act of 1943 will regulate the rights of the parties so that adjustments for expenses incurred, and benefits received, are possible.

(b) *Damage*

6.26   What happens if goods are accidentally damaged while they are still at the seller's risk? This problem could arise if, *e.g.* the furniture ordered by the buyer is damaged when the delivery van is involved in a road accident for which the seller is not responsible. Presumably the buyer can refuse to accept the damaged goods and then bring an action for non-delivery. The precise

---

[32] *cf.* s.6, which deals with goods perishing *before* contract, *i.e. res extincta* and common mistake.
[33] s.7.
[34] Above, para. 6.20.
[35] *Fibrosa Spolka Akcyjna v. Fairbairn, Lawson Combe Barbour Ltd* [1943] A.C. 32.
[36] Below, Chap. Eight.
[37] Above.

nature and the precise legal basis of the buyer's rights do not appear to have been analysed in any reported case; perhaps it is based on an implied undertaking by the seller that the quality of the goods delivered will correspond precisely with the quality of the goods when the buyer agreed to take them.[38]

4. THE PLUMBER WAS A COWBOY

The contract of "work and materials" (installation of central heating, double-glazing, etc.) was briefly examined in Chapter 4.[39] It will be recalled that such a contract can be divided into two parts—the "goods" part and the "work" part and the legal rules for the two parts are different (although in practice the difference may well be slight). The "work" part of such a contract can be classified as a contract for services. The list of such contracts includes repair, decoration, servicing, maintenance, cleaning, building, storage, carriage of goods and passengers, insurance, the provision of accommodation, entertainment and the whole range of professional services—legal, banking, accountancy, medical, dental, surveying, valuing and so on. A report published by the National Consumer Council (*Service Please*)[40] in 1981 highlighted three main areas of dissatisfaction—the quality of the work, the time it took to do it and the cost. This section of this chapter is only concerned with the first of these—unsatisfactory performance. The Report referred to above shows that, for example:

6.27

(1) Out of 50 garages only two came anywhere near to carrying out a full service in line with the maker's specifications.[41]
(2) Out of 10 repair men called in to mend defective washing machines only two did so effectively.
(3) A "plumber" connected an office coffee machine to a lavatory pipe.

Until fairly recently there was no statutory obligation on the supplier of a service to carry out his work with reasonable care and skill but this was rectified by section 13 of the Supply of Goods and Services Act 1982.[42] It reads:

> In a contract for the supply of a service where the supplier is acting in the course of a business there is an implied term that the supplier will carry out the service with reasonable care and skill.

The section was intended to confirm and codify the existing common law.

---

[38] For a somewhat similar principle in a slightly different context see *Financings Ltd v. Stimson* [1962] 1 W.L.R. 1184, CA (damage to car between hirer's initial offer and its acceptance by the finance company).
[39] Above, para. 4.28.
[40] Above, para. 1.05.
[41] See *Motoring Which*, January 1981.
[42] For the background to, and commentary on, the 1982 Act see Woodroffe, *Goods and Services—The New Law* (1982).

It was not intended to enlarge existing areas of liability. Accordingly, section 12(4) gives the Secretary of State power to make orders excluding particular groups of persons from the "services" provisions of the Act (*i.e.* ss.13–15). An Order has been made (S.I. 1982 No. 1771) which provides that section 13 shall not apply to the following services:

    (i) the services of an advocate in court or before any tribunal, inquiry or arbitration or in carrying out any preliminary work directly affecting the conduct of the hearing[43]; or

    (ii) the services rendered to a company by a director of the company in his capacity as such.

A second Order (S.I. 1985 No. 1) has been made taking arbitrators outside the scope of section 13.[44]

We revert now to the basic question—does the consumer have to pay the price if the work of the plumber, electrician, etc., is unsatisfactory? In the vast majority of cases the answer will be "no"; the plumber, etc., will be in breach of the implied duty of care and skill under section 13 and the consumer may well be able to treat himself as discharged from the contract altogether or alternatively he can set off his claim for damages against the claim for the charge or fee. The matter is examined more fully in Chapter 7 (below, paras 7.14–7.15).

5. They Turned Up Late

6.28 Late performance, whether by sellers, electricians, builders, plumbers, carriers or holiday operators, is a frequent source of complaint by consumers. The legal principles governing this topic can be summarised as follows:

(1) If the contract specifies a date for performance, a supplier of goods or services who fails to perform by that date will be liable for damages for breach of contract (unless this liability has been effectively excluded or unless the contract is frustrated). This claim for damages can be pleaded by way of set-off or counter-claim in an action by the supplier for the price.[45]

(2) If the contract does not specify a date for performance the supplier must perform within a "reasonable" time. This statutory obligation is imposed on business suppliers by section 14 of the Supply of Goods and Services Act 1982.[46] The question of reasonableness is a question of fact[47]; even a long delay will not necessarily amount to a breach of contract if it was due to

---

[43] See *Rondel v. Worsley* [1969] 1 A.C. 191 for the advocate's immunity in such cases. The immunity is not limited to barristers: Courts and Legal Services Act 1990, s.62. It may soon be challenged under the European Convention on Human Rights.
[44] An arbitrator is immune from liability unless he acts in bad faith: Arbitration Act 1996, s.29.
[45] For the assessment of damages, see below, paras 7.31–7.42.
[46] This section codified the existing common law rule.
[47] *ibid.*

circumstances beyond the supplier's control. In one case a car owner took his car to a garage for repair following an accident. A normally competent repairer would have taken five weeks; the garage gave priority to other work and took eight weeks. It was held by the Court of Appeal that they had failed to carry out the work within a reasonable time and were therefore liable in damages.[48]

(3) Can the consumer go further and claim to be discharged from the contract altogether? This depends on whether time is "of the essence", *i.e.* a vital term or, in sale of goods language, a condition. The following statement in *Halsbury's Laws of England* has recently received judicial approval:

> Time will not be considered to be of the essence unless (1) the parties expressly stipulate that conditions as to time must be strictly complied with, or (2) the nature of the subject-matter of the contract or the surrounding circumstances show that time should be considered to be of the essence.[49]

It is probably true to say that under a contract to supply goods or services to a consumer a failure to observe the agreed performance date is not of itself a repudiation of the contract. There can, of course, be difficult cases; what about an operator who agrees to provide his client with a 15-day holiday in Majorca starting on August 1, but is prevented from carrying out that obligation by reason of industrial action for which he is not responsible? It could be argued that if he is unable to transport his clients on August 1, he will have broken an essential term of the contract which enables the clients to treat the contract as discharged; alternatively, it might be argued that the contract has been frustrated.[50]

(4) If a reasonable time has elapsed, or if the breach of an essential time clause has been waived, the consumer can serve a notice fixing a time for performance. The time limit in this notice must itself be a reasonable one, but subject to this the consumer can treat the contract as discharged if the supplier fails to perform by the date specified in the notice.[51]

Thus the consumer should always make it clear, in appropriate cases, that the date for performance is vital, *e.g.* by stating expressly that "time is of the essence".

6. THE PRICE SEEMS RATHER HIGH

In the case of sale of goods it is fairly rare to find an agreement without a **6.29**

---

[48] *Charnock v. Liverpool Corporation* [1968] 1 W.L.R. 1498; s.14, above, would now apply to such a case.
[49] *Halsbury's Laws of England* (4th ed.), Vol. 9, para. 481, approved by Lord Simon in *Universal Scientific Holdings Ltd v. Burnley Council* [1978] A.C. 904, HL. See also *Bunge Corporation v. Tradax S.A.* [1981] 1 W.L.R. 711, HL.
[50] In practice the contract will usually deal with the matter in accordance with the Codes of Practice discussed in Chap. Ten, below.
[51] *Charles Rickards Ltd v. Oppenheim* [1950] 1 K.B. 616, CA.

price; indeed the absence of a price may indicate that the parties are still negotiating and that consequently there is no contract at all.[52] Section 8 of the 1979 Act, which is more appropriate to a commercial contract, provides that the price can be fixed by the contract itself, or in manner thereby agreed, or by usage. It then goes on to provide that if the price is not fixed in this way the buyer must pay a reasonable price.

In the case of services, it is rather more common to call in a repairer, or to take a suit to the cleaners or a car for a service without agreeing a price in advance. In such a case the supplier is entitled to claim a reasonable charge by virtue of section 15 of the Supply of Goods and Services Act 1982.[53] This, of course, is much easier said than done. If a consumer feels that the price is too high the onus will be on him to find expert evidence to substantiate his claim. He will also be put to great practical inconvenience if the supplier has the goods in his possession and refuses to release them until he has been paid. The consumer should also be very careful to limit his potential liability. Instead of saying "the car is starting badly—put it right" he should say "tell me if the work is going to cost more than £50".

Incidentally, what about an "estimate"? If an estimate amounts to an offer which is accepted, the estimate will become the contract price.[54] This, however, is rather unusual and the general rule is that the estimate is not legally binding; if however the estimate is a long way short of the final bill, the court might take the estimate into account in fixing a "reasonable price". In contrast, a quotation is more likely to be an offer to do the job for the quoted price.[55]

Can a supplier of services claim an additional amount if additional work is required? This again depends on what the parties have agreed. If, for example, a builder is employed to convert a loft the onus will be on him to ensure that the work will comply with the local bye-laws and building regulations. If it turns out that the local authority require extra work to be done (for example, fireproofing) he will generally be unable to recover any additional payment for this extra work from the owner—he should have checked on the point before fixing his price.

There may also be special rules to protect the consumer in particular professions. Thus, for example, a client who is dissatisfied with a solicitor's bill for non-contentious business can insist that the solicitor has the bill assessed by the Law Society (a "remuneration certificate") or by an official of the court (a "detailed assessment" of the bill).

---

[52] *May and Butcher v. R.* [1934] 2 K.B. 17.
[53] Provided that there is a "contract" for the service it does not have to be in the course of a business—although it usually is.
[54] *Croshaw v. Pritchard* (1899) 16 T.L.R. 45.
[55] See, *e.g.* Motor Industry Code, below, para. 10.15.

Chapter Seven

"WHAT ARE MY REMEDIES?"

In the previous five chapters we have considered some of the supplier's basic **7.01**
obligations. We now come to the subject of remedies which, as stated in the
Preface to the First Edition, is what this book is all about; it is also the area in
which the consumer is most likely to seek legal advice. In practice three
questions most frequently arise, namely (a) what are the consumer's remedies, (b) can they be excluded, and (c) how can they be enforced? These
topics are considered in this chapter and the four following ones.

One preliminary point can be made. This chapter and the next two are
concerned with questions of strict law. In Chapter 10 we shall see that in
many cases consumers may be able to sidestep the worry, uncertainty and
expense of litigation as a result of voluntary codes of practice drawn up by a
number of trade and professional associations with the encouragement of the
Office of Fair Trading. We shall also see that a complaint to a trading standards inspector can lead to a prosecution in certain cases and that this, in turn,
can lead to a compensation order.[1]

This chapter is divided into three parts, namely:

(1) Remedies for misrepresentation.
(2) Remedies for breach of contract.
(3) Remedies in tort.

The Sale and Supply of Goods Act 1994 (which has already been considered when dealing with satisfactory quality in Chap. 4[2]) will be considered
again in appropriate places in this chapter.

1. Remedies for Misrepresentation

The remedies for misrepresentation can be summarised as follows: **7.02**

(1) Fraudulent misrepresentation:
    (a) damages in tort for deceit;
    (b) rescission.
(2) Negligent misrepresentation:

---

[1] Below, paras 13.58 and 16.02.
[2] Above, paras 4.18–4.19.

      (a)   damages under section 2(1) of the Misrepresentation Act 1967;

      (b)   rescission (or damages in lieu under s.2(2) of the 1967 Act).

  (3) "Innocent" misrepresentation (*i.e.* neither fraudulent nor negligent): rescission (or damages in lieu under s.2(2) of the 1967 Act).

These matters will now be considered.

Fraudulent misrepresentation

7.03   A person commits the tort of deceit (or fraud) if he makes a false statement of fact knowingly, or without belief in its truth, or recklessly (*i.e.* careless whether true or false) with the intention that it should be acted upon by the plaintiff who does act on it and thereby suffers damage.[3] In practice, fraud is notoriously hard to prove. If, however, the consumer can prove that, for example, the dealer deliberately misrepresented the age or mileage of a car then, as we have seen, he may have the remedies of damages and/or rescission.[4] If he rescinds the contract he can claim to be put back into his pre-contractual position, so that, for example, he can recover any part of the price which he has paid. The action for damages can be considered (a) if the innocent party does not wish to rescind, (b) if it is too late to rescind,[5] or (c) if he has suffered damage over and above the price.

What is the measure of damages for fraudulent misrepresentation? The rules are designed to prove compensation for all loss flowing directly from the fraud, whether reasonably foreseeable or not. Thus, in a sale of goods or land the starting point is the difference (if any) between the price paid by the consumer and the true value of the goods or land.[6] Money spent on repair and improvement before discovering the fraud can also be recovered[7] but not damages for loss of bargain.[8] Damages for personal injury or damage to property can also be recovered.[9]

Negligent misrepresentation

7.04   Until the passing of the Misrepresentation Act 1967 the court had no general power to award damages for a non-fraudulent misrepresentation—hence the importance of proving that there had been a breach of a contractual term.[10] A Law Reform Committee recommended a change in the law and accordingly section 2(1) of the 1967 Act was passed to give a statutory right to damages in certain cases. It reads:

---

[3] See the leading case of *Derry v. Peek* (1889) 14 App.Cas. 337, HL.
[4] Above, para. 3.03.
[5] See below, paras 7.05–7.06.
[6] *Doyle v. Olby (Ironmongers) Ltd* [1969] 2 Q.B. 158—a case of the sale of a business.
[7] *ibid.*
[8] *East v. Maurer* [1991] 1 W.L.R. 461 (another business sale; damages awarded for the profits which the plaintiff would have earned if the false statement had not been made).
[9] *Langridge v. Levy* (1838) 4 M. & W. 337—exploding gun.
[10] Above, para. 3.03.

Where a person has entered into a contract after a misrepresentation has been made to him by another party thereto and as a result thereof he has suffered loss then if the person making the representation would be liable in damages in respect thereof had the representation been made fraudulently, that person shall be so liable notwithstanding that the misrepresentation was not made fraudulently, unless he proves that he had reasonable grounds to believe and did believe up to the time that the contract was made that the facts represented were true.

It is clear from the case of *Howard Marine & Dredging Co. Ltd v. A. Ogden & Son (Excavation) Ltd*[11] that a section 2(1) claim is a claim in tort, and the approach in relation to a claim for damages is the same as for fraud.[12] We have seen that the object of damages in tort is to put the innocent party in the same position *as if the contract had never been made*. This can be contrasted with a different rule in contract where the damages are designed to put the innocent party in the same position *as if the contract had been performed*. Thus damages for loss of bargain are appropriate to contract but not to tort; the case of *Watts v. Spence*,[13] where damages for loss of bargain were awarded under section 2(1) of the 1967 Act, must be regarded as wrongly decided.

Rescission

We can now turn to the equitable remedy of rescission. This has already been mentioned[14] and it only remains to consider the cases where it is not available. There are four well-established bars to rescission and these can be summarised as follows:　　　　　　　　　　　　　　　　　　　　　　**7.05**

(a) where the parties can no longer be restored to their previous position. Thus the right to rescission would disappear if goods were destroyed before the buyer had elected to rescind;
(b) where third party rights have been acquired. Perhaps the clearest example is where B, by misrepresentation, persuades S to sell the goods to B and then resells the goods to C[15];
(c) where the innocent party has affirmed the contract with knowledge of the misrepresentation[16];
(d) where the innocent party has been guilty of unreasonable delay. In the well-known case of *Leaf v. International Galleries*,[17] the buyer of a

---

[11] [1978] Q.B. 574. See also *Naughton v. O'Callaghan* [1990] 3 All E.R. 191 (misdescription of racehorse).
[12] *ibid.* at p. 197. See also *Royscot Trust Ltd v. Rogerson* [1991] 2 Q.B. 297, CA.
[13] [1976] Ch. 165.
[14] Above, para. 7.03.
[15] See Sale of Goods Act 1979, s.23, above, para. 2.07.
[16] *Long v. Lloyd* [1958] 2 All E.R. 402. *Cf.* Acceptance and loss of the right to reject for breach of condition, where knowledge is irrelevant: below, para. 7.25.
[17] [1950] 2 K.B. 86.

painting which was described as by J. Constable sought to rescind for misrepresentation five years after making the contract on discovering that it was the work of another artist. The Court of Appeal held that it was far too late to rescind. In the words of Jenkins L.J.:

> "If he is allowed to wait five, ten or twenty years and then re-open the bargain, there can be no finality at all."

If the buyer had claimed damages under section 13 of the Sale of Goods Act[18] the claim would presumably have been unanswerable.

Statutory restriction on rescission

7.06   If none of these four bars apply, the general rule is that the innocent party can rescind the contract. The exercise of this remedy can have far-reaching results.

> Suppose that P buys a house from V for £80,000. V makes a non-fraudulent misrepresentation relating to the drains; the defect will cost £200 to put right. V has spent the whole of the £80,000 in buying another house.

If P were to rescind, V would have to find £80,000 (and might well be rendered homeless) because of a statement which caused damage of only £200. It was clearly with this kind of case in mind that section 2(2) of the Misrepresentation Act was enacted. It provides that:

> where a person has entered into a contract after a misrepresentation has been made to him otherwise than fraudulently, and he would be entitled, by reason of the misrepresentation, to rescind the contract, then, if it is claimed in any proceedings arising out of the contract, that the contract ought to be or has been rescinded, the court or arbitrator may declare the contract subsisting and award damages in lieu of rescission, if of opinion that it would be equitable to do so, having regard to the nature of the misrepresentation and the loss that would be caused by it if the contract was upheld, as well as to the loss that rescission would cause to the other party.

Thus, in the above example, the court would probably refuse rescission and award P damages of £200.

This power to award discretionary damages only applies where a person "would be entitled . . . to rescind the contract". In the previous editions of this book we suggested that damages could only be awarded under section 2(2) if the innocent party had a subsisting right to rescind at the date of the hearing, but in a recent High Court case[18a] Jacob J. has reached the opposite conclusion.

---

[18] Above, para. 3.08. But see *Harlingdon and Leinster Enterprises v. Christopher Hull Fine Art*, above, para. 3.09.

[18a] *Thomas Witter Ltd v. TBP Industries*, [1996] 2 All E.R. 573.

"Innocent" misrepresentation

If the misrepresentation is neither fraudulent nor negligent, the only poss- **7.07**
ible remedy is rescission. This is subject to the usual equitable bars[19] and the
court's discretionary power under section 2(2) to award damages in lieu of
rescission.

Exclusion clauses

A clause excluding liability for misrepresentation or cutting down the con- **7.08**
sumer's remedies for misrepresentation is only valid if it satisfies the test of
"reasonableness".[20]

Misrepresentation and breach of contract

It is clear from section 1 of the Misrepresentation Act 1967 that the inno- **7.09**
cent party will have remedies for misrepresentation even though the representation has become a term of contract. The precise relationship between
the two sets of remedies has yet to be worked out but presumably they are
complementary.[21] It has recently been held that a clause stating "this agreement contains the whole contract between the parties" does not oust a claim
for misrepresentation.[22] The court expressly decided that such a clause was
not an exemption clause within section 8 of the Unfair Contract Terms Act
1977 (below, para. 8.33), but presumably the reasoning in this case would
apply to an exemption clause.

2. REMEDIES FOR BREACH OF CONTRACT

This topic will be considered under four main headings, namely: **7.10**

    (1) Can I make him perform the contract?
    (2) Can I have the goods repaired or replaced?
    (3) Can I get my money back?
    (4) Can I get compensation?

(1) Can I make him perform the contract?

Let us suppose that a consumer has ordered goods from a supplier, or work **7.11**
from a builder, and the supplier or builder has failed to perform. We have
already seen that the consumer may be able to serve a notice making time of
the essence; if the supplier or builder then fails to perform by the stipulated
date the consumer may be able to treat the contract as discharged.

Let us suppose, however, that the consumer does not want to do this—

---

[19] Above, para. 7.04.
[20] See above, n. 18a.
[21] See *Naughton v. O'Callaghan*, above, para. 7.05, n. 11. See also n. 18a.
[22] *McGrath v. Shah* (1988) 57 P. & C.R. 452.

what he wants is to compel the supplier or builder to perform the contract. In practical terms this may be more trouble than it is worth—the consumer may be better advised to obtain the goods or work elsewhere and claim compensation from the defaulting party.[23] If, however, the consumer insists on performance can the law help him? Historically the courts of common law granted only the remedy of damages, but the courts of equity supplemented this by granting decrees of specific performance in cases where damages would not be an adequate remedy. In the case of sale of goods the power to award specific performance is now enacted in section 52 of the Sale of Goods Act 1979 as follows:

> In any action for breach of contract to deliver specific or ascertained goods the court may, if it thinks fit, on the plaintiff's application ... direct that the contract shall be performed specifically, without giving the defendant the option of retaining the goods on payment of damages. ...

Two points must be stressed. In the first place the goods must be specific or ascertained. We have already seen that goods are specific if they are identified and agreed upon at the time of the contract.[24] Although the term "ascertained" is not defined in the Act it probably refers to goods which are identified *after* the making of the contract.[25] Thus if a consumer merely orders "a deep freeze" or "a heated trolley" and the seller, who is out of stock, fails to obtain one, the remedy of specific performance would not be available.[26] Secondly, the remedy of specific performance is, and has always been, a discretionary remedy and a court will not grant it if damages would be an adequate remedy. In the vast majority of consumer contracts the buyer can get similar goods elsewhere and any loss can be compensated by an award of damages. Accordingly, specific performance would not be granted. It follows that the scope of the remedy, in practical terms, is extremely limited.

In the case of a contract for services (*e.g.* building, cleaning or repairing) the remedy is even less appropriate[27] and it is difficult to think of any case in which it will be granted.

(2) Can I have the goods repaired or replaced?

7.12   In considering this problem there is a vast difference between law and practice. If, for example, a car, television set or a lawnmower proves to be defective, the consumer will usually take it to the seller and ask for it to be

---

[23] Below, para. 7.31.

[24] s.61, above, para. 6.16.

[25] See Atkin L.J. in *Re Wait* [1927] 1 Ch. 606. See also n. 21, para. 6.23 above.

[26] *ibid.*

[27] There used to be a rule that specific performance (or a mandatory injunction) would not be granted if this required constant supervision of the defendant's work (*Ryan v. Mutual Tontine Westminster Chambers Ass.* [1993] 1 C.L. 116). The rationale of this rule has always been questionable and it is clear that it no longer exists: *Shiloh Spinners Ltd v. Harding* [1973] A.C. 721 at 724, HL.

repaired or replaced.[27a] In practice the seller (or the manufacturer in guarantee cases) will endeavour to repair it. Alternatively, the seller may take the goods back and give the consumer a replacement or a credit note; in the case of a car, however, it is very rare for the car to be taken back. All this is a matter of business practice; *there is no legal right to have the goods repaired or replaced*. The Law Commission Report[28] does not put forward any proposals to change the law on this point. However, an E.U. Directive *will* confer such a right (see para. 28.12 below).

What happens if the buyer's expensive dishwasher breaks down and the seller tells him "we can't replace the defective part because this particular model has been discontinued"? The Report referred to above confirms that the retailer is under no legal duty to keep a stock of spare parts and servicing facilities and does not recommend that the retailer should be placed under such a duty.[29] However, such an obligation is being gradually adopted on a voluntary basis (see, *e.g.* the electrical Codes of Practice).[30]

(3) Can I get my money back?

When a consumer makes a contract for the purchase of goods or services **7.13** he is under a basic obligation to pay the contract price. Thus, if he has booked a holiday at a seaside hotel, he cannot simply cancel his booking. If he does so then, as a matter of strict law, the hotel can forfeit his deposit, and can even sue him for damages if they have suffered additional loss by reason of his cancellation and have been unable to mitigate the loss by reletting the room.

There may, however, be cases where the consumer is relieved of his basic duty to pay the price; in these cases he can recover the price (or a deposit) if he has already paid it. This will be so in at least three cases:

(a) where the contract is rescinded for misrepresentation[31];
(b) where specific goods perish before the risk has passed to the buyer[32];
(c) where a contract for the sale of goods is discharged as a result of the supplier's breach.

Discharge by breach

If one party breaks a contractual term (express or implied) the innocent **7.14** party can claim damages. In some cases he can go further and claim that the entire contract has been discharged by the breach. Once that happens the innocent party can regard himself as excused from further performance and can also claim damages in respect of the past breach. His right to get his

---

[27a] The buyer's agreement to its repair is no longer deemed to be acceptance of the goods: see below, para. 7.22.
[28] *Sale and Supply of Goods*, Law Com. No. 160 (1987).
[29] *op. cit.* para. 3.66. Nor does a manufacturer have such a duty.
[30] Below, para. 10.27.
[31] Above, para. 7.05.
[32] Above, para. 6.25.

money back, however, is only available if the contract so provides or if there has been a total failure of consideration.

In deciding whether a contract has been discharged by breach we must start by looking at the general law and then at the special rules which apply to the sale of goods and (probably) to analogous contracts. Under the general law, a contract is discharged by a breach if the innocent party has been deprived of substantially the whole benefit which it was intended that he should obtain from the contract.[33] In other words the question is not "how was this term classified when the contract was made?" but—much more sensibly—"what effect did the breach have on the innocent party?" Even if the breach was a repudiatory breach, the innocent party may well have received *some* benefit under the contract and therefore has no right to recover money paid by him—although he will have a claim for damages which could well be equal to, or greater than, the amount of payments made.

Sales of goods

7.15   If we now turn to sale of goods we find the matter complicated by the condition/warranty classification. By section 61(1) of the 1979 Act a warranty is defined as:

> an agreement with reference to goods which are the subject-matter of a contract of sale, but collateral to the main purpose of such contract, the breach of which gives rise to a claim for damages but not to a right to reject the goods and treat the contract as repudiated.

In contrast, section 11(3) states that:

> Whether a stipulation in a contract of sale is a condition, the breach of which may give rise to a right to treat the contract as repudiated, or a warranty . . . depends in each case on the construction of such contract.

This wording, with its emphasis on "the construction of the contract" appears to leave no scope for the flexibility shown by the *Hong Kong* case (above), where the remedies available to the innocent party depend on the severity and consequences of the breach. (We use the words "appear to leave" because neither the courts nor the Law Commission seem to have considered the word "may" in the above definition—this might enable the *Hong Kong* principle to apply after all.)

Nevertheless in the case of *express* terms the courts have succeeded[34] in breaking out of the statutory straitjacket by holding that a clause could be neither a condition nor a warranty but an "intermediate stipulation" or "innominate term" to which the *Hong Kong* principles apply. Nevertheless there is no scope for such flexibility in the case of the statutory *implied* terms

---

[33] *per* Diplock L.J. in *Hong Kong Fir Shipping Co. Ltd v. Kawasaki* [1962] 2 Q.B. 26 at 66.
[34] *Cehave v. Bremer* [1976] Q.B. 44, C.A.

and, as we have seen in Chapters 2 to 4, the most important of the implied terms are classified as conditions. It remains to add that a buyer who rejects the goods for breach of condition can recover the price paid because there has been a total failure of consideration (see s.54).

Other supply of goods contracts

In the case of hire-purchase, hire and other contracts for the supply of goods the relevant statutes[35] use the condition/warranty terminology but do not define it. It is possible therefore (but unlikely) that a court would feel free to construe the words in a more flexible way. The case law makes it clear that a breach relating to fitness for purpose, etc., does not necessarily amount to a total failure of consideration. Accordingly the innocent party has no direct cause of action to recover payments made but instead he must seek to recover them indirectly by means of an action for damages.[36] If, however, the hirer under a hire-purchase agreement discovers the owner has no right to sell, we have seen that he *can* recover all his payments on the basis of total failure of consideration (see para. 2.14 above).

7.16

Supplies of services

Finally in contracts for services the statutory obligations as to care and skill, time for performance and price are referred to by the neutral word "term".[37] It is clear therefore that the flexible *Hong Kong* test will apply to them: they are innominate terms or intermediate stipulations.

7.17

The Law Commission: slight breaches

Minor defects can create a problem. On the one hand, a consumer should not be required to take goods which have minor defects (such as scratches on the bodywork of a car). On the other hand, the remedy of rejection may be so out of proportion that a court might be tempted to hold that the condition of "satisfactory quality" was not broken at all[37a]—with the result that the buyer could neither reject nor claim damages. We pointed out this problem in relation to the implied condition as to description in Chapter Three (above, para. 3.10).

7.18

The Law Commission in their report recommended that the law be changed for non-consumers[38] but not for consumers[39] and their proposals have now been enacted in the Sale and Supply of Goods Act 1994. Section

---

[35] Supply of Goods (Implied Terms) Act 1973 for hire-purchase and the Supply of Goods and Services Act 1982 for the other types of contract.
[36] See Law Commission Working Paper No. 85, paras. 2.41–2.43 and cases there cited.
[37] Supply of Goods and Services Act 1982, ss.13–15.
[37a] *Cehave v. Bremer* (above, n. 34, para. 7.15) is a commercial example, where the buyer was awarded damages for breach of an *express* term.
[38] *op. cit.* para. 4.21.
[39] *op cit.* para. 4.41.

4(1) inserts into the Sale of Goods Act a new section 15A(1) which provides that:

> Where in the case of a contract of sale—
> (a) the buyer would, apart from this subsection, have the right to reject goods by reason of a breach on the part of the seller of a term implied by section 13, 14 or 15[40] above, but
> (b) the breach is so slight that it would be unreasonable for him to reject them,
> then, if the buyer does not deal as consumer, the breach is not to be treated as a breach of condition but may be treated as a breach of warranty.

This section breaks new ground by drawing a distinction between consumers and non-consumers; the rest of the Act applies indiscriminately to consumers and non-consumers alike.

Loss of right to reject—sale of goods

7.19   Section 11(4) of the 1979 Act cuts down the buyer's rights if the goods (or part) have been accepted. As originally drafted section 11(4) reads as follows:

> Where a contract of sale is not severable and the buyer has accepted the goods or part of them . . . the breach of any condition to be fulfilled by the seller can only be treated as a breach of warranty, and not as a ground for rejecting the goods and treating the contract as repudiated, unless there is an express or implied term of the contract to that effect.

The Sale and Supply of Goods Act 1994 now allows the buyer a right of partial rejection in certain cases (see below, para. 7.26).

When is a contract severable?

7.20   The opening words of the subsection refer to a contract which is "severable". Thus, if a consumer made a contract with a supplier for the delivery of a 12-part encyclopedia, one part to be delivered each month and to be *separately paid for*, this would be a severable contract. The result would be that the acceptance of one instalment would not prevent the buyer from rejecting a later one on the grounds that, for example, a number of pages were blank.

A further question then arises; does a breach with regard to one or more instalments amount to a repudiation of the entire contract or is it merely a severable breach? In other words, can a buyer who rejects instalment number two be compelled to accept the remaining 10 instalments? There is no clear cut answer to this question; by section 31(2):

> it is a question in each case depending on the terms of the contract and the circumstances of the case.

In this example the buyer might well be able to refuse further instalments

---

[40] s.15 relates to sale by sample.

if, for example, the set as a whole is useless without the missing part. This raises a further unsettled point; if a seller tenders a defective instalment which is lawfully rejected, can he put the matter right by delivering a non-defective instalment? On principle, the answer ought to be "yes"—provided that he is not in breach of an essential time clause.

What is acceptance?

In the overwhelming majority of consumer sales the contract will be non- **7.21** severable so that the buyer will lose the right to reject when he accepts the goods.[41] The 1994 Act makes a number of changes in favour of the buyer as proposed by the Law Commission. The statutory provisions are contained in sections 34 and 35(1) of the 1979 Act (as amended). Section 34 gives buyers the right to examine the goods. It now reads as follows:

> Unless otherwise agreed, when the seller tenders delivery of the goods to the buyer, he is bound, on request, to afford the buyer a reasonable opportunity of examining the goods for the purpose of ascertaining whether they are in conformity with the contract and, in the case of a contract for sale by sample, of comparing the bulk with the sample.

This section is clearly of considerable importance to consumers. It would apply, for example, to a purchase by mail order; it would also apply to a purchase of a cooker or washing machine where the consumer had merely examined a demonstration model. In practice, the goods themselves are usually delivered in a large closed box and the consumer is required to sign a form stating that the contents are satisfactory.

In the Third Edition of this book we felt that the court would look at the reality of the situation. The problem has now been resolved in the consumer's favour by section 2(1) of the 1994 Act which inserts two new subsections in section 35 as follows:

> (2) Where goods are delivered to the buyer, and he has not previously examined them, he is not deemed to have accepted them . . . until he has had a reasonable opportunity of examining them for the purpose—
>   (a) of ascertaining whether they are in conformity with the contract, and
>   (b) in the case of a contract for sale by sample, of comparing the bulk with the sample.
> (3) Where the buyer deals as consumer . . . the buyer cannot lose his right to rely on subsection (2) above by agreement, waiver or otherwise.

The three types of acceptance

The remainder of the revised section 35 (inserted by s.2(1) of the 1994 Act) **7.22** reads as follows:

> (1) The buyer is deemed to have accepted the goods subject to subsection (2) below—

---

[41] But the right to damages remains untouched. See below, para. 7.31.

(a) when he intimates to the seller that he has accepted them, or

(b) when the goods have been delivered to him and he does any act in relation to them which is inconsistent with the ownership of the seller.

(4) The buyer is also deemed to have accepted the goods when after the lapse of a reasonable time he retains the goods without intimating to the seller that he has rejected them.

(5) The questions that are material in determining for the purposes of subsection (4) above whether a reasonable time has elapsed include whether the buyer has had a reasonable opportunity of examining the goods for the purposes mentioned in subsection (2) above.

(6) The buyer is not by virtue of this section deemed to have accepted the goods merely because—

(a) he asks for, or agrees to, their repair by or under an arrangement with the seller, or

(b) the goods are delivered to another under a sub-sale or other disposition.

(7) Where the contract is for the sale of goods making one or more commercial units a buyer accepting any goods included in a unit is deemed to have accepted all the goods making the unit; and in this subsection "commercial unit" means a unit division of which would materially impair the value of the goods or the character of the unit.

Let us now examine the forms of "acceptance".

7.23 (i) **Intimation of acceptance.** There has been no reported case on this topic; it is felt that there must be conduct on the part of the buyer which makes it clear to the seller that the goods have been accepted. One example might be a letter asking the seller to carry out modifications. On the other hand, a form signed by the consumer stating "I accept these goods" would only amount to "acceptance" if the conditions of section 35(2) (see above) were satisfied.

7.24 (ii) **Act after delivery inconsistent with the seller's ownership.** The leading cases are concerned with commercial contracts under which a delivery to a sub-buyer has destroyed the right to reject.[42] The underlying principle appears to be an inability to restore the goods to the seller. Thus, if a consumer receives a large consignment of wood and starts sawing it up in order to build a shed, the act of cutting it up would destroy his right to reject if he then discovers that, for example, the wood does not answer the contract description. Another grey area concerns negligent damage. What happens if the buyer of a defective suit stains it with ink when he wears it for the first time? If the stain is indelible it could affect his right of rejection, since it would prevent him from returning the goods in their original form.

It must, however, be remembered that all forms of acceptance are now subject to the "opportunity to examine" rule in subsection (2). Under the statutory wording an act done by the buyer before he has had a reasonable

---

[42] See, *e.g. Ruben v. Faire Bros* [1949] 1 K.B. 254 but note that s.35(6)(b) above has altered the law on this point.

opportunity for examination will not destroy the right to reject; it is possible that some of the earlier cases[43] might now be decided differently.

(iii) **Retention beyond a reasonable time.**   This is the most contentious type of acceptance in the consumer context. The main bone of contention is whether "a reasonable time" begins to run only after the buyer has *discovered* the defect (or other breach of contract) or at some earlier stage. This is of crucial importance if the goods contain a latent defect which will not show up until some months or even years of use have elapsed.

  Suppose that a carpet wears through or a bed collapses after only a year or two of normal use. What if the bearings of a washing machine or the motor of a lawn mower break down after 18 months? Even though it can be shown that the goods must have been unmerchantable at the date of delivery—this is evidenced by their subsequent failure to be durable enough—can the buyer still reject the goods? The consumer's answer would be "Of course! How can the right to reject for breach of condition be lost before the consumer can realise that there has been a breach?" The legal answer, however, may well be otherwise. The misunderstanding arises from confusing "acceptance" in section 35 with affirmation, waiver, laches, etc., which operate at common law or in equity to bar rescission[44] only if the plaintiff treats the contract as continuing *after* discovery of the breach or misrepresentation.

  It must be remembered that we are dealing with a commercial statute which has to do service in consumer transactions too. "The general legal proposition that there should, wherever possible, be finality in commercial transactions" was stressed by Rougier J. in *Bernstein v. Pamson Motors (Golders Green) Ltd.*[45]

> B bought a new Nissan Laurel from P for £8,000. It was delivered on December 7, 1984. B was ill over Christmas and unable to use it. On January 3 with 140 miles on the odometer the car broke down with a seized camshaft. Next day B wrote to P rejecting the car on the grounds that it was not merchantable. P resisted B's claim on the grounds that (1) the car was merchantable and (2) anyway it was too late to reject the car as B had accepted it. P repaired the car under the manufacturer's warranty. B sued for rescission and damages.[46]

Giving judgment for B on the first point (the car was unmerchantable) and for P on the second (it was too late to reject) Rougier J. upheld P's submission that "once a buyer has had the goods for a reasonable time, *not*, be it noted, related to the opportunity to discover any particular defect, he is deemed to have accepted them."

  He went on to say:

---

[43] *ibid.* The earlier cases were decided under the 1893 Act. As originally drafted, an "inconsistent act" destroyed the right to reject even though the buyer had not had a reasonable opportunity of examination.

[44] *Long v. Lloyd*, see n. 16 in para. 7.05 above.

[45] [1987] 2 All E.R. 220.

[46] The action was really fought between the AA, backing B, and Nissan, backing P.

7.25

"In my judgment, the nature of the particular defect, discovered *ex post facto*, and the speed with which it might have been discovered, are irrelevant to the concept of reasonable time in s.35 as drafted. That section seems to me to be directed solely to what is a reasonable practical interval in commercial terms between a buyer receiving the goods and his ability to send them back, taking into consideration from his point of view the nature of the goods and their function, and from the point of view of the seller the commercial desirability of being able to close his ledger reasonably soon after the transaction is complete. The complexity of the intended function of the goods is clearly of prime consideration here. What is a reasonable time in relation to a bicycle would hardly suffice for a nuclear submarine."[47]

Applying those principles to the facts, Rougier J. held that three weeks (discounting the period of illness) was a reasonable time for a new car:

"Reasonable time means reasonable time to examine and try out the goods in general terms."[48]

The decision seems a harsh one and some commentators regard it as suspect on the basis that an appeal was settled out of court on terms which acknowledged that the right to reject had not been lost (see (1987) 137 N.L.J. 962). Nevertheless, it must be admitted that the alternative view (*i.e.* that the buyer has a continuing right to reject until he discovers the defect) has one fundamental weakness—it would enable a buyer to reject and *recover his full price* even though he had used the goods for a considerable time. The Law Commission considered the problem extensively in their Report[49] and reached the conclusion that the present rule should continue; for no one had suggested, and no other common law system provided, a better answer.

Considerable room for judicial maneouvre exists because "what is a reasonable time is a question of fact".[50] This gives flexibility, although as three weeks was reasonable for a complex piece of machinery (a new car), an even shorter period might be reasonable for simple products like a pen, pie or pair of pants.

It is easy to concentrate so fiercely on the loss of the right to reject that damages are forgotten. In the *Bernstein* case the car was repaired free of charge. In addition damages were awarded: £33 for the taxi fare home and a wasted tank of petrol, £50 for five days' loss of use until a hire car was made available and £150 "for a totally spoilt day, comprising nothing but vexation".

In the Third Edition of this book we forecast that the law would soon be changed by allowing consumers a continuing right to reject.[51] It seems that on this occasion we were wrong!

[47] At p. 230.
[48] *ibid.*
[49] *op. cit.* paras. 5.14 to 5.19.
[50] s.59.
[51] See 3rd ed., p. 108.

The next point concerns the effect of complaints. Let us suppose that an expensive camera fails to work. The consumer will usually ask the supplier (or manufacturer) to repair it. What happens if the defect persists after (say) 10 attempts to repair it? Alternatively, what happens if a large number of different defects manifest themselves after purchase? The buyer is certainly entitled to wait for a time to see if the defects can be put right. Thus in *Lee v. York Coach and Marine Ltd*[52] the critical factor which destroyed the right to reject was the delay of six months after the final repair. It will be recalled that a mere request for repair is not of itself acceptance, but if the defect does persist for a substantial time, the buyer will have to decide "do I keep the goods or not?" Accordingly, the buyer should make it clear at the outset that he will reject the goods if the defects are not rectified.[53]

Rejection of part

Subject to the "commercial unit" point in new section 35(7) (above, **7.26** para. 7.22), the buyer can now reject part of goods supplied under a non-severable contract. Section 3 of the 1994 Act introduces a new section 35A and the four subsections of that section provide as follows:

(1) If the buyer—
    (a) has the right to reject the goods by reason of a breach on the part of the seller that affects some or all of them, but
    (b) accepts some of the goods, including, where there are any goods unaffected by the breach, all such goods,
he does not by accepting them lose his right to reject the rest.
(2) In the case of a buyer having the right to reject an instalment of goods, subsection (1) above applies as if references to the goods were references to the goods comprised in the instalment.
(3) For the purposes of subsection (1) above, goods are affected by a breach if by reason of the breach they are not in conformity with the contract.
(4) This section applies unless a contrary intention appears in, or is to be implied from, the contract.

Absence of title

If the supplier of goods has no right to sell, the consumer can recover the **7.27** price on the basis of total failure of consideration. His right to do this is not lost by "acceptance"—as Atkin L.J. pointed out in *Rowland v. Divall*.[54] He will, however, lose his right to get his money back if the defect in title is put right before he purports to reject.[55] This is reasonable enough—it would obviously be wrong to allow a claim based on "total failure of consideration" if the buyer has received substantially what he paid for, *i.e.* the property in the goods.

---

[52] Above, para. 4.13.
[53] As happened in the hire-purchase case *Farnworth Finance Facilities v. Attryde*, below, para. 7.28.
[54] [1923] 2 K.B. 500 and see, above, para. 2.12.
[55] *Butterworth v. Kingsway Motors* [1954] 1 W.L.R. 1286.

Loss of right to reject—other supply contracts

7.28   There is nothing in the Consumer Credit Act 1974 nor in the Supply of
Goods (Implied Terms) Act 1973 nor in the Supply of Goods and Services
Act 1982 regulating the remedies of the consumer. The position is governed
by the common law principles of waiver or affirmation which, unlike acceptance, operate only when the consumer becomes *aware* of the defect in the
goods. The cases at common law show a fairly broad approach. In *Farnworth
Finance Facilities v. Attryde*[56]:

> Mr Attryde took a new motorcycle on hire-purchase terms on July 11, 1964.
> There were a very large number of defects and finally on November 23 he pur-
> ported to reject it and claimed the return of all payments.

Counsel for the defendants argued that by driving the motorcycle for 4,000
miles, Mr Attryde had affirmed the contract so as to lose his right to reject.
The Court of Appeal rejected this argument. In the words of Lord Denning
M.R.[57]:

> "Affirmation is a matter of election. A man only affirms a contract when he
> knows of the defects and by his conduct elects to go on with the contract despite
> them. In this case Mr Attryde complained from the beginning of the defects and
> sent the machine back for them to be remedied. He did not elect to accept it
> unless they were remedied. But the defects were never satisfactorily remedied.
> When the rear chain broke it was the last straw."

As already stated, there is nothing in hire-purchase law comparable to section 11(4) of the Sale of Goods Act. The Law Commission acknowledge that
the right to reject is more readily available than in a sale and recommend that
this regime, which is more favourable to customers than the sale of goods
regime, should not be disturbed.[58]

Where a "conditional sale agreement" (below, para. 18.05) is a "consumer
sale" (below, para. 8.25) the rules governing rejection are similar to those for
hire-purchase: see the Supply of Goods (Implied Terms) Act 1973, s.14. In
Rogers v. Parish (Scarborough) Ltd (above, para. 4.11) the buyer was
allowed to reject after using the car for six months and driving 5,500 miles. It
must be noted, however, that the seller's counsel did not raise the matter[58a]
and one wonders what would have happened if he had done so.

Section 30: additional remedies

7.29   What happens if some of the goods are satisfactory while others are not?
We have seen that under a non-severable contract the buyer can now accept
part and reject part.[59]

---

[56] [1970] 1 W.L.R. 1053.
[57] p. 1059.
[58] Report No. 160, paras. 5.43 to 5.46.
[58a] The Court of Appeal refused to allow him to do so because he had not done so in his defence or
in the court below.
[59] Above, para. 7.26.

It is also necessary to refer to section 30 which can be summarised as follows:

(a) If the seller supplies *too many* goods, the buyer can (i) reject all the goods, (ii) reject the surplus, or (iii) keep all the goods and pay for them at the contract rate.

(b) If the seller tenders *too little*, the buyer can (i) reject the goods, or (ii) keep them and pay at the contract rate.

(c) If the seller tenders the contract goods *mixed* with goods of a different description, the buyer can (i) reject all the goods or (ii) reject the goods not answering the description. There is no statutory right to keep the latter goods, but the courts might treat the delivery as an offer to sell them. If the buyer accepted this offer, he would be liable to pay a reasonable price.[60] Alternatively if the buyer did not initially accept the offer, he might be able to take advantage of section 1 of the Unsolicited Goods and Services Act 1971 which was considered in Chapter 6.

Section 4(2) of the 1994 Act now prevents a non-consumer from exercising his right to reject where the defect is so slight that rejection would be unreasonable. This adds little to section 15A above[61] because the quantity of the goods will normally form part of their description (above, para. 3.10).

Practical considerations

There will, in many cases, be practical barriers to repudiation in cases where the price has already been paid. Section 36 of the 1979 Act provides that the buyer can send the seller a notice of rejection; if the property and risk have passed to the buyer the effect of the notice is to re-transfer them to the seller. In practice, however, the seller is likely to dispute the buyer's right to reject. This can mean that the buyer will have neither his money nor the use of the goods until his right to reject has been upheld by a court and until the judgment for the return of the price has been satisfied.   **7.30**

(4) **Can I get compensation?**

The consumer is always entitled to damages if the other party has broken a term of the contract, express or implied, and the consumer has suffered loss. It is irrelevant whether the term is a condition, warranty or intermediate stipulation. When we turn to the difficult question of quantifying the claim we must consider two closely related problems, namely (a) for what items of loss is the defendant liable? and (b) on what principles should the compensation be assessed?   **7.31**

---

[60] s.8.
[61] Above, para. 7.18.

For what loss is the defendant liable?

7.32   The general principles governing remoteness of damage were laid down more than 100 years ago in *Hadley v. Baxendale*[62] and more recently by the House of Lords in *Koufos v. Czarnikow Ltd (The Heron II)*.[63] The defendant is clearly liable for damage arising naturally from the breach (normal loss— first rule). He is also liable for other damage which can fairly and reasonably have been within the contemplation of both parties, at the time they made the contract, as the probable result of the breach of it (unusual loss—second rule). It has been held that where the general *type* or kind of damage was within the contemplation of the parties, the defendant is liable even though the precise *extent* of the damage, or the precise form of the damage, was outside his contemplation.[64]

Mitigation

7.33   Another basic rule is that of mitigation—the injured party must take reasonable steps to mitigate his loss. Thus, to take an obvious example, a buyer of a defective product could not sue the seller for the cost of having it repaired by a third party if the seller had previously offered to repair it free of charge or presumably if a free repair (parts *and* labour) was available under a manufacturer's guarantee.

General principles of compensation

7.34   If the damage is not too remote under the rules set out above, the general principle is that damages should, so far as possible, place the injured party in the same position as if the contract had been performed properly. Thus, where a negligent survey causes a buyer to pay too much for a house the damages will be the difference between the price paid and the lower (defective) value; in *Watts v. Morrow*[64a] a claim based on the cost of repair when the defects were discovered was rejected.

Non-delivery

7.35   In the case of sale of goods the buyer may have an action for damages against the seller (a) if the seller fails to deliver, or (b) if the seller breaks a condition or warranty. In all these cases the general principles laid down in *Hadley v. Baxendale*[65] appear in statutory form; thus section 51(2) which deals with non-delivery provides that:

---

[62] (1854) 9 Exch. 341 at 354.
[63] [1969] 1 A.C. 350.
[64] *Parsons (Livestock) Ltd v. Uttley Ingham & Co.* [1978] 1 Q.B. 791 (sale and construction of hopper for feeding nuts to pigs; ventilator left unopened; nuts became mouldy; pigs died; supplier of hopper liable). See also *Vacwell v. B.D.H. Chemicals* [1971] 1 Q.B. 88.
[64a] [1991] 1 W.L.R. 1421, CA.
[65] Above, para. 7.32.

> The measure of damages is the estimated loss directly and naturally resulting, in the ordinary course of events, from the seller's breach of contract.

As an example of this, section 51(3) provides that:

> Where there is an available market for the goods in question the measure of damages is prima facie ... the difference between the contract price and the market or current price of the goods at the time or times when they ought to have been delivered, or (if no time was fixed) at the time of refusal to deliver.

Let us suppose that John agrees to buy a new Ford Escort car from a dealer for £8,000. The contract provides that the car must be delivered by May 1 but the dealer fails to deliver. By that date the price of Ford Escorts has increased by £500. If John has to pay an extra £500 to buy one from another dealer, this sum will prima facie be his damages under section 51(3).

The second rule of *Hadley v. Baxendale*, damage within the reasonable contemplation of the parties, is preserved by section 54 which reads:

> Nothing in this Act affects the right of the buyer or the seller to recover interest or special damages in any case where by law interest or special damages may be recoverable....

Thus, if, as a result of the non-delivery of the car, John loses a valuable business contract, that would be "special damages" and the defaulting dealer will only be liable for it if it was brought to his attention before the agreement was made.

Damages for breach of warranty

In this situation damages arising naturally are covered by section 53(2) while "contemplated" damages are covered by section 54.[66] Where the warranty relates to quality the damages are prima facie the difference between the actual value of the defective goods and their value if they had answered the warranty.[67] It is clear, however, that damages are not necessarily confined to that amount. Thus, for example, damages for personal injury or death can be recovered on a sale of a defective toy.[68] Then, if a defective car is "off the road" for repair, the buyer will be able to recover from the seller not only the cost of repair but also the cost of hiring a substitute car[69] during this period. The magazine *Which?* has cited a case where a buyer of a leaking caravan

7.36

---

[66] Above, para. 7.32.
[67] s.53(3) and see *Lee v. York (Coach and Marine) Ltd*, above, para. 4.13.
[68] *Godley v. Perry* [1960] 1 W.L.R. 9.
[69] Some car hire companies provide cars free of charge on condition that the consumers co-operate with them in bringing proceedings and pays the hire-charges out of damages awarded. The deferment of the hirer's payment obligation amounts to "credit" and the hire agreement will usually be regulated under the Consumer Credit Act 1974 (para. 19.03 below). If the agreement is "improperly executed" (para. 21.02 below) the hirer cannot recover the hire charges from the other driver: *Dimond v. Lovell, The Times*, May 3, 1999, CA.

spent large sums of money on petrol on numerous journeys to have it repaired. He also planned to have a caravan holiday but was compelled to move into a guest house when the defects reappeared. He successfully recovered both the cost of petrol and the boarding house expenses in county court proceedings.

If the seller is in breach of the condition of "right to sell",[70] the damages recoverable by the buyer can include not merely the price paid but also the cost of necessary repairs.[71]

The principles set out above apply equally where the seller is in breach of a condition which the buyer elects to treat, or is compelled to treat, as a breach of warranty.

Mental distress

7.37   A novel head of damages which no legal adviser should forget in a consumer dispute is mental distress, upset, disappointment and injured feelings. The seminal case on this topic was *Jarvis v. Swan Tours*, a heart-rending case.[72]

> The plaintiff, on a fortnight's holiday in the Swiss Alps, spent an entire week surrounded by foreigners who could not speak English! As a further insult instead of Swiss cakes he was served crisps and desiccated nut rolls. (As their Lordships pointed out during the hearing, "You don't have to go to Switzerland to get those": Stephenson L.J. "You can get them at Crewe": Edmund Davies L.J.—*The Times*, October 19, 1972.) Damages of £125 were awarded, double the cost of the holiday, by the Court of Appeal.

Holiday contracts continue to be a fruitful area for this type of loss.[73]

Damages have also been awarded in proceedings for negligence against a solicitor who failed to obtain a non-molestation injunction for a client.[74]

The first sale of goods case was *Jackson v. Chrysler Acceptances*.[75] This has been followed recently by two other car cases where the damages were by no means nominal.[76]

Even so, the courts seem likely to approach this area cautiously, as can be gleaned from the remarks of Staughton L.J. in *Hayes v. Dodd*[77] where the Court of Appeal disallowed this head of damage in a business dispute:

> "Damages for mental distress in contract are, as a matter of policy, limited to

---

[70] Above, para. 2.12.
[71] *Mason v. Burningham* [1949] 2 K.B. 545.
[72] [1973] 1 Q.B. 233.
[73] For further examples, see below, para. 7.39.
[74] *Heywood v. Wellers* [1976] Q.B. 446.
[75] [1978] R.T.R. 474. A consumer told a dealer that he wanted a car for a holiday. The car was defective. The county court judge awarded (*inter alia*) £75 for a spoilt holiday. Although the award was varied on appeal there was no suggestion that such damages could not be recovered.
[76] *Bernstein v. Pamson Motors*, above, para. 7.28: £150 for spoilt day. *UCB Leasing v. Holtom* [1987] R.T.R. 362, CA: £500 for distress where hire car had three complete electrical failures in four months.
[77] [1990] 2 All E.R. 815 at 824.

certain classes of case. I would broadly follow the classification provided by Dillon L.J. in *Bliss v. South East Thames Regional Health Authority* [1987] I.C.R. 700 at 718:

> '... where the contract which has been broken was itself a contract to provide peace of mind or freedom from distress ....'

It may be that the class is somewhat wider than that. But it should not, in my judgment, include any case where the object of the contract was not comfort or pleasure, or the relief of discomfort, but simply carrying on a commercial activity with a view to profit."

In *Watts v. Morrow*[78] the Court of Appeal rejected the argument that a contract for the survey of a house was a contract to buy peace of mind. In this type of case damages for distress should be limited to a modest sum for physical discomfort; the Court reduced the award from £4,000 to £750.

It is clear from the cases that damages for distress will be kept within narrow limits. Thus it has recently been held[79] that customers suing a bank could not claim damages for distress resulting from alleged unauthorised withdrawals from service-till machines. Similarly, the undoubted pleasure of a car owner in driving a Rolls Royce did not give rise to a distress claim when the car was badly repaired.[79a]

Hire-purchase

The principles set out above are equally relevant to hire-purchase trans-   **7.38**
actions. Thus in *Yeoman Credit Ltd v. Apps*[80] the hirer of a car which took one-and-a-half hours to do three or four miles successfully sued for damages. The damages were assessed at the difference between what the car should have been worth and what it was actually worth; on that basis the hirer recovered all his payments, less a very small allowance for use.

Holiday contracts

If the customer finds, on arrival at his resort, that his room has been double-   **7.39**
booked, or that the hotel does not exist, he can claim the cost of having to stay at an equivalent hotel plus (as already stated) damages for mental distress. If the hotel exists but does not have the promised facilities, the remedy will be damages. In appropriate cases damages can include losses suffered by members of the plaintiff's family.[81]

An interesting recent case is *Spencer v. Cosmos Air Holidays*.[82]

---

[78] [1991] 1 W.L.R. 1421.
[79] *McConville v. Barclays Bank, The Times*, June 30, 1993. The court formerly known as the Official Referee court has now been renamed the Technology and Construction Court.
[79a] *Alexander v. Rolls Royce Motor Co. Ltd* [1996] R.T.R. 95.
[80] [1962] 2 Q.B. 508.
[81] *Jackson v. Horizon Holidays* [1975] 1 W.L.R. 1468, CA. A four-week family holiday in Sri Lanka proved to be a disaster, with very distasteful food apparently cooked in coconut oil, and a shower and no bath. The holiday price was £1,200. Damages of £1,100 were awarded for breach of contract to cover the distress of the husband, wife and child.
[82] *The Times*, December 6, 1989.

The plaintiff booked two weeks' holiday in Spain with the defendants for £266. After about a week the hotelier wrongfully ejected her and her two female companions. They spent two nights sleeping on the beach before the defendants found them alternative, inferior accommodation at a less pleasing resort.

The Court of Appeal awarded her £1,000 for her distress, misery and humiliation, reducing by half the award by the trial judge.

Cleaners

7.40   If a cleaner negligently ruins or loses a blanket, a carpet or a suit, the damages will be based on the cost of acquiring a replacement, but this will be subject to a discount for age and use.

Builders

7.41   If a builder, decorator or plumber does a job badly, the damages will normally include not only the money paid to another firm to have it put right but also damages for the resulting inconvenience.[83] If the work is done extremely badly, the consumer may be entitled to refuse to pay anything at all.[84] If, however, the cost of repair or reconstruction is out of all proportion to the resulting benefit, the court will award damages based on "diminution of value" (if any) plus a modest sum for loss of amenity.[84a]

3. REMEDIES IN TORT

7.42   Perhaps the most likely case of a tort claim would be where the consumer has a claim against the manufacturer for negligence or under the Consumer Protection Act 1987. In personal injury cases the damages would include loss of actual and future earnings, medical expenses, pain and suffering, and loss of amenities. For further details readers are referred to the standard textbooks on tort and to *McGregor on Damages*.

In a case where the same facts give rise to liability in both contract and tort the rules as to damages are being brought very close together.[85]

---

[83] See, *e.g. Batty v. Metropolitan Realisations* [1978] Q.B. 554.
[84] See, *e.g. Bolton v. Mahadeva* [1972] 1 W.L.R. 1009.
[84a] See the swimming pool case of *Ruxley Electronics v. Forsyth* [1995] 3 All E.R. 268, HL.
[85] *Parsons (Livestock) Ltd v. Uttley Ingham & Co.*, above, para. 7.32.

CHAPTER EIGHT

"THEY SAY THAT I HAVE SIGNED AWAY MY RIGHTS"

Exemption clauses have been widely used in standard form contracts **8.01** in the past 50 years or so and have come in for severe criticism from the courts and other bodies. The courts have developed certain techniques to control the legal effect of these clauses. Unfortunately the control exercised by the courts has been unsatisfactory because, with the exception of Lord Denning M.R., they have felt themselves unable to break out of the straitjacket of freedom of contract. Accordingly, the use of exemption clauses has been increasingly controlled by statute and the overwhelming majority of these clauses are now controlled by the Unfair Contract Terms Act 1977. These controls are supplemented by the Unfair Terms in Consumer Contracts Regulations which are dealt with in Chapter Nine.

Examples

The first three examples are taken from Law Commission Working Paper **8.02** No. 39, pp. 74–88.

(1) The shipowner shall be exempt from all liability in respect of any detention, delay, overcarriage, loss, expenses, damage, sickness or injury of whatever kind, whenever and wherever occurring, and however and by whomsoever caused of or to any passenger, or of or to any person or child travelling with him or her or in his or her care, or of or to any baggage, property, goods, effects, articles, matters or things belonging or carried by, with or for any passenger or any such person or child.

(2) [The ferry company] shall not be liable for the death or any injury, damage, loss, delay or accident . . . wheresoever, whensoever and howsoever caused and whether by negligence of their servants or agents or by unseaworthiness of the vessel.

(3) The contractors shall not under any circumstances be liable for any loss or damage caused by or resulting from or in connection with fire, howsoever caused.

(4) All cars parked at owner's risk.

(5) In the case of loss or damage the liability of the company is limited to the value of the garment.

(6) All claims within seven days.

Justification

8.03   In deciding on the price of his product a supplier is bound to consider the question of loss apportionment. He can also cut down very substantially on administration overheads by having standard form contracts (thus avoiding the need to negotiate each contract separately) and by avoiding litigation. A survey carried out by Yates in *Exclusion Clauses in Contracts* contains the following passage (2nd ed., p. 25):

> "The desire to avoid court proceedings in the event of a dispute was also a reason advanced for using exemption clauses which, it was often felt, gave each party a clearer indication of where they stood. ... Distrust of lawyers' and more especially judges' ability to understand the businessman's problems was very marked."

Criticism

8.04   When due allowance has been made for the points set out above there is no doubt that exemption clauses are open to abuse. The following passage is taken from the Law Commission's Second Report on Exemption Clauses No. 69, para. 11, on which the Unfair Contract Terms Act 1977 was based:

> We are in no doubt that in many cases they operate against the public interest and that the prevailing judicial attitude of suspicion, or indeed of hostility, to such clauses is well founded. All too often they are introduced in ways which result in the party affected by them remaining ignorant of their presence or import until it is too late. That party, even if he knows of the exemption clause, will often be unable to appreciate what he may lose by accepting it. In any case he may not have sufficient bargaining strength to refuse to accept it. The result is that the risk of carelessness or of failure to achieve satisfactory standards of performance is thrown on to the party who is not responsible for it or who is unable to guard against it. Moreover, by excluding liability for such carelessness or failure the economic pressures to maintain high standards of performance are reduced.

Scheme of this chapter

8.05   It is proposed to start by examining the attitude of the courts to exemption clauses and then to consider the statutory controls imposed by the Unfair Contract Terms Act. The broad scope of the Act has made the former topic far less important and accordingly it will be examined fairly briefly. A short reference to other legislation will be made at the end of this chapter.

1. JUDICIAL CONTROL OF EXEMPTION CLAUSES

8.06   The reasons for judicial hostility to exemption clauses have already been mentioned: ignorance, non-negotiation and inequality of bargaining power. Perhaps the first of these points is the strongest. After all, the law of contract is, or should be, about agreement. If the consumer were asked "do you know that you have signed away your right to complain if the cleaners lose the carpet?" or "do you know that you will receive no compensation at all if the carriers damage your furniture?" it is unlikely that his reply could be printed in this book; at all events it is likely to include the word "no". When he made the contract he would reasonably have expected that the work would be done with reasonable care, and that he would receive compensation if this was not so. His expectations may have been increased by a glowing advertisement in a newspaper or magazine or on television. Accordingly exemption clauses, which are often inconsistent with his reasonable expectations, are closely scrutinised by the courts.

The courts have to decide two basic problems, namely:

(1) was the clause duly incorporated into the contract? and
(2) does it, on its true construction, cover the event which has occurred?

(1) **Incorporation**[1]

The general contractual principles relating to incorporation have been well **8.07** established for a considerable time. Thus:

(a) *Signed document*

If the contractual document is signed, this operates as an incorporation of **8.08** all the terms which appear on that document or which are referred to in it.[2] The signer will not be bound, however, if he signed the document without negligence and it turns out to be a document of a fundamentally different kind from the document which he thought that he was signing.[3]

(b) *Unsigned document or notice*

If the consumer has not signed a contractual document, a clause will only **8.09** be incorporated if reasonable steps were taken before contract to bring it to his notice. The following cases illustrate how this principle has been applied.

(i) In the case of *Thompson v. L.M.S. Railway*[4] a lady bought a railway excursion ticket containing the words "For conditions see back". The back of the ticket referred to conditions in the railway timetables which were available for purchase. Had Mrs Thompson obtained and read it (by which time she would certainly have missed her train) she would have seen an exclusion clause excluding liability for negligence. The Court of Appeal held that the exemption clause had been incorporated into the contract.

(ii) The case of *Chapelton v. Barry U.D.C.*[5] concerned an exclusion

---

[1] For a recent summary of the rules see the judgment of Boreham J. in *John Snow & Son Ltd v. Woodcroft Ltd* [1985] B.C.L.C. 48.
[2] The leading case is *L'Estrange v. Graucob* [1934] 2 K.B. 394.
[3] *Saunders v. Anglia Building Society* [1971] A.C. 1039, in which the House of Lords emphasised that this so-called "*non est factum*" defence must be confined within narrow limits.
[4] [1930] 1 K.B. 41. Such a clause might now be "unfair" under Schedule 3 of the 1994 Regulations: see below, paras 9.20–9.21.
[5] [1940] 1 K.B. 532. In any case it was post-contractual and so ineffective.

clause on a deckchair receipt. It was held that there was no incorporation; this was not the type of document on which the consumer could reasonably expect to find conditions and therefore the local authority had not taken sufficient steps to bring the clause to the consumer's attention. The court reached a similar "no incorporation" result in two more recent cases where words appeared on the inside of a cheque book[5a] and on time sheets.[5b]

(iii) In *Olley v. Marlborough Court Hotel*[6] a consumer booked a hotel room. After he had done so he saw an exemption notice in the bedroom. It was held that there was no incorporation since the clause had been introduced too late. The position might have been different if the notice was prominently displayed at the reception desk or if the customer had stayed at the hotel on previous occasions. In the latter case the notice might have been incorporated on the basis of a previous course of dealing. Nevertheless, this principle, which can readily be implied in commercial contracts,[7] is very rarely applied in consumer contracts.[8]

8.10   (iv) *Thornton v. Shoe Lane Parking Co. Ltd*[9] is perhaps the best modern example of how the basic rules of "contract" are being adapted, in a realistic way, to standard form consumer transactions.

> Mr Thornton went to park his car at a new multistorey car park—he had not been there before. When he arrived opposite the ticket machine a ticket popped out, the light turned from red to green and he went through and parked his car. The ticket referred to conditions displayed on the premises. These conditions (*inter alia*) excluded liability for personal injuries caused by negligence. There was an accident caused partly by the defendants' negligence and Mr Thornton was injured.

The Court of Appeal held that the defendants had not taken reasonable steps to bring this particular clause to the notice of Mr Thornton. In the words of Lord Denning M.R. at p. 170:

> "It is so wide and destructive of rights that the court should not hold any man bound by it unless it is drawn to his attention in the most explicit way.... In order to give sufficient notice, it would need to be printed in red ink with a red hand pointing to it—or something equally startling."

Megaw L.J. gave an equally vivid example when he said at p. 173:

> "It does not take much imagination to picture the indignation of the defendants if their potential customers ... were one after the other to get out of their cars leaving the cars blocking the entrance to the garages in order to search for, find

---

[5a] *Burnett v. Westminster Bank* [1965] 3 All E.R. 81.
[5b] *Grogan v. Robin Meredith Plant Hire* [1996] C.L.C. 1127, CA.
[6] [1949] 1 K.B. 532.
[7] *Spurling v. Bradshaw* [1956] 1 W.L.R. 461.
[8] See, *e.g. McCutcheon v. David MacBrayne Ltd* [1964] 1 W.L.R. 125, HL, a notable case, if only because of the appearance in it of a Mr McSporran!
[9] [1971] 2 Q.B. 163.

and peruse the notices! Yet unless the defendants genuinely intended that potential customers should do just that it would be fiction, if not farce, to treat those customers as persons who have been given a fair opportunity, before the contracts are made, of discovering the conditions by which they are to be bound."

Lord Denning M.R. went so far as to hold that the contract was made when the customer dropped his money into the machine, with the result that the conditions on the ticket were introduced too late.[10] The trouble with this approach is that in many cases the customer does *not* put money into the slot—he merely collects a ticket and pays later. Nevertheless both Lord Denning M.R. and Sir Gordon Willmer were influenced by the finality of a contract made with a machine. To quote again from Lord Denning:

> "The customer pays his money and gets a ticket. He cannot refuse it. He cannot get his money back. He may protest to the machine, even swear at it. But it will remain unmoved. He is committed beyond recall."

These interesting problems may never be decided because it may be unnecessary to do so. If the facts of *Thornton* were to recur, a clause excluding liability for death or personal injury resulting from negligence would in any event be void[11] and accordingly the question of incorporation would have no practical importance. The point might, however, remain relevant if the customer suffered damage to his property. In that case the exemption clause would be valid if reasonable[12] and accordingly the customer might well raise the argument of "no incorporation" as his first line of attack.

(v) In *Interfoto Picture Library Ltd v. Stiletto Visual Programmes Ltd*[13] (a non-consumer case) the Court of Appeal had to consider the situation where one clause in a set of conditions was particularly onerous.

8.11

> SVP, an advertising agency, telephoned IPL, a photographic library, requesting photographs of the 1950s for a presentation for a client. IPL sent by hand 47 transparencies in a bag with a delivery note stating that they must be returned within 14 days.
>
> Across the bottom of the note were printed nine conditions in four columns, under the fairly prominent heading "CONDITIONS". Condition 2 stated that all transparencies must be returned within 14 days and that "A holding fee of £5.00 plus VAT per day will be charged for each transparency which is retained by you longer than the said period of 14 days. ...."
>
> SVP accepted delivery, but did not use them and by an oversight kept them for 28 days. When IPL sent an invoice for £3,783.50, SVP refused to pay, for most libraries charged less than 50p per day.

Hitherto the general approach in the "ticket cases" had been to ask whether the supplier has taken reasonable steps to bring the conditions *as a whole* to

---

[10] *cf. Olley v. Marlborough Court Hotel*, above, para. 8.09.
[11] Unfair Contract Terms Act 1977, s.2(1): below, para. 8.23.
[12] *ibid.* s.2(2).
[13] [1988] 1 All E.R. 348.

the notice of the consumer. However, Lord Denning M.R. had signposted a different route with his "red ink—red hand" approach in *Thornton v. Shoe Lane Parking Ltd*.[14] Following that route the Court of Appeal held in the *Interfoto* case that condition 2, imposing an exorbitant holding fee, was not part of the contract. Dillon L.J. stated the principle thus[15]:

> "It is in my judgment a logical development of the common law into modern conditions that it should be held, as it was in *Thornton v. Shoe Lane Parking Ltd*, that, if one condition in a set of printed conditions is particularly onerous or unusual, the party seeking to enforce it must show that that particular condition was fairly brought to the attention of the other party."

Bingham L.J., agreeing that "the plaintiffs did not do what was necessary to draw this unreasonable and extortionate clause fairly to their attention", seemed to be of the view that a more general principle of fairness was being applied[16]:

> "The tendency of the English authorities has, I think, been to look at the nature of the transaction in question and the character of the parties to it; to consider what notice the party alleged to be bound was given of the particular condition said to bind him; and to resolve whether in all the circumstances it is fair to hold him bound by the condition in question. This may yield a result not very different from the civil law principle of good faith, at any rate so far as the formation of the contract is concerned."

The actual decision (treating the clause as unduly onerous merely because other libraries charged less) is certainly debatable but, subject to this, three final points can be made. First, the clause was not an exemption clause[17] and it will be interesting to see how far the courts will use this "non-incorporation" tool to protect consumers in areas where Parliament has chosen not to do so. Secondly, we have already seen how non-incorporation can be used to out-flank the Unfair Contract Terms Act (above, para. 8.07). Finally, it remains to be seen how far the principle discussed in *Interfoto* (and particularly the fairness point raised by Bingham L.J.) can be called in aid by someone who has *signed* a contract—even though up to now the principle of bringing the conditions to the notice of the consumer has not been relevant in this situation. In other words, *L'Estrange v. Graucob*[18] may not be an impassable barrier.

---

[14] Above, para. 8.10. See also his dictum to similar effect in *J. Spurling Ltd v. Bradshaw* [1956] 1 W.L.R. 461 at 466, and the comments of Bramwell and Mellish L.JJ. in *Parker v. South Eastern Rly. Co.* (1877) 2 C.P.D. 416.

[15] At p. 620.

[16] *ibid*. The concept of "good faith" in the context of the Unfair Terms in Consumer Contracts Regulations is considered below, see para. 9.08.

[17] The Unfair Contract Terms Act 1977 could not be used to control the clause for that very reason—see below, para. 8.22.

[18] Above, para. 8.08.

(2) **Does the clause cover the event which has occurred?**

Even if the clause has been incorporated into the contract it is not automati-   **8.12**
cally effective. The courts have evolved a number of techniques to counter
their effect. These techniques may still be relevant in some cases but it must
be strongly emphasised that times have changed and, with the arrival of the
Unfair Contract Terms Act 1977, the courts will be less concerned with these
matters (see below, para. 8.18).

(a) *Privity*

After earlier doubts the House of Lords have held that an exemption clause   **8.13**
in a contract between A and B could not protect C, even if C was an employee
or contractor employed by B to perform the contract.[19] It seems, however,
that this can be outflanked by having a clause whereby a party contracts, as
agent for his employees, etc., that they shall have the benefit of the clause. As
a matter of strict legal analysis this can create a separate contract between the
employees and the other party and the performance of the main contract will
provide the consideration for it.[20]

The position will also be altered when the Contract (Rights of Third Parties) Bill becomes law. Under this Bill (which we noted in para. 4.05) a non-
contracting party can enforce a "benefit" in his favour and the term "benefit"
includes a clause limiting or excluding his liabilities.

(b) *Strict construction and the* contra proferentem rule

A party seeking the protection of an exemption clause must show that the   **8.14**
wording is clear enough to cover the alleged breach. This is well illustrated
by three cases involving sale of goods.

In *Wallis, Son and Wells v. Pratt and Haynes*[21] a commercial contract for
the sale of seed excluded "all warranties". The seller supplied seed of a different description and the buyer claimed damages. The House of Lords held that
the seller had broken a *condition* and that a clause referring only to *warranties* did not protect him. The mere fact that the buyer, in ignorance of the
breach, had "accepted" the goods, and was therefore compelled to treat the
breach as a breach of warranty,[22] was immaterial.

In *Andrews Bros. (Bournemouth) Ltd v. Singer & Co. Ltd*[23] the seller sold a
"new Singer car" with a clause excluding "implied conditions and warranties". The seller supplied a car which was not new. The Court of Appeal held
that he had broken an *express* condition and accordingly a clause which
merely referred to *implied* conditions did not protect him.

---

[19] *Scruttons v. Midland Silicones Ltd* [1962] A.C. 446.
[20] *New Zealand Shipping Co. Ltd v. Satterthwaite & Co. Ltd* [1975] A.C. 154, P.C.
[21] [1911] A.C. 394. See also *Southern Water Authority v. Carey* [1985] 2 All E.R. 1077 where the
    same result was reached by a different route.
[22] Above, para. 7.19.
[23] [1934] 1 K.B. 17.

In *Nichol v. Godts*[24] the sellers agreed to supply rape oil "warranted only equal to sample". Sellers supplied a mixture of rape oil and hemp oil which matched the sample. It was held that the exclusion clause did not protect them from their overriding duty to supply rape oil in accordance with the description.

The rule of strict construction leads on naturally to the so-called "*contra proferentem*" rule which provides that an ambiguity must be construed against the party who wishes to rely on the clause. Thus if a plaintiff has two distinct claims against the defendant (one in contract and one in tort for negligence) an exemption clause may well be construed so as to cover only the former and not the latter.[25] Even words like "the company will not be liable for damage caused by fire" may merely operate as a warning that the company will only be liable if negligent.[26] It follows that clear words are required to cover liability for negligence, for example, "howsoever caused" or "whether or not due to negligence".

(c) *Inconsistent oral promise*

8.15   An exemption clause will be overridden by an oral promise which is inconsistent with it. Thus in *Mendelssohn v. Normand*[27] a suitcase was stolen from a car which the plaintiff had parked at the defendants' car park. An employee of the defendants promised the plaintiff that he would lock the car, but he failed to do so. The Court of Appeal held that a clause excluding "loss or damage howsoever caused" was ineffective.

(d) *Misrepresentation*

8.16   The courts will not allow a party to rely on an exemption clause if he has misrepresented its effect to the consumer.[28] On the other hand, the consumer may find himself faced with a clause which says that "no employee of the company has any authority to add to or vary these terms." Such a clause is legally binding.[29]

(e) *Fundamental breach*

8.17   In a number of cases decided before the Unfair Contract Terms Act 1977 the courts sought to relieve the consumer from the harsh effects of an exemp-

---

[24] (1854) 10 Exch. 191.
[25] See, *e.g. White v. John Warwick* [1953] 1 W.L.R. 1285 and more recently *The Zinnia* [1984] 2 LL.L.R. 211.
[26] *Hollier v. Rambler Motors (AMC) Ltd* [1972] 2 Q.B. 71.
[27] [1970] 1 Q.B. 177. See also *J. Evans & Son (Portsmouth) Ltd v. Andrea Merzario Ltd* [1976] 1 W.L.R. 1078, CA.
[28] *Curtis v. Chemical Cleaning and Dyeing Co.* [1951] 1 K.B. 805, CA.
[29] *Overbrooke Estates Ltd v. Glencombe Properties Ltd* [1974] 1 W.L.R. 1335 (a case on auction particulars). In practice, however, the exemption clause can sometimes be overridden by the employee's apparent authority.

tion clause by holding that it did not cover the breach of a fundamental term[30] or a fundamental breach.[31] The legal reasoning for this doctrine was highly dubious. The House of Lords has twice rejected it[32] and reaffirmed the basic rule that the scope of an exemption clause is always a question of construction and that there is no rule of law preventing the exclusion of a fundamental breach. In a more recent case the House of Lords has warned against the danger of reintroducing the doctrine under another name.[33]

(f) *The new approach*

The most recent cases herald a new approach to the construction of exemp- **8.18** tion clauses; in future the courts will be less willing to adopt a policy of judicial control of exemption clauses because the need for it has gone. Thus in a case decided on the previous law (but with knowledge that the 1977 Act had been passed) Lord Diplock said as follows:

> "My Lords the reports are full of cases in which what would appear to be very strained constructions have been placed upon exclusion clauses, mainly in what today would be called consumer contracts or contracts of adhesion. As Lord Wilberforce has pointed out, any need for this kind of distortion of the English language has been banished by Parliament, having made these kinds of contract subject to the Unfair Contract Terms Act."[34]

Quite apart from this, it seems that a clause limiting damages to a fixed amount (a "limitation clause") will not be construed as strictly as a full exclusion clause.[35] It must be said, however, that the reasoning is not convincing.[36]

2. UNFAIR CONTRACT TERMS ACT 1977

The Act is largely based on the Law Commission's Second Report on **8.19** Exemption Clauses, but it differs from the Law Commission's Draft Bill in several material respects.

Scope of the Act

The Act operates in five overlapping areas, namely: **8.20**

---

[30] "Something narrower than a condition—something which underlies the whole contract:" *per* Devlin J. (as he then was) in *Smeaton Hanscomb & Co. Ltd v. Setty (Sassoon) Sons & Co.* [1953] 1 W.L.R. 1468 at 1470.
[31] See, *e.g. Karsales (Harrow) Ltd v. Wallis* [1956] 1 W.L.R. 936.
[32] *Suisse Atlantique v. N.V. Rotterdamsche Kolen Centrale* [1967] 1 A.C. 361; *Photo Production v. Securicor Transport* [1980] A.C. 827.
[33] *George Mitchell (Chesterhall) Ltd v. Finney Lock Seeds Ltd* [1983] 3 W.L.R. 163.
[34] *Photo Production Ltd v. Securicor Transport* [1980] A.C. 827 at 851.
[35] *Ailsa Craig Fishing Co. Ltd v. Malvern Fishing Co. and Securicor (Scotland)* [1983] 1 W.L.R. 964—a House of Lords decision on appeal from Scotland.
[36] *ibid.* at p. 966 (Lord Wilberforce) and at p. 970 (Lord Fraser).

(a) negligence;
(b) contractual obligations;
(c) terms implied in contracts for the sale of goods, hire-purchase and certain analogous contracts;
(d) guarantees and indemnities;
(e) misrepresentation.

Before considering these areas it is necessary to mention some preliminary points.

Preliminary matters

8.21   (1) The Act does not create new duties—it merely controls clauses which cut down a duty which would otherwise exist or which exclude or modify the remedies available on breach of that duty.

> Let us suppose that Richard parks his car in a car park and keeps the key. There is a large notice at the entrance "The company is not liable for any loss or damage to vehicle or contents, whether or not due to negligence of the company or its servants or agents." When Richard comes back to collect his car it cannot be found.

The notice set out above would be controlled by section 2 of the Act[37] and would be subject to the reasonableness test. This, however, is likely to be completely irrelevant; the company can avoid liability on the more basic ground that the transaction was a mere licence and not a bailment and therefore they owed Richard no duty of care. That was the position before the Act[38] and, as already stated, the Act does not create new duties.

(2) The name of the Act is misleading—it is both too narrow and too wide. It is too narrow because it only refers to "contract"; the Act also applies to negligence both at common law and under the Occupiers' Liability Act 1957. It is too wide because it does not control all "unfair terms"; it merely controls exemption clauses and notices.

(3) With very minor exceptions the key provisions of the Act (ss.2–7) only apply to "business liability". By section 1(3) this means:

> liability for breach of obligations or duties arising—
> (a) from things done or to be done by a person in the course of a business (whether his own business or another's); or
> (b) from the occupation of premises used for business purposes of the occupier.

When we turn to section 14 we find that the term "business" includes a profession and the activities of any government department or local or public authority.

The term "business" crops up at various points in this book. Thus we have

---

[37] See below, para. 8.23.
[38] *Ashby v. Tolhurst* [1937] 2 K.B. 242.

already come across it in connection with (a) supply of goods—implied conditions of quality and fitness,[39] and (b) unsolicited goods and services.[40] We shall meet it again later in this chapter when considering the phrase "deals as consumer".[41] It is also critical for certain provisions of the Consumer Credit Act, for example, non-commercial agreements[42] and the licensing provisions.[43] There are bound to be borderline cases. Is a landlord carrying on a "business" when he lets a block of flats? Is a charity "bazaar" a business? The tax cases show that the key factors include the frequency of the transaction, the manner of operation and the profit motive. It is felt that, on these criteria, a charity bazaar would not be a business, whereas a landlord might well be carrying on a business—especially if he provided services for the tenants.

Reverting now to section 1(3) the question arises as to whether the Act would apply to the premises of a professional man who worked from his home. The answer is "yes", because the Act does not require the premises to be used *exclusively* for business purposes. The point is rather academic since the home is unlikely to be plastered with exclusion notices.

(4) Sections 2 to 4 do not apply to certain contracts listed in Schedule 1. For the consumer the two most important are (a) contracts of insurance, and (b) any contract so far as it relates to the creation, transfer or termination of an interest in land.[43a] The words "so far as" are important. If, for example, a landlord of a block of flats remains the occupier of the common staircase, a notice stating that "visitors enter these premises at their own risk" would be controlled: thus if the landlord negligently allows the staircase to fall into disrepair, he would be liable in damages to an injured visitor under the Occupier's Liability Act 1957, s.2(2), and the exemption notice would be void by the Act of 1977, s.2(1) (below, para. 8.23).

8.22

In relation to insurance the industry successfully lobbied the Government to exclude insurance policies from the Act and in return they issued their Statements of Practice covering life and non-life insurance respectively. There is no corresponding exemption from the Unfair Terms in Consumer Contracts Regulations 1994 which are considered in the next chapter.

(5) The Act repeatedly refers to a clause which "excludes or restricts liability". This clearly covers a clause that "no liability is accepted for any loss or damage howsoever caused" or "liability shall be limited to the cost of replacing the appliance and all liability for consequential loss is excluded". Then when we turn to section 13(1) we find that:

> To the extent that this Part of this Act prevents the exclusion or restriction of any liability it also prevents

---

[39] Above, para. 4.08.
[40] Above, para. 6.03.
[41] Below, para. 8.25.
[42] Below, para. 19.08.
[43] Below, para. 20.03.
[43a] See *Electricity Supply Nominees v. IAF Group* [1993] 3 All E.R. 372—clause in lease excluding tenant's right of set-off not controlled by the Act.

    (a) making the liability or its enforcement subject to restrictive or onerous
        conditions;

    (b) excluding or restricting any right or remedy in respect of the liability, or
        subjecting a person to any prejudice in consequence of his pursuing any
        such right or remedy;

    (c) excluding or restricting rules of evidence or procedure.

Thus the following would be caught:

    (a) "all claims within seven days";

    (b) "before starting proceedings the customer must pay £1,000 into a
        joint bank account";

    (c) "no rejection";

    (d) "if you sue us we will see that you get no further supplies";

    (e) "the report by our engineer shall be conclusive".

Section 13(1) then concludes with these words:

> and (to that extent) sections 2 and 5 to 7 also prevent excluding or restricting
> liability by reference to terms and notices which exclude or restrict the relevant
> obligation or duty.

What does this mean? How can the Act control a clause which prevents a duty
from arising? What is "the relevant obligation or duty"? In the earlier editions
of this book we suggested that the answer is to adopt the approach of Lord
Denning M.R. in *Karsales (Harrow) Ltd v. Wallis*[44] and look at the contract or
activity apart from the clause. If, for example, it is a contract giving rise to a
condition of reasonable fitness or a duty of reasonable care, the Act would
control a clause or notice providing that "no condition of fitness is implied
herein" or "the occupier shall be under no duty of care". The House of Lords
has recently confirmed in *Smith v. Eric S. Bush*[45] that this is the correct
interpretation. Affirming the decision of the Court of Appeal[46] that the disclaimers did not prevent the surveyors having a duty of care Lord Jauncey
commented on the concluding words in section 13(1) as follows[47]:

> "These words are unambiguous and are entirely appropriate to cover a dis-
> claimer which prevents a duty coming into existence."

Lord Griffiths adopted a "but for" test[48]:

> "They indicate that the existence of the common law duty to take reasonable care

---

[44] [1956] 1 W.L.R. 936.
[45] [1989] 2 All E.R. 514. The facts are given above, p. 31. A similar construction was adopted by
Slade L.J. in *Phillips Products Ltd v. Hyland* [1987] 1 W.L.R. 659, CA.
[46] [1987] 3 All E.R. 179.
[47] At p. 543.
[48] At p. 530.

... is to be judged by considering whether it would exist 'but for' the notice excluding liability."

Three final points can be made on this topic. First, an agreement in writing to submit present or future disputes to arbitration is *not* a clause "excluding or restricting liability".[49] Secondly, it is thought that the Act does not apply to a genuine "liquidated damages" clause. Thirdly, it has recently been held[49a] that the Act does not control a genuine settlement out of court ("I accept this sum [or credit note] in full and final settlement of all claims").

(6) The common law rules as to incorporation, privity and construction mentioned earlier in this chapter remain unaffected, although, as already stated,[50] they will become of far less practical importance. There may, of course, be cases where the common law rules will still be relevant. Thus if the exemption clause is controlled by the reasonableness test[51] this gives the court a wide discretion; so if the consumer can prove non-incorporation, this will of itself defeat the exemption clause and the question of discretion will not arise.

The five areas affected by the Act

(a) *Negligence*

Section 1(1) defines negligence as the breach: **8.23**

    (a) of any obligation, arising from the express or implied terms of a contract, to take reasonable care or exercise reasonable skill in the performance of the contract;

    (b) of any common law duty to take reasonable care or exercise reasonable skill (but not any stricter duty);

    (c) of the common duty of care imposed by the Occupiers' Liability Act 1957....

In practice the most important example of (a) is to be found in section 13 of the Supply of Goods and Services Act 1982 (above, para. 6.27).

We can now consider section 2—one of the most important sections of the Act. It reads as follows:

(1) A person cannot by reference to any contract term or to a notice given to persons generally or to particular persons exclude or restrict his liability for death or personal injury resulting from negligence.

(2) In the case of other loss or damage, a person cannot so exclude or restrict his liability except in so far as the term or notice satisfies the requirement of reasonableness.

(3) Where a contract term or notice purports to exclude or restrict liability for negligence a person's agreement to or awareness of it is not of itself to be taken as indicating his voluntary acceptance of any risk.

---

[49] s.13(2).
[49a] *Tudor Grange v. Citibank* [1991] 4 All E.R. 1.
[50] Above, paras 8.12 and 8.18.
[51] Below, para. 8.34.

The scope of section 2 is wide. Examples include architects, surveyors, builders, carriers, cleaners, dancehalls, cinemas, garages, decorators and holiday tour operators. In all these cases—and there are many more—an exemption clause or notice will be totally void in cases of *death or personal injury*.

If the negligence results in damage to *property* or economic loss, the clause or notice will only be effective if it satisfies the reasonableness test.[52] No distinction is made between contracts with consumers and contracts with businesses—in either case the test is the same.[53]

(b) *Contractual obligations*

8.24   The other really far-reaching provision in the Act—and one bristling with problems—is section 3. It reads as follows:

> (1) This section applies as between contracting parties where one of them deals as consumer or on the other's written standard terms[54] of business.
> (2) As against that party, the other cannot by reference to any contract term—
>   (a) when himself in breach of contract, exclude or restrict any liability of his in respect of the breach; or
>   (b) claim to be entitled—
>   (i) to render a contractual performance substantially different from that which was reasonably expected of him, or
>   (ii) in respect of the whole or any part of his contractual obligations, to render no performance at all,
> except in so far as (in the cases mentioned above in this subsection) the contract term satisfies the requirement of reasonableness.

This section is based on the recommendation of the Law Commission in their Second Report on Exemption Clauses[55] and is discussed on pages 52 to 62 of that Report. It applies to a contract (1) between a businessman and a person dealing as consumer, or (2) between two businessmen where it is made on the written standard terms of business of one of them. Thus in the consumer situation there is no distinction between a standard form contract and a negotiated contract (although a negotiated contract is more likely to be upheld as being "reasonable").

8.25   **Deals as consumer.**   The term "deals as consumer" is defined in section 12 as follows:

> (1) A party to a contract "deals as consumer" in relation to another party if—
>   (a) he neither makes the contract in the course of a business nor holds himself out as doing so; and
>   (b) the other party does make the contract in the course of a business; and

---

[52] s.11, below, para. 8.34.
[53] *cf.* ss.3, 4, 5, 6 and 7, where the distinction is crucial.
[54] See article in Professional Negligence (1993), Vol. 9, No. 1 at p. 28 citing *The Chester Grosvenor Hotel Co. Ltd v. Alfred Macalpine Management Ltd* (1992) Building Law Reports 115.
[55] Law Com. No. 69.

    (c) in the case of a contract governed by the law of sale of goods or hire-purchase, or by section 7 of this Act, the goods passing under or in pursuance of the contract are of a type ordinarily supplied for private use or consumption.

(2) But on a sale by auction or competitive tender the buyer is not in any circumstances to be regarded as dealing as consumer.

(3) Subject to this, it is for those claiming that a party does not deal as consumer to prove that he does not.

In most cases it is easy to see whether these factors are present, as the definition is aimed at the everyday consumer situation where (a) the customer is a private consumer; (b) the supplier is in business; and (c) if the contract concerns goods (rather than services) they are ordinary consumer goods.

So if a private individual buys a camera from a shop, acquires a car on hire-purchase from a finance company, has central heating installed in his house by British Gas or books a holiday with a tour operator, in each case he "deals as a consumer".

Equally obviously a manufacturing company does not deal as consumer where it buys machinery for its factory, leases cars for its sales force or uses a security company to provide guards for its premises. Taking the three factors in order we see that a customer will *not* be dealing as consumer where:

(a) the customer is a business[56] customer; or

(b) the supplier is a private person (although exemption clauses are rare here, except perhaps "sold as seen" on a used car);

(c) the goods are not ordinarily supplied for private use, *e.g.* a van or coach, to be converted into a touring home. This part of the definition may give rise to problems, *e.g.* in the case of DIY materials. Are wiring, cisterns, cement, cement mixers and other builder's tools of that type? Here—and in the difficult areas discussed below—section 12(3) should swing the balance in favour of the consumer, for it is for the supplier to prove that a consumer does *not* deal as such.

There are two main areas of difficulty, both concerned with the precise meaning of "in the course of a business" in section 12(1)(a) and (b). First, suppose a solicitor, accountant or other professional person buys a car through his business, but to be used for mixed business and private use. Secondly, assume that a retailer or estate agent buys a carpet or chair for his office—a rare event. In none of these cases are the goods part of their stock-in-trade, but in every case the goods are ordered through the business and doubtless tax allowances are claimed. Are the goods bought "in the course of a business"? On a straightforward reading of the words, particularly in view of use of the indefinite article, the answer is "yes". The Act does not require the business to deal in goods of the relevant type. Surprisingly the Court of Appeal has

---

[56] No sale by auction or competitive tender is a consumer dealing, even though the buyer is a private person: s.12(2).

recently decided that cases of this type will be classed as consumer transactions.

In *R & B Customs Brokers Co. Ltd v. United Dominions Trust*[57]:

> R & B, shipping brokers, was a private company whose only directors and share-holders were a married couple. R & B bought a Colt Shogun for personal and company use from UDT under a conditional sale agreement. (R & B had previously acquired one or two other vehicles on credit terms.) They both signed the agreement on behalf of the company. It contained an exemption clause excluding (*inter alia*) the implied condition as to fitness for particular purpose. The vehicle leaked badly in breach of the Sale of Goods Act 1979, s.14(3). When UDT sought to rely on the exclusion clause, R & B argued that it was void under the UCTA, s.6(2), as R & B was "dealing as consumer".

The Court of Appeal gave judgment for R & B. On first impression the court was convinced by the argument put forward above that the company bought in the course of a business.[58] In the end, however, the court was persuaded that there should be consistency of meaning for the same words in different statutes dealing with consumer protection (a line of reasoning which has since been disapproved—see para. 4.04 above) and that they should follow the guidance given by the House of Lords in *Davies v. Sumner*,[59] a case on the Trade Descriptions Act 1968. The court did not overlook the point that the techniques of construction of criminal and civil Acts are different; the judgment of Dillon L.J. underlines the court's approach most clearly[60]:

> "Under the Trade Descriptions Act 1968 any person who in the course of a trade or business applies a false trade description to goods is, subject to the provisions of that Act, guilty of an offence. It is a penal Act, whereas the 1977 Act is not, and it is accordingly submitted that decisions on the construction of the 1968 Act cannot assist on the construction of s.12 of the 1977 Act. Also the legislative purposes of the two Acts are not the same. The primary purpose of the 1968 Act is consumer protection, and the course of business referred to is the course of business of the alleged wrongdoer. But the provisions as to dealing as a consumer in the 1977 Act are concerned with differentiating between two classes of innocent contracting parties (those who deal as consumers and those who do not) for whom differing degrees of protection against unfair contract terms are afforded by the 1977 Act. Despite these distinctions, however, it would, in my judgment, be unreal and unsatisfactory to conclude that the fairly ordinary words 'in the course of business' bear a significantly different meaning in, on the one hand, the 1968 Act and, on the other hand, s.12 of the 1977 Act. In particular, I would be very reluctant to conclude that these words bear a significantly wider meaning in s.12 than in the 1968 Act."

8.26   So when is a purchase by a business customer outside section 12? The answer is that it must be an *integral part of the business carried on* (see

---

[57] [1988] 1 All E.R. 847.
[58] *ibid.* at p. 857, *per* Neill L.J.
[59] See below, para. 13.05, for the facts and discussion. Dillon and Neill L.JJ. cited with approval the words of Lord Keith set out there.
[60] *ibid.* at p. 853. See also Neill L.J. at p. 859.

below). This will be so if (a) it is a one-off adventure in the nature of a trade, or (b) a regular pattern of purchases has emerged. So presumably a firm of solicitors buying a typewriter or word processor or a firm of accountants buying a micro computer would be "dealing as consumer" unless a regular pattern of such purchases could be shown. Referring to the words of Lord Keith in *Davies v. Sumner*[61] and of Lord Parker C.J. in *Havering L.B.C. v. Stevenson*,[62] Dillon L.J. said[63]:

> "In the 1977 Act also, the words 'in the course of business' are not used in what Lord Keith called 'the broader sense.' I also find helpful the phrase used by Lord Parker C.J. and quoted by Lord Keith, 'an integral part of the business carried on.' The reconciliation between that phrase and the need for some degree of regularity is, as I see it, as follows: there are some transactions which are clearly integral parts of the businesses concerned, and these should be held to have been carried out in the course of those businesses; this would cover, apart from much else, the instance of a one-off adventure in the nature of trade where the transaction itself would constitute a trade or business. There are other transactions, however, such as the purchase of the car in the present case, which are at the highest only incidental to the carrying on of the relevant business; here a degree of regularity is required before it can be said that they are an integral part of the business carried on and so entered into in the course of that business."

One final comment of Dillon L.J. is worthy of note—that if the husband had personally bought the car for domestic and business use, it would have been difficult to argue that he was not dealing as consumer; so it would be anomalous to reach a different result just because it was bought by a company for such use by its two directors: "It could well be appropriate to pierce the corporate veil and look at the realities of the situation."[64]

While we should applaud this interpretation by the Court of Appeal on the grounds that it assists the consumer, the quirky and unexpected effect on the supplier seems to have been overlooked. The use of such a written exemption clause is a *criminal* offence.[65] Yet how can a supplier know whether the customer has regularly bought such goods in the past or whether they are an essential part of the business? Such a careful examination of the extrinsic circumstances of the sale would be impracticable.

The trader's solution to this danger is perhaps to be found in the wording of the defendants' exemption clause in the *R & B Customs Brokers* case: "If the buyer deals as consumer within section 12 of the Unfair Contract Terms Act 1977 . . . the buyer's statutory rights are not affected" by the following clause. Thus the trader gets it both ways, but leaves the buyer in doubt as to whether or not he is protected by the 1977 Act.

[61] See above.
[62] See below: another Trade Descriptions Act case.
[63] *ibid.* at p. 854.
[64] *ibid.* at p. 855.
[65] Consumer Transactions (Restrictions on Statements) Order 1976, below, para. 17.13. Remember that neither *R & B* nor *Davies v. Sumner* affect the words "in the course of a businesss" under section 14 of the Sale of Goods Act—*Stevenson v. Rogers*, para. 4.04, above.

Returning to section 3 itself, let us assume that the client does deal as consumer. In that case section 3 applies the reasonableness test in three cases. The first case is where the trader is in breach of contract and the clause excludes or restricts his liability (for example, liability limited to £100). The second case is where the trader relies on a clause giving him the right to render a contractual performance substantially different from that which was reasonably expected of him. This would apply to a condition on a theatre ticket whereby "the management reserve the right to alter the performance of any member of the cast". In the case of holidays the section would apply to a clause like the one in *Anglo-Continental Holidays Ltd v. Typaldos Lines (London) Ltd*[66] "Steamers, Sailing Dates, Rates and Itineraries are subject to change without notice." The final case covered by section 3 is where a contractual term gives the trader the right to offer no performance at all. It would seem that this provision is wide enough to cover the so-called "force majeure" clause which is very common in practice. It may provide that "the seller shall not be liable for non-delivery if delay is caused by strikes, lockouts or other acts beyond the seller's control". Even a clause giving the right of cancellation might be caught by this provision.[67]

One final comment may be made: if a trader tenders a performance substantially different from that "reasonably expected of him", can the clause which allows him to do so ever be reasonable? The question of reasonableness is considered later[68] but it might be reasonable if it formed part of an arm's-length business contract between two traders where the trader attacking the clause had exactly the same provision in his own standard terms.

(c) *Implied terms*

8.27 **Sale of goods.**   In Chapters 2, 3 and 4 we examined the terms implied by sections 12 to 14 of the Sale of Goods Act 1979. Until 1973 the parties had complete freedom to exclude these obligations, because section 55, as it appeared in the original Sale of Goods Act 1893, provided that "where any right, duty or liability would arise under a contract of sale by operation of law it can be modified or varied by express agreement or by the course of dealing between the parties or by usage if the usage be such as to bind both parties to the contract". This provision was radically altered by the Supply of Goods (Implied Terms) Act 1973 and the controls introduced by that Act are substantially re-enacted by section 6 of the Unfair Contract Terms Act. There are three basic rules:

(i) The conditions and warranties in section 12 (right to sell) can *never* be excluded.

(ii) Where the buyer deals as consumer (above, para. 8.25) the conditions

---

[66] [1967] 2 Lloyd's Rep. 61.
[67] See Law Com. No. 69, para. 146.
[68] Below, para. 8.34.

under sections 13 (description), 14 (quality and fitness) and 15[69] can never be excluded. Hence they are often called the consumer's "inalienable rights".[70]

(iii) Where the buyer does not deal as consumer, a clause excluding or restricting the obligations referred to in (ii) above will only be valid if it satisfies the test of reasonableness.

Despite section 6 a limited amount of "contracting out" is permitted by the sections themselves. Thus it will be recalled that under section 12 the seller can agree to transfer only such title as he himself has, while section 14(2) allows the seller to avoid liability for satisfactory quality in relation to particular defects by drawing the buyer's attention to those defects before the contract is made.

Private sales.   As an exception to the general rule section 6 also applies   **8.28**
where the seller is *not* acting in the course of a business.[71] This is unlikely to be of great practical importance because private sales are unlikely to contain exemption clauses and because, in relation to quality and fitness, there will nothing to exclude.[72] Thus the significance of this provision is limited to attempts to exclude liability under sections 13 and 15.

Hire-purchase.   The terms implied into a hire-purchase agreement are vir-   **8.29**
tually identical to those set out above[73] and section 6 of the 1977 Act controls them in exactly the same way as it does in sales of goods.

Other supply contracts.

(1) *Title.*   It will be recalled that under a contract of hire the owner does not   **8.30**
give an undertaking that he has a "right to sell".[74] An exemption clause controlling the more limited form of title undertaking in hire cases is controlled by the reasonableness test and is not subject to an outright ban.[75] Subject to this, the controls are virtually identical to those for sale and hire-purchase.[76]

(2) *Description, quality, fitness, sample.*   It will also be recalled that the implied terms are virtually identical to those implied in sale and hire-purchase cases.[77] Similarly, the controls on exemption clauses contained in section 7 of the 1977 Act are virtually identical to those in section 6—the

---

[69] This relates to sales by sample.
[70] Such an exemption clause, if written, is a criminal offence: below, para. 17.13.
[71] See s.6(4).
[72] Above, para. 4.03.
[73] Above, paras 2.14–2.15. 3.13 and 4.22–4.29 and below paras 23.08–23.10.
[74] Above, para. 2.15.
[75] Act of 1977, s.7(4).
[76] *ibid.* s.7(3A).
[77] See Supply of Goods and Services Act 1982, above, paras 3.13 and 4.27–4.29.

exemption clause is void where the buyer "deals as consumer" and it is controlled by the reasonableness test in other cases.

If a consumer has a complaint relating to a "work and materials" contract (*e.g.* repairs to a car) it will be necessary to find out what was wrong. If the *materials* themselves were defective, there may be strict liability and an exemption clause would be void under section 7. If, however, the complaint relates to the *work* itself, the supplier will only be liable if negligent and a clause excluding this liability will be subject to the "reasonableness" test under section 2(2) (or totally void if the negligence causes personal injury or death).

(d) *Guarantees and indemnities*

8.31   (i) **Indemnities.**   Perhaps one of the most unreasonable clauses imaginable was formerly used by a ferry company. It said in effect "if we (the company) incur liability to a third party in carrying your car, you (the consumer) must indemnify us—even if the liability was entirely due to our negligence". Not surprisingly such clauses are now controlled—perhaps the only surprising thing is that they are not subject to an outright ban. Section 4(1) provides that:

> A person dealing as consumer cannot by reference to any contract term be made to indemnify another person (whether a party to the contract or not) in respect of liability that may be incurred by the other for negligence or breach of contract, except in so far as the contract term satisfies the requirement of reasonableness.

The section is expressed to apply not only where the liability is to a third party but also where the liability is to the consumer himself. This could give rise to a conflict between section 4 and other provisions of the Act. To take an extreme case let us suppose that goods are supplied subject to the following condition: "the buyer agrees that if the goods are unsatisfactory the buyer will indemnify the seller against any damages and costs payable under any judgment obtained by the buyer against the seller". This would be an attempt to exclude the non-excludable condition of satisfactory quality[78] and would be totally void under section 6 (read with the definition of exemption clause in section 13). It would be extraordinary if the clause were saved by section 4.

8.32   (ii) **Guarantees.**   As already stated,[79] it was common practice for a manufacturer's guarantee to exclude negligence liability. The result was that the consumer, who thought that he was gaining valuable rights, was in effect giving up valuable rights in return for something which might well be far less valuable. Lord Denning M.R. severely criticised such clauses in *Adams v. Richardson*.[80] In ringing tones he declared that "If he wished to excuse himself from liability he should say so plainly. Instead of heading it boldly

---

[78] Above, para. 8.07.
[79] Above, para. 5.04.
[80] [1969] 1 W.L.R. 1645 at 1649.

'GUARANTEE' he should head it 'NON-GUARANTEE'; for that is what it is."

Fortunately, this type of problem should now be a thing of the past in respect of the supply of goods because section 5 of the 1977 Act nullifies a large number of such clauses. By section 5(1):

> In the case of goods of a type ordinarily supplied for private use or consumption, where loss or damage—
> (a) arises from the goods proving defective while in consumer use; and
> (b) results from the negligence of a person concerned in the manufacture or distribution of the goods,
> liability for the loss or damage cannot be excluded or restricted by reference to any contract term or notice contained in or operating by reference to a guarantee of the goods.

It will be appreciated that this provision neatly sidesteps the question of whether a guarantee is a contract; even if it is not a contract the purported exclusion notice will be ineffective to exclude liability for negligence.

Two further points should be noted. First, goods are "in consumer use" when a person is using them, or has them in his possession for use, otherwise than exclusively for the purpose of a business.[81] Thus if the buyer of a car and his wife are injured while the car is being used on a combined business-and-pleasure journey, section 5 would control a clause in the guarantee excluding liability for the manufacturer's negligence. Presumably, if the negligence resulted in damage to property, the "outright ban" in section 5 would override the section 2 "reasonableness" test. Secondly, the section does not apply as between the parties to a contract under or in pursuance of which possession or ownership of the goods passed.[82] In such cases the consumer would have the benefit of section 2 in relation to negligence and sections 6 and 7 in relation to the implied terms.

(e) *Misrepresentation*

Exemption clauses relating to misrepresentation have been controlled **8.33** since the passing of section 3 of the Misrepresentation Act 1967. Section 3 is redrafted by section 8 of the Unfair Contract Terms Act so that it now reads as follows:

> If a contract contains a term which would exclude or restrict—
> (a) any liability to which a party to a contract may be subject by reason of any misrepresentation made by him before the contract was made; or
> (b) any remedy available to another party to the contract by reason of such a misrepresentation,
> the term shall be of no effect except in so far as it satisfies the requirement of reasonableness as stated in section 11(1) of the Unfair Contract Terms Act 1977;

---

[81] s.5(2)(a). See the example given by Neill L.J. in *R & B Customs Brokers Co. Ltd v. U.D.T.* (above, para. 8.25) at p. 858.
[82] s.5(3).

and it is for those claiming that the term satisfies that requirement to show that it does.

The first point to notice here is that the law is to be found in section 3 of the Misrepresentation Act 1967 (as amended) and not in the Unfair Contract Terms Act. It follows that the section applies to all contracts (including those excluded from the Unfair Contract Terms Act) and it is not confined to "business liability".

What type of clauses are caught by section 3? Some cases are obvious: "The purchaser shall have no right to rescind this agreement" or "All liability for misrepresentation is excluded". On the other hand a clause stating that "no employee of the company has any authority to make representations on the company's behalf" might be effective.[83] Finally, the contract might state that "although every care has been taken the vendors do not warrant the accuracy of these particulars and the purchaser shall not rely on them." If such a clause were outside section 3 it would severely limit the scope of the section. It seems that if the other party does rely on the incorrect particulars there will be a misrepresentation and the clause will be treated as an exemption clause to which section 3 applies.[84]

The reasonableness test

8.34   Sections 2, 3, 4, 6, 7 and 8 all refer to the reasonableness test. The concept is not a new one; it has applied to misrepresentation since 1967 and it has applied to the implied terms of sale of goods and hire-purchase since 1973. Section 11 draws a distinction between contractual clauses and non-contractual notices. In the case of contract the person claiming that the term is reasonable must prove that:

> the term shall have been a fair and reasonable one to be included having regard to the circumstances which were, or ought reasonably to have been, known to or in the contemplation of the parties when the contract was made.[85]

Thus the critical date is the date of the contract. For example, a limitation of damages clause which was reasonable at the date of the contract will be upheld even though by the time of the hearing it has become hopelessly inadequate by reason of inflation or by reason of the plaintiff's loss being far greater than expected.

Three more preliminary points are significant. First, the question is whether the clause is reasonable in relation to *this particular contract*[86]; so what may be reasonable between a supplier and one customer may be unreasonable as against another, *e.g.* because there may be equality of bar-

---

[83] See *Overbrooke Estates Ltd v. Glencombe Properties Ltd* [1974] 1 W.L.R. 1335, above, para. 8.16.

[84] *Cremdean Properties Ltd v. Nash* (1977) 244 E.G. 547, CA.

[85] s.11(1).

[86] See Slade L.J. in *Phillips Products Ltd v. Hyland* [1987] 2 All E.R. 620 at 628.

gaining power in the one case and not in the other. This poses considerable problems for the draftsman of standard form contracts in that there is no such thing as a clause which is fair and reasonable in itself.

Secondly, the burden of proving reasonableness lies on the supplier; if the factors are evenly balanced, the customer wins the day.[87] This point equally applies to non-contractual notices and disclaimers where the party relying on the notice (*e.g.* a building society surveyor with a potential liability to a house buyer in the tort of negligence) must show that:

> it should be fair and reasonable to allow reliance on it, having regard to all the circumstances obtaining when the liability arose or (but for the notice) would have arisen.[88]

Finally, the term must be looked at *as a whole*. Thus in *Stewart Gill v. Myers*[89] the plaintiff sought to rely on a clause excluding various remedies including a right of set-off. The Court of Appeal held that the clause read as a whole was unreasonable.

The role of the courts

The concept of reasonableness appears in many areas of the law, including unfair dismissal, matrimonial finance, negligence claims and housing. In relation to the Unfair Contract Terms Act Lord Bridge has emphasised that more than one view is possible. His Lordship dealt with the matter as follows: **8.35**

> "The court must entertain a whole range of considerations, put them in the scales on one side or the other and decide at the end of the day on which side the balance comes down. There will sometimes be room for a legitimate difference of judicial opinion as to what the answer should be and where it will be impossible to say that one view is demonstrably wrong and the other demonstrably right. It must follow in my view that when asked to review such a decision the appeal court should treat the decision with the utmost respect and refuse to interfere unless it is satisfied that it proceeded upon some erroneous principle or was plainly and obviously wrong."[90]

Guidelines

In any case involving the reasonableness test the court has a wide discretion and must consider all the relevant circumstances; presumably if the matter comes to court the defendant should be advised to plead the facts on which he relies to support his claim of reasonableness. Schedule 2 contains a non-exhaustive list of guidelines. They apply only to contracts controlled by   **8.36**

---

[87] *ibid.* See s.11(5).
[88] s.11(3).
[89] [1992] 2 All E.R. 257.
[90] *George Mitchell (Chesterhall) Ltd v. Finney Lock Seeds Ltd* [1983] 3 A.C. 803 at 816. The case was actually decided on an earlier Act but this does not reduce its importance in the present context.

sections 6 and 7, *i.e.* to supplies of *goods* where the plaintiff's claim relies on the *statutory implied* terms.[91] They are as follows:

"GUIDELINES" FOR APPLICATION OF REASONABLENESS TEST

The matters to which regard is to be had in particular for the purposes of sections 6(3), 7(3) and (4), 20 and 21 are any of the following which appear to be relevant—

(a) the strength of the bargaining positions of the parties relative to each other, taking into account (among other things) alternative means by which the customer's requirements could have been met;

(b) whether the customer received an inducement to agree to the term, or in accepting it had an opportunity of entering into a similar contract with other persons, but without having to accept a similar term;

(c) whether the customer knew or ought reasonably to have known of the existence and extent of the term (having regard, among other things, to any custom of the trade and any previous course of dealing between the parties);

(d) where the term excludes or restricts any relevant liability if some condition is not complied with, whether it was reasonable at the time of the contract to expect that compliance with that condition would be practicable;

(e) whether the goods were manufactured, processed or adapted to the special order of the customer.

The first three are of greatest importance. Their broad effect is that if a business buyer, large enough to have bargaining power and with a choice of potential suppliers with whom to negotiate terms, enters into a disadvantageous contract with his eyes open, the court is unlikely to rush to his assistance. The buyer has made a bad bargain and is stuck with it. In contrast if the buyer is a small business, perhaps dealing with a monopoly or with a supplier who belongs to a trade association whose members all adopt standard terms, and does not notice or cannot understand the exemption clause, then the court will probably strike down the clause. He had no real choice—it was a "take it or leave it situation".[92]

No specific guidelines are laid down by the Act in other cases, *e.g.* contracts for *services*, breach of *express* terms. However, by analogy the courts are applying similar guidelines with particular emphasis on the first three criteria—bargaining power, choice and knowledge. Lord Wilberforce stressed the significance of the first factor in the pre-Act case of *Photo Production Ltd v. Securicor Transport*[93]:

"After this Act, in commercial matters generally, when the parties are not of

---

[91] Where the customer is "dealing as consumer", any exemption clause is void in respect of such terms: above, paras 8.27–8.30.

[92] See Slade L.J. in *Phillips Products Ltd v. Hyland* at p. 629 (clause was one of 43 clauses of plant hire company's terms; used by all members of trade association; not fair and reasonable).

[93] [1980] A.C. 827. The respondents' employee purposely set fire to a factory which he was supposed to be guarding!

unequal bargaining power, and when risks are normally borne by insurance, not only is the case for judicial intervention undemonstrated, but there is everything to be said, and this seems to have been Parliament's intention, for leaving the parties free to apportion the risks as they think fit and for respecting their decisions."

The size of print would also be relevant,[94] and a clause is unlikely to be upheld if it is out of line with a Code of Practice adopted by the trader's trade association.[95] The continued use of immensely wide exemption clauses could influence the court in a case involving the reasonableness test. It may be that a clause that "the seller can cancel this agreement in the event of strikes, etc." should now be redrafted so as to give a mutual right to rescind. It is also possible that the contract will specify the factors on which the trader relies in support of his claim of reasonableness. Perhaps we may see the emergence of a dual price contract, £X with full responsibility or £Y without it. We may also see "split clauses"—different clauses dealing with consequential loss, limitation of liability and time-limits for claims.

Limitation of damages clauses

A number of small traders (including travel agents) felt very uneasy about   **8.37** the possibility of having to meet very large claims and accordingly Lord Hailsham introduced a new clause which is now section 11(4). It reads:

> Where by reference to a contract term or notice a person seeks to restrict liability to a specified sum of money, and the question arises (under this or any other Act) whether the term or notice satisfies the requirement of reasonableness, regard shall be had in particular ... to—
> (a) the resources which he could expect to be available to him for the purpose of meeting the liability should it arise; and
> (b) how far it was open to him to cover himself by insurance.

This provision, if it is ever litigated, is bound to cause problems. Do the "resources" of a sole trader or partner include his private assets? How far afield does he have to search to find insurance? What happens if the premium would destroy or seriously reduce the commercial viability of the transaction? In spite of such difficulties it seems likely that the courts will view more sympathetically a limitation clause whereby the supplier accepts some liability than an exclusion clause where the supplier in cavalier fashion refuses to contribute at all to the consumer's loss.[96]

The emerging case law

The Act was passed to give added protection to consumers who are nearly   **8.38**

---

[94] In *The Zinnia* [1984] 2 LL.L.R. 211, Staughton J. was minded to strike down the clause on the grounds of (a) size of print, and (b) complexity of language. Unfortunately counsel for the party attacking the clause did not raise this point!
[95] Below, para. 10.06.
[96] See *Ailsa Craig Fishing Co. v. Malvern Fishing Co.*, above, para. 8.18, n. 35.

always in a weak bargaining position. The problem of widely drawn exemption clauses has not gone away[97] but we are not aware of a single post-Act consumer case in which an exemption clause has been upheld as reasonable. The following cases show the attitude of the courts.

The first is the latest and most important in that the House of Lords has now given valuable guidance on the operation of the reasonableness test in a consumer context.

Smith v. Bush.[98] We have already discussed the first point in this case, namely, whether the surveyors owed a duty of care in tort to the house buyers. To this question the House of Lords unanimously answered "yes".

We now turn to the second point—were the surveyors able to prove that their exemption clauses satisfied the reasonableness test? Again the House of Lords answered the question in favour of the consumers: "no". The judgments of Lords Griffiths and Templeman deserve careful examination. Although Lord Griffiths admitted that it is impossible to draw up an exhaustive list of relevant factors for the court to take into account when applying the reasonableness test, the following extract is crucial for the legal adviser, since he states that these matters should "always be considered"[99]:

"(1) Were the parties of equal bargaining power? If the court is dealing with a one-off situation between parties of equal bargaining power the requirement of reasonableness would be more easily discharged than in a case such as the present where the disclaimer is imposed on the purchaser who has no effective power to object.

(2) In the case of advice, would it have been reasonably practicable to obtain the advice from an alternative source taking into account considerations of costs and time? . . .

(3) How difficult is the task being undertaken for which liability is being excluded? When a very difficult or dangerous undertaking is involved there may be a high risk of failure which would certainly be a pointer towards the reasonableness of excluding liability as a condition of doing the work. A valuation, on the other hand, should present no difficulty if the work is undertaken with reasonable skill and care. . . .

(4) What are the practical consequences of the decision on the question of reasonableness? This must involve the sums of money potentially at stake and the ability of the parties to bear the loss involved, which, in its turn, raises the question of insurance. There was once a time when it was considered improper even to mention the possible existence of insurance cover in a lawsuit. But those days are long past. Everyone knows that all prudent professional men carry insurance, and the availability and cost of insurance must be a relevant factor when considering which of two parties should be required to bear the risk of a loss."

The effect of this decision is that an exemption clause will not protect a surveyor "in respect of a dwelling house of modest value". The position may

[97] See Chap. Nine below.
[98] [1990] 1 A.C. 831, above, para. 3.05.
[99] At p. 858.

well be different where other types of property are valued "such as industrial property, large blocks of flats or very expensive houses",[1] where it may be reasonable for the mortgagee's surveyor to exclude or limit his liability to the buyer/mortgagor.

Spencer v. Cosmos Air Holidays.[2] We discussed this case earlier in relation to damages for distress. The agreement contained a clause whereby the defendants excluded responsibility "for any injury, death, loss or damage which is caused by any negligence of the management or employees of an independent contractor". Without amplifying their reasons the Court of Appeal brushed the clause aside. In the words of Farquharson L.J.:

> "It does not bear upon the case at all and does not affect the plaintiff's contractual rights against the defendants—namely, to enjoy 14 days' holiday in the hotel she had chosen."

Walker v. Boyle.[3] During negotiations for the sale of V's house V told P that there was no boundary dispute. This was an innocent misrepresentation which induced P to buy. On discovering the facts P refused to proceed whereupon V claimed specific performance in reliance on Condition 17 of the National Conditions of Sale, which provided that "no misdescription can annul the sale". P claimed that the clause was unreasonable. His claim was upheld. Even though the clause was in the National Conditions of Sale it was not the product of negotiation between the parties or their representatives.

South Western General Property Co. v. Marton.[4] Property was described in auction particulars as "long leasehold building land". The particulars failed to disclose major restrictions on development and the buyer would never have bought the property if he had known of this. The particulars provided that the statements were made without responsibility and were statements of opinion only and that it was up to intending purchasers to satisfy themselves as to their accuracy. Croom-Johnson J. held that the clause failed to pass the reasonableness test. His Lordship laid great stress on the vital importance of the matter for the buyer. He also pointed out that many prospective buyers attended auctions at short notice and would obviously have no opportunity to check out the particulars.

Waldron-Kelly v. British Railways Board.[5] The defendants agreed to carry   **8.39**

---

[1] *per* Lord Griffiths, at p. 859.
[2] *The Times*, December 6, 1989, CA, above, para. 7.39.
[3] [1982] 1 W.L.R. 495.
[4] (1982) 263 E.G. 1090.
[5] [1981] C.L.Y. 303.

the plaintiff's suitcase on "owner's risk" terms. It disappeared. The Board sought to limit their liability by a clause which referred only to the weight of the suitcase (£27) and not to its value (£320). The learned county court judge held that the clause failed to pass the reasonableness test.

Woodman v. Photo Trade Processing Ltd.[6] Mr Woodman took photographs of a friend's wedding. The shop to which he brought the film for development displayed a notice limiting liability to the cost of the film. The film came back ruined and Mr Woodman (with the support of the Consumers' Association) claimed that the clause was unreasonable. The learned county court judge upheld his claim and awarded £75 for disappointment.

St Albans D.C. v. ICL.[6a] Although not a consumer case, it provides helpful guidance on the "reasonableness" test. ICL were a very substantial company with turnover of £1109 million, profit of £100 million and world-wide liability insurance of £50 million. The contract contained a clause limiting liability to £100,000 (less than their normal standard clause). Scott-Baker J. after considering the bargaining strength of the parties, the likely losses of the plaintiffs and other factors, held that the clause failed the reasonableness test: "I do not think it is unreasonable that he who stands to make the profit should carry the risk."[6b] The Court of Appeal agreed.

The message from these cases comes through loud and clear—the standard form, non-negotiated consumer exemption clause has had its day. In none of the above cases was there any negotiation; in none of them was the clause expressly brought to the consumer's notice. In only one of them (*Waldron-Kelly*) did the consumer have anything in the nature of a choice. Indeed the most significant feature of the *Woodman* case was the fact that, in the opinion of the learned judge, it should have been possible for the processing industry to offer their customers a choice—£X with limited liability or £Y with greater liability.[7] The Act may therefore mark a return to basic principles of contract law by destroying the fiction that a party has "agreed" to a term if (1) he did not know it was there, (2) even if he had known, he would not have understood it, and (3) even if he would have understood it, he would never have agreed to it without modification.

3. OTHER CONTROLS

8.40   Although the Unfair Contract Terms Act 1977 is by far the most important example of statutory control of exemption clauses there are many other statu-

---

[6] *Times Business News*, June 20, 1981; *Which?*, July 1981.
[6a] [1995] F.S.R. 686. The case is also relevant on the meaning of "written standard terms of business" (see para. 8.24 above) see [1997] F.S.R. 251.
[6b] *ibid.* at p. 711.
[7] The so-called "two-tier system".

tory controls. One of these, section 3 of the Misrepresentation Act 1967, has already been mentioned. There are also a number of other Acts relating to the carriage of passengers by public service vehicle, rail and air (see particularly the Carriage by Air Act 1961). Other examples include the Occupiers' Liability Act 1957, the Defective Premises Act 1972, the Road Traffic Act 1988, the Consumer Credit Act 1974 and the Solicitors Act 1974. For a summary of the statutory controls readers are referred to *Chitty on Contracts*, Vol. I, paras. 1022–1028.

4. THE E.C. DIMENSION

On July 1, 1995 the Unfair Terms in Consumer Contracts Regulations 1994, **8.41** giving effect to the Unfair Contract Terms Directive, came into force alongside the Act. It will be fully analysed in the next chapter.

Chapter Nine

"THESE SMALL PRINT TERMS SEEM VERY UNFAIR"

On July 1, 1995 the Unfair Contract Terms Directive became part of English **9.01** law. This was done by statutory instrument—namely the Unfair Terms in Consumer Contracts Regulations 1994 (S.I. 1994 No. 1359). The Regulations enable a consumer (or, in certain cases, the Director General of Fair Trading acting on behalf of consumers) to challenge certain contractual terms as being "unfair"—a concept new to English law. If the challenge succeeds, the clause will be ineffective but the rest of the contract will remain in force if this is possible (see reg. 5). Schedule 3 to the Regulations lists 17 clauses which *may* be unfair; the list is not exhaustive.

For the English lawyer/adviser it is vital to appreciate that the new legislation exists alongside the other controls, notably the Unfair Contract Terms Act 1977 which has been fully discussed in the previous chapter. Three points can be made:

(1) In some respects the Regulations go beyond the 1977 Act (UCTA) because (a) UCTA is largely concerned with *exemption clauses* whereas the Regulations are not so limited and (b) the Regulations control a number of contracts (such as insurance) to which UCTA does not apply at all.

(2) In four respects UCTA is wider than the Regulations. Thus (a) UCTA is not limited to contracts—it also covers non-contractual disclaimers; (b) UCTA is not limited to non-negotiated terms; (c) UCTA can apply even though the party attacking the clause is a company; and (d) UCTA applies not only to consumer sales but also to business sales.

(3) There is a substantial area of overlap and Article 8 of the Directive provides that: "Member States may adopt or retain the most stringent provisions compatible with the Treaty in the area covered by this Directive, to ensure a maximum degree of protection for the consumer." It follows that if a clause is struck down as *void* by UCTA, the consumer is not concerned with the Regulations. If, however, the clause is controlled by the "reasonableness" test (*e.g.* UCTA, s.3), the court will have to decide whether the test of "fairness" goes beyond the test of reasonableness. The language of Article 3, which refers to a clause causing a "significant imbalance in the parties' rights and obligations arising under the contract to the detriment of the consumer",

is strikingly similar to paragraphs 1 and 4 of Lord Griffiths' UCTA guidelines in *Smith v. Bush* (above, para. 8.38).

1. THE EUROPEAN BACKGROUND

9.02   The Directive has had an (interrupted) gestation period of some 19 years. Work on it started as long ago as 1975, but it was then halted when a large number of Member States (including the U.K.) introduced domestic legislation in this area. When the dust of this legislation had been given a chance to settle work on the Directive started again; not surprisingly the comments (especially from industry) were not entirely uncritical.

An E.C. Directive is normally preceded by Preambles setting out the thinking behind the Directive. This one has a very large number and in this book we have numbered them 1 to 40 for ease of reference. There seems little doubt that these Preambles will be referred to by a court faced with a problem of interpretation. Preambles 5 to 9 provide some of the flavour:

(5) Whereas, generally speaking, consumers do not know the rules of law which, in other Member States than their own, govern contracts for the sale of goods or services;

(6) Whereas this lack of awareness may deter them from direct transactions for the purchase of goods or services in another Member State;

(7) Whereas, in order to facilitate the establishment of the internal market and to safeguard the citizen in his role as consumer when acquiring goods and services under contracts which are governed by the laws of Member States than his own, it is essential to remove unfair terms from those contracts;

(8) Whereas sellers of goods and suppliers of services will thereby be helped in their task of selling goods and supplying services, both at home and through the internal market;

(9) Whereas competition will thus be stimulated, so contributing to increased choice for Community citizens as consumers.

One general observation can be made; the attempt by the Directive to boost cross-border trade is unlikely to succeed, because the Directive has nothing to say on the vital question of enforcement. In most cases a consumer who is dissatisfied with his purchase must sue in the supplier's home state: see the Convention on Jurisdiction and the Enforcement of Judgments (which now forms part of English law under the Civil Jurisdiction and Judgments Act 1982), Arts. 2 and 5.

Interpretation

9.03   This Directive (like all Directives) is addressed to Member States and requires them to enact the relevant legislation by a specified date (in this case December 31, 1994). A question may then arise as to what remedies are available to a consumer if a Member State fails to implement the Directive correctly, or in time, or at all. This is a very live issue; in two recent cases involving the rights of employees on a business transfer and in case of collective redundancies the E.C. Commission took the U.K. Government before the European Court which held that the U.K. Government had failed to implement Directives correctly in no less than six respects.[1] Where does this leave the consumer under the Directive which we are discussing? From the highly creative law-making of the European Court three principles emerge:

(1) The English courts must construe domestic law (the Regulations) in such a way as to give effect to the *purpose* of the Directive. This principle was laid down by the House of Lords in *Litster v. Forth Dry Dock*[2] and by the European Court in *Marleasing*[3] and most recently in *Faccini Dori*.[4] Since one of the objects of the Directive is to approximate the laws of Member States the courts may well give particular words such as "good faith" a European meaning; anyone putting forward an argument in this area should not do so in purely Anglo-Saxon terms.

(2) If the Regulations cannot be construed as set out in (1) above, the question arises as to what remedy (if any) is available to a consumer if the Directive has not been correctly implemented. As previously stated, the European Court has been extremely creative and as a result the consumer may have two possible remedies:

(a) If the claim is brought against a public body (an "emanation of the State") the claimant can enforce the Directive directly in the English courts; the public body cannot shelter behind the Government's failure to implement it. The leading case[5] concerned a Health Authority and the concept of "public body" has been widely interpreted to cover public utilities both before[6] and after[7] privatisation.

(b) Quite apart from this, an aggrieved party may sue the Government for failure to implement the Directive correctly, if the relevant provision was enacted for his benefit and if the failure has caused him loss. The ramifications of the historic *Francovitch* decision on this point[8] are still being worked out.[9]

Chapter 11 of this book focuses on what has (at least until recently) been the central weakness of consumer law in this country—the time, cost and

---

[1] *Commission v. U.K.* [1994] I.R.L.R. 392 and 412
[2] [1990] 1A.C. 546.
[3] *Marleasing SA v. La Commercial* [1992] 1 C.M.L.R. 305.
[4] [1995] All E.R. (EC) 1, ECJ.
[5] *Marshall v. Southhampton Area Health Authority* [1986] Q.B. 401.
[6] *Foster v. British Gas* [1988] C.M.L.R. 697.
[7] *Griffin v. South West Water Services* [1995] I.R.L.R. 15.
[8] *Francovitch v. Italian Republic* [1992] I.R.L.R. 84, ECJ.
[9] In the *Factortame* case [1991] A.C. 603 the U.K. Government was held to be in breach of E.C. law because the Merchant Shipping Act 1988 discriminated against non-U.K. nationals. Spanish fishermen are suing the U.K. Government under *Francovitch* (n. 8, above) and a decision on damages is likely in the near future.

aggravation of getting the matter dealt with if the trader decides to fight all the way (especially as the cost of litigation will nearly always far exceed the amount in dispute). Article 7 of the Directive requires Member States to ensure that "adequate and effective means exist to prevent the continued use of unfair terms". Initially the Department of Trade and Industry proposed to take no action under this Article at all but, in response to widespread criticism, it decided something had to be done; accordingly Regulation 8 enables the Director General of Fair Trading to apply to the court for an injunction to ban the continued use of the offending term or terms. This narrow provision was criticised by other consumer bodies (including the Consumers Association) seeking enforcement powers; the Government has bowed to this pressure and Regulation 8 will shortly be widened to meet these demands.

The Department of Trade and Industry has published guidance notes setting out their views on some unsettled points. Not all their views are a model of clarity.

2. What Contracts are Caught?

9.04   The Regulations apply to "any term in a contract concluded between a seller or supplier and a consumer where the said term has not been individually negotiated." When we turn to the definitions in regulation 2(1) we find that:

> "consumer" means a natural person who, in making a contract to which these Regulations apply, is acting for purposes which are outside his business;
> "seller" means a person who sells goods and who, in making a contract to which these Regulations apply, is acting for purposes relating to his business;
> "supplier" means a person who supplies goods or services and who, in making a contract to which these Regulations apply, is acting for purposes relating to his business;
> "business" includes a trade or profession and the activities of any Government Department or local or public authority."

Several points call for comment. The first two both relate to the *R&B* case (above, para. 8.25). This case would be decided differently under the Regulations because (a) a company can never be a "consumer" for the purpose of the Regulations, and (b) in any event the buyer would be unable to prove that he was acting for purposes outside his business. It follows that a sole trader buying a car for his manager would not have the protection of the Regulations. To avoid confusion, we must repeat that the non-application of the Regulations will not affect the rights of a consumer under UCTA where that Act applies. In other words, the actual decision in *R. & B.*, based on UCTA, would be unaffected.

This leaves three unsettled questions. First, what about mixed use? What happens if a solicitor or estate agent buys a car for private use but uses it occasionally for business purposes? Secondly, what happens if the private nature of the purchase is unknown to the supplier (as where the order is given on business stationery)? In the light of what has been said above (para. 9.03) the court can be directed to other European texts where similar terms appear.[10] On that basis, the first question may well be answered by applying a proportionality test, so that if the car was employed overwhelmingly for private use the Directive would apply. On the second point the obvious inference must be that a buyer who leads the seller to believe that it is a business sale must take the consequences. Finally, the wording is wide enough to cover a case where the business "seller" is acting as a buyer in the particular transaction. This is the DTI view (Guidance Notes para. 4.8) and we agree.

3. WHAT CONTRACTS ARE EXCLUDED?

Schedule 1 of the Regulations gives effect to the rather curious provisions of Recitals 14 and 15 of the Directive which read as follows: **9.05**

> Whereas [uniform rules of law in the matter of unfair terms] should apply to all contracts concluded between sellers or suppliers and consumers;
> Whereas as a result *inter alia* contracts relating to employment, contracts relating to succession rights, contracts relating to rights under family law and contracts relating to the incorporation and organization of companies or partnership agreements must be excluded from this Directive.

Presumably the words "contracts relating to the incorporation and organisation of companies" would not cover shares sold across the counter, so that the Regulations would apply. The Regulations also apply to contracts of insurance (which are outside UCTA). Also, the supply of an interest in land by a "business" supplier to a consumer would appear to be controlled (although the point is not free from doubt) so that, for example, a very one-sided service charge in a lease granted to a consumer, or a hefty default provision in a tenancy, or a clause that "discovery of defects shall not be a ground for refusing to complete" could all be caught. The DTI Guidelines are cautious but they consider it prudent to assume that the Regulation can apply (para. 3.20).

4. WHAT TERMS ARE NOT CAUGHT?

Three points must be noted.   **9.06**
  (1) The Regulations apply only to terms which have not been "individually negotiated". This is considered below.
  (2) The Regulations do not apply to a term incorporated in order to comply with or which reflects (a) mandatory, statutory or regulatory provisions of the United Kingdom or (b) the provisions or principles of International Conventions to which the Member States or the Community are party. An obvious example of (a) would be a contractual term inserted to comply with the Con-

---

[10] See, *e.g.* the Official Report (Guilano-Lagarde) on the Rome Choice of Law Convention, where the point is discussed in relation to Art. 5 of that Convention.

sumer Credit Act (as to which see below, para. 18.01). A further example would be a contract incorporating terms laid down by a regulatory authority (such as Lautro) under the Financial Services Act. An example of (b) above would be a clause giving effect to the Warsaw Convention on carriage by air.

(3) The Regulations are only designed to cover ancillary clauses rather than "core" provisions. Thus, regulation 3(2) gives effect to Preamble 31 to the Directive by providing that:

> in so far as it is in plain intelligible language, no assessment shall be made of the fairness of any term which—
> (a) defines the main subject-matter of the contract, or
> (b) concerns the adequacy of the price or renumeration, as against the goods or services sold or supplied.

The basic principle is clear enough; a consumer cannot allege unfairness merely because he has made a bad bargain. That said, there is bound to be scope for argument as to which terms are core terms and so outside the Regulations. If one takes the case of a clause in a motor policy stating that "the car can only be used by a driver over 25 for social, domestic or pleasure purposes and the insured must pay the first £100 of any claim", it would be a "core" provision, whereas a clause stating that "all claims must be notified within 48 hours" would be non-core. Even in the former case the Regulations would apply, if the core provision was not expressed in plain intelligible language.

The emphasis on plain language is to be welcomed and, although the Regulations do not mention it, the other consumer horror (tiny print) will presumably be taken into account in evaluating good faith and fairness.

5. Not Individually Negotiated

9.07 We have seen that the Regulations only control a term which has not been individually negotiated. Regulation 3 tells us that:

> (3) For the purposes of these Regulations a term shall always be regarded as not having been individually negotiated where it has been drafted in advance and the consumer has not been able to influence the substance of the term.
> (4) Notwithstanding that a term or certain aspects of it in a contract has been individually negotiated these Regulations shall apply to the rest of a contract if an overall assessment of the contract indicates that it is a pre-formulated standard contract.
> (5) It shall be for any seller or supplier who claims that a term was individually negotiated to show that it was.

If a consumer contract contains any express terms at all (other than subject matter, price and time for performance) all such terms will in practice be controlled except in those very rare cases where the consumer persuades the supplier to alter the term. The words "in advance" presumably mean "before the document was presented to the consumer" and the concluding words "and the consumer has not been able to influence the substance of the term" do not appear to impose an additional requirement; the Directive links the two clauses by inserting the word "therefore" so that it reads:

> . . . drafted in advance and the consumer has therefore not been able to influence the substance of the term.

If the consumer's request for a variation is met with the reply "sorry, we can't change these terms" the clause would clearly be controlled. The same would apply if the supplier said "we can't alter the term but we will give you £20 off the price"; this will clearly be relevant in deciding whether the term was fair.

6. WHEN IS A TERM UNFAIR?

Regulation 4 gives effect to Article 3.1 of the Directive. It provides as follows:

9.08

(1) In these Regulations, subject to paragraphs (2) and (3) below "unfair term" means any term which contrary to the requirement of good faith causes a significant imbalance in the parties' rights and duties under the contract to the detriment of the consumer.

(2) An assessment of the unfair nature of the terms shall be made taking into account the nature of the goods or services for which the contract was concluded and referring, as at the time of the conclusion of the contract, to all circumstances attending the conclusion of the contract and to all the other terms of the contract or of another contract on which it is dependent.

(3) In determining whether a term satisfies the requirement of good faith, regard shall be had in particular to the matters specified in Schedule 2 to these Regulations.

(4) Schedule 3 to these Regulations contains an indicative and non-exhaustive list of the terms which may be regarded as unfair.

It is clear from the Directive and the Regulations that the fairness of a term must not be looked at in isolation but in the context of the contract as a whole—including the price and the consumer's reasonable expectations. The reference to "another contract on which it is dependent" would enable the court to examine the terms of a contract between a lender and a debtor when assessing the fairness of a term in a contract of guarantee or indemnity. The Regulations mirror section 11 of UCTA (see above, para. 8.34) by making the time of the contract the critical time for assessing fairness. This time is also crucial in deciding what damage is reasonably foreseeable (see Chap. 7, para. 7.32, above).

The concept of "good faith" is familiar to continental lawyers: it involves fair dealing and the absence of "sharp practice".[11] Schedule 2 lists four matters and the first three of them are strikingly similar to those in Schedule 2 of UCTA (see above, para. 8.36). The list reads as follows:

---

[11] See the judgment of Bingham L.J. in the *Interfoto* case [1988] 2 WLR 615 at 620.

(a) the strength of the bargaining position of the parties;
(b) whether the consumer had an inducement to agree to the term;
(c) whether the goods or services were sold or supplied to the special order of the consumer;
(d) the extent to which the seller or supplier has dealt fairly and equitably with the consumer.

It may well be that paragraph (d) will often be crucial in that a supplier should take steps to make the consumer aware of the relevant term before the contract is made; a failure to do so may well indicate a lack of "good faith".

7. PLAIN LANGUAGE AND CONSTRUCTION

9.09 We have already come across one reference to plain language in relation to the core provisions. Regulation 6 contains two provisions of general application. It provides that:

> A seller or supplier shall ensure that any written term of a contract is expressed in plain, intelligible language, and if there is doubt about the meaning of a written term the interpretation most favourable to the consumer shall prevail.

As the Regulations are essentially concerned with standard form contracts, the words "plain, intelligible language" will presumably be given an objective meaning so that a clause which meets the standards of the "Plain English campaign" should pass the regulation 6 test. Knowledge that the particular consumer does not speak English, or that English is not his first language, will be taken into account in assessing good faith and fairness.

The requirement of plain language is greatly to be welcomed. Although the Regulations do not provide any sanction for the use of obscure language (apart from subjecting the "core" to statutory scrutiny) it seems clear that lack of plain language will be highly relevant to good faith and fairness.

The Fifth OFT Bulletin on Unfair Contract Terms (see para. 9.11 below) states that the use of plain, intelligible language "not only meets the specific statutory requirement set out in Regulation 6 but also makes it less likely that terms which protect suppliers' interests will be considered to create a contractual imbalance contrary to the requirement of good faith" (p. 13). Pages 115–122 contain examples of how particular terms have been improved by the use of plain English and the avoidance of legal jargon; in one car rental case a clause containing 164 words was reduced to 39.

In what we believe to be the first case on the Regulations to reach the courts[11a] a judge in Northern Ireland has struck down an "early repayment penalty" clause in a loan agreement. One of the grounds for doing so was that it was not expressed in plain, intelligible language. Unfortunately, the relevant part of the judgment also failed that test; there were no less than 59 words separating the subject from the verb!

[11a] *Kidlance Ltd v. Murphy* (unreported) Northern Ireland High Court, Chancery Division.

Choice of law evasion

Article 6.2 requires Member States to ensure that a consumer will not be   **9.10**
deprived of the benefit of the Directive by the choice of a foreign system of
law to govern the contract, if the contract has a close connection with the
territory of a Member State. Regulation 7 contains a provision to that effect.

8. The Role of the OFT

We have seen that Regulation 8 enables the Director-General of Fair Trading   **9.11**
to take steps to ban the continued use of unfair terms. The OFT have devoted
a great deal of time and energy to this task and have achieved a significant
measure of success. Nevertheless, "there remains a serious problem in the
United Kingdom in that the large majority of consumer contracts which come
under scrutiny prove to be unfair."[11b] Their fifth Bulletin on Unfair Contract
Terms (see below) states "since the inception of the Regulations in July 1995
more than 1200 terms have been successfully challenged and the number of
businesses that have undertaken to drop or amend questionable terms continues to grow." The terms in question have been used and challenged in a
vast number of areas including car sale and rental agreements, home
improvements, gas supplies, burglar alarms, satellite and cable TV, loan
agreements and leisure facilities. They have no power to deal with individual
complaints; their powers are purely generic and they will exercise those powers in the following way:

(1) If they receive a complaint from a consumer, a trading standards
    department or any organisation, they will examine the relevant term
    in the context of the contract as a whole.
(2) If they consider that the term is potentially unfair they will seek to
    persuade the trader (with or without the relevant trade association) to
    alter it or to stop using it altogether.
(3) The "persuasion" may in appropriate cases be coupled with threats of
    court proceedings; this often produces results.
(4) Finally, the OFT can take proceedings under Regulation 8 for an
    injunction banning the continued use of the disputed term. The reluc-
    tance of the OFT to take this step has been criticised[11c] and now they
    have finally taken the plunge by applying for a hotly-contested
    injunction to ban a term in a loan agreement under which contractual
    interest continues to accrue even after a "time order" reducing the
    instalments and extending the payment period (these orders are con-
    sidered in Part IV of this book—see para. 25.04 below).

The OFT also gives wide publicity to its activities by publishing regular

[11b] Pat Edwards, Legal Director OFT, in an address reproduced in Bulletin 4 at p. 26.
[11c] Richard Colley in [1998] N.L.J. 46.

Bulletins (available free of charge) which describe and illustrate their work. A key feature is the "naming and shaming" of traders who have been using potentially unfair terms—the Bulletins set out a large number of potentially unfair terms and then describes how they were modified or abandoned after discussions with the OFT. Some examples of these "before and after" clauses will be given in the following pages—but it must be stressed that they are merely examples of potentially unfair terms and nothing more—they have no legal force.

9. Clauses Which may be Unfair

9.12   As already stated (above, para. 9.08), Regulation 4(4) provides that Schedule 3 to these Regulations contains an indicative and non-exhaustive list of the terms which may be regarded as unfair. In the following paragraphs each of these clauses is followed by a comment and, in some cases, by an OFT example. The words "indicative and non-exhaustive" should be constantly borne in mind—see OFT Bulletin 5, pp. 107–114 for examples of clauses which they consider as potentially unfair even though they are not mentioned in the Schedule.

1. Terms which have the object or effect of:

   (a) excluding or limiting the legal liability of a seller or supplier in the event of the death of a consumer or personal injury to the latter resulting from an act or omission of that seller or supplier;

9.13   **Comment.**   This situation is already largely covered by sections 2, 6 and 7 of UCTA—but the Regulations go beyond the Act by conferring the OFT enforcement powers described in para. 9.03 above. Thus in one case the OFT achieved the deletion of the following clause:

> The company does not accept responsibility for the failure of any fire protection equipment in the event of a fire.

In another case, a clause stated that persons using the equipment or facilities at a gymnasium did so at their own risk. It was amended so that it started with the words, "In the absence of any negligence or other breach of duty ..."

   (b) inappropriately excluding or limiting the legal rights of the consumer *vis-à-vis* the seller or supplier or another party in the event of total or partial non-performance or inadequate performance by the seller or supplier of any of the contractual obligations, including the option of offsetting a debt owed to the seller or supplier against any claim which the consumer may have against him;

9.14   **Comment.**   The ground covered by this provision is similar to that covered by section 3(2) of UCTA in those cases where UCTA applies. It will be recalled that that section is not limited to cases of *breach* by the supplier; it could also catch a one-sided "force majeure" clause giving the supplier a right to suspend performance, or even to terminate the contract, if performance is prevented or delayed for reasons beyond the supplier's control. The reference to set-off is not mirrored in UCTA and under the general law the position is as follows:

(1) Set-off is a procedural device which allows a defendant to put forward a claim (*e.g.* for damages for unsatisfactory quality) in reduction or extinction of the plaintiff's claim (*e.g.* for the price).
(2) If the supplier and the consumer have *liquidated* claims against each other, set-off is allowed.
(3) If the two claims arise out of the *same* transaction (a builder claims the invoice price and is met with a claim that his workmen caused damage to the consumer's house) set-off is allowed.
(4) In other cases, *e.g.* where the consumer claims damages for defective performance and the supplier seeks to set-off a debt due under an *earlier* transaction, set-off is not allowed.

The OFT has launched a campaign to ban "full payment in advance" terms in home improvement contracts, as these terms destroy the consumer's valuable right to set-off a claim for defective work against the price.

The following example of a paragraph (b) term relating to Microsoft software is a good illustration of a change in substance and in the use of plain intelligible language.

Before:

> LIMITED WARRANTY. MICROSOFT warrants that the support provided hereunder shall be substantially as described. THIS WARRANTY IS EXCLUSIVE AND IS IN LIEU OF ALL OTHER WARRANTIES AND MICROSOFT DISCLAIMS ALL OTHER WARRANTIES, EXPRESS OR IMPLIED, INCLUDING, BUT NOT LIMITED TO, WARRANTIES OF MERCHANTABILITY AND FITNESS FOR A PARTICULAR PURPOSE.

After:

> LIMITED WARRANTY. MICROSOFT warrants that it will provide Support with reasonable care, within a reasonable time and substantially as described in this Agreement. MICROSOFT does not make any other promises or warranties about Support service.

This is a good illustration of balancing the interests of supplier and consumer; the OFT acknowledge that the supplier also needs to protect his interests—but not to the extent provided by the original term. This group of potentially unfair terms is by far the largest section of the OFT illustrations;

the Bulletin contains no fewer than 179 examples identified by the OFT in just one year (1998); they include terms excluding or limiting liability for defective performance, non-performance or delay, time limits, excluding or restricting set-off and using "guarantees" to restrict liability. We must once again stress two essential points which apply to every illustration; they merely represent the opinion of the OFT and not the opinion of a court, and each term under discussion must be considered in the context of the contract as a whole and not in isolation.

> (c) making an agreement binding on the consumer whereas provision of services by the seller or supplier is subject to a condition whose realisation depends on his own will alone;

9.15   Comment.   This could catch a servicing agreement where the consumer was required to pay an annual fee even though the supplier might decide to discontinue carrying spare parts for that particular item (see OFT Bulletin No. 5 at p. 76).

> (d) permitting the seller or supplier to retain sums paid by the consumer where the latter decides not to conclude or perform the contract, without providing for the consumer to receive compensation of an equivalent amount from the seller or supplier where the latter is the party cancelling the contract;

9.16   Comment.   This highlights one of the key concepts of "unfairness", namely the one-sided nature of a particular provision. Essentially the clause covers three distinct situations, namely a term giving the seller or supplier the right to forfeit (1) a pre-contractual deposit, (2) a deposit liable to be forfeited if the consumer "cancels" and (3) a deposit liable to be forfeited if the consumer breaks the agreement. Under the general law (1) a pre-contractual deposit is recoverable by a consumer as of right if the contract does not happen, (2) a "cancellation" deposit is presumably forfeitable as of right as being the price paid by the consumer for a right not available to him or her under the general law and (3) a deposit payable on breach can be forfeited unless it amounts to a penalty. In all these cases a deposit (being a payment indicating that the consumer "means business") must be distinguished from a part-payment which the consumer can recover (subject to a set-off for damages) if the event giving rise to payment has not yet arrived.

The Regulations now provide that a deposit forfeiture clause may be unfair if it is not matched by a "reverse deposit"—a totally new concept. Here is an OFT illustration (omitting the company's name).

Before:

No order which has been accepted by (the Company) may be cancelled by (the Customer) except on terms that the customer shall indemnify (the Company) in full against any losses and costs incurred by (them) as a result of cancellation. A MINIMUM CANCELLATION CHARGE of 25% OF THE CONTRACT PRICE WILL BE PAYABLE BY THE CUSTOMER IN THE EVENT THAT (THE COMPANY) ACCEPTS SUCH CANCELLATION.

After:

> You cannot cancel an order unless you … pay any losses and costs we suffer because of the cancellation. If we cancel the contract, we must pay you any losses or costs you suffer because of the cancellation.

Readers will be familiar with cases where a cancellation charge is imposed by, *e.g.* a hotel without any attempt by them to re-let the accommodation or to calculate the costs saved by the cancellation. Such terms can now be open to challenge.

> (e) requiring any consumer who fails to fulfil his obligation to pay a disproportionately high sum in compensation;

Comment.   Under a loan agreement the *initial* rate of interest is a "core"   **9.17** provision and therefore falls outside the Regulations if it is expressed in plain, intelligible language (and it may well be that a reference to a "flat" rate without a reference to the "true" rate based on the amount from time to time outstanding could be attacked). Paragraph (e) relates to the rate of *default* interest (which might be attacked under the general law as a penalty). The word "disproportionate" must refer to the size of the transaction, the extent of the default and to the loss that this causes to the other party. The OFT have persuaded traders to reduce the amount of default interest and to replace a "termination" clause by a "suspension" clause.

> (f) authorizing the seller or supplier to dissolve the contract on a discretionary basis where the same facility is not granted to the consumer, or permitting the seller or supplier to retain the sums paid for services not yet supplied to him where it is the seller or supplier himself who dissolves the contract;

Comment.   This lack of mutuality as a key feature of unfairness has already   **9.18** been mentioned in relation to paragraph (d). An obvious example would be a clause in a policy of insurance giving the insurer (but not the insured) a discretionary right to cancel the policy during the period of insurance. The OFT give a number of illustrations of one-sided termination rights covering a wide variety of activities including blinds, computer systems, football club membership and satellite TV. In a widely publicised success story, the OFT has persuaded Sky TV to change its terms of business so that (1) Sky will have no right to terminate during the "minimum period" unless the customer is in breach and (2) more significantly, the customer will have a termination right if, for example Sky varies the conditions or withdraws one of the Channels falling within the Option chosen by the customer.

 (g) enabling the seller or supplier to terminate a contract of indeterminate duration without reasonable notice except where there are serious grounds for doing so.[11d]

9.19 **Comment.** A contract of hire or storage or a contract for the provision of accommodation may give the supplier the right to terminate without notice. Clearly such a clause, which could put the consumer into great difficulty, is potentially unfair unless serious grounds exist for it. Examples of the latter would include the consumer becoming bankrupt or his cheques being dishonoured.

 (h) Automatically extending a contract of fixed duration where the consumer does not indicate otherwise, when the deadline fixed for the consumer to express this desire not to extend the contract is unreasonably short;

9.20 **Comment.** A contract of hire or a maintenance contract for one year might provide that "this contract will be automatically extended to three years unless the consumer informs the company in the first three months that he does not wish this to occur".

In the vast majority of cases the consumer would be blissfully unaware of this provision until it was too late.

 (i) irrevocably binding the consumer to terms with which he had no real opportunity of becoming acquainted before the conclusion of the contract;

9.21 **Comment.** One obvious example would be a clause in a train ticket stating that "passengers are carried on our conditions of carriage which can be inspected at our Head Office" (see the *Thompson* case, above, para. 8.09). Then again, terms not expressed in plain, intelligible language or put in minute print could be unfair under this provision. This can be regarded as one of the most important of the Schedule 3 terms. In the words of the OFT (Bulletin 4, p. 10):

> "We interpret a 'real' opportunity as something more than the theoretical right to refer to a book held by the operator. While it is not practicable to put much information legibly on the back of a normal sized ticket, it is by no means impossible to take reasonable steps—for example by displaying posters in ticket offices—to alert consumers to, and summarise, significant provisions which they might not otherwise realise applied to them, and ignorance of which could cause them detriment.

One potential trap for consumers is the possibility that they may place an order by phone, fax or internet and then find themselves bound by conditions of sale of which they were unaware. There is a strong argument that, under general principles of contract law, the conditions will not bind the consumer because they were introduced too late (see paras 8.09–8.10, above). Quite

---

[11d] But see below, paras 9.30–9.31.

apart from this, the OFT have persuaded a supplier to give the consumer a "money-back" seven-day cancellation right for unopened and unused goods if he does not agree to the hidden conditions.

> (j) enabling the seller or supplier to alter the terms of the contract unilaterally without a valid reason which is specified in the contract[12];

Comment.   Under the general law neither party can vary the terms of a   **9.22** concluded contract, unless the contract itself gives such a right. The exercise of such a right (*e.g.* altering the duration of the contract or the time fixed for performance) would clearly undermine what the consumer expects and it may therefore be unfair.

The OFT attitude is that "any term in any kind of contract that effectively gives an unrestricted power to vary significant terms for captive consumers creates a contractual imbalance that is likely to be considered unfair." (Bulletin 5, p. 10). This was written when criticising the terms of business of Northern Rock Plc which (1) gave Northern Rock the right to restructure their customers' accounts (involving a reduction in the rates of interest) without notice to the customers and (2) prevented the customers from moving their money to another account without incurring a penalty. The OFT have now persuaded Northern Rock to change this policy. They have also persuaded BSkyB to modify a "right to vary" clause and they have persuaded a ladies' health club to delete the following term:

> We reserve the right to alter hours of business if found necessary and change the annual membership system and/or price structure.

> (k) enabling the seller or supplier to alter unilaterally without a valid reason any characteristic of the product or service to be provided;

Comment.   If a building contract specifies the materials to be used, a clause   **9.23** giving the builder the right to substitute different materials may well be unfair.

A kitchen company was persuaded to restrict a substitution clause from "if for any reason the company is unable to supply a particular piece of furniture" to "if for any reason beyond the company's reasonable control . . ." The OFT also examined the following term in the conditions of a ferry company (name has been omitted):

> The company accepts no liability for any inaccuracy in the information contained in this publication, which may be altered at any time without prior notice, and also reserves the right to alter, amend, or cancel any of the arrangements shown in this publication.

This was changed to:

> We reserve the right, **before you book**, to vary the services described in our

---

[12] See below, para. 9.32.

brochures, including prices and departure dates, and to designate a different ferry for a particular journey.

    (l) providing for the price of goods to be determined at the time of delivery or allowing a seller of goods or supplier of services to increase their price without in both cases giving the consumer the corresponding right to cancel the contract if the final price is too high in relation to the price agreed when the contract was concluded[13];

9.24   **Comment.**   It is common to find a price escalation clause as, for example, "the price quoted is the price prevailing at the date of the contract and the seller reserves the right to increase the price if this should prove necessary by reason of increases in the cost of work or materials". Such a clause may be unfair, unless it gives the consumer the option of pulling out.

The OFT have persuaded traders to modify price increase terms by (1) making the increases index linked (2) giving the customer a termination right if the price is increased or (3) improving that right. They also came across a term used by a trader with the improbable name of .0.0.0.0.0.0.1.A.A.A. Abbeyflow Ltd stating that "the quoted prices will be adjusted to meet any price variation in labour or materials occurring after the date of quotation". The term was deleted.

    (m) giving the seller or supplier the right to determine whether the goods or services supplied are in conformity with the contract, or giving him the exclusive right to interpret any term of the contract;

9.25   **Comment.**   In cases involving breach such a provision (*e.g.* "the certificate of the company's surveyor shall be conclusive") is already controlled by UCTA. Thus in relation to goods supplied to a consumer the clause would be void (see ss.6 and 7 read with s.13) while a corresponding clause relating to services would be controlled by the test of reasonableness (s.3 read with s.13). Such terms can easily mislead a consumer and Regulation 8 enables them to be modified or banned without the need for litigation.

    (n) limiting the seller's or supplier's liability to respect commitments undertaken by his agents or making his commitments subject to compliance with a particular formality;

9.26   **Comment.**   A clause might provide "we are not responsible for any statements made by our agents or employees in negotiating this contract unless authorised in writing by a director". Under the general law a clause limiting the authority of an agent is effective (see above, para. 8.33, n. 29) but in a consumer transaction the consumer is likely to rely heavily on the salesman and a "small print" clause of this type may well be unfair under the Regulations.

A common clause, which can operate unfairly, is the so-called "entire agreement" clause which effectively prevents the consumer relying on any

---

[13] See below, para. 9.34.

other document, letter or oral statement (especially promises made by an enthusiastic salesman). The matter is discussed in a five-page survey in the OFT Bulletin 2 at p. 14. An advertising company has agreed to delete a clause which bluntly stated that "no verbal agreements will be honoured" and a security company has agreed to the following plain-English variation. Before:

> All the terms of the Contract between the Company and the Customer are contained in the Contract and in these conditions and no oral or written arrangements ... not contained in the Contract shall be in any way binding on the Company.

After:

> The Company intends to rely upon the written terms set out here and on the other side of this document. If you require any changes, please make sure that you ask for these to be put in writing. In this way we can avoid any problems surrounding what the Company and you the Customer is expected to do.

> (o) obliging the consumer to fulfil all his obligations where the seller or supplier does not perform his;

Comment. The unfairness of such a provision (which overlaps with (c) **9.27** above) is self-evident.

> (p) giving the seller or supplier the possibility of transferring his rights and obligations under the contract, where this may serve to reduce the guarantees for the consumer, without the latter's agreement;

Comment. Under the general law the burden of a contract cannot be **9.28** assigned; the *assignor* remains liable to perform. If the contract does confer a right to assign obligations, the consumer might thereby lose the value of a long-term guarantee. The clause may therefore be unfair.

> (q) excluding or hindering the consumer's right to take legal action or exercise any other legal remedy, particularly by requiring the consumer to take disputes exclusively to arbitration not covered by legal provisions, unduly restricting the evidence available to him or imposing on him a burden of proof which, according to the applicable law, should lie with another party to the contract;

Comment. This provision overlaps paragraph (m) above and the ground is **9.29** already largely covered by section 13 of UCTA and by the Consumer Arbitration Act 1996 (see below, para. 10.61).

Modifications

Paragraph 2 of Schedule 3 modifies three of the preceding provisions ((g), (j) **9.30** and (l)); a clause which satisfies the modifying provisions is less likely to be unfair. However, it must be stressed that:

> "any standard term will be seen as being unfair, whether or not it appears in (or is

excluded from) the list if it fails the unfairness test in Regulation 4 ... The purpose of the Schedule is to *illustrate this test* ... Similarly, the restrictions to the scope of the Schedule found particularly in paragraph 2 ... exemplify situations in which—despite their apparent similarity to what is included in the Schedule—certain kinds of terms may nonetheless not produce 'imbalance, detriment or lack of good faith'." (OFT Bulletin 5 at p. 10.)

The modifications are set out below.

   2. Scope of sub paragraphs (g), (j) and (l):

     (a) Subparagraph (g) is without hindrance to terms by which a supplier of financial services reserves the right to terminate unilaterally a contract of indeterminate duration without notice when there is a valid reason, provided that the supplier is required to inform the other contracting party or parties thereof immediately.

9.31 **Comment.** The "valid reason" can be contrasted with "serious grounds" in paragraph (g). Presumably the reason is not limited to default or insolvency by the consumer but can include reasons personal to the lender (such as a decision to withdraw from house mortgage loans). Although the proviso is not expressed in plain, intelligible language, the spirit of the Regulations suggests that the reason must be set out as part of the termination terms.

     (b) Subparagraph (j) is without hindrance to terms under which a supplier of financial services reserves the right to alter the rate of interest payable by the consumer or due to the latter, or the amount of other charges for financial services without notice where there is a valid reason, provided that the supplier is required to inform the other contracting party or parties thereof at the earliest opportunity and that the latter are free to dissolve the contract immediately.

9.32 **Comment.** On a strict reading of this proviso (and the placing of the comma) the words "where there is a valid reason" appear to qualify the words "other charges" but not the words "rate of interest"; in other words a term that "the lender may by written notice increase the rate of interest payable to the lender or decrease the rate of interest payable to the borrower" would not be within paragraph (j) provided that it also allowed the consumer to respond to the notice by terminating the contract. This seems surprising and the French text (which omits the commas) points to a different conclusion.

     Subparagraph (j) is also without hindrance to terms under which a seller or supplier reserves the right to alter unilaterally the conditions of a contract of indeterminate duration, provided that he is required to inform the consumer with reasonable notice and that the consumer is free to dissolve the contract.

9.33 **Comment.** It will be recalled that a term may very well be unfair if it gives the supplier the right to alter the terms of the agreement and to hold the consumer to a bargain different from the one he originally made.

If the supplier finds it necessary to alter a term in a contract of indeterminate duration, this proviso allows him to insert a contractual term to that effect provided that the consumer is then given the option of walking away from the contract. This proviso is not limited to contracts for financial services.

    (c) Subparagraphs (g), (j) and (l) do not apply to:
        — transactions in transferable securities, financial instruments and other products or services where the price is linked to fluctuations in a stock exchange quotation or index or a financial market rate that the seller or supplier does not control;
        — contracts for the purchase or sale of foreign currency, traveller's cheques or international money orders denominated in foreign currency.

Comment. These two provisos permit sellers or suppliers to insert alter- **9.34** ation/termination clauses in cases where the seller/supplier's calculations can go wildly wrong as a result of share or currency fluctuations beyond his control.

    (d) Subparagraph (l) is without hindrance to price-indexation clauses, where lawful, provided that the method by which prices vary is explicitly described.

Comment. A general price escalation clause may well be unfair under **9.35** paragraph (l) above, but a clause for price adjustment by reference to (for example) the retail price index might not be caught.

Burden of Proof

The Regulations provide (reg. 3(5)) that the burden of proving that a term **9.36** was individually negotiated is on the seller/supplier. It does not deal with the burden of proving that "Schedule 3" terms are fair. Although, as already stated, the Regulations merely state that these terms "may" be unfair, one has the strong feeling that a court (and especially a county court where most of these cases are likely to be litigated) would treat such clauses as potentially unfair and would look to the seller/supplier to prove that this is not so.

Conclusion

There is a Latin maxim "*ubi ius, ibi remedium*" which basically means that **9.37** a right without a remedy is not a right at all. Whether the Regulations are to be a strong weapon or a damp squib will depend entirely on whether the enforcement machinery (see above, para. 9.03) will work effectively. The whole question of enforcement (which lies at the heart of consumer protection) is considered in the next two chapters.

Chapter Ten

"HOW DO I ENFORCE MY RIGHTS WITHOUT GOING TO COURT?"

In the previous chapters we have considered the consumer's rights and rem- **10.01**
edies and attempts to exclude them or to cut them down. We come now to the
all-important question—how can the rights be enforced? The lawyer tends to
think immediately of court proceedings but in this branch of the law the
courts should only be used as a last resort—if only because the cost of proceedings may exceed the amount in dispute.

Scheme of this chapter

A short introduction will be followed by an examination of the codes of **10.02**
practice prepared in consultation with the Office of Fair Trading—one of the
most important developments in the consumer field in recent years. This
leads on to a brief summary of proposed new legislation strengthening consumer rights and remedies in relation to public activities. Our discussion will
then focus on the Ombudsman schemes which play an increasingly significant role in consumer redress. This will be followed by sections dealing with
arbitration, alternative dispute resolution and contingency fees.

1. How to Start

The obvious first step is to contact the supplier. If the client himself does not **10.03**
receive satisfaction he might call in to see his solicitor, Citizen's Advice
Bureau, Consumer Advice Centre or the Trading Standards Department
(Consumer Protection Department) of the local authority. A letter, fax or
e-mail sent to the head office, or to the managing director, might produce
results. Alternatively, a member of the staff of the Trading Standards Department might make a telephone call or visit the shop to see what the shop has to
say. These Departments are anxious to adopt a neutral role—to play the part
of conciliator rather than advocate. They do, of course, compile lists of complaints and forward them from time to time to the Office of Fair Trading.

If the suppliers are not co-operative, the next step might be to contact their
trade association. This is especially relevant if they are members of a trade
association with a code of practice supported by the OFT. This is considered
below.

Mention must also be made of the press, both local and national, radio and
television. Many of these bodies have someone dealing with consumer mat-

ters and if they are satisfied that the consumer has had a raw deal, they will print or publish a story about it. Needless to say they will take great care to get their facts right because damages for defamation can be very high.

2. Codes of Practice

A. *Introduction*

10.04   One method of improving standards of business practice across the board is to introduce legislation (with criminal sanctions) on such matters as trade descriptions and safety.[1-2] A second method is to use subordinate legislation under Part II of the Fair Trading Act 1973 to correct particular abuses, although after an early burst of activity this procedure has fallen into disuse in the 1980s and 1990s.[3]

A third method is to leave it to the different sectors of commerce to put their own houses in order by the introduction of voluntary codes of practice by the various trade associations. The development of voluntary codes can be regarded as one of the most significant contributions which the Fair Trading Act 1973 has made to the protection of individual consumers and accordingly it may be useful to examine this topic in some detail.

Section 124(3) of the Fair Trading Act places a duty upon the Director General to encourage associations "to prepare, and to disseminate to their members, codes of practice for guidance in safeguarding and promoting the interest of consumers". So far, following negotiations with the relevant associations, the OFT has given its support to 49 codes. These include cars, electrical appliances, travel, laundries and cleaners, mail order trading and double glazing. A complete list of the codes is given in the following table; the names of the sponsoring trade associations and their addresses are set out in Appendix 1.[4] No further codes are likely to receive OFT support in the future in view of the change in policy discussed below (para. 10.07).

Operative from	Code
1974	AMDEA (Association of Manufacturers of Domestic Electrical Appliances): Principles for Domestic Electrical Appliance Servicing.
1975	ABTA (Association of British Travel Agents): Codes of Conduct.
1975	VBRA (Vehicle Builders and Repairers Association): Code of Practice for Vehicle Body Repair (Motor Car and Caravan Sector).
1976	RMI (Retail Motor Industry Federation Ltd): SMTA (Scottish Motor Trade Association): SMMT (Society of Motor Manufacturers & Traders): Code of Practice for the Motor Industry.

[1-2] See below, para. 12.01 *et seq.*
[3] Below, para. 17.06 *et seq.*
[4] Below, para. A1.01.

1976   NAMSR (National Association of Multiple Shoe Repairers):
Society of Master Shoe Repairers:
Code of Practice for Shoe Repairs.

1976   TSA (Textile Services Association Ltd):
Code of Practice for Domestic Laundry and Cleaning Services.

1976   FDF (Footwear Distributors Federation):
Code of Practice for Footwear.

1976   RETRA (Radio, Electrical and Television Retailers' Association (RETRA) Ltd):
Code of Practice for the Selling and Servicing of Electrical and Electronic Appliances.

1978   MOTA (Mail Order Traders' Association):
Catalogue Mail Order Code of Practice.

1979   Photographic Industry Code of Practice.

1980   DSA (Direct Selling Association Ltd):
Direct Selling Code of Practice.

1981   GGF (Glass and Glazing Federation):
Code of Ethical Practice.

1984   Motorcycle Code.

1987   FLA (Finance and Leasing Association):
Code of Practice.

1988   CCTA (Consumer Credit Trade Association):
Code of Practice.

1988   NCCF (National Consumer Credit Federation):
Code of Practice.

1988   CCA (Consumer Credit Association of the United Kingdom):
Code of Practice.

1989   LPFA (London Personal Finance Association Ltd):
Code of Practice.

1989   British Holiday and Home Parks Association Ltd:
National Caravan Council:
Code of Practice for Letting Holiday Caravans.
Code of Practice for Selling and Siting Holiday Caravans.

1989   SMMT (Society of Motor Manufacturers and Traders):
Code of Practice for Mechanical Breakdown Insurance Schemes.

1989   BDMA (British Direct Marketing Association Ltd):
Direct Marketing Code of Practice.

1991   CSA (Credit Services Association):
Code of Practice.

1995   BVRLA (British Vehicle Rental and Leasing Association):
Code of Conduct.

1995   BRC (British Retail Consortium):
Code of Practice for Extended Warranties on Electrical Goods.

1996   ABIA (Association of British Introduction Agencies):
Code of Practice for Introduction Agencies.

1997   STAR (Society of Ticket Agents and Retailers):
Code of Practice.

1998   OEA (Ombudsman for Estate Agents Scheme):
Code of Practice for Residential Estate Agents.

1998   NTDA (National Tyre Distributors Association):
Code of Practice for Tyre and Fast Fit Trade.

Advantages?

10.05   Whether voluntary codes are to be preferred to legislation is a matter of debate. The advantage from the point of view of industry is that traders are allowed to police themselves, but this in turn may be disadvantageous to the consumer. It is clear from the results of monitoring exercises undertaken by the OFT that, predictably, not every member of a trade association honours its code and, more surprisingly, not every trade association checks to ensure that its members follow the code.[5]

Another serious disadvantage of relying on voluntary methods is that, even if all members of an association comply with their obligations, the rogues in the trade may well not be members. This is particularly true of the motor trade. The Director General must then turn to other weapons in his armoury, *e.g.* seeking an assurance under Part III of the Fair Trading Act 1973[6] or under the Unfair Terms in Consumer Contracts Regulations 1994[6a] or refusing a credit brokerage licence under the Consumer Credit Act 1974.[7]

However, some advantages can be cited. (1) Legislation would necessarily be of a general nature and inappropriate for setting precise standards for a particular industry, for example, pre-delivery inspections of cars or service calls within three days for electrical appliances. (2) Businessmen are more likely to comply with their own optional rules than with statutory obligations imposed against their will. (3) Codes can be improved by re-negotiation; for example, the ABTA Code was amended after a year to include surcharges and overbooking, both common causes of complaint. (4) Codes go beyond the existing law, in recommending practices which impose on suppliers obligations or restrictions not otherwise attaching to them, and thus consumers' rights are enhanced; for example, the laundry code bans all exemption clauses.[8] (5) The opportunity for conciliation and arbitration affords a cheap and quick mode of resolving disputes instead of taking action in the courts.[9]

Sanctions for non-compliance

10.06   An increasingly important question is how codes of practice should be enforced. We have seen that by no means all members of a trade association adhere to the recommended practices. The most obvious way is for the trade association itself to deal with recalcitrant members. Some associations have very wide powers, including fines and expulsion, and are prepared to use

[5] On monitoring and other aspects of codes see Woodroffe, "Government Monitored Codes of Practice in the United Kingdom" (1984) 7 *Journal of Consumer Policy* 171; Cranston, *Consumers and the Law* (2nd ed.), pp. 31–42.
[6] Below, para. 17.20.
[6a] Above, para. 9.11.
[7] Below, para. 20.05.
[8] Below, para. 10.25. For further examples, see Woodroffe, n. 5, above.
[9] For an assessment of trade arbitrations, see *Simple Justice*, National Consumer Council (1979), especially pp. 71–82.

them, as can be seen from the activities of the Retail Motor Industry Federation and the Association of British Travel Agents. In contrast sponsors of the Footwear Code and the Society of Motor Manufacturers and Traders can do little more than apply the "club" threat of social ostracism by their peers.

It has been suggested, optimistically in our view, that an individual consumer may enforce a code against a member of a trade association by claiming that a breach of contract occurs when a trader fails to comply with a practice, on the basis that the contract includes an implied term that the trader will comply with the code. In view of the limitations placed by the courts on implied terms such a plea is unlikely to succeed.[10] Of course, it is possible for a consumer to incorporate a code expressly when making the contract, but it would be unrealistic to expect all but the most enthusiastic and well-informed consumers to remember to refer to the point in their conversation when taking a pair of shoes for repair or a car for servicing.

In contrast, the criminal law may provide a more hopeful route following the 1980 decision in *Shropshire County Council Trading Standards Department v. Telford (Vehicles) Ltd*: a motor dealer was convicted by the Wrekin magistrates' court of an offence under section 14 of the Trade Descriptions Act 1968 for failing to comply with the Motor Industry Code of Practice although stating that he subscribed to the code.[11]

On the assumption that self-regulation is not as effective a method of controlling business suppliers as it should be, two solutions have been canvassed to give teeth to the codes. The less ambitious proposal was to amend section 34 of the Fair Trading Act 1973[12] so as to extend the definition of "unfair" beyond contravention of criminal and civil duties to include non-compliance with a code of practice supported by the OFT. The virtue of such a change would be that the codes would then be made to apply to *all* members of a particular trade, not merely those who choose to join a trade association. This very change was recommended by the National Consumer Council in 1997 in its report *Unfair Trading*.

A much more far-reaching proposal, embracing the extension of section 34, is to impose on traders a statutory "duty to trade fairly". A suggestion to this effect was put forward by Lord Borrie, the then Director General of Fair Trading, in a lecture[13] discussing the self-regulatory system of advertising control:

"The duty not to publish misleading advertisements could be seen as a precursor to a more general statutory duty to trade fairly in consumer transactions, a duty which would not be enforceable apart from sectoral or general retail codes of practice giving it practical expression. Such codes could be prepared by the

[10] The narrow "business efficacy" test in *The Moorcock* (1889) 14 P.D. 64.
[11] Unreported. See Lawson, *The Supply of Goods and Services Act 1982*, p. 131.
[12] Discussed in Chap. 17, below, para. 17.23.
[13] "Laws and Codes for Consumers" [1980] J.B.L. 315 at 324.

DGFT after consultation with relevant trade associations and the codes would need to be given some form of ministerial or parliamentary approval before becoming effective. Under Part III of the Fair Trading Act, persistent breaches of the new statutory duty could result in the DGFT requiring assurances or court orders and, of course, the new statutory duty would be applicable to all traders and not just those who belong to the relevant trade associations. It would be for consideration whether the statutory duty should also be enforceable: (i) by local authorities, or by the DGFT in respect of individual breaches, and (ii) by an individual seeking damages against a trader. In both cases the court would presumably need to look at the codes for guidance when interpreting the duty."

The Office of Fair Trading floated the idea in March 1982 in *Home Improvements: A Discussion Paper* and followed this up in 1986 with a discussion paper *A General Duty to Trade Fairly*. However, it is no surprise to discover that such a bold approach was not welcomed by industry in a period of free market economy. Indeed the Government's policy at the time can be discerned from the titles of two White Papers—*Lifting the Burden* and *Building Business ... not Barriers*.[14] In the end the Director General reluctantly admitted in *Trading Malpractices*[15] that "the original proposals were over-ambitious in aiming in one provision both to raise trading standards generally and to improve the prospects for consumer redress" and came down in favour of a complete overhaul of Part III of the Fair Trading Act 1973. The latest proposals are discussed in Chapter 17 (below, para. 17.23).

"Raising Standards" and future policy

10.07   The early optimism engendered by self-regulation and the proliferation of codes supported by the OFT has subsided in the late 1990s. At the end of 1996 the OFT issued a consultation paper *Voluntary Codes of Practice*. This was followed in February 1998 with its report *Raising Standards of Consumer Care—Progressing beyond codes of practice*. In his foreword John Bridgeman, the Director General of Fair Trading, strikes a cautionary note:

"While not perfect, the standards within the codes of practice I support contain examples of businesses setting themselves demanding targets to give their customers a fair deal. The practical operation of these codes is far less satisfactory, as the responses to my Office's earlier consultation paper showed. Too many businesses can operate to inferior standards and consumers can find it hard to distinguish the better trader from the rest."

The OFT's probable change in policy is set out on p. 5 of the report:

The main change suggested is to introduce standards to replace codes, with a core standard applicable to all business and sectoral versions where necessary. A

---

[14] Cmnd. 9571 (1985) and Cm. 9794 (1986) respectively.
[15] OFT (July 1990), para. 1.5. The arguments for and against the general duty appear on p. 21. The duty is not unlike the European concept of "good faith". See above, para. 9.08.

key element would be access to effective, low-cost independent redress, without recourse to the courts. The standards would be drawn up under the British Standards Institution, and all those with a direct interest would participate. To administer the new scheme, the OFT proposes the creation of a new approval body that would vet all applicants, monitor their behaviour and deal with complaints. Successful applicants would be required to agree to follow the relevant standard. In return, they would be able to use a new, cross-sectoral quality logo. The logo and the underlying scheme should quickly become familiar to the vast majority of consumers in the United Kingdom. The scheme would have the potential to allow traders offering a higher level of service to be distinguished from competitors and to reap the appropriate commercial rewards.

These proposals were discussed at an OFT-sponsored conference in Cambridge in September 1998, on which the OFT published a report in February 1999. This promised a further report "in the next few months". However, further progress is now on hold because the Secretary of State for Trade and Industry announced in March that the Government will publish a White Paper in the summer setting out the Government's Consumer Strategy. This will have three strands:

- Better information for consumers on their rights and to help them make well-informed decisions;
- Effective enforcement of consumer protection laws to drive out rogue traders; and
- Better assurance of redress.

We await the proposals for legislative reform with interest.

Conciliation

All the codes provide conciliation procedures and most provide arbitration **10.08** as a last resort. Generally conciliation procedures conform to the same pattern (suggested in Pt. 1 of this chapter). Dissatisfied customers should first bring their complaints to the attention of the manager, partner, proprietor or director of the business. If the complaint is not resolved, then it may be appropriate to seek the help of a trading standards officer, Consumer Advice Centre or Citizens' Advice Bureau. If the complaint relates to new goods, the customer may agree to the manufacturer being brought in. Where the dispute is still not settled and the trader is a member of a trade association, the customer should ask the association to conciliate. No charge is made for this service.

However, it should be remembered that the association may appear to the consumer, rightly or wrongly, to lack impartiality and to be prejudiced in favour of its own member.[15a] If only for this reason an opportunity to put the matter before a truly independent arbitrator is valuable where conciliation fails.

[15a] cf. Ombudsmen schemes, where independence and impartiality are prerequisites to membership of BIOA (below, para. 10.55).

Arbitration

10.09   Where a code provides for arbitration, the customer is required to pay a fee of about £40, often refundable where the claim is upheld: this is the limit of liability where the arbitration is on the basis of "documents only". The fee does not cover the full cost of arbitration, the balance being borne by the trade association. The arbitrator will usually be appointed by the Chartered Institute of Arbitrators. Normally the arbitration will be "documents only". The expense of attended oral arbitrations is so great that they are discouraged both by the associations and by the Director General, for the purpose of writing arbitration procedures into the codes is to provide an inexpensive and quick adjudication of the dispute.

To discover how well these arrangements for settling consumer disputes were working the OFT undertook a review in 1980 and published the conclusions in December 1981 in *Redress Procedures under Codes of Practice*.[16] The main conclusions of the report were that arbitration should be on a documents-only basis, as litigants desiring an attended hearing may always resort to the County Court arbitration scheme; that in view of the concern expressed about the slow progress of both the conciliation and arbitration stages, targets should be set of a maximum of three months for the conciliation stage dealt with by the trade associations and 12 weeks for the arbitration stage if undertaken by the Institute of Arbitrators (28 days for the claimant to submit details of the claim, 28 days for the respondent to reply and 28 days for the arbitrator to deliver his decision); that arbitrators should always give reasons for their decisions; and that a standard scale of arbitration fees be introduced. As a result a new "model" arbitration scheme was developed by the Institute in consultation with the OFT who in September 1983 made it known that the Institute would be contacting various trade associations with a view to amending their arbitration arrangements accordingly.

Publicity

10.10   It is not enough to introduce legislation and codes of practice to bolster the consumer in his perpetual confrontation with the business world. Such rights are useless unless he knows of them and can exercise them. To ensure that as far as possible the consumer is made aware of his rights the Director General is empowered by section 124(1) to arrange for the publication "of such information and advice as it may appear to him to be expedient to give to consumers" in so far as the matters fall within his duties under section 2(1).[17] From its inception the OFT has enthusiastically exercised this power.

---

[16] A recent NCC report on research into arbitration schemes, *Out of Court*, is discussed by Goriely in (1991) N.L.J. 535.

[17] *cf.* the Consumer Credit Act 1974, s.4, which imposes a *duty* on the Director to disseminate information and advice about the operation of the Act and the credit facilities available to the public.

Numerous pamphlets and posters are available free of charge to inform the consumer and trader of their respective rights and obligations in respect of goods or services.

It is difficult to know whether the effect of consumer legislation and the codes has been to improve the quality of goods and services. The statistics given in the Director General's Annual Reports show a fairly steady level of complaints running at about 600,000 a year during the 1970s and 1980s. For example, there were 591,000 complaints in 1976–1977 and 623,000 in 1988–1989, an increase of 5 per cent. The 1993 Annual Report revealed that 769,518 complaints were received by trading standards departments and Citizens Advice Bureaux in 1992–1993, an increase of 10.5 per cent over the previous year. This upward trend has continued—the 1998 Annual Report discloses that consumer complaints notified to the OFT increased by 17 per cent over the intervening five years to 896,901 for the year ending September 30, 1998. What is significant is that "research indicated that only about one per cent of people who felt they had a reason to complain about goods or services" sought the help of these agencies.[18] Clearly the reported figures are merely the tip of the iceberg.

The main culprits have regularly been motor vehicles, furniture and floor coverings, household appliances and electronic equipment, and clothing and footwear, with secondhand cars usually taking the gold or silver medal. One area giving an increasingly major headache to consumers, particularly in view of the large sums of money usually at risk, is that of home improvements (including double glazing); it continues to figure prominently in the top ten of this unenviable "top of the pops".

B. *Particular codes*

Caravans

There are two codes drawn up in 1989 by the British Holiday and Home Parks Association Ltd and the National Caravan Council. One relates to letting and the other to selling and siting holiday caravans, *i.e.* permanently sited on a park licensed for recreational use (not mobile homes). **10.11**

Letting Code

The Code of Practice for Letting Holiday Caravans is binding on members of the two trade associations mentioned above whether they let caravans owned by themselves (as park owners) or as agents for individual owners. The main provisions are these: **10.12**

Caravan park. Facilities must be well maintained with staff available during all reasonable hours.

[18] OFT Press Release, June 27, 1991.

Caravans. They must be in good condition with equipment functioning properly. They should be thoroughly cleaned between hirings. Breakages should be replaced and gas supplies maintained.

Information. The owner must send to enquirers detailed information on park facilities, caravan type and equipment (the appendix to the code gives a suggested list), and the charges, including additional charges for swimming pools, insurance, etc.

Disclaimers. If they are void under the Unfair Contract Terms Act 1977, they are prohibited; otherwise they are apparently permissible. Thus a disclaimer relating to damage or loss of property caused by negligence may be introduced into the contract.

Complaints. Free conciliation, and low cost, documents-only arbitration are available.

Selling and Siting Code

10.13   The Code of Practice for Selling and Siting Holiday Caravans is to protect the caravan owner in his dealings with the park owner.

Sale of caravan. If a prospective buyer will have to sub-let his caravan as a condition of the purchase, he must be given detailed information before making a binding contract.

Written agreement. On the first purchase of a caravan the buyer must be offered a written agreement to occupy a pitch for at least five years, renewable annually for another five years provided the caravan is in good condition. A long list is set out of the contents of the agreement, including the right of the caravan owner to assign the pitch to a buyer of the caravan: such resale of caravans is specially provided for.

Complaints. The procedures are the same as in the Letting Code.

Cars

10.14   There are four codes:[18a]

> Code of Practice for the Motor Industry
> VBRA Code of Practice for Vehicle Body Repair
> Mechanical Breakdown Insurance.
> Vehicle Rental.

[18a] The Tyre Code is discussed below, para. 10.51.

The Motor Industry Code[19]

This Code was drawn up by the Retail Motor Industry Federation (RMI), **10.15**
the Scottish Motor Trade Association (SMTA) and the Society of Motor
Manufacturers and Traders (SMMT). It governs the conduct of manufacturers, importers, distributors and retail dealers. It covers the supply of new
and used cars, petrol, parts and accessories, and servicing and repair. Its main
provisions are set out below.

New cars. Dealers should carry out the pre-delivery inspection required by
the manufacturer and give a copy of the PDI check list to the customer. Order
forms must make clear the total price payable to put the car on the road and
their conditions must be fair and reasonable.

Manufacturers' warranties. The dealer should draw the terms of the warranty to the attention of the consumer. It must state that it does not adversely
affect the consumer's remedies against the seller.[20] Transfer to subsequent
owners should be allowed. The consumer may take the car to any franchised
dealer for rectification work. An extension of the warranty period may be
given when the car has been off the road for an extended period or if faults
worked upon during the warranty period recur later.

Used cars. Dealers are reminded of their obligations under the Sale of
Goods Act 1979. Guarantees should not purport to take away the consumer's
rights and should state that they are in addition to his statutory rights.[21] Copies
of information provided by previous owners about the car's history should be
passed on, *e.g.* service records. Advice is given about odometers and the form
of disclaimer to be used. (These aspects are of great practical importance
under the Trade Descriptions Act 1968.)[22]

One major effect of the 1981 revision of the code was to strengthen the
requirements about pre-sales inspections. The dealer should inspect the car
before sale in accordance with an approved checklist, which should be completed and displayed in a prominent place in the car[23]; a copy should be given
to the customer. (This is generally known as a PSIR—pre-sales information
report.) Unfortunately only a minority of RMI members complied with this
procedure, prompting the Director General of Fair Trading to make the following remarks in his 1982 Annual Report:

> "It seems to me in this instance that self-regulation is *not* an effective substitute
> for law and that if, as I believe, there is a strong case for consumers to be given a

---

[19] Revised in 1981. Reproduced in an Appendix to previous editions of this book.
[20] This is a statutory requirement under the Consumer Transactions (Restrictions on Statements)
Order 1976: see below, para. 17.14.
[21] See n. 20.
[22] Below, para. 13.21.
[23] Such a system operates in a number of states of the USA, *e.g.* Wisconsin.

more detailed written description of a used car at the point of sale than is common now, it must be done by law and therefore be enforceable against *all* used car dealers."

The OFT report *The Motor Code—A Report on a Monitoring Survey* in September 1986 disclosed that still only 20 per cent of members displayed the checklist.

Servicing.   A distinction is drawn between quotations and estimates. Although the words "estimate" and "quotation" generally have no well-settled legal meaning, the code clarifies their use in this context, "an estimate is a considered approximation of the likely cost involved whereas a quotation constitutes a firm price for which the work will be done". A firm quotation should be given for a major repair. Where estimates are given, it should be made clear that they are only estimates. In either case the VAT position must be clarified. If a charge is to be made for the estimate, for example, to cover dismantling, the consumer should be notified in advance. No attempt should be made to exclude liability for loss or damage to cars or contents[24] which must be adequately protected and insured. Repairs must be guaranteed for a specific mileage or period.

Complaints.   The following procedure is laid down:

(a) First refer the complaint to the dealer, addressing it to a senior executive, director, partner or proprietor.
(b) If it relates to a new car warranty and the dealer does not resolve the matter, contact the manufacturer direct.
(c) If no satisfactory solution is reached, write to the relevant trade association provided the dealer is a member:
    new car warranty claim—SMMT
    dealer in Scotland—SMTA
    dealer in the rest of the United Kingdom—RMI.
(d) The trade association will try to effect a settlement between the consumer and its member.
(e) If conciliation fails, the association will arrange for arbitration. The arbitration will normally be "documents only"—the cost of oral arbitration is prohibitive. A written award is made which is enforceable in the courts.
(f) Consumers must be advised that they may sue in the courts instead of choosing arbitration.

Monitoring.   The trade associations are required to analyse all complaints

---

[24] Such a clause would be controlled by the Unfair Contract Terms Act 1977, ss.2 and 3: see above, para. 8.23.

about the code or other matters referred to them for conciliation or arbitration.

Body repairs[25]

The VBRA Code of Practice for Vehicle Body Repair is, as its title dis-   **10.16**
closes, much more limited in its scope than the Motor Industry Code. In cases where the garage is a member of both the RMI and VBRA, the consumer will have the benefit of both codes where a body repair is involved.

In many respects it is similar to the Motor Industry Code. It deals with estimates. Guarantees must last for at least 12 months or 12,000 miles, whichever occurs first, and be transferable to later owners.

The complaints procedure follows the pattern outlined earlier. First complain to the trader. Next seek the advice of a trading standards officer, CAB, Consumer Advice Centre, etc. Then proceed to use the VBRA Conciliation Service under which the complaint may be referred to an independent examiner appointed by the Institute of Automotive Engineer Assessors. No fee is payable for conciliation. If a member has ceased trading and cannot comply with a settlement recommended under the Conciliation Service, the association will pay up from its "Contingency Fund" established for the purpose.

As a last resort arbitration is available. It is normally on a "documents only" basis.

Mechanical breakdown insurance

The third of the codes relating to vehicles was drawn up by the SMMT in   **10.17**
1989: The Code of Practice for Mechanical Breakdown Insurance Schemes.

Insurers.   All schemes must be underwritten by an authorised insurer or Lloyds.

Policy.   The policy must be written as a direct contract between the consumer and the insurer (in some schemes it has been difficult to work out against whom the consumer's rights lie). The documentation given to the consumer must set out the contractual position in a clearly displayed panel.

Assignment.   The policy should be transferable to a subsequent owner, if the insurer approves: the latter point weakens this aspect.

Claims.   Consumers must be informed of the result of their claims within seven days, if possible.

Complaints.   Conciliation is provided by the SMMT. However, after that

---

[25] Revised 1989 following a *The Motor Code—A Report on a Monitoring Survey* published by the OFT in November 1986.

the consumer will have to turn to the relevant insurance body. Ultimately the Insurance Ombudsman may be asked to adjudicate.

Vehicle rental

10.18   The last of the four car codes was introduced in 1995. The British Vehicle Rental and Leasing Association's Code of Conduct covers cars and commercial vehicles.

Age or mileage.   Cars should have been bought new and be less than three years old with under 60,000 miles on the clock. Commercial vehicles' history varies with the weight, *e.g.* up to 1.8 tonnes, 85,000 maximum mileage (age is not specified here).

Complaints.   Staff should "adopt a friendly, positive approach"! Complaints should usually be resolved within 15 working days. Conciliation by the BVRLA's Conciliation Committee comes next, with its decision given to the customer within 30 working days. Arbitration is not mentioned.

Credit

10.19   There are six Codes of Practice relating to credit. The first five cover the relationship of creditors and debtors, contain virtually identical provisions and so will be explained together. They regulate the business operations of the following associations:

> Finance & Leasing Association
> Consumer Credit Trade Association
> National Consumer Credit Federation
> Consumer Credit Association of the U.K.
> London Personal Finance Association.

The sixth code of the Credit Services Association is concerned with debt collection and will be explained separately.

In broad terms the five codes require the associations' numerous members to comply with legislation and to conduct their businesses with integrity. The following obligations are noteworthy at a time when thousands of debtors are finding it difficult to cope with their financial commitments.

Plain English.   So that they are readily intelligible, all communications and agreements should be in plain English. This is now a crucial factor in view of the Unfair Terms in Consumer Contracts Regulations 1994.[26]

Credit brokers.   A member must satisfy itself that credit-brokers have

---

[26] See above, para. 9.09.

integrity and competence. Clearly it is in the interest of creditors to vet such intermediaries carefully, if only as a matter of self-interest, *e.g.* in view of their possible liability under section 75 of the Consumer Credit Act 1974.[27]

Ability to repay.   A frequent criticism of moneylenders is that they tempt the improvident into borrowing more than they can afford. The codes state that members must not pressurise customers into loans which they may find difficult to repay. Before granting credit they should take "all reasonable steps to satisfy themselves as to the customer's ability to repay". Particular care should be taken in relation to young applicants.

Complaints.   Conciliation is available as a first resort, after the chief executive of the member has considered the complaint. Then the usual "documents only" arbitration comes into play.

Debt collection

Members of the Credit Services Association are businesses which as agents collect debts for their clients from consumers or business debtors. Its Code of Practice contains provisions dealing with the conduct of members in relation to their business clients as well as the following provisions to protect consumer debtors.   **10.20**

The Code requires members to respond sympathetically to consumers in financial difficulties and its Guidelines require them to accept all reasonable offers to pay by instalments.

The Guidelines prohibit such infamous practices as parking outside the debtor's house a vehicle displaying "Debt Collectors" on its side—members must not embarrass debtors or disclose their indebtedness to neighbours, relatives or employers. Nor may members falsely imply that civil action has been instituted—collection letters sometimes look remarkably similar in colour and style to a County Court claim form.

For complaints, conciliation is available and then a disciplinary committee of the Association's Council may become involved. Arbitration is not available.

Direct marketing

The various activities described as "direct marketing" are covered by a code drawn up jointly in 1989 by the British Direct Marketing Association (BDMA) and the Association of Mail Order Publishers (MOPA). These Associations adopted a separate version for each as there are some minor differences to suit the individual constitutions of the two bodies.   **10.21**

As the meaning of "direct marketing" is not self-evident we give the explanation set out in Annex 2 of each code:

---

[27] Below, para. 23.05.

Marketing comprises the whole range of activities in providing the public with goods and services. **Direct Marketing** has the same broad function except that it requires the existence and maintenance of a database of information to record names of customers, actual and potential; and to provide the means for continuing direct communication with the customer. It may take place where the buyer responds to the seller's advertisement in a newspaper, on television or on the radio, or by postal advertising; it may take place when the seller contacts the buyer—direct selling; it may take place when the buyer contacts the seller and places an order by post; it may take place where the advertiser makes use of a mailing list.

This includes mail order selling, but is confined to the supply of books and records, *e.g.* by book clubs, the Reader's Digest.

Two other codes should be borne in mind in this area of activity:

The MOTA Code relating to *mail order catalogue* trading[28]
The DSA Code relating to *party plan* selling.[29]

As the BDMA and MOPA versions of the code are so similar, we shall deal with them together and pick out just a few features of these lengthy documents.

Samples.   Samples of goods, including bespoke or made-to-measure goods, should be available for public inspection.

Free gifts and prizes.   In view of the prevalence of these inducements, special rules are set out concerning free gifts, premiums, prize draws and competitions: the last two items have special appendices devoted to them.

On approval.   If goods are offered on "free" approval or trial, return postage and carriage must be refunded.

Prepayments.   The name and address of the member must be given. Orders must normally be despatched within 28 days.

Club schemes.   There are special rules for club schemes (*e.g.* book clubs) and for a continuing series with an open-ended commitment.

Collectables.   Advertisements for facsimiles of swords, antique guns, etc., or other "collectibles" [*sic*], where emphasis is placed on their scarcity or aesthetic quality, are dealt with in an appendix.

Telephone selling.   Guidelines on telephone marketing appear in an appendix.

---

[28] Below, para. 10.32.
[29] Below, para. 10.23.

Complaints. The BDMA has its own free conciliation service, but no arbitration scheme. The MOPA code is supervised and monitored by the Mail Order Publishers' Authority (MOPA) under an independent chairman, not by the Association itself. MOPA has a free conciliation scheme and arrangements for arbitration by the Chartered Institute of Arbitrators.

E.C. Distance Selling Directive

When the Directive on the Protection of Consumers in respect of Distance **10.22** Contracts (Directive 97/7/EC) is implemented—and this must happen by June 4, 2000—self-regulation of mail order and other distance contracts will be overtaken by legislation.

Distance contract. This is defined in Article 2 and means that the business supplier and private consumer make the contract "without the simultaneous physical presence" of the parties. Annex 1 gives some examples, *e.g.* printed matter, catalogue, telephone, e-mail, fax, teleshopping.

Prior information. Article 4 entitles the consumer to specified information "in good time prior to the conclusion" of the contract, *e.g.* identity of supplier, main characteristics of the goods or services, prove, delivery costs, right of withdrawal. It must be provided "in a clear and comprehensible manner", but not necessarily in writing—it may be a telephone call.

Written confirmation. Article 5 provides that the consumer must receive, at the latest at the time of delivery, confirmation in writing or "in another durable medium available" to him (unless already given in such form) most of the prior information, and also additional matters such as after-sales service.

Right of withdrawal. A cooling off period of seven working days is given by Article 6. The consumer may have to pay the cost of returning goods, but nothing else. The right is excluded in certain cases, *e.g.* personalised goods (engraved pewter tankard), software unsealed after purchase, magazines.

Performance. The supplier has 30 days after the day when the order was "forwarded" to execute the order, unless otherwise agreed. The Department of Trade and Industry put out a consultation paper *Distance Selling* in June 1998 proposing options and seeking views on the implementation of the Directive. This will be done by Regulations made under the European Communities Act 1972, s.2(2).

Direct selling

The Direct Selling Code of Practice was drawn up in 1980 by the Direct **10.23**

Selling Association in consultation with the Office of Fair Trading after an OFT study had identified consumer problems arising out of party plan selling.

Liability insurance.   Suppliers should have adequate public liability and product liability insurance and indemnify the hostesses against any claims arising out of such parties.

Cancellation and deposits.   Members should not insist on payment in full when the order is placed. Customers are given a 14-day cancellation period; any deposit is then to be refunded. However, customers may now be in a better position by reason of the Consumer Protection (Cancellation of Contracts Concluded away from Business Premises) Regulations 1987.[31–32]

Copies.   A copy of the order should be given to the customer when it is placed. Copies of the code should be available for inspection.

Complaints.   There is an unusual complaints procedure which is an improvement on the usual conciliation procedure, although no arbitration scheme is included. Initially a complaint will be referred to the Association. If it is not resolved by the chief executive of the member company within 21 days, it passes to the Association's Code Administrator, a post created especially for this purpose. Unlike arbitration, however, if the customer is dissatisfied with the Administrator's decision, it is still open to him to seek redress in the county court. Failure by a member to comply with his decision could lead to expulsion from the DSA.

Double glazing

10.24   The home improvement sector has figured prominently in consumer complaints in recent years. Double glazing contractors appear to have been one of the main causes of dissatisfaction. The Office of Fair Trading has identified the main problems as high-pressure salesmanship, delays in installation, unexpected price increases, lost deposits and poor workmanship. Accordingly, a Code of Ethical Practice was introduced by the Glass and Glazing Federation in November 1981.[33]

Cancellation.   Whether or not credit is involved, a customer may cancel a contract. The code points out that the statutory rights must be notified to the customer: here again the 1987 Regulations should be considered.[34]

[31–32] See above, para. 6.04.
[33] Revised 1988.
[34] See n. 31, above.

Price. If after placing an order a survey by the contractor reveals that additional work is required, thus increasing the price, the customer may cancel the contract with a refund of the deposit.

Deposits. A supplier taking deposits must be covered by the GGF Deposit Indemnity Fund. If a member cannot carry out work for which a deposit has been taken, the GGF will arrange for the work to be completed at a fair price or refund the deposit. This covers deposits up to £2,500.

Quotations. A written quotation should be given to a customer where the contract is negotiated away from business premises.

Quality and guarantees. The material should conform to relevant BSI and GGF standards. The guarantee period should be clearly stated.

Delivery dates. These provisions are not of much benefit to consumers. Although suppliers should quote a completion date, it is not to be of the essence of the contract unless otherwise agreed. If it is not met, the customer can give notice making time of the essence and the code itself provides that six weeks' notice "would be reasonable". (The customer could do this in any case, and at common law reasonable notice might be even shorter.[35]) At the end of the six week period the customer may cancel "without penalty to the householder". Of course the customer should not be liable to the supplier, for the supplier himself has broken the contract by failure to perform on time! These rights must be set out in customers' contracts.

Complaints. The code has the normal complaints procedure including conciliation and low cost, documents only arbitration.

Dry cleaners and laundries

The Code of Practice for Domestic Laundry and Cleaning Services was **10.25** drawn up by the Textile Services Association.

Exclusion clauses. Members will not exclude or limit their liability for negligence.[36] They will reprocess free of charge any article which has been processed unsatisfactorily due to their fault. Where loss or damage is caused by fire or burglary, even though the trader is not negligent, compensation will be paid unless the customer has his own insurance cover; this goes beyond the supplier's legal liability for negligence.

Prices. A list of prices for standard articles should be displayed.

[35] Above, para. 6.28.
[36] See above, n. 24.

Delay.   Where an article has been mislaid and not returned within a reasonable time, a reduction in the charge is recommended to compensate for the customer's inconvenience.

Complaints.   The TSA has a Customer Advisory Service to which unresolved complaints should be referred in writing. If the TSA considers that a laboratory test is necessary, this will be made free of charge; otherwise a fee is payable. Arbitration is not available.

Electrical goods

10.26   There are three codes:

RETRA Code of Practice for the Selling and Servicing of Electrical and Electronic Appliances.
AMDEA Principles for Domestic Electrical Appliance Servicing.
British Retail Consortium Code of Practice on Extended Warranties on Electrical Goods

In the trade such goods fall into two categories: "white goods", *i.e.* domestic appliances, such as washing machines, refrigerators, cookers and toasters; and "brown goods" such as radios, televisions and stereo systems. All the codes cover white goods; only the AMDEA code does not include brown goods as well.

RETRA Selling and Servicing Code

10.27   The Radio, Electrical and Television Retailers' Association (RETRA) is an association of retailers and represents thousands of shops. The code covers both the sale of goods and their servicing and repair. The following are some of its more important provisions.

Sale of goods.   Prices should be clearly indicated. Refunds are encouraged even where a customer has simply changed his mind and has no right to his money back. Where a retailer receives a deposit, he should indicate the delivery period and, if delivery is not made in time, offer the customer a refund.
A guarantee of new goods must be given, covering parts and labour for a minimum period of a year. This is additional to the buyer's rights under the Sale of Goods Act 1979 and under any manufacturer's guarantee. If the retailer cannot effect a repair within 15 working days from the date of notification of the defect, he should normally lend a similar item or, if this is impracticable, extend the guarantee period. Where a customer moves away, the guarantee should be transferred on request to a local retailer.

Repairs and servicing.   The retailer should accept for repair goods sold by him but not necessarily other goods (*e.g.* bought from a rival discount store?).

Customers will be told the minimum service charge when they ask for service. Estimates should be offered in the case of major repairs. The code points out that quotations when accepted constitute a contract binding upon both parties. Customers are encouraged to return faulty goods to the workshop, which should be so organised as to be able to complete 80 per cent of all repairs within five working days.

Where they request a visit, this should be made within three working days; if the repair cannot be effected then, it should normally be completed within a further 15 working days. (Is the association's aim of providing prompt and efficient after-sales service fulfilled when it may take three weeks to repair such essential equipment as a washing machine?) The retailer will guarantee repairs on products outside the normal guarantee period for three months for parts and labour.

Life expectancy.   The code states that "most electronic equipment can be expected to last about seven years and in certain cases this period may be longer". Presumably "electronic equipment" means brown goods. It is arguable that this provides a guide as to the meaning of "satisfactory quality" in this context, *i.e.* that the retailer will be liable if the goods prove to be beyond economic repair within that period.

No guide is given in respect of the life expectancy of domestic appliances. However, a table is included of the availability of functional parts after the date when production of the appliance ceases, which at least gives an indication of the durability of the appliances in the list. "Functional parts" are electrical and mechanical parts which are essential to the continued operation and safety of the appliance.

Small appliances.	5–8 years
Cleaners, direct acting space heaters, refrigerators and freezers, spin and tumble driers and wash boilers.	8 years
Cookers, dishwashers, washing machines.	10 years
Thermal storage space heating.	15 years

Complaints.   The now familiar sequence is suggested. First, complain to the retailer or service agent. Next try the CAB, trading standards officer or Consumer Advice Centre. Finally, complain in writing to the Secretary of RETRA under its Conciliation Service. If he cannot resolve the dispute, it may be referred to the RETRA Conciliation Panel. No fee is payable. However, arbitration is not available. If conciliation is unsuccessful, the customer will have to resort to the courts.

AMDEA Servicing Code

The code of the Association of Manufacturers of Domestic Electrical   **10.28**

Appliances (AMDEA) covers only "white" goods. Its aim is to ensure that users of domestic appliances receive the same high standard of service whatever the source of the product and whether the service is provided directly by the manufacturer or indirectly by major retailers or specialised servicing organisations.

Its provisions are similar to the RETRA code, but there are some detailed differences, *e.g.* guarantees. The main improvements made in 1984 were: (1) the first home repair visit should be made within three working days "wherever possible"; (2) the customer should be notified of minimum charges at the outset and be given a written quotation on request; (3) repairs should be guaranteed for 12 months (except "small appliances," three months only).

It improves on the RETRA code in one respect, namely by offering independent arbitration, not merely conciliation, for a "nominal fee". It is on a documents only basis.

Extended warranties

10.29   Both manufacturers[37] and retailers offer extended warranties or guarantees on electrical goods. Often manufacturers give better value and consumers need to check which is cheaper before committing themselves, bearing in mind that goods must be of satisfactory quality and durable[38] and also that manufacturers usually give a free guarantee for at least a year.

For years consumer organisations have expressed anxiety about retailers' selling methods. Are consumers aware of their statutory rights? Are they sold warranties to give them "peace of mind" without realising that often most of the cost of the warranty goes into the pocket of the retailer as commission for arranging the insurance rather than into a pot to cover maintenance and repairs?

After publication in 1994 of its Report on *Extended Warranties on Electrical Goods* the Office of Fair Trading invited the British Retail Consortium to develop a code of practice. The code described below is also supported by RETRA and the Association of British Insurers. Not surprisingly it has some similarities with the Code of Practice for Mechanical Breakdown Insurance schemes for cars (above, para. 10.17).

Point of sale.   Retailers must draw attention by notices to their range of warranties, including manufacturers'. They should clearly display leaflets with information about, *e.g.* prices, period of cover, whether the warranty is insured and the cancellation period. Sales staff must not apply undue pressure.

Documentation.   Warranty contracts must contain the above information

---

[37] See above, para. 5.03, on the legal effect of manufacturers' guarantees.
[38] See above, para. 4.15.

and state with whom the contract is being made. They should indicate how disputes are dealt with, *e.g.* by the Insurance Ombudsman.

Monitoring. Retailers must provide annually information about complaints to their trade associations, which in turn must submit an annual report to the OFT on the operation of the Code.

Estate agents

The Residential Estate Agency Code of Practice for the Ombudsman for Estate Agents (OEA) Scheme is unique among the codes supported by the OFT in that it was prepared by an Ombudsman Scheme. Initially it covered corporate estate agents only, *e.g.* the national agencies owned by building societies. The OEA since 1998 is open to independent residential estate agents who have chosen to join the OEA; the Code applies to them too. **10.30**

Further, members of the following three associations are in effect bound by the Code, even though they may have chosen not to belong to the OEA; for each of the associations has adopted a code identical to the OEA Code.

Incorporated Society of Valuers and Auctioneers (ISVA)
National Association of Estate Agents (NAEA)
Royal Institution of Chartered Surveyors (RICS).

The Code applies only to residential buildings sold with vacant possession. It protects the public against many malpractices hitherto rife in this sector. Of its many, detailed and valuable provisions we highlight the following.

Instructions. Agents must give their clients written details of their fees and expenses. The fees will be due only if a purchaser contracts to buy the property, unless otherwise stated. Phrases such as "sole agency" must be explained in writing. They must not misrepresent the value of the property to gain instructions—asking prices must reflect market conditions.

Offers. They must tell clients quickly about all offers. When an offer is accepted subject to contract, they must ask the seller whether to withdraw it from the market; if it is not withdrawn, they must advise the buyer in writing.

Conflict of interest. The common malpractice of agents buying properties from their clients surreptitiously, perhaps through a nominee, is banned: they must inform the client and his solicitor in writing, before negotiations begin, of the conflict.

Introduction agencies

The Code of Practice for Introduction Agencies covers dating agencies **10.31** and marriage bureaux—in the latter case the main objective is to find a spouse. It applies to members of the Association of British Introduction Agencies (ABIA).

Information.   Before the agreement is made the client must be given a copy of the Code and a description of the service and fees.

Number of introductions.   The agency must give clients a realistic indication of the likely number of introductions and, upon request, how many people they have available in the client's age group and area.

Complaints.   ABIA provides conciliation; then documents only arbitration is available. A disciplinary sub-committee[39] of the ABIA Council, with a majority of independents, can impose sanctions, including expulsion on members for non-compliance with the Code.

Mail order[40]

10.32   This code was adopted by the Mail Order Traders Association in 1978. The MOTA code is concerned with buying goods from mail order catalogues of such organisations as Great Universal Stores and Littlewoods. The following are the main provisions.

Prices.   Prices must be VAT-inclusive and it should be made clear whether postage and packing are included.

Cancellation.   Unless otherwise stated, goods should be dispatched "on approval" giving the customer the right of cancellation within a period of at least 14 days after receipt of the goods. A full refund should then be made promptly of the "purchase price", which presumably does not include postage and packing.

Damage in transit.   Where goods are damaged in transit the customer will receive a replacement, if available, or otherwise a full refund, including carriage costs.

Delivery.   If a quoted delivery date is not met, the customer has a right to cancel the order and obtain a full refund.

Complaints.   The usual procedure is adopted, including conciliation and low-cost arbitration.

---

[39] Geoffrey Woodroffe, co-author of this book, was a member from 1996 to 1999.
[40] The MOPA code also covers mail order, *inter alia:* above, para. 10.21.

Motorcycles

This code was prepared by the RMI, SMTA, Motorcycle Retailers Associ-   **10.33**
ation and Motor Cycle Association. It came into effect in October 1984.

Not surprisingly, bearing in mind some of its sponsoring associations, it
bears a close resemblance to the Motor Industry Code.[41] Thus it deals with the
sale of new and used motorcycles and spare parts as well as their servicing
and repair. In view of the similarity we do not propose to spell out in detail its
provisions, covering such matters as manufacturers' warranties, checklists
and mileages on used motor cycles, quotations and estimates, and the availability of spare parts.

In two respects, however, this code differs from the car code. First, it deals
specifically with delayed delivery and recommends that where a delivery
date of a vehicle is not met, the buyer should be offered a refund. As regards
repairs, it requires dealers to give an indication of the time to be taken, where
possible, and to notify customers of the reason for any undue delay; in this
respect the code goes beyond the dealers' legal duties.

Secondly, the code takes account of the fact that many buyers of motorcycles are young. It advises dealers to try to persuade first-time riders to
choose a sensible type of vehicle and to undertake formal training. Where a
minor cannot obtain his parents' consent to the purchase, dealers should
promptly refund any deposit.

As usual under the codes, free conciliation is available together with arbitration procedures.

Photography

The Code of Practice for the Photographic Industry covers a wide range of   **10.34**
sales and services relating to photography—the sale and repair of cameras
and other photographic equipment, film processing and professional photographers. Eight trade associations[42] subscribe to the code. In view of the
disparate activities covered by the code we shall highlight only its main
points.

Sales of equipment

The retailer.   Prices should be VAT-inclusive. When a deposit is taken on   **10.35**
an order, the price will be the price at that date unless the contrary is made
clear, and the delivery period should be made known in writing. (This suggests, wrongly, that when no deposit is taken on an order, retailers are at
liberty to increase the price on delivery.)

Second-hand equipment should be given an adequate pre-sales inspection

---

[41] Above, para. 10.15.
[42] See list in Appendix 1, below.

before sale and a suitable guarantee should be provided commensurate with the price and condition of the goods—a weak provision of doubtful value.

Manufacturers and importers. They will provide a guarantee covering parts and labour but no period is recommended. It should be transferable to new owners.

Repairs

10.36   *Retailers.* They should tell the customer how long a repair will take and give the consumer a written estimate (if the cost is known) or otherwise offer to obtain an estimate.

Manufacturers, importers and independent repairers. Repairs should normally be effected within 21 days. Manufacturers and importers should keep stocks of spares for a minimum period of five years following the last sale to the trade and for 10 years "for expensive equipment". A written guarantee should be given covering parts and labour, but again no period is recommended.

Film processing

10.37   The retailer should display his prices and give the name and address of the processing laboratory if requested. There is an ambiguous provision relating to compensation for films lost or damaged: "The consumer may be informed of the reasonable compensation offered." Presumably this means that the consumer should always be entitled to reasonable compensation, although he need not necessarily be informed of this right. This part of the code would be clearer, if it stated specifically that suppliers should not attempt to exclude or limit liability.

Where the customer has informed the retailer that a film has exceptional value or importance, the retailer should advise the laboratory, as "there may be a special service combined with higher prices". This provision was an important factor in *Woodman v. Photo Trade Processing*[43] in deciding that the defendants' limitation clause was unreasonable. Judge Clarke pointed out that it was not necessary for the defendants to set up their own special service of a higher quality at extra cost, but at least they should have informed their customers that such a service was available from other specialised laboratories:

> "In the light of the Code of Practice I reach the conclusion that some such form of two-tier system is not only reasonable but practicable."

---

[43] Above, para. 8.39.

Professional photography

The photographer should ensure that clients understand his fee structure   **10.38**
and give them a statement of the completion date for the work. In contrast
with the repairer it is clearly stated that he should not restrict his legal
liability.

Complaints

Conciliation is undertaken by the appropriate trade association. An   **10.39**
arbitration scheme is operated under the aegis of the Chartered Institute of
Arbitrators, on a documents only basis.

Shoes

There are two codes: **10.40**

> FDF Voluntary Code of Practice for Footwear.
> Code of Practice for Shoe Repairs.

Sales

The Code of Practice for Footwear was drawn up by the Footwear Dis-   **10.41**
tributors Federation and sponsored by the FDF and two other associations
concerned with the manufacture, distribution and retailing of footwear.[44] Its
more significant features are these:

Prices.   These must be VAT-inclusive. Reductions must be on the retailer's
previous price or the manufacturer's recommended price. Deposits are
returnable within seven days of an unmet delivery date.

Exclusions.   Notices appearing to limit customers' rights are banned; for
example, "No goods exchanged".[45]

Fitting.   Measuring facilities should be available where children's shoes are
sold.

Labels.   The materials used in the uppers and soles and the country of origin
must be marked on the shoes or labels.

Complaints.   There are no conciliation or arbitration procedures. However,
an independent report may be obtained from the Footwear Testing Centre for
a fee of a few pounds.
Perhaps the most important question is whether adherence to the code

---

[44] See list in App. 1.
[45] This notice is not void, and so not illegal: below, para. 17.15.

should be obligatory on all members of the sponsoring associations as is the case with all the other codes. As it is, if a member subscribing to the code fails to comply, he can be removed from the *scheme*, not from membership. Thus if he finds the code too burdensome, he shrugs it off. What disincentive is there to such an irresponsible attitude?

Repairs

10.42   Members of the National Association of Multiple Shoe Repairers and the Society of Master Shoe Repairers are governed by the Code of Practice for Shoe Repairs. It applies not only to their repair services but also to their sales: in the latter case its guidance is almost identical to the FDF code discussed above.

Its repairing provisions are similar to the Laundry Code explained earlier (they came into operation within two months of each other). In the case of a complaint the associations are prepared to conciliate and to obtain an independent test report, apparently free of charge, but arbitration is not available.

Ticket agencies

10.43   The Code of Practice of the Society of Ticket Agencies and Retailers (STAR), introduced in 1997, covers both ticket agents re-selling tickets and box offices. Theatres, concerts, exhibitions and sporting events are included.

Booking fees.   The worst sharp practice was perpetrated by touts and agents who loaded the face value of a ticket with an exorbitant service charge without informing the customer how the total price was made up. Now the STAR Code requires agents to inform customers of this breakdown when taking bookings, including by telephone.

Complaints.   They must be dealt with in five working days. Conciliation is available, and arbitration too but unhappily by a sub-committee of STAR. Will the public be wise to trust such in-house arrangements?

Travel

10.44   The ABTA Code of Practice consists of two Codes of Conduct—the Tour Operators' Code and the Travel Agents' Code. It was first introduced in January 1975, but was amended a year later to take account of criticisms by the OFT with regard to surcharges and overbooking. The latest 1993 revision makes further improvements in respect of surcharges and liability.

However, the ABTA Code does not provide the only protection for tourists. What is more important now is the statutory protection given to them by the Package Travel, Package Holidays and Package Tours Regulations

1992.[46] Our discussion of these regulations follows our analysis of the two Codes of Conduct.[47]

Tour Operators' Code[48]

Brochures. Considerable detail is set out in the code and its appendix **10.45** "Standards on Brochures" on the information required in brochures. For example, they must mention the arbitration scheme.

Liability. Times have changed significantly for the better. Gone are the days of disclaimers. Instead the code positively states that in respect of foreign inclusive holidays the contract must include a term "accepting responsibility for acts and/or omissions of their employees, agents, sub-contractors and suppliers". However, liability may be limited in compliance with international conventions in respect of the transportation elements, *e.g.* air, rail.

Cancellation and alteration. Problems have often been caused by holidays being cancelled or rearranged by the tour operator at the last minute. Now a cancellation must not be made after the date when the balance of the price becomes due; but if the tour operator does cancel so late, he must pay compensation on "a rising scale . . ., *i.e.* the nearer to departure, the higher". If it occurs before that date, customers must be informed as soon as possible and offered a choice between a comparable alternative holiday and a full refund. Exceptionally it may be necessary to cancel as a result of force majeure as in the Gulf War: again a choice should be offered of an alternative holiday or a refund.

There are comparable provisions relating to material alterations to holiday arrangements. That is as it should be; for what is the difference to a customer with a holiday booked in Acapulco between cancelling it and offering him a holiday in Rhyl? In either case the holiday in Mexico is cancelled, either specifically or by a unilateral variation.[49]

Overbooking. Cancellation and alteration caused by overbooking of hotels, which may be the fault of the tour operator or the hotel management, are dealt with by separate provisions of the code. Where this occurrence is beyond the control of the tour operator, the code imposes different obligations depending on whether or not he knows of the overbooking before the departure of the customer. (1) If he is aware at that stage, he must immediately inform the customer and offer an alternative holiday or full refund as

---

[46] S.I. 1992 No. 3288.
[47] Below, para. 10.49.
[48] Reproduced in the Appendices to previous editions of this book.
[49] Clauses excusing the tour operator in such cases would be open to attack, if not reasonable, under the Unfair Contract Terms Act 1977, s.3. See *Spencer v. Cosmos Air Holidays*, above, para. 10.50.

above. (2) If it is discovered only on arrival, the customer must be offered alternative accommodation plus "disturbance" compensation where the location or facilities are inferior.

The code proceeds on the basis that the tour operator has complied with the code by taking all reasonable steps to ensure that arrangements are not cancelled or altered, *i.e.* he can show that the overbooking is beyond his control. Presumably if he is at fault, the customer will be treated at least as generously.

Surcharges.   Surcharges resulting from fluctuations in fuel costs or rates of exchange have been a major cause of discontent amongst holidaymakers. The code was strengthened in 1976 to prohibit such surcharges, unless made more than 30 days before departure. In 1988 a separate document, "Standards on Surcharges", was added to the code. Tour operators must now absorb increased costs up to two per cent of the holiday price. If they exceed 10 per cent, the customer may cancel and obtain a refund.

Building works.   Resorts which turn out to be more like a massive building site than a place for a holiday have been a common problem. The code requires the tour operator to notify customers when he becomes aware of building works which may "seriously impair the enjoyment of the holiday" and to offer them an alternative or their money back.

Bonds.[50]   The code notifies customers of the ABTA Scheme of Protection in Appendix 1. All tour operators must provide bonds or guarantees. If they become insolvent and an air package is involved, the Civil Aviation Authority will reimburse advance payments on prospective holidays and, where a holiday is in progress, try to arrange for the holiday to continue and return travel: otherwise ABTA[50a] will do so.

If the customer has paid by credit card and so can claim against the credit card company under section 75 of the Consumer Credit Act,[51] ABTA may require the customer to pursue that claim first.

Arbitration.   ABTA no longer has a conciliation service, but arbitration is provided. Its availability should be included as a term of the contract in booking conditions so that customers are aware of this facility. It covers claims up to £1,500 per person or £7,500 per booking form.

"Documents only" arbitration is the norm. Originally attended hearings

---

[50] See also below, para. 8.38 on insolvency.
[50a] In *Bowerman v. ABTA, The Times,* November 24, 1995, the Court of Appeal held that a contract existed between ABTA and a tour operator's customer because of a notice stating "ABTA arranges for you to be reimbursed the money you have paid in respect of your holiday arrangements".
[51] See below, para. 23.06. See also Rutherford, "Travel agents and the use of credit cards in the travel trade" (1994) 144 N.L.J. 668.

were available with the disincentive of the prospect of paying unlimited costs, but they were rare and expensive. Accordingly the OFT recommended that attended hearings be withdrawn from the scheme[52]; this change took place in 1982.

Travel Agents' Code

The code relating to the conduct of travel agents covers such matters as **10.46** ensuring that counter staff "carefully study travel brochures" to provide accurate information to customers (yet how often is the customer simply given an armful of glossy brochures and left to work out for himself which operator offers the best terms for children, off-peak holidays, etc.?); passing on immediately alterations to travel arrangements; advising on insurance, visas and health requirements; and generally acting as intermediaries in negotiations and disputes between the tour operators and the customers. So presumably it is now unheard of for an agent, having booked a holiday and earned his commission, to wash his hands of the matter and to tell the customer to go direct to the tour operator/supplier in case of difficulty!

The code also brings travel agents within the arbitration procedure.

Disciplinary procedures

The ABTA Codes of Conduct give the association the power to investigate **10.47** infringements of the codes and to impose penalties ranging from a reprimand to a fine or even termination of membership.

Legal relationship between the parties

The Law Commission Second Report on Exemption Clauses[53] touches on **10.48** an interesting and difficult question—the precise legal relationship between the customer and the other organisations involved in providing his holiday (the travel agent, the tour operator, the hotel and the airline).

It is suggested that generally the position is as follows. The customer makes only one contract with one legal entity—the tour operator.[54] This is effected via the travel agent who acts on behalf of the tour operator, not the customer.[54a] As the agent is known to be acting for a named principal, he will incur no personal responsibility to the customer on the contract.

The contracts for accommodation and transportation are made by the tour operator on his own account: only he is responsible to the hotelier and airline for these costs, even though the services will be supplied by them to the tour

---

[52] A general recommendation to the same effect was made in *Redress Procedures under Codes of Practice* (OFT, 1981).

[53] Law Com. No. 69 (1975), para. 126.

[54] See Lord Scarman in *Wings Ltd v. Ellis* [1984] 3 All E.R. 577 at 586, discussed below, para. 13.39.

[54a] For a discussion of this tripartite relationship, particularly in relation to payment by credit card, see *Connected Lender Liability* (OFT, March 1994), pp. 28–30.

operator's customer. Clearly the tour operator is under an implied obligation to his customer to pay the necessary sums to the carrier and hotelier to enable the customer to travel and to stay at his chosen resort without additional payment; if he fails to do so, so that the carrier or hotelier refuse to provide their services to the customer unless the customer himself pays for them direct, the tour operator will have broken his contract with the customer and be liable in damages for such additional charges. Of course, if he does not provide the promised accommodation and facilities, he will be liable for breach of contract too,[55] as well as risking a prosecution under the Trade Descriptions Act 1968.[56]

Although the travel agent is not a party to the main holiday contract, he may incur liability to the customer in other ways. If he makes untrue statements to the customer about the subject-matter of the contract, for example, hotel amenities, he may be liable (1) in tort for deceit or negligence, or (2) for breach of an implied warranty of authority if the statement is outside his actual or ostensible authority. Further, he may be in breach of a collateral contract between himself and the customer—a contract collateral to the main contract between the tour operator and the customer. Such rights against the travel agent are unlikely to be needed unless the tour operator is unable to meet his responsibilities under the main contract, *e.g.* because he is bankrupt or in liquidation.

Package Travel Regulations

10.49   The consumer's position has been considerably strengthened by legislation passed to comply with the E.C. Directive on Package Travel, Package Holidays and Package Tours (90/314/EEC). This was adopted by the E.C. Council in June 1990 and had to be brought into force by the end of 1992.

The Directive was implemented in the United Kingdom by the Package Travel, Package Holidays and Package Tours Regulations 1992.[57] They came into force on December 23, 1992, with a week to spare! They keep closely to the wording of the Directive. Clearly the Government is anxious not to be taken to the European Court of Justice, as happened in the field of employment law and sex discrimination, for failure properly to translate European law into national law; the safest route then is to use the same phrases as the Directive.

Most of their provisions can already be found in the ABTA Code of Practice, which no doubt was revised in 1990 to take account of the initiatives in Brussels. We shall comment on the main provisions, particularly where they improve the consumer's position.

Package.   The Regulations do not apply to travel or accommodation

---

[55] See the cases cited above, para. 7.39.
[56] Below, para. 13.38.
[57] S.I. 1992 No. 3288.

booked separately, for example, a flight or hotel. Regulation 2(1) defines "package" as follows:

> "package" means the pre-arranged combination of at least two of the following components when sold or offered for sale at an inclusive price and when the service covers a period of more than twenty-four hours or includes overnight accommodation:
> (a) transport;
> (b) accommodation;
> (c) other tourist services not ancillary to transport or accommodation and accounting for a significant proportion of the package.

It can be seen that there must be at least two of the three elements. Generally, of course, the package will comprise travel by aircraft, coach, ship or train coupled with accommodation[57a] in a hotel, apartment or even on the ship itself in the case of a cruise. However, it is not vital for transport to be included as the package may consist of items (b) and (c). An example given in the Consultation Document *Implementation of E.C. Directive on Package Travel, Package Holidays and Package Tours (Arts. 1–6)* (February 1992) put out by the Department of Trade and Industry suggests that a weekend at a hotel where the price included access to fishing rights or to a golf course, where residents do not generally have these benefits, would be "other tourist services" thus making the arrangement a "package".

Organiser and retailer.   These terms are used in regulation 2(1) to describe the tour operator and travel agent.

Information.   There are a number of regulations about information to be given to the consumer. Regulation 5 coupled with Schedule 1 prescribes the information to be included in brochures, *e.g.* type of accommodation, inclusion of meals, itinerary, price and deposit.

Regulation 7 deals with information to be provided "before a contract is concluded". This covers such matters as passport and visa requirements, health formalities, and importantly "the arrangements for security for the money paid over and (where applicable) for the repatriation of the consumer in the event of insolvency". This is supplemented by regulation 8 which deals with information to be provided "in good time before the start of the journey", for example, the times and places of intermediate stops and transport connections, and the name, address and telephone number of any local representative or agent.

We now come to the contents and form of the contract itself which is governed by regulation 9. A written copy of the terms of the contract must be supplied to the consumer. Depending on the nature of the package, the con-

---

[57a] In *Administrative proceedings concerning AFS Intercultural Programs Finland ry, The Times*, March 4, 1999, the ECJ decided that the Directive did not apply to a student exchange, where the student was treated as a member of the host family free of charge.

tract must contain at least the elements specified in Schedule 2. This is set out verbatim below in view of the importance of these details to the consumer or adviser.

Elements to be included in the contract if relevant to the particular package

(1) The travel destination(s) and, where periods of stay are involved, the relevant periods, with dates.

(2) The means, characteristics and categories of transport to be used and the dates, times and points of departure and return.

(3) Where the package includes accommodation, its location, its tourist category or degree of comfort, its main features and, where the accommodation is to be provided in a member State, its compliance with the rules of that member State.

(4) The meals which are included in the package.

(5) Whether a minimum number of persons is required for the package to take place and, if so, the deadline for informing the consumer in the event of cancellation.

(6) The itinerary.

(7) Visits, excursions or other services which are included in the total price agreed for the package.

(8) The name and address of the organiser, the retailer and, where appropriate, the insurer.

(9) The price of the package, if the price may be revised in accordance with the term which may be included in the contract under regulation 11, an indication of the possibility of such price revisions, and an indication of any dues, taxes or fees chargeable for certain services (landing, embarkation or disembarkation fees at ports and airports and tourist taxes) where such costs are not included in the package.

(10) The payment schedule and method of payment.

(11) Special requirements which the consumer has communicated to the organiser or retailer when making the booking and which both have accepted.

(12) The periods within which the consumer must make any complaint about the failure to perform or the inadequate performance of the contract.

Regulation 9(3) states that it is "an implied condition" that the other party complies with the provisions of the regulation, so the consumer will be able to rescind the contract in the event of non-compliance—a serious sanction which should encourage organisers to keep to the rules.

10.50   *Prices.*   Regulation 11 deals with price revisions. Prices are fixed unless the contract "states precisely how the revised price is to be calculated". Even then price revisions are permitted only for variations in transport costs, taxes or exchange rates. No increase can be made during the 30 days before departure or if less than 2 per cent.

Cancellation and alteration.   There are ABTA-like provisions in Regulations 12 and 13 entitling the consumer to cancel or to accept an alternative package, with compensation if appropriate, *e.g.* if the organiser "is constrained to alter significantly an essential term"; force majeure excuses the organiser.

Implied warranties.   Regulation 6 also provides that "the particulars in the brochure ... shall constitute implied warranties ... for the purposes of any contract to which the particulars relate." The effect is that a consumer will be able to recover damages for breach of warranty, where the services provided by the organiser do not precisely match their description. There will be no need for the consumer to resort to the Supply of Goods and Services Act 1982, s.13, by proving that the organiser had not exercised reasonable care and skill in the provision of the services, for the warranty implied by regulation 6 imposes strict liability. There is one catch, however, for the consumer: there is no implied warranty where the brochure contains an express statement that changes may be made in the particulars contained in it and such changes are "clearly communicated to the consumer before a contract is concluded".

Liability for sub-contractors.   Regulation 15 provides that the organiser "is liable to the consumer for the proper performance of the obligations under the contract, irrespective of whether such obligations are to be performed by that other party or by other suppliers of services". As explained above, this is already the legal position in the United Kingdom, but it does no harm for the regulation to spell this out.

Unfortunately it goes on to permit limitation clauses which are "not unreasonable". This is the same as the U.K. position under section 3 of the Unfair Contract Terms Act 1977, but worse than under the ABTA Code which outlaws disclaimers.

One point for the consumer to watch is that complaints must be speedy—"at the earliest opportunity" to the organiser and to the supplier of the services.

Assignment.   One valuable new right is that the consumer may transfer his booking to a third party. However, regulation 10 confines this possibility to a case where "the consumer is prevented from proceeding with the package". Will this cover only force majeure circumstances, *e.g.* illness? It would appear so. A change of mind would not be enough.

Insolvency.   We have already drawn attention to the problem of insolvency, which has underlined the value of booking a holiday with an ABTA tour operator to take advantage of its Scheme of Protection. Of course, not all businesses are members of ABTA.

Article 7 of the Directive requires the organiser to prove that there is "security" for refunds and repatriation in the event of insolvency. Regulation 16 obliges the other party to the contract to "be able to provide sufficient evidence of security" for these matters. The organiser is given the option of pursuing a number of different routes: regulations 17 to 20 permit bonds, insurance[57b] or trust funds to be used. Further, none of these requirements

---

[57b] See Package Tours (Amendment) Regulations 1995 (S.I. 1995 No. 1648).

apply where the package is covered by the Civil Aviation (Air Travel Organisers' Licensing) Regulations.[58]

Enforcement and Penalties.   Apart from giving the consumer certain contractual rights for breach of the implied terms the Regulations may result in criminal sanctions against the organiser or retailer. Various criminal offences are scattered throughout the Regulations. As usual with consumer protection legislation they are enforced by trading standards officers. The penalty for contravention is a fine; a prison sentence cannot be imposed even where the defendant is convicted on indictment. ~

Tyres

10.51   The latest code supported by the OFT is the Code of Practice for the Tyre and Fast Fit Trade. Introduced in 1998 by the National Tyre Distributors Association (NTDA) it covers over 65 per cent of the relevant trade.

Cash price.   A clear indication of cash price must be available to the customer.

Exemption clauses.   Suppliers must not avoid liability for loss or damage by disclaimers and must insure against their liability. This improves on the legal position, as such clauses are never void, *e.g.* under the Unfair Contract Terms Act 1977, s.2(2) (see para. 8.23).

Complaints.   The first step is the member's own in-house procedures, with a suggested six months' maximum for this stage. Then follows conciliation by the NTDA: any dispute "must be settled within 9 months of the completion of the work". What happens if a tyre collapses or shows unusual wear after, say, a year? Is conciliation not available? It appears not.
    Arbitration is possible as a last resort.

3. Public Utilities—New Consumer Councils

10.52   In September 1998 the Government published a consultation paper setting out proposals for consumer councils for the energy, water and telecommunications sectors. More than 130 responses were received and the government has now announced that it will introduce legislation to implement the proposals. The councils will assist consumers in three ways:

(a) they will act as independent and influential consumer advocates with a voice at the heart of the regulatory system—advising utility regulators, utility companies and others on consumer issues;

(b) they will have the specific task of handling consumer complaints

---

[58] S.I. 1972 No. 223.

against utility companies where they have not been resolved by the company concerned. They will be expected to mediate a satisfactory outcome wherever possible; if enforcement action is necessary they will pass the complaint to the relevant regulatory authority. They will also be expected to work with the utility companies to reduce the causes of complaints. Hopefully, the councils will succeed in resolving disputes without the need for litigation;

(c) they will provide consumers with good quality information and advice on how to get the best deal from the utility markets; influential councils and well-informed consumers can play a key part in driving standards up and prices down.

Energy Minister John Battle has recently told consumers to put behind them the traditional British reluctance to complain. He urged them to "expect and demand good service, remembering that you can take your business elsewhere. In the United Kingdom, the most open energy market in the world, it's cool to complain." (DTI Press Notice P/99/617).

4. OMBUDSMAN SCHEMES

Comparison with codes of practice

We have already suggested that from the consumer's point of view codes   **10.53**
of practice suffer from the disadvantage that they do not appear to provide a completely impartial method of resolving disputes. As conciliation is carried out by employees of the relevant trade association, there may be some justification for the scepticism of consumers in believing that he who pays the piper calls the tune.

Of course, where a code of practice gives a complainant the opportunity of going to arbitration—and we have seen that not all codes do so—then without doubt the arbitrator will act independently and reach a fair and impartial conclusion. However, it should be remembered that although conciliation by the trade associations is free, the consumer must pay for arbitration. Then again a decision by an arbitrator is binding on the parties and final—the claimant cannot ignore it and later sue in the courts. None of these disadvantages is present in the ombudsmen schemes discussed below. All of the ombudsmen are independent and impartial. In every case the service is provided free of charge. If the complainant rejects the ombudsman's decision, litigation in the courts is still available.

We have already drawn attention to the fact that in recent years the OFT too has become disenchanted with codes, partly because of the trade associations' conflict of interest. As the report *Raising Standards* (above para. 10.07) states;

"We are led to conclude that trade associations, set up for the benefit of members, will frequently be neither comfortable nor effective in the role of sectoral regulator. The inherent conflict between the tasks of a regulator and their representational and promotional duties, as well as their lack of necessary power over their membership, militate against choosing this route, save in exceptional circumstances." (para. 2.23)

If then codes of practice do not provide consumers with suitable redress procedures, are other routes of alternative dispute resolution (usually nowadays blessed with the acronym ADR) to be preferred? *Raising Standards* comes down firmly in favour of ombudsmen schemes:

"Use indicates that ombudsmen schemes are more popular with consumers than is trade-association-sponsored independent arbitration. There are a number of perceived benefits. They include: the fact that they are free to consumers; the ombudsman's ability to investigate cases as well as adjudicate on them; and the general perception (perhaps largely based on the objective stance perceived to have been taken by the better known operators in the financial services sector) that ombudsmen appear to be impartial. In response to the OFT's earlier consultation paper, some consumer bodies felt that arbitration was not suitable for consumer problems. Their view was that the nature of the process, with the element of legal confrontation, was off-putting. They also considered that successful arbitration required some semblance of equity in the knowledge and abilities of the parties, which is seldom present in consumer cases. Ombudsmen schemes also seem preferable from the OFT's perspective." (para. 3.43)

This official support for ombudsmen was preceded by judicial support in the shape of Lord Woolf, whose proposed reforms of litigation—case management, practice, procedure, costs—came into force in April 1999. *Access to Justice*, his interim report to the Lord Chancellor in June 1995, recommended:

"63. The retail sector should be encouraged to develop private ombudsman schemes to cover consumer complaints similar to those which now exist in relation to service industries; the government should facilitate this.
64. The relationship between ombudsmen and the courts should be broadened, enabling issues to be referred by the ombudsman to the courts and the courts to the ombudsman with the consent of those involved."

It is obvious which way the wind is blowing as far as consumer redress is concerned.

Background

10.54   The origins of ombudsman schemes can be found in the Nordic countries. In the United Kingdom most of the schemes have been set up by statute and many, particularly the earlier schemes, are concerned with complaints about the activities of public bodies, including central and local government. Others, though, are voluntary and were set up at the expense of the businesses concerned to deal with complaints about particular sectors of the service industries such as banking and insurance. All the schemes have one thing in common, namely they exist to deal with complaints from members of the public about the way in which members of the schemes carry out their business, *e.g.* delay, carelessness, inefficiency or discourtesy. Ombudsmen must not be confused with regulators such as OFTEL and OFGAS, as their sole function is to provide redress to individuals, not to control or supervise a business sector.

Ombudsman Association

The use of the term "Ombudsman" can be misleading in that it gives the **10.55** impression that, whenever the word is used, the adjudicator will be impartial. It is a matter of regret that sometimes the term is used to describe someone who is concerned with handling complaints either on behalf of a trade association or even on behalf of a single organisation such as a newspaper or local authority; obviously in neither of these cases is the person independent.

To enable the public to identify genuine, independent ombudsmen the British and Irish Ombudsman Association was set up. Only those schemes are admitted to membership which satisfy its strict criteria, namely independence, effectiveness, fairness and public accountability. Of these four factors the crucial one is independence and it is this which distinguishes recognised ombudsmen schemes from other complaints procedures.

So far 22 schemes have satisfied the Association's criteria; of these 19 operate within the United Kingdom and are listed in Appendix Three.

An invaluable guide to all the schemes was published in 1997 by the National Consumer Council: *A–Z of Ombudsmen*. The book gives such details as jurisdiction, terms of reference, powers and time limits.

Finally, before turning to some common features, it should be noted that once the Financial Services and Markets Bill is enacted, the Financial Services Authority will have a single "super" Financial Services Ombudsman; such well-known schemes as the Banking and Insurance Ombudsmen will be encompassed by the new arrangements. This reform aims to simplify matters for consumers of financial services by giving a single entry point to one scheme—at present the borderline between the different schemes sometimes seems difficult to discern.

Jurisdiction and powers

The extent of the jurisdiction of a particular ombudsman depends on the **10.56** particular scheme. For example, the private sector schemes do not usually cover all members of a particular industry. Thus, the Ombudsman for Estate Agents was initially concerned only with the large chains of estate agents owned by banks, building societies and insurance companies and could not deal with complaints against independent estate agents. The OEA has now extended its scope to those independent estate agents whose principals are members of any of the three associations listed in para. 10.30 and who choose to join the OEA too. In contrast, the Funeral Ombudsman Scheme covers all members of the Funeral Standards Council, the Funeral Planning Council and the Society of Allied and Independent Funeral Directors plus those other funeral and crematorium businesses who have applied to join the FOS directly.

To discover the extent of the jurisdiction, powers and duties of a particular scheme the consumer adviser will normally need to peruse its terms of reference which where appropriate will reflect the memorandum and articles of association of the company operating the scheme. By way of example we have set out in Appendix Two the Terms of Reference of the Funeral Ombudsman Scheme.

Usually complaints have to be brought within a specified time-limit and cannot be dealt with if the complainant has already issued court proceedings.

Procedures

10.57   Here again the adviser must look at the details of the particular scheme. However, generally the ombudsman cannot consider a complaint until he or she is satisfied that the complainant has given the business concerned the opportunity to try to resolve the complaint by its own in-company complaints procedure. Once the ombudsman is satisfied that such procedures have been exhausted, he will then try to resolve the dispute by acting as a conciliator.

If conciliation fails, the ombudsman will commence his formal investigation and collect all the relevant evidence. Generally there will not be an oral hearing and the adjudication will be based on written evidence only. On reaching his decision the ombudsman will take into account such matters as the terms of the contract, codes of practice, previous decisions and in some schemes what is "fair and reasonable".

Remedies

10.58   One of the main aims of the ombudsman is to try to improve the quality of service in a particular organisation or industry. Thus if the ombudsman upholds a complaint, he may well make a recommendation that the business practices or procedures of the respondent organisation should be altered and improved to prevent a repetition of the problem. Sometimes an apology by the business will satisfy a complainant— it is strange how frequently an organisation, though at fault, will be absolutely certain that it has acted properly and efficiently and refuse to budge, while all the complainant desires is a formal apology that a mistake had been made. Often, though, the complainant will seek financial compensation. The maximum which can be awarded depends on the scheme; for example, the Insurance Ombudsman may award up to £100,000. Failure by an organisation to carry out its services carefully and efficiently may cause distress to the complainant and some schemes contain express power for the ombudsman to award compensation for aggravation and distress. Often this sum has a maximum of £750, but the Funeral

Ombudsman[58a] may award up to £5,000 for the obvious reason that this is an area of activity where, if the quality of service falls down, severe upset may be caused to members of the family.

Sanctions

Throughout this chapter we are concerned with the effectiveness of procedures, so what can be done if a recommendation or award by an ombudsman is ignored by the respondent organisation? The answer depends on the particular scheme. In some a monetary award is legally binding on the organisation. In other schemes the recommendation and award by an ombudsman is not legally enforceable, because an ombudsman is not an arbitrator. In the latter situation, which is normally the position with regard to the voluntary, non-statutory schemes, the business organisation with rare exceptions complies with the ombudsman's decision.

10.59

The ultimate sanction for non-compliance is publicity. Every ombudsman publishes an annual report, which will normally give examples of complaints made in the previous year and statistics on the number and type of complaints without naming the organisations involved. However, if an organisation were to fail to comply with a decision, in some schemes the ombudsman would have the power to name the culprit; it is the fear of the commercial effect of such adverse publicity which stimulates businesses into compliance.

5. ARBITRATION

Cheap, quick, informal?

Until 1971 the consumer, faced with a supplier who was not prepared to meet his proper obligations, had no choice but to abandon his complaint unless he was determined enough to launch himself upon the uncertain seas of litigation. The prospect of such action caused the consumer considerable anxiety for three principal reasons. First, it was likely to be expensive because of the level of legal fees. Secondly—and a related point—although he could save legal fees by conducting the case himself, he was put off playing the role of the litigant in person by the formality and complexity of court proceedings. Thirdly, he knew litigation to be a long-winded affair and was unhappy at having the doubtful outcome hanging over him like the sword of Damocles for years on end. Thus, the layman saw access to his legal rights guarded by a Cerberus whose three heads were expense, delay and formality.

10.60

These disadvantages were particularly identified in the 1960s and fully discussed in *Justice out of Reach* the crucial report by the Consumer Council

---

[58a] He is currently Geoffrey Woodroffe, co-author of this book.

published in 1970. The report proposed a nationwide system of small claims courts, drawing partly upon experience in North America. (It is salutary to recall that the county courts were set up in 1846 to provide the sort of forum being ardently espoused a century and a quarter later.) The nearest we have come so far to such a system incorporating the triple desiderata of cheapness, speed and informality are the voluntary small claims arbitration schemes introduced in Manchester (1971) and Westminster (1973) and the county court arbitration scheme inaugurated in 1973. The Manchester and Westminster schemes, however, were short-lived and ceased in 1979 when financial support was withdrawn by the local authorities then funding them: a sad end to a successful experiment.[59] The small claims track now caters for court-based small claims.[60]

The consumer adviser must remember, however, that many of the codes of practice discussed in the previous section provide for low cost, documents only arbitration arranged by the relevant trade association. It must be stressed, though, that if consumers agree to their disputes being resolved by arbitration, they are bound by the arbitrator's decision. They cannot ignore it and then try the courts later in the hope that the district judge adopts a different attitude. This is the crucial distinction between arbitration and the ombudsman schemes.

Nor should the European dimension be overlooked. As the habit develops of consumers buying goods as well as services abroad, so the likelihood of trans-border disputes increases. The European Commission remarked in its 1993 Green Paper[61-62]:

> Access to justice is at once a human right and a prerequisite for an effective legal order.
>
> However, it follows from Article 7 of the Treaty that the national courts must be equally accessible to all individuals, without discrimination on grounds of nationality, and that the divergences between existing national procedures— which as such are quite legitimate—should not be such as to affect the equality of treatment of Community subjects in different countries who invoke respect of one and the same Community provision.
>
> It is up to the national courts to enforce Community law in the context of their powers and using their own procedures. But this means that if access to justice at national level is impeded, the effectiveness (and non-discriminatory application) of Community law is placed in jeopardy.

We suggest though that the task of harmonising judicial procedures is so complex that any European changes will not occur until well into the next millennium.

---

[59] Details of these schemes are given in the 1st ed. of this book, pp. 145–149.
[60] Below, para. 11.07.
[61-62] "Access of Consumers to Justice and Settlement of Consumers' Disputes in the Single Market" COM (93) 576.

Consumer Arbitration

The codes of practice supported by the OFT do not compel consumers to **10.61** take advantage of an arbitration scheme, if available, and point out that the complainant is free to take the alternative route of suing in the courts. This contrasts with the type of clause common in commercial contracts which makes arbitration a condition precedent to action in the courts (the so-called "*Scott v. Avery*"[63] clause).

Such clauses can operate unfairly and legislation to control them has been in force since 1988. Under section 91 of the Arbitration Act 1996 a clause referring present or future disputes to arbitration is to be treated as "unfair" under the Unfair Terms in Consumer Contracts Regulations 1994 (which we discussed in Chapter Nine) where the value in dispute does not exceed a specified amount—currently £3,000 (S.I. 1996 No. 3211).[63a]

Two points can be made. First, the 1996 Act is wider than the Regulations because, by section 90, the term "consumer" includes a company or partnership. Secondly, it has been suggested that the £3,000 ceiling is a breach of E.U. law as it derogates from the Directive (see *Arbitration Law* published by Lloyd's of London, at para. 1.47).

6. ALTERNATIVE DISPUTE RESOLUTION

In Chapter Ten of our fourth Edition we wrote that ADR was "increasingly in **10.62** the news as the cost of legal aid continues to rise faster than general inflation". Much water has flowed under the bridge in the four years since then as clients and the courts have sought to avoid the cost and delay of litigation. The Civil Procedure Rules, which are considered in the next Chapter, give the court wide powers to stay a case so that the parties can explore ADR; also, an unreasonable refusal to consider ADR (both before and after the start of proceedings) will be taken into account when the court awards costs. For small claims the cost of litigation is usually out of all proportion to the amount in dispute—hence the value of ADR. At the time of going to press there are two main ADR organisations—namely the Centre for Dispute Resolution (CEDR) and ADR Group; the latter is probably more suitable for smaller cases.

The procedure varies from one mediation to another but essentially it involves getting the parties to reach their own agreement—rather than leaving it to a third person (the judge). A typical mediation will proceed as follows:

(1) Before the mediation starts the parties will be asked to prepare written position statements and to sign the mediation agreement; this con-

---

[63] (1856) 5 H.L.C. 811.
[63a] This will shortly be increased to £5,000 to mirror the small claims track under the new Civil Procedure Rules—see Chap. Eleven.

firms that anything said during the mediation is, and will remain, confidential.

(2) The parties will then come together and meet the mediator; he will ask each of them to make an opening statement.

(3) The parties then retire to separate rooms and the mediator will shuttle between them—exploring the strength and weakness of each party's case in more detail and finding out what their main concerns are. In these separate discussions he will endeavour to get the parties to narrow their differences until an agreement emerges and this will then be recorded in writing.

7. CONTINGENCY FEES—"NO WIN, NO FEE"

10.63   There has been a great deal of debate and legislation on whether solicitors should be allowed to run cases on the basis of (1) charging no costs if the case is lost and (2) charging increased costs, or taking a slice of the amount recovered, if the case is won. The legislation and the rules of professional conduct are limited to "contentious business" and only become relevant if proceedings actually start. In other words, a client can validly instruct a solicitor on a "contingency fee" basis to negotiate with the other side to obtain an acceptable settlement without having to go to court. Such an agreement can provide for the solicitor to be paid by either of the methods set out in (2) above.

Chapter Eleven

"WHAT HAPPENS IF I GO TO COURT?"

1. Funding the Action

A. *Legal aid*

The Labour Government of 1945 introduced the legal aid scheme under **11.01** the Legal Aid and Advice Act 1949. This was designed to enable persons of limited means to take their cases to court. Now, as we go to press, the legal aid scheme is in the process of being completely restructured (and, in personal injury cases, abolished). There are three major developments:

(1) Under the Access to Justice Act 1999 the responsibility for civil legal aid will pass to a new body—the Legal Services Commission. This body will establish, maintain and develop a Community Legal Service which can fund information, advice and assistance with settlement. The geographical spread of legal aid will be monitored by regional legal services committees. For the first time, the legal aid budget will be "capped".

(2) The provision of civil legal aid will be confined to firms and advice agencies who meet certain quality standards and are franchised. It is proposed to drastically reduce the number of eligible firms by awarding contracts on an exclusive basis to a limited number of firms.

(3) Legal aid is currently available for all types of civil work except defamation if (1) the applicant qualifies financially and (2) he or she has a reasonable chance of success. This so-called "merits test" is to be drastically tightened under a "funding code" published by the Legal Aid Board. This code requires the applicant to clear no less than sixteen hurdles before legal aid is granted. These include:

    (a) the prospects of success—are they very good (80 per cent or more), good (60 to 80 per cent), moderate (50 to 60 per cent) or less than even

    (b) the benefit which the applicant will gain from the proceedings and the likely costs—*i.e.* a cost–benefit ratio which will prove fatal in many consumer cases

    (c) the likelihood of the case being referred to the small claims track (see para. 11.07, below) in which case funding will usually be refused

    (d) the availability of other sources of funding.

If legal aid is granted, the applicant will obtain the services of a legal representative who will be paid by the Legal Services Commission. If the applicant's income is above a certain limit, he or she will have to pay a contribution. Finally, and this is vitally important, the Commission will have a "statutory charge" on money or property recovered or preserved in the proceedings. If, for example the assisted person recovers £5,000 from the defendant, and if the cost of the case to the Commission is £2,000 (money paid to the legal representative less the assisted person's contribution and costs recovered from the other side) the first £2,000 of the award will go to the Commission.

B. *Conditional fees*

11.02   We have seen that U.S.-style contingency fees (no costs if you lose but a slice of the compensation if you win) are permitted for non-contentious work (see p. 10.63, above). Once proceedings become necessary the position is different—contingency fees are not permitted. Instead, a solicitor can enter into a "conditional fee agreement" with his or her client under powers contained in the Courts and Legal Services Act 1990 and Orders made under that Act. Essentially, the agreement will provide that (1) no costs are payable if the case is lost and (2) the solicitor can charge his usual profit costs plus a success fee if the case is won. The amount of the success fee is a matter for agreement but it can be as high as 100 per cent of the usual charging rate; The Law Society has recommended that the success fee should be capped at 25 per cent of the compensation awarded and this is widely followed. The widely used words "no win, no fee" are seriously misleading for two reasons. First, the agreement will normally be limited to the solicitors' profit costs and will not normally include court fees and other outgoings such as experts' fees (although some experts are now accepting instructions on a "no win, no fee" basis). Secondly, the client must realise that he may have to pay the other side's costs if he loses (although this is unlikely if the case is allocated to the small claims track as to which see para. 11.07, below) and insurance is essential to cover this risk. Under the Access to Justice Act 1999 (many legal aid lawyers and their clients will wince at this title) both the success fee and the insurance premium will be recoverable from the other side if the case is won.

Under the conditional fee regime, the client's chances of legal representation will depend on the willingness of a solicitor to take the case and this will usually depend on finding an insurer who is prepared to do so.

2. PROCEDURE

Introduction

11.03   An entirely new procedural code came into force on 26 April, 1999. It is based to a large extent on Lord Woolf's Report "Access to Justice" published

in 1996 which sought to eradicate the three evils of litigation at that time—
delay, cost and uncertainty. The new regime is to be found in three sources—
the Civil Procedure Rules, Practice Directions and Protocols; no doubt there
will soon be a fourth source—court decisions clarifying the many uncer-
tainties which will arise as the new rules start to bite. The rules are expressed
in plain English and Latin terminology is abolished (when the rules were
published at the end of January 1999 the legal correspondent of *The Times*
wrote an article under the headline "Legal Latin outlawed pro bono
publico").

The new regime has six key features, namely:

(1) openness and "cards on the table"—no more last minute ambush;
(2) co-operation with the court and the other side and early disclosure of
    documents;
(3) proportionality;
(4) on-going attempts to settle—using the courts as a last resort;
(5) case management by the court; and
(6) pre-action protocols.

Some matters are currently not covered by the new regime; they include one
item of considerable importance to consumers and others—the enforcement
of a judgment. The matter is under review.

The overriding objective

The Rules are divided into 51 Parts and many of them are supplemented by   **11.04**
Practice Directions—a number of which are longer and more detailed than
the Rules themselves. Part 1 sets out the overriding objective which must be
constantly borne in mind both before and during the conduct of the case. It
reads as follows:

1.1(1) These rules are a new procedural code with the overriding objective of
       enabling the court to deal with cases justly.
   (2) Dealing with a case justly includes, so far as is practicable:
       (a) ensuring that the parties are on an equal footing;
       (b) saving expense;
       (c) dealing with the case in ways which are proportionate:
             (i) to the amount of money involved;
            (ii) to the importance of the case;
           (iii) to the complexity of the issues; or
            (iv) to the financial position of each party;
       (d) ensuring that it is dealt with expeditiously and fairly; and
       (e) allotting to it an appropriate share of the court's resources, while
           taking into account the need to allot resources to other cases.
1.2 The court must seek to give effect to the overriding objective when it:
       (a) exercises any power given to it by the rules; or

(b) interprets any rule.

1.3 The parties are required to help the court to further the overriding objective.

1.4(1) The court must further the overriding objective by actively managing cases.

(2) Active case management includes:—

    (a) encouraging the parties to co-operate with each other in the conduct of the proceedings;

    (b) identifying the issues at an early stage;

    (c) deciding promptly which issues need full investigation and trial and accordingly disposing summarily of the others;

    (d) deciding the order in which issues are to be resolved;

    (e) encouraging the parties to use an alternative dispute resolution procedure if the court considers this appropriate and facilitating the use of such procedures;

    (f) helping the parties to settle the whole or part of the case;

    (g) fixing timetables or otherwise controlling the progress of the case;

    (h) considering whether the likely benefit of taking a particular step justifies the cost of taking it;

    (i) dealing with as many aspects of the case as it can on the same occasion;

    (j) dealing with the case without the parties needing to attend at court;

    (k) making use of technology; and

    (l) giving directions to ensure that the trial of a case proceeds quickly and efficiently.

Two observations can be made. First, much of the necessary technology to assist the court in managing cases is not yet in place (although there is likely to be increased use of the telephone and hearings by video-link). Secondly, these management powers are supplemented by Part 3 which contains sanctions for non-compliance with a court order or direction; these include striking out a claim or defence or ordering a defaulting party to pay money into court.

Pre-action protocols

11.05   There are currently only two pre-action protocols (personal injury and clinical negligence) but even where there is no protocol (and consumer cases are an obvious example) the parties must behave as if there was one—and if the case does have to go to court there can be penalties if the protocols have not been observed. (See rule 3.1(4).) They have been structured with one central aim—to encourage the early settlement of cases. If we take the personal injury protocol as an example, we can pick out five points:

(1) The claimant must send two copies of a letter of claim to the defendant as soon as sufficient information is available to substantiate a realistic claim and before questions of quantum are addressed in detail.

(2) The defendant must reply and identify his insurer within 21 days.

(3) The insurer must reply within three months stating whether liability is denied and, if so, giving reasons.

(4) If the defendant denies liability his denial must be accompanied by any documents in his possession which are relevant to the issues.

(5) Part 36 of the rules enables either party to make an offer to settle and there may be serious costs consequences if the matter comes to court and it is found that a party has unreasonably failed to make or to accept an offer.

What happens next?

If court proceedings become necessary the next stages are as follows: **11.06**

(1) The claimant will file a "claim form" at the appropriate court—this will generally be (a) the county court if he is unlikely to recover £15,000 or more (or £50,000 in personal injury cases) and (b) the High Court in other cases.

(2) The particulars of claim can form part of the claim form or they can be served separately. They will contain details of such matters as the defects in the goods and the loss or damage sustained by the claimant. Both the claim form and any separate particulars must be verified by a "statement of truth".

(3) The court will issue the claim form (on payment of the appropriate fee) and will serve it on the defendant (unless the claimant wishes to serve it himself).

(4) Within 14 days of service of the particulars the defendant must file:
    (a) an admission; or
    (b) a defence; or
    (c) an acknowledgement of service (giving him a further 14 days to file a defence).
    Failure to take steps (b) or (c) can lead to a default judgment.

(5) As soon as a defence is filed, the court will send to the parties a detailed allocation questionnaire. This must be completed and returned by a specified date not earlier than 14 days after service—and the possibility of applying for summary judgment should be considered at this stage before allocation has taken place.

(6) Part 26 of the Rules deals with the vital question of allocation. The procedural judge will consider the claim form, the defence and the completed questionnaires and will then allocate the case into one of the three tracks—small claims, fast or multi. For consumers and their advisers the small claims track will be the most important one; this is the normal track where the amount in dispute is £5,000 or less (an increase from the previous ceiling of £3,000 for small claims arbitration). The fast track (and fast is the operative word) is for cases where the amount in dispute is between £5,001 and £15,000 and the hearing will not last more than one day). The multi track is for cases (1) over £15,000 or (2) cases in the fast-track band which will take more than one day. The claim form must indicate the band into which

the claim falls and Part 26 sets out the matters which must be taken into account. Note that the value of the claim is not the only relevant factor; thus, for example a "small" claim may be allocated to a different track if it involves the construction of an exemption clause which will affect many other cases.

In the remainder of this Chapter we will look in some detail at the small claims track and then briefly at the fast and multi tracks.

Small claims track (Part 27)

11.07   Although there are some differences of detail (including the right to apply for summary judgment), the basic approach is similar to that in the former County Court Rules Order 19, rule 7; the emphasis is on informality and on costs limitation—so that a person with a small claim can bring it to the court without the need to instruct a solicitor. (For a summary of the previous procedure readers are referred to pages 209–210 of the Fourth Edition of this book.)

To achieve the object set out above, Part 27 of the Civil Procedure Rules contains the following provisions:

(1) A number of the rules which apply elsewhere will not apply in the small claims track. They include (a) disclosure of documents, (b) the strict rules of evidence, (c) most of the rules about experts, (d) most of the rules about hearings and (e) the provisions of Part 36 relating to offers to settle and payment into court (these have costs consequences which are not appropriate to small track cases).

(2) At the allocation stage the procedural judge may:

    (a)   give "standard directions" in the Notice of Allocation and fix a date for hearing;

    (b)   give "special directions" in the Notice of Allocation and fix a date for hearing;

    (c)   fix a date for a preliminary hearing (if, for example he feels that the claim or the defence has no reasonable chance of success); or

    (d)   give notice that he or she proposes to decide the case on the papers without a hearing and invite the parties to notify the court by a specified date if they agree.

"Standard directions" will include a direction that each party shall, at least fourteen days before the hearing, file and serve on each other party copies of all documents (including experts' reports) on which he intends to rely. The term "special directions" covers such matters as the inspection of documents, experts, witness statements and video evidence; it also covers directions appropriate to the type of case which have been provided for by Practice Directions including vehicle repairs, holiday and wedding claims—see Appendix A to Practice Direction 27, para. 2.2 for further detail.

(3) The case will normally (but not invariably) be heard by a district judge in his room; the general rule is that hearings should be open to the public but this will not not be so if (a) the hearing is held away from the court or (b) the judge orders a hearing in private—he can do this if the parties agree or on certain other grounds listed in Part 39.

(4) A party can present his or her case personally, or by a lawyer or lay representative (if the party is present), or by any other person with permission of the judge.

(5) As stated above, the strict rules of evidence do not apply. Thus, for example evidence need not be on oath and a party can rely on a witness statement even though the witness is not present—although the statement must be verified by a statement of truth. Expert evidence can only be used if the court has granted permission—and this will usually be limited to a single expert jointly instructed.

(6) The judge can adopt any method of proceeding that he or she considers fair and can limit cross-examination. Judges have traditionally taken a very pro-active role in small claims cases (especially as many of the claimants will not have a lawyer to present their case) and the new rules reflect this (see Rule 27.8 and Practice Direction 27, para. 4.3).

(7) If a party is unable or unwilling to attend the hearing, he or she can, at least seven days before the hearing, give written notice to the court that he or she will not be attending and asking the court to decide the case in his or her absence. A failure to send this notice is likely to lead to the case being struck out—although the rules allow the absent party to apply within fourteen days to have a judgment set aside if he or she can show a good reason for non-attendance and a reasonable chance of success at the hearing.

(8) If a party is dissatisfied with the decision of a district judge, he or she can appeal to a circuit judge within fourteen days on the ground that (a) there was a serious irregularity affecting the proceedings or (b) the court made a mistake of law.

(9) A person with a small claim may be reluctant to use the courts for two reasons—fear of the complexity and fear of having to pay the other side's costs if he or she loses. The new rules (like their predecessors) seek to overcome both of these fears. We have already dealt with informality; we must now mention that the general power to award costs to the winner is heavily circumscribed in the small claims track. Under rule 27.14 the court can order a party to pay to the other party:

    (a)   fixed costs on the issue of proceedings (see Part 44),

    (b)   costs assessed summarily on an appeal (see 8 above); and

    (c)   such further sum as the court may assess summarily and order to be paid by a party who has behaved unreasonably (an unreasonable failure to settle the case, or failing to turn up at the hearing, are obvious examples).

In addition, the court can order a party to pay:

(i) any court fees paid by another party;
(ii) expenses which a party or witness has reasonably incurred in travelling to and from a hearing or staying away from home for the purpose of attending a hearing;
(iii) a sum not exceeding £50 for loss of earnings sustained by a party or witness due to attending a hearing or to staying away from home for that purpose; and
(iv) a sum not exceeding £200 for an expert's fee.

If the parties have agreed to a "small track" allocation even though the amount in dispute exceeds the normal small track ceiling, the case is to be treated for costs purposes as proceeding in the fast track.

This general inability to recover costs from the other side, and the need to balance the value of the claim against the cost of enforcing it, are key issues for solicitors consulted in small claims cases (the problems are much less acute if the client has legal expenses insurance). The solicitor may feel that he or she should take a "behind the scenes" advisory role, perhaps drafting the letter of claim and/or the claim form. This division of functions is known in the USA as "unbundling" and it will be interesting to see whether it takes off here (see an article by Suzanne Burn in *Busy Solicitors' Digest*, July 1999).

The fast track (Part 28)

11.08   We have mentioned the need to reduce delay as being one of the central aims of the new regime and the fast track is a prime example. This is the normal track for cases where:

(1) the value of the amount in dispute is between £5,001 and £15,000.
(2) the trial is likely to last for no longer than one day; and
(3) oral expert evidence at the trial (where allowed) will be limited to (a) one expert per party in any expert field and (b) expert evidence in two expert fields.

Once a case has been allocated to the fast track (see para. 11.06, above) the district judge will consider whether further details of the claim or defence are necessary, whether the case can be disposed of summarily and whether a preliminary hearing is necessary. Subject to this, he will make an order for directions which is likely to include a strict (and largely immovable) timetable; this will be geared to a fixed trial date not more than 30 weeks from service of the directions.

There are detailed rules as to disclosure of documents, exchange of witness statements, exchange of experts' reports, a "listing questionnaire" and the preparation of a "trial bundle" limited to those documents which are really required. Also (and this is of great importance) the court will have an on-going power to control the cost of litigation; the rules require the parties to prepare costs estimates (present and future) on every court appearance.

It is also important to appreciate that under Part 46 an award of costs for the trial advocate is severely limited—£350 for claims from £3,001 to £10,000, £500 for claims from £10,001 to £15,000 and a mere £750 for claims above £15,000. Also, if the case is not finished in one day (and a day is normally limited to five hours), there is no scope for increasing the figures set out above. Bearing in mind the ways in which a hearing can so often go off in unexpected directions, solicitors should think long and hard before expressing a preference for the fast track in the allocation questionnaire.

The multi-track (Part 29)

This is the normal track for (a) claims in excess of £15,000 and (b) claims **11.09** within the fast track band where the case is likely to last for more than one day or where the rules relating to expert evidence (see above) are not satisfied. The cases in this track are not subject to the severe time constraints of the fast track and there may be two occasions on which the judge will meet with the parties' lawyers (and in many cases the clients will also be present) to plan the conduct of the case. The first of these meetings is the Case Management Conference at which the judge is likely to give directions—this can involve approving directions which the parties have agreed between themselves. The second meeting is known as the Pre-Trial Review and it will take place after completion of a Listing Questionnaire. The trial advocates will meet the trial judge about 8–10 weeks before the hearing date (a) to explore the possibility of settlement before the full trial costs are incurred and, (b) if settlement is not possible, to prepare an agenda for the trial. At both of these meetings the judge will be fully prepared and he or she will expect the same of the lawyers. In moving the case forward at these meetings the rule 1 overriding objective must be constantly borne in mind by all concerned.

Part II

THE CONSUMER AND THE CRIMINAL LAW

CHAPTER TWELVE

INTRODUCTION

In Part I we have examined the position of consumers as far as the civil law is **12.01** concerned. We saw that it is not enough for them to show that they have a right of action, for example, for breach of contract or negligence. Their main problem is how to enforce that right. It is evident from the figures given at the end of Chapter 10 that the proportion of complainants who are prepared to sue to enforce their rights is small. This encourages traders to assume that they can adopt careless and sloppy practices with impunity. If they can get away with providing shoddy goods and incompetent service, traders will be enticed into lowering their standards by the prospect of increased profitability. Not only is this clearly contrary to the interests of consumers; it is equally unfair to the honest trader who endeavours to maintain high standards and at the same time to compete with the rogues operating in the same line of business.

In pursuing its twofold aim—to protect consumers and to ensure that honest traders are able to make a living on equal terms without the need to resort to the malpractices of their dishonest competitors—Parliament has increasingly turned to the sanctions of criminal law in its search for control. This approach has the significant advantage for the consumer that the expensive and time-consuming process of regulating the rogue is entrusted to public officials who in recent legislation usually have a duty to enforce its provisions. If the provisions of the criminal law also enable consumers to obtain full compensation,[1] it will be unnecessary for them to rely on the rights explained in Part I: they will be superfluous.

The full range of criminal controls is very extensive. The following examples show some of their ambit.

(1) The Food Safety Act 1990[2] controls the quality of food. Section 14 prohibits the sale of "any food which is not of the nature or substance or quality demanded by the purchaser", for example, containing maggots, mould or metal.

(2) The Weights and Measures Act 1985 empowers trading standards inspectors to test weighing and measuring equipment, and also makes it an offence to deliver short weight when goods are sold by weight, number or other measurement.

---

[1] Below, para. 16.02.
[2] Repealing most of the Food Act 1984.

(3) The Trade Descriptions Act 1968 controls business activities at large in so far as they involve descriptions of goods or services. Criminal sanctions are imposed for non-compliance.[3]

(4) The Fair Trading Act 1973, Pt. II, enables orders to be made outlawing general trade practices which adversely affect the economic interests of consumers, for example, the use of certain exemption clauses invalidated by the Unfair Contract Terms Act 1977. A trader who contravenes one of these orders commits a criminal offence.[4]

(5) The Consumer Credit Act 1974 creates a large number of criminal offences (*e.g.* carrying on a consumer credit business without a licence).[5]

(6) The Consumer Protection Act 1987 imposes a general safety requirement prohibiting the supply of unsafe goods. It is an offence to fail to comply.[6]

12.02   In Part II we propose first in Chapter 13 to look in detail at the Act which has resulted in recent years in more consumer complaints than all the other criminal legislation put together—The Trade Descriptions Act 1968—and then in Chapter 14 to proceed to Part III of the Consumer Protection Act 1987 which controls misleading prices in place of the repealed section 11 of the 1968 Act. Next in Chapter 15 we survey those statutory provisions which protect the consumer against unsafe goods, now to be found in Part II of the 1987 Act. Finally in Chapter 16 we consider the important question of compensation for the victims of criminal offences. How can they obtain financial redress for any loss which they may have suffered as a result of the convicted person's failure to comply with his statutory obligations under the criminal law? Two aspects are examined—orders for compensation under the Powers of Criminal Courts Act 1973 and the right to bring civil proceedings for breach of statutory duty.

[3] See para. 13.01 below.
[4] See para. 17.09 below.
[5] See para. 20.06 below.
[6] See para. 15.19 below.

CHAPTER THIRTEEN

"THE DESCRIPTION MISLED ME"

1. INTRODUCTION

This chapter is primarily concerned with the Trade Descriptions Act 1968 **13.01** and the two types of criminal offence to which it gives rise—misdescriptions of goods and of services.

Originally the 1968 Act also contained the provisions relating to misleading prices, but they are now separately controlled by the Consumer Protection Act 1987, Pt. III, and discussed in Chapter 13.

In the Review of the Trade Descriptions Act 1968 published in 1976 the Director General of Fair Trading stated that "by and large, the Act has achieved what its authors and Parliament intended it to do: encourage high standards of truthfulness in describing goods and services".[1] Although the Review contained numerous recommendations to strengthen the Act, the Director General emphasised that "widely as the Act had been drawn, it was never intended to be a panacea for all consumer ills."[2]

Clearly it did not prove to be so, as was evidenced by the Director General's Annual Report for 1977.[3] Consumer complaints notified to the Office of Fair Trading numbered well over half a million in 1977, an increase of 26 per cent on the previous 12 months. (The Report was unclear whether the increase was "due to a general rise in the level of consumer dissatisfaction, a greater readiness by consumers to seek aid from the enforcement and advisory bodies, or a combination of both".) The analysis of consumer complaints by criminal legislation contained in the Report showed that by far the largest single category continued to be complaints under the 1968 Act. A comparison with the figures given in the Annual Report for 1998 shows that the position has not improved in the intervening period. Complaints for that year[4] reached nearly 900,000 and trade descriptions offences still figure prominently among the convictions obtained under consumer protection legislation.

Background to the Act

As early as 1423 an Act was passed regulating the marking of silver plate. **13.02**

---

[1] Cmnd. 6628, para. 1.
[2] *ibid.* para. 2.
[3] H.C. Paper No. 228, Session 1977/78, App. 1.
[4] See above, para. 10.10, for further statistics.

Others dealt with the marking of gold and other precious metals, cutlery and linen. The first statute to cover goods in general was the Merchandise Marks Act 1862 which was replaced in 1887 by an Act of the same name. This was added to by later statutes culminating in the Merchandise Marks Act 1953.

Apart from these statutes dealing specifically with marking, there are related Acts dealing with other aspects of the supply of goods. For example, the Weights and Measures Act 1985, replacing earlier legislation, as its name implies, is particularly concerned with the *quantity* of goods being sold, *e.g.* coal and petrol, and with ensuring that weighing and measuring equipment is accurate, *e.g.* petrol pumps, whereas the Trade Descriptions Act 1968 is also concerned with *quality*. There is one major similarity between the two Acts, namely, that their provisions are enforced by trading standards officers[5] (formerly known as inspectors of weights and measures) employed by local authorities but responsible at ministerial level to the Department of Trade and Industry (as to which see above, para. 1.04). Whilst it is true that the above legislation has the effect of protecting the consumer, most of the legislation, like that relating to patents and trade marks, was passed with the intention of protecting one trader or manufacturer against unfair competition from another who would otherwise be tempted to make business use of the goodwill attaching to a particular mark or brand-name.

The position with regard to trade descriptions generally was looked into by the Committee on Consumer Protection, generally known as the Molony Committee, which published its Final Report in 1962.[6] It paid particular attention to the working of the Merchandise Marks Acts and highlighted a number of defects:

(a) Consolidation was desirable in view of the law being contained in a multiplicity of Acts.

(b) The Acts were limited in their scope since they were relevant only where a description had been "applied" to goods, *i.e.* where goods had been physically marked with labels, dies, blocks, etc. Thus oral statements[7] and many advertisements were not covered.

(c) Whatever the merits of the Acts, they were not generally enforced. The Acts of 1891 and 1894 gave the Board of Trade and Ministry of Agriculture, Fisheries and Food respectively the *power* to enforce the regulations; the Local Government Act 1933 gave a similar power to local authorities, and an individual could bring a private prosecution. Yet nobody was under a *duty* to enforce them. The Committee found that only about a dozen prosecutions were brought each year by the Board of Trade, though a larger number were brought by local authorities.

---

[5] See below, para. 13.57.
[6] Cmnd. 1781.
[7] But see now 1968 Act, s.4(2), below, para. 13.10.

These defects were cured by the passing of the Trade Descriptions Act 1968.

Purpose and ambit

The beginning of the preamble to the Act sets out its essential purpose and scope: **13.03**

> An Act to replace the Merchandise Marks Act 1887 to 1953 by fresh provisions prohibiting misdescriptions of goods, services, accommodation and facilities provided in the course of trade.

The preamble discloses the two main offences[8]:

(a) applying a false trade description to *goods* or supplying goods with such a description[9];

(b) making a false statement as to the provision of *services*, accommodation or facilities.[10]

Before considering these offences in detail, two important general features of the Act need to be grasped. First, the Act operates in the criminal area only: it does not give any direct civil remedy to the misguided consumer.[11] Secondly, it applies only to suppliers in the course of a trade or business, *i.e.* not to private suppliers.[12] However, it is irrelevant whether or not the recipient of the goods or services is a private consumer or a trader: the Act protects all and sundry—domestic consumers, sole traders, partnerships and corporations.

In the course of a trade or business

As mentioned above, the Act applies to business suppliers only. Section 1[13]   **13.04**
includes an express limitation to persons "in the course of a trade or business" and section 14[14] has an almost identical limitation to persons "in the course of any trade or business": presumably the two expressions have the same meaning.

A question giving rise to slight doubt had been whether the professions fall within the scope of the Act. Unlike the Fair Trading Act 1973, s.137, and the Consumer Credit Act 1974, s.189, no definition of "business" is given so as to make it clear that professional practice is included. This point was recently clarified by the Court of Appeal in *Roberts v. Leonard*[15]: professions are covered. As Simon Brown L.J. stated, he had not the least doubt that the term

---

[8] s.11 created a third offence and controlled misleading *prices*, but has now been repealed: see below, para. 14.01.

[9] s.1.

[10] s.14.

[11] See below, para. 13.61. For the possibility of a compensation order see below, para. 16.02.

[12] The by-pass provision (s.23) is an exception.

[13] Below, para. 13.06.

[14] Below, para. 13.37.

[15] *The Times*, May 10, 1995 (vets' descriptions of exported calves).

"trade or business" was "apt to include professions as well. There is no suf-ficient reason to exclude professional men from the scope of the legislation nor for their being any better placed than others in its application".

Clearly the Act applies where the essence of the business is the supply of the goods or services in question. Yet the Act is wider. Provided the trans-action occurs in the course of *a* business, it may be caught even though it does not form part of the primary activities of the business. Thus in *Havering L.B.C. v. Stevenson*[16]:

> The defendant ran a car hire business. When the cars were about two years old, his practice was to sell them and to use the proceeds to buy new cars. He sold a car with a false description as to the mileage. When prosecuted he argued that the sale was outside section 1, since he did not carry on the business of a car dealer. The Divisional Court was unmoved. When a car hire business as part of its nor-mal practice[17] buys and sells cars, the sale of a car with the related application of a trade description is an integral part of (and thus in the course of) the car hire business.

13.05   A more difficult question is posed where the sale or other transaction is an isolated occurrence or is not part of the trader's normal practice. Suppose that an electrician inaccurately describes the mileage on his van when selling it to purchase a new one, an infrequent event. Or perhaps a solicitor, refurbishing her office, misdescribes an old desk in an advertisement as "used by Lord Chief Justice Widgery when an articled clerk". Clearly the transaction involves an asset of the business, for which no doubt tax allowances have been claimed. At first sight the transaction falls within the wide wording of section 1(1) as the phrase "a trade or business" is not in terms limited to businesses which normally deal in goods of the type in question. The House of Lords, however, adopted a narrow interpretation of the provision in *Davies v. Sumner*[18]:

> The defendant was a self-employed courier whose whole activity was trans-porting films and other material round Wales for Harlech Television. In June 1980 he bought a new Ford car; he had previously hired a car for a few months. In July 1981 he offered the car in part exchange for a new car and was given an allowance on the basis of the mileage of 18,100 shown on the odometer. The defendant failed to disclose that the true mileage was 118,100, as the odometer had gone right round the clock. He was convicted by the Clwyd Justices of hav-ing applied a false description to the car in that he represented that it had travelled the lower mileage. His appeal on the grounds that the description was not applied "in the course of a trade or business" was allowed by the Divisional Court and the prosecutor's appeal to the House of Lords was dismissed.

Lord Keith, with whose judgment the other members of the court agreed, accepted that in a sense any disposal of a chattel held for the purposes of a

---

[16] [1970] 1 W.L.R. 1375.
[17] *cf. Devlin v. Hall* [1990] R.T.R. 320, DC (taxi proprietor owned two taxis; his *first* sale did not establish "normal practice", though three later sales did).
[18] [1984] 3 All E.R. 831.

business might be said to be in the course of that business, whether it was acquired for resale, for consumption or as a capital asset. However, section 1(1) is not intended to cast such a wide net. Lord Keith, accepting that the *Havering* case was correctly decided, distinguished it from the present case on a number of grounds[19]:

> "The expression 'in the course of a trade or business' in the context of an Act having consumer protection as its primary purpose conveys the concept of some degree of regularity, and it is to be observed that the long title of the Act refers to 'misdescriptions of goods, services, accommodation and facilities provided in the course of trade.' Lord Parker C.J. in the *Havering* case clearly considered that the expression was not used in the broadest sense.
>
> The reason why the transaction there in issue was caught was that in his view it was 'an integral part of the business carried on as a car hire firm.' That would not cover the sporadic selling of pieces of equipment which were no longer required for the purposes of a business. The vital feature of the *Havering* case appears to have been, in Lord Parker's view, that the respondent's business *as part of its normal practice* bought and disposed of cars.
>
> The need for some degree of regularity does not, however, involve that a one-off adventure in the nature of trade, carried through with a view to profit, would not fall within section 1(1) because such a transaction would itself constitute a trade."[20]

There were other differences too. In the present case the defendant might well revert to hiring a car as he had previously done; the outcome would apparently have been different had the prosecution been able to establish that as part of his normal practice the defendant had bought and disposed of cars at regular intervals. Again in the *Havering* case the defendant had exploited his stock-in-trade (the hire cars), whereas the defendant here was merely using his car as a piece of equipment in providing his courier service.

From the point of view of the consumer the House of Lords re-strictive interpretation is disappointing. Had the draftsman of the 1968 Act wished to limit its application to the supply of goods in a business which normally deals in goods of that type, it would not have been difficult to find an appropriate formula. For example, the wording of section 14(2) of the Sale of Goods Act 1893 was limited in this way before it was amended in 1973 to widen its scope. The decision can be justified on the basis that here we are dealing with criminal legislation where a narrow interpretation in favour of the defendant is appropriate, but surprisingly the Court of Appeal followed *Davies v. Sumner* in a civil case on the interpretation of the same expression in section 12 of the Unfair Contract Terms Act 1977.[21]

---

[19] *ibid.* p. 833.

[20] *Quaere* whether *Blakemore v. Bellamy* [1983] R.T.R. 303, DC is still good law. (Postman's hobby of buying, refurbishing and selling numerous cars. No significant profit. Not "trade or business".)

[21] *R & B Customs Brokers Co. Ltd v. United Dominions Trust* [1988] 1 All E.R. 847. For a full discussion, see above, para. 8.25. However, recently the Court of Appeal gave a wide meaning to the phrase "in the course of a business" in section 14(2) of the Sale of Goods Act 1979 (see above, para. 4.04).

2. Goods

13.06   Section 1(1) prohibits false trade descriptions of goods:

> Any person who, in the course of a trade of business—
>   (a) applies a false trade description to any goods; or
>   (b) supplies or offers to supply any goods to which a false trade description is applied;
> shall, subject to the provisions of this Act, be guilty of an offence.

Business suppliers

13.07   As we saw above, an offence is committed only by a person acting "in the course of a trade or business". The provision does not catch supplies by private persons.[22]

Strict liability

13.08   The offences created by section 1 are offences of strict liability. Although charges under these provisions often involve an element of dishonesty, as was pointed out by the Divisional Court in *Alec Norman Garages Ltd v. Phillips,*[23] it is not necessary for the prosecution to prove dishonesty.

Two offences

13.09   Section 1 covers two different offences: first, the application of a false trade description to goods; secondly, the supply of goods to which such a description has already been applied. Thus the first offence would be committed by a manufacturer incorrectly labelling goods, while the second offence would occur when a retailer displays or sells those same goods.

Applying a false trade description: section 1(1)(a)

13.10   The first of the offences occurs when a person "applies a false trade description to any goods". A wide meaning is given by section 4 to the word "applies":

> (1) A person applies a trade description to goods if he—
>   (a) affixes or annexes it to or in any manner marks it on or incorporates it with—
>   (i) the goods themselves, or
>   (ii) anything in, on or with which the goods are supplied; or
>   (b) places the goods in, on or with anything which the trade description has been affixed or annexed to, marked on or incorporated with, or places any such thing with the goods; or
>   (c) uses the trade description in any manner likely to be taken as referring to the goods.

---

[22] Above, para. 13.03.
[23] [1985] R.T.R. 164.

(2) An oral statement may amount to the use of a trade description.
(3) Where goods are supplied in pursuance of a request in which a trade description is used and the circumstances are such as to make it reasonable to infer that the goods are supplied as goods corresponding to that trade description, the person supplying the goods shall be deemed to have applied that trade description to the goods.

It covers:

 (i) markings on the goods themselves, *e.g.* labels;
 (ii) markings on anything in which the goods are supplied, *e.g.* packaging[24];
(iii) markings on anything in which the goods are placed, *e.g.* display units, vending machines, point-of-sale material;
(iv) oral statements, specifically mentioned in section 4(2).

The inclusion of oral descriptions is one of the major differences between the 1968 Act and the Merchandise Marks Acts which were limited to the physical application of descriptions to goods.[25] This extension of the law was effected against the recommendation of the Molony Committee whose reasons for the preservation of the status quo are set out in paragraph 659 of their Report.

Descriptions used by customers in their requests for goods, when it is reasonable to infer that the goods are supplied as goods corresponding to such descriptions, are deemed to have been applied by the supplier.[26] Thus if a customer asks for a cotton shirt and is supplied with a polyester shirt, the shopkeeper applies the description "cotton" to the shirt even if he says nothing and the shirt is not labelled.

In most cases the trader has quite clearly described the goods and thus applied a description to them. However, "applies" was given a much wider meaning by the Divisional Court in *Tarleton Engineering Co. Ltd v. Nattrass*[27]:

> A dealer sold a car with a false odometer reading. He had not altered the odometer himself. He did not know it was false nor did he repeat the reading or vouch for it. Held, he had applied a false trade description to the car.

It is difficult to justify such a wide interpretation of any of the expressions used in section 4. It would have been preferable to bring a prosecution under

---

[24] In the unreported *Astral* case (1981) A & F Pears Ltd was convicted of a s.1 offence for selling jars of face cream 30 per cent larger in volume than their contents which were correctly given as 54 grams on their labels. Presumably the goods described themselves by their packaging. For a critical analysis, see Woodroffe, *"False Bottoms, Thick Skins"*, 79 L.S.Gaz. 62.
[25] See *Coppen v. Moore (No. 1)* [1898] 2 Q.B. 300.
[26] s.4(3). See *R. v. Ford Motor Co.* [1974] 1 W.L.R. 1220: description in order form completed by supplier. See below, para. 13.36.
[27] [1973] 1 W.L.R. 1261. *Cf. Newham L.B.C. v. Singh* [1988] R.T.R. 359, DC: dealers not aware of alteration—no offence.

section 1(1)(b) on the grounds that the trader had supplied the car with a false trade description.

Nevertheless it now seems to be settled beyond doubt that a person "applies" a description to goods, even in the absence of a written or oral statement, if he fails to take steps to correct a misunderstanding which is induced by a description borne by the goods themselves. Thus in *Davies v. Sumner*[28] the defendant applied a false description to the car, in that "he represented that it had travelled 18,100 miles when the true mileage was 118,100 miles", by merely standing by and not disclosing the truth.

Supplying goods with a false trade description: section 1(1)(b)

13.11   The second of the two offences contained in section 1 is committed when a person "supplies or offers to supply any goods to which a false trade description is applied". The offence is most likely to occur where a retailer sells goods with a description applied by a manufacturer, importer or another distributor earlier in the commercial chain.

Offer to supply

13.12   To resolve the problem that, where goods are in a shop window, on a supermarket shelf or put up at an auction,[29] no offer for sale is made in a contractual sense by the prospective supplier—there is only an invitation to treat to customers who then make an offer to buy—section 6 provides that "a person exposing goods for supply or having goods in his possession for supply shall be deemed to offer to supply them".

Knowledge

13.13   It appears from *Cottee v. Douglas Seaton (Used Cars) Ltd*[30] that a supplier does not commit this offence if he neither applied the description to the goods himself nor knew or had means of knowing that this had been done by another. However, where a supplier knows that a description has been applied, even though he does not know that it is false, he is liable, *e.g.* selling a car with an inaccurate odometer.

The facts of the *Cottee* case were as follows:

> Dealer A patched up the bodywork of a car which he sold to dealer B. The repair was so skilfully done that B did not discover it. B sold it to C. Held, B had not committed an offence under section 1(1)(b) as he was unaware of the defect. Knowledge that a trade description was applied was essential. Accordingly, A was acquitted of an offence under section 23[31] which depended upon the commission of an offence by B.

---

[28] Above, para. 13.05, *per* Lord Keith of Kinkel at p. 832.

[29] Shop window—*Fisher v. Bell* [1961] 1 Q.B. 394. Supermarket—*Pharmaceutical Society of G.B. v. Boots Cash Chemists (Southern)* [1952] 2 Q.B. 795. Auction—*Payne v. Cave* (1789) 3 Term Rep. 148.

[30] [1972] 1 W.L.R. 1408. The "description" in this case consisted of the covering up of the defect by A.

[31] See below, para. 13.53. B could have relied on the s.24(3) defence: *ibid.*

In short, knowledge of the *existence* of the description is a prerequisite, but not knowledge of its *falsity*.

Time of application

No offence is committed under section 1 where the description is applied **13.14** to goods *after* they have been supplied. Thus in *Hall v. Wickens*[32] the Divisional Court upheld the acquittal of a motor dealer who had falsely described a car as not being in need of repair 40 days after supplying it to a customer. The description must precede or be contemporaneous with the supply of goods.

Meaning of trade description

Section 2(1) defines a trade description as "an indication" of any of the **13.15** matters exhaustively listed in its 10 paragraphs and amplified in section 2(2) and (3):

(1) A trade description is an indication, direct or indirect, and by whatever means given, of any of the following matters with respect to any goods or parts of goods, that is to say—
- (a) quantity, size or gauge;
- (b) method of manufacture, production, processing or reconditioning;
- (c) composition[33];
- (d) fitness for purpose, strength, performance, behaviour or accuracy;
- (e) any physical characteristics not included in the preceding paragraphs;
- (f) testing by any person and results thereof;
- (g) approval by any person or conformity with a type approved by any person;
- (h) place or date of manufacture, production, processing or reconditioning;
- (i) person by whom manufactured, produced, processed or reconditioned;
- (j) other history, including previous ownership or use.

(2) The matters specified in subsection (1) of this section shall be taken—
- (a) in relation to any animal, to include sex, breed or cross, fertility and soundness;
- (b) in relation to any semen, to include the identity and characteristics of the animal from which it was taken and measure of dilution.

(3) In this section "quantity" includes length, width, height, area, volume, capacity, weight and number.

There are special provisions relating to seeds, agriculture and food and drugs.[34]

---

[32] [1972] 1 W.L.R. 1418. *Cf. R. v. Haesler* [1973] Crim.L.R. 586.
[33] "Composition" includes the way in which components are arranged: *Queensway Discount Warehouses Ltd v. Burke* (1986) 150 J.P. 17, DC (furniture in newspaper advertisement—picture showed it ready assembled but it was not).
[34] s.2(4) and (5).

Examples

13.16 The following examples may assist readers; the lettering follows that in section 2(1):

  (a) size of shoes, shirts, dresses or other clothing;
  (b) Axminster or Wilton carpet;
  (c) shirt labelled "65% polyester, 35% cotton";
  (d) "top speed 102 mph, 28 mpg";
  (e) car equipped with "five-tone horn playing 'Colonel Bogey' ";
  (f) "tested by the Road Research Laboratory";
  (g) tennis racket "as used by Sampras"[35];
  (h) 1990 Audi Quattro;
  (i) "tuned by High Performance Motors Ltd";
  (j) "only one private owner[36]; 46,000 miles".

Review recommendations

13.17 The Review considered the suggestion of replacing the list in section 2 with a general offence of misdescribing goods or services with the object of catching the misdescription of any feature not included in the list. However, such a suggestion was rejected on the grounds that "it seems a good principle when creating criminal offences that the offence is defined as precisely as possible."[37-38]

Definition orders

13.18 Difficulties can arise where a term is used which has a special meaning and is not meant as a literal description of the goods, *e.g.* "Dover Sole" not from Dover or "Bombay Duck" which is neither duck nor from Bombay. The problem was discussed in a case under the Merchandise Marks Acts, *Lemy v. Watson*,[39] in which it was held to be a false trade description to describe brisling as "Norwegian sardines". Darling J. used as an illustration the "Holy Roman Empire"—a description of an institution which was neither holy nor Roman nor an Empire.[40]

  To alleviate this problem section 7 gives the Department of Trade and Industry power to make definition orders assigning definite meanings to expressions used as part of a trade description.

Is it false?

13.19 Let us assume that (a) there is a trade description within the meaning of

---

[35] See also s.3(4).
[36] See *R. v. Inner London Justices, ex p. Wandsworth L.B.C.* [1983] R.T.R. 425, DC: "One owner" car sold by leasing company after leasing to five successive hirers. Acquittal quashed. "One owner" means that the car has been controlled and maintained by only one person.
[37-38] Para. 121.
[39] [1915] 3 K.B. 731.
[40] See also *Kat v. Diment* [1951] 1 K.B. 34 (non-brewed vinegar).

section 2; (b) the defendant has either applied it or supplied goods to which it has been applied within section 1(1); and (c) the defendant has done so in the course of a trade or business.

The next question to consider is whether the trade description is a *false* trade description. Section 3(1) states simply and clearly that "a false trade description is a trade description which is false to a material degree." These last four words were considered by the Divisional Court in *Donnelly v. Rowlands*[41]:

> Rowlands was a Welsh dairy farmer and milk retailer. He bottled his milk in various types of bottles, some of which were embossed Express, C.W.S., Northern and Goodwins. The foil cap on every bottle was embossed with the words "Untreated milk. Produced from T.T. cows. Rowlands" and the name of his farm. A prosecution was brought by an Inspector of Milk Vessels Recovery Limited (not by a trading standards officer) under section 1(1)(b). The justices decided that no offence had been committed on the basis that, as the description on the foil cap was accurate, the false description on the bottle was not false "to a material degree". The Divisional Court dismissed an appeal by the prosecutor.

The court, while agreeing that it was possible to approach the problem by looking at the description as a whole on both the bottle and the cap, took a different line. In their view the trade description was not false to any degree at all.[41a] The words on the foil cap were an accurate trade description of the milk; the words on the bottle did not refer to the milk but merely conveyed that the bottle belonged to the company whose name was embossed.[42]

The meaning of "false trade description" is extended by section 3(2) and (3):

> (2) A trade description which, though not false, is misleading, that is to say, likely to be taken for such an indication of any of the matters specified in section 2 of this Act as would be false to a material degree, shall be deemed to be a false trade description.
> (3) Anything which, though not a trade description, is likely to be taken for an indication of any of those matters and, as such an indication, would be false to a material degree, shall be deemed to be a false trade description.

The latter subsection was considered by the Divisional Court in *Holloway v. Cross*,[43] another of the numerous cases relating to clocked cars:

> A motor dealer bought a car with an odometer reading 716 miles, although unknown to him the true mileage was over 70,000 miles. He told an interested customer that he would make inquiries as to the true mileage. Later he told the customer that in his opinion it was probably about 45,000 miles and wrote on the invoice "recorded mileage 716, estimated mileage 45,000 miles". He was con-

---

[41] [1970] 1 W.L.R. 1600.
[41a] See also *R. v. Bull (Carl)* [1996] Crim.L.R. 438, below, para. 13.22.
[42] *cf. Stone v. Burn* [1911] 1 K.B. 927 where an offence was committed under the Merchandise Marks Acts when Bass beer was sold in another brewer's bottles with Bass labels.
[43] [1981] 1 All E.R. 1012.

victed of offences under section 1(1)(a) and (b) by the Chatham Justices who considered that, as the estimate was an opinion, it was not "an indication" falling within section 2(1)(j) but was within the extension to the concept of a false trade description provided by section 3(3); the disparity between the actual and estimated mileages was sufficiently large to render the estimate false to a material degree.

Donaldson L.J. thought it debatable that the estimate was not caught by section 2(1). In any case the dealer's estimate was likely to be taken by the buyer as an indication of the history of the vehicle and amounted to a false description within section 3(3). The dealer's appeal against conviction was dismissed.

Advertisements

13.20   The Act does not create a separate offence relating to advertisements incorporating a false description. However, this is not to say that manufacturers or retailers may include false descriptions in their publicity material with impunity; they run the risk of committing offences under section 1(1)(a) and (b). The importance of section 5 of the Act, which is concerned solely with advertisements, is its relation to the section 1 offences and also to section 4 which, as we have seen, defines the ways in which a trade description may be applied.

It is to be remembered that section 4(1)(c) states that a person applies a trade description to goods if he "uses the trade description in any manner likely to be taken as referring to the goods." Section 5 provides an answer when one is trying to ascertain whether an advertisement relates to those goods which are the subject-matter of proceedings: it states that where a trade description is used in an advertisement in relation to any class of goods, the description "shall be taken as referring to all goods of the class, whether or not in existence at the time the advertisement is published."[44] Factors to be taken into account in deciding whether a customer would think of his goods as belonging to the relevant class are the form and content of the advertisement and the time, place, manner and frequency of its publication.

Example

A manufacturer launches a national television advertising campaign in relation to certain goods. A retailer supplies goods of that type with knowledge of the advertisement. The retailer commits an offence under section 1(1)(b) if the advertisement includes false information. If the goods are accompanied by point-of-sale material which also includes a false trade description, the retailer will in addition commit an offence under section 1(1)(a), for he will have applied

[44] s.5(2).

the description within the meaning of section 4(1)(b) by placing such material with the goods.

It should be noted that the meaning of "advertisement" is defined in section 39, the interpretation section, as including a catalogue, circular and price list.

Disclaimers and odometers

The Review reveals that the most prevalent offence dealt with by enforce-   **13.21**
ment authorities involves tampering with odometers (or milometers) to understate the true mileage.[45] Accordingly, it is proposed to look particularly at this type of offence. Further, as the cases involving disclaimers are, in the main, concerned with false odometer readings, this area will be considered at the same time.

The first question is whether a false odometer reading can in law be a false trade description. Counsel's submission that it cannot be so was described as "bold but hopeless" by Lawton L.J. in *R. v. Hammertons Cars Ltd.*[46] The Divisional Court decided that an odometer reading is an indication of the use which the car has had and is "other history, including previous ownership or use" within section 2(1)(j).[47]

Effect of disclaimer

An important limitation on the use of disclaimers is that they may assist   **13.22**
defendants only where a section 1(1)(b) "supplier" offence is charged. The common law doctrine of disclaimer has no application where the defendant himself is the culprit who "applies" the description. Thus in *Newman v. Hackney L.B.C.*[48] a motor dealer turned back an odometer from 46,328 to 21,000 and then stuck a disclaimer over it; this later action did not prevent the commission of an offence under section 1(1)(a).

However, the Court of Appeal in *R. v. Bull (Carl)*[49] allowed an appeal by a dealer convicted under section 1(1)(a) on the grounds that, although he had applied a description, the prosecution had not established that it was false.

> The defendant sold a car with an odometer reading of 47,526 miles. The sales invoice contained a box with a heading "Odometer reading" which the defendant completed with the figure 47,526. Next to the figure was an asterisk and, immediately below, this explanation: "Trade Descriptions Act 1968. We have been unable to confirm the mileage on this odometer and therefore it must be considered incorrect."

[45] Para. 160.
[46] [1976] 1 W.L.R. 1243 at 1246.
[47] But a statement in an MOT certificate as to mileage, etc., is not an indication of the vehicle's history: *Corfield v. Sevenways Garage Ltd* [1985] R.T.R. 109, DC. Such a statement as to year of manufacture may be: *R. v. Coventry City Justices, ex p. Farrand* [1988] R.T.R. 273, DC.
[48] [1982] R.T.R. 296, DC. Approved by Court of Appeal in *R. v. Southwood* [1987] 1 W.L.R. 1361.
[49] [1996] Crim.L.R. 438.

Waterhouse J. stated, "The real question was whether or not the qualification of the figure was properly to be regarded as part of the trade description or as a mere disclaimer." It follows that a "qualification" preventing the description being false is effective, whereas a disclaimer is not. *Newman* was distinguished on the grounds that "very different circumstances" applied.

Disclaimer in time?

13.23   To be effective a disclaimer must be introduced by the trader before he "supplies" the goods, the word used in section 1(1)(b). It is tempting to apply by analogy the contractual rules relating to the incorporation of terms and to take the view that, if a disclaimer is introduced after the contract has been made, it is entirely ineffective. However, the test is not a contractual one. Clearly if the disclaimer is sufficiently brought to the attention of the customer at an early stage during the negotiations, it will be successful. Equally clearly a disclaimer after the buyer has taken possession of the goods will fail, for a disclaimer must be made before the goods are supplied.

The most difficult problem occurs where the trader endeavours at the moment of delivery to disclaim responsibility by telling the buyer only then that the odometer reading is unreliable. Supply and delivery are not to be equated, as can be seen from the judgment of Lawton L.J. in *R. v. Hammertons Cars Ltd.*[49a] Such an oral statement at the delivery stage may not be enough to displace the impression given by the odometer reading which may linger on in the buyer's mind. "The issue for the court of trial is whether when the purchaser takes possession of the goods he gets them with a false trade description applied to them."[50] So while it is possible for a trader to disclaim when making delivery, he will have great difficulty by delaying so late in persuading a court that a false trade description has not been applied.

It is to be noted that a disclaimer can be implied from a previous course of dealing or because of an understanding between the parties, at least when both of them are experienced car dealers.[51]

General tests

13.24   A number of tests have been propounded in the cases to assist in deciding whether in a particular case a disclaimer is effective. In *Norman v. Bennett* Lord Widgery C.J. stated that the disclaimer must be "as bold, precise and compelling as the trade description itself" and "must equal the trade description in the extent to which it is likely to get home to anyone interested in receiving the goods."[52] Lawton L.J.'s instruction to dealers who do not want prospective purchasers to take any notice of odometer readings is that "they must take positive and effective steps to ensure that the customer understands

---

[49a] [1976] 1 W.L.R. 1243.
[50] *ibid.* at p. 1248, *per* Lawton L.J.
[51] *Norman v. Bennett* [1974] 1 W.L.R. 1229.
[52] *ibid.* at p. 1232.

that the milometer reading is meaningless."[53] Lord Widgery C.J. returned to the problem in *Waltham Forest London Borough Council v. T.G. Wheatley (Central Garage) Ltd (No. 2)*[54] when he said, "The purpose of the disclaimer is for it to sit beside, as it were, the false trade description and cancel the other out as soon as its first impression can be made on the purchaser."[55]

All these tests come to the same thing. At the moment of delivery at the latest the buyer must be fully aware that he should place no reliance at all on the odometer reading which has been effectively neutralised or cancelled by the disclaimer, be it oral or contained in a notice, agreement or other document.

Particular disclaimers

Oral.   For two reasons an oral disclaimer is least likely to be effective. First, **13.25** there is the evidential problem of proving what the seller said. Secondly, a casual remark in the course of negotiations will hardly satisfy the general criteria mentioned above. In *R. v. Hammertons Cars Ltd*:

> Car dealers sold two cars to a customer. The odometers showed 25,600 miles and 25,300 miles, whereas the true mileages were 53,714 miles and 34,000 respectively. At the time of delivery the buyers were given a printed document headed "SPECIFIC GUARANTEE OF USED MOTOR VEHICLE." At the bottom of the document in small print under the heading "MILEAGE AND DATE" appeared: "any estimate or opinion of the mileage . . . which the Suppliers may have given to the Customer during negotiations . . . was given according to their best information and belief. (The suppliers are not answerable for the mileage shown on the vehicle's milometer.)" The salesman also gave evidence that he had clearly given the purchasers to understand that the mileage as shown on the odometer was not guaranteed but his evidence was rejected by the jury. Held, the dealers had committed an offence under section 1(1)(b). A casual remark in the course of oral negotiations or small print in a contractual document are unlikely to be sufficient disclaimers.

Documents.   As has just been seen, disclaimers in small print will not pro- **13.26** tect the dealer. Presumably, disclaimers printed boldly in documents read by the buyer before the goods are supplied will suffice. However, here again a distinction must be drawn between the contractual rules relating to the incorporation of terms, *e.g.* exemption clauses, and the present situation. In view of the statement of Lord Widgery C.J. in *Norman v. Bennett*[56] that the disclaimer "must be effectively brought to the notice" of the customer, it seems that the dealer will not be able to rely on the fact that the customer happened to sign the relevant document. Thus to have the desired neutralising effect the clause must be both boldly printed and brought clearly to the attention of the customer.

[53] *R. v. Hammertons Cars Ltd* [1976] 1 W.L.R. 1243 at 1248.
[54] [1978] R.T.R. 333.
[55] *ibid.* at p. 339.
[56] Above, n. 51.

13.27 **Notices.** In a number of cases dealers have attempted to rely on disclaimers in notices on their premises. Thus in *Zawadski v. Sleigh*[57]:

> Dealers auctioned three cars with false odometer readings. Disclaimers as to the mileage of the cars appeared both in the auction entry forms and in notices in the auction premises. A Divisional Court held that the general notices were insufficient to be disclaimers.

Similarly, in *Waltham Forest L.B.C. v. T.G. Wheatley (Central Garage) Ltd*[58] a notice in the dealer's office was held to be an insufficient disclaimer. One difficulty is that prospective buyers looking at vehicles on the forecourt or in the showroom may not enter the dealer's office and so will not have an opportunity of seeing the notice. Even so the dealer is offering to supply the goods within the meaning of section 1(1)(b). It may be that prominent notices placed in close proximity to the relevant goods are apt to neutralise the odometer reading. Clearly the safest method to adopt is to place the disclaimer notice next to or over the odometer so that it does "sit beside the false description". If, in addition, there is a written contract with a boldly printed clause to the same effect and both the clause and the notice are pointed out to customers, then with this belt and braces technique the dealer is unlikely to run the risk of committing an offence.

13.28 A case where a rogue dealer deserved to escape liability, if ingenuity were the criterion, is *Corfield v. Starr*[59]:

> A motor dealer purchased a car for resale and substituted an odometer showing a misleadingly low mileage. He attached a notice to the dashboard stating, "With deep regret due to Customer's Protection Act we can no longer verify that the mileage shown on this vehicle is correct." The Divisional Court allowed the prosecutor's appeal against acquittal, as the notice with its reference to the non-existent Act was misleading and fell far short of disclaiming the unmistakable representation given by the odometer.

13.29 **Zeroing.** One practice adopted by some motor dealers is to zero the odometer. Clearly the reading is then false. Has the trader applied a false trade description and committed an offence? Doubtless traders would argue that it is not false to a material degree, as it can mislead no one.[60] Their position is more secure if they use a disclaimer too, as in *Lill Holdings v. White*[61]:

> The defendants zeroed an odometer reading 59,000 miles, attached a disclaimer and sold it to A. A resold it to B, who resold to C with a reading of some 5,000 miles. The Divisional Court allowed the defendants' appeal against conviction under section 23,[62] as they had not been guilty of any "act or default".

---

[57] [1975] R.T.R. 113.
[58] [1978] R.T.R. 333.
[59] [1981] R.T.R. 380.
[60] But see the comments of Lord Lane C.J. in *R. v. Southwood* [1987] 3 All E.R. 556 at 564: "The person who 'zeroes' the instrument is applying a false trade description as much as the man who reduces the reading."
[61] [1979] R.T.R. 120.
[62] See below, para. 13.53, for the "by-pass" provision.

Defences

Even where a prima facie offence has been committed because the dis-   **13.30**
claimer fails in its purpose, the defendant may be able to take advantage of
the defences available under section 24(1). These are discussed later.[63] The
only point to be made at this stage is that in *Simmons v. Potter*[64] the Divisional
Court held that a car dealer who had not published a disclaimer had failed to
take an obvious precaution and therefore could not rely on the statutory
defence. It appears then to be advantageous for dealers to use disclaimers. On
the one hand they may well prevent an offence being committed in the first
place. On the other hand even if they fail in that primary objective, a dealer's
attempt to disclaim responsibility may itself enable him or her more readily
to call in aid the section 24 defence.

Illustrative cases on section 1

In all the following cases a prima facie offence was committed under sec-   **13.31**
tion 1, although in some of them the defendant was able to rely on the section
24 defence.

Beckett v. Kingston Bros. (Butchers) Ltd[65]

Butchers sold a turkey labelled "Norfolk King Turkey". It had in fact come   **13.32**
from Denmark. It was held to be an offence under section 1(1)(b).

British Gas Corporation v. Lubbock[66]

In response to her inquiry at a corporation showroom about a Parkinson   **13.33**
cooker, a customer was given a brochure which stated "ignition is by the
hand-held battery torch supplied with the cooker". She ordered a cooker
which was supplied without a torch. It was held that the brochure referred to a
"package" of goods which included the torch. The description in the brochure was an indication as to "composition" under section 2(1)(c); alternatively, an indication of "physical characteristics not included in the preceding
paragraphs" under section 2(1)(e). An offence was committed under section
1(1)(a). (Presumably there was also an offence under section 1(1)(b), as the
appellants supplied the goods as well as applying the description.)

Sherratt v. Geralds The American Jewellers Ltd[67]

The jewellers sold a watch described as a "diver's watch" and engraved   **13.34**
"waterproof". The purchaser tested the watch by immersing it in a bowl of
water; it filled with water and stopped. Held, an offence under section
1(1)(b).

---

[63] See below, para. 13.44.
[64] [1975] Crim.L.R. 354.
[65] [1970] 1 Q.B. 606.
[66] [1974] 1 W.L.R. 37.
[67] (1970) 114 S.J. 147.

Fletcher v. Budgen[68]

13.35   A private seller wished to sell his car to a car dealer. The dealer said that there was no possibility of repairing the car; repairs would not make the car safe; and the only possible course of action was for the car to be scrapped. So the car was sold to him for £2. The dealer spent £56 repairing it and then advertised it at a price of £135. It was held to be an offence under section 1(1)(a), the description falling within section 2(1)(e). The Act applied even though the description was applied by a prospective trade *buyer*, the reverse of the normal situation.

R. v. Ford Motor Co.[69]

13.36   Fords supplied a "new" car to a dealer who resold it to a customer. It had been damaged after leaving their factory and while in the hands of their forwarding agents, and properly repaired at a cost of £50. Fords were charged under section 1(1)(b) (and also under section 23 because of the dealer's section 1(1)(b) offence). The Court of Appeal held that no offence was committed. The description "new" is not false where the damage is superficial, or limited to parts which can be simply replaced by new parts, and is perfectly repaired so that the car is as good as new.[70]

3. Services

13.37   An area not covered by the Merchandise Marks Act nor by the Molony Report is services. This novel extension of criminal liability from goods to services doubtless accounts for a more tentative approach in section 14 as compared with section 1. The offence of making false or misleading statements about services is not an offence of strict liability, as can be seen from the wording of section 14(1):

> It shall be an offence for any person in the course of any trade or business—
>   (a) to make a statement which he knows to be false; or
>   (b) recklessly to make a statement which is false;
> as to any of the following matters, that is to say—
>   (i) the provision in the course of any trade or business of any services, accommodation or facilities;
>   (ii) the nature of any services, accommodation or facilities provided in the course of any trade or business;
>   (iii) the time at which, manner in which or persons by whom any services, accommodation or facilities are so provided;
>   (iv) the examination, approval or evaluation by any person of any services, accommodation or facilities so provided; or

---

[68] [1974] 1 W.L.R. 1056.
[69] [1974] 1 W.L.R. 1220.
[70] *cf. Raynham Farm Co. Ltd v. Symbol Motor Corp. Ltd, The Times*, January 27, 1987 (a civil case; "new" Range Rover damaged by fire and repaired; not restored to new condition; buyer obtained rescission).

(v) the location or amenities of any accommodation so provided.

Like section 1 the Act applies only to the provision of services in the course of a trade or business. As has been seen, it is now certain that this expression includes services rendered by members of the professions.[71] Again like section 1 this section includes oral as well as written statements.

However, although a statement made *after* the supply of goods has been completed is not an offence under section 1,[72] section 14 has a wider application, as is shown by *Breed v. Cluett*.[73]

> A builder built a bungalow, sold it and afterwards falsely stated that it was covered by an NHBRC 10 years' guarantee. The Divisional Court held that such a statement could be a statement as to the provision of services within section 14.

The distinction between this case and the later section 1 decision in *Hall's* case[74] is that the provision of services may involve continuing obligations and, had there been an NHBRC guarantee, the builder could have been called upon to provide services during the guarantee period.

This connection between the supply of services and the defendant's statement was recently emphasised by the Court of Appeal in *R. v. Bevelectric Ltd*; *R. v. Broad (Norman)*; *R. v. Broad (Stirling)*.[75]

> The three defendants were a company carrying on a washing machine repair business, a director and an employee. Their statements that motors needed to be replaced implied that a genuine assessment had been made of the extent of any necessary repairs. They argued that the word "provided" in section 14(i)(b)(iii) covered statements as to services which traders were offering to supply or were in the course of supplying, but not those which had been provided in the past. The Court of Appeal disagreed with their argument and upheld their conviction.

"A false statement about services already provided", said Staughton L.J., "is within the section if it is connected or associated with the supply of the services in question."

Recklessly

Another distinction between this offence and the section 1 offences is that **13.38** section 14 is not an offence of strict liability. Section 14 requires that the person making the false statement knows it to be false or makes it recklessly. A reckless statement is defined by section 14(2)(b) as "a statement made regardless of whether it is true or false . . . whether or not the person making it had reasons for believing that it might be false". Lord Parker C.J. in *Sunair*

---

[71] Above, n. 15. See also *R. v. Piper* [1995] Crim.L.R. 827 (using logo of Guild of Master Craftsmen on notepaper).
[72] *Hall v. Wickens Motors (Gloucester) Ltd* [1972] 1 W.L.R. 1418. See above para. 13.14.
[73] [1970] 2 Q.B. 459.
[74] Above, n. 72.
[75] [1993] Crim.L.R. 155.

Holidays Limited v. Dodd[76] stated *obiter* that the Act imported the common law definition of "reckless".

> Tour operators in their brochure described accommodation offered at a hotel as "all twin-bedded rooms with private bath, shower, w.c. and terrace". They had a contract with the hotel to provide such accommodation. Two couples booked holidays with them on this basis, but on arrival were given rooms without terraces. It was held by the Divisional Court that no offence had been committed. At the time the statement was made the accommodation existed and the statement was perfectly true. Nothing which happened afterwards could alter the accuracy of the description when it was made. Further, the definition of reckless does not include negligence.

However, a different view was taken by the Divisional Court in *MFI Warehouses v. Nattrass*[77]:

> A mail order company advertised goods "on 14 days' free approval" and "carriage free". These offers were intended to cover only some of the goods in the advertisement but appeared to relate to all of them. The company's conviction for recklessly making false statements as to the provision of facilities was upheld on appeal. The court considered that the chairman of the company had given insufficient care to his perusal of the advertisement so that the company had been reckless as to its contents.

While this case to an extent throws doubt on the dictum of Lord Parker and appears to give a wider meaning to the words "recklessly", the main point of *Sunair Holidays Limited v. Dodd* still stands. No offence is committed merely because the trader fails to provide services which accord with the description. Provided the services or accommodation existed when the statement was made and provided that he then had an intention of providing them,[78] the statement is not false and no offence occurs.

It is important to distinguish the two related points. First one asks the question, "Is the statement false?" If the answer is "no", as in *Sunair Holidays Limited v. Dodd*, then one need not proceed further: there is no offence. If the answer is "yes", then one goes on to ask, "Did the trader know that the statement was false when he made it or make it recklessly?" If the answer to either alternative is "yes", an offence has occurred.

Knows to be false

13.39   In *Wings Ltd v. Ellis*[79] the House of Lords were called upon to consider the wording of section 14(1)(a), namely, "to make a statement which he knows to be false". The certified question for the opinion of the court was, "Whether a

---

[76] [1970] 1 W.L.R. 1037.
[77] [1973] 1 W.L.R. 307.
[78] "The state of a man's mind is as much a fact as the state of his digestion": *per* Bowen L.J. in *Edgington v. Fitzmaurice* (1885) 29 Ch.D. 459 at 483.
[79] [1984] 3 All E.R. 577.

Defendant may properly be convicted of an offence under section 14(1)(a) of the Trade Descriptions Act 1968 where he has no knowledge of the falsity of the statement at the time of its publication but knew of the falsity at the time when the statement was read by the complainant." The case is one of the many cases relating to tour operators.

> The respondents published a brochure in May 1981 describing the Seashells Hotel, Sri Lanka, as having air conditioning in the bedrooms. This was untrue, but the respondents at the time believed it to be true. In June 1981 on discovering the error the respondents took steps to prevent potential customers from reading the false statement. Even so in January 1982 a customer read a copy of the brochure in its original form and booked a holiday on the strength of it. The respondents argued successfully in the Divisional Court[80] that no offence was committed because, when the brochure was published, they did not know that the statement was false and, when it was read by the customer, they honestly believed that a member of the public would read it in its corrected and accurate form so that they did not knowingly make a false statement.

The House of Lords, allowing the prosecutor's appeal, answered the question as follows (*per* Lord Scarman)[81]:

> "A statement which was false was made by the respondent company in the course of its business when it was read by Mr Wade, an interested member of the public doing business with the respondent company on the basis of the statement. The offence was committed on that occasion because the respondent company then knew that it was false to state that the hotel accommodation was air-conditioned. The fact that the respondent was unaware of the falsity of the statement when it was published as part of the brochure in May 1981 is irrelevant."

In reaching this conclusion the court interpreted the words according to their literal and natural meaning. As Lord Scarman pointed out, "The subsection says not that it is an offence knowingly to make the statement but that it is an offence to make the statement."[82] There is therefore an important difference between section 14(1)(b), under which an offence is committed only if the trader recklessly makes a statement, and section 14(1)(a) where an offence may be committed even though the statement is not *made* knowingly. In his judgment Lord Scarman succinctly explains the current state of the law together with the policy reasons behind it.[83]

> "The respondent submits that the essence of the offence is knowingly making a false statement. The appellant submits that it suffices to prove that the statement was made on a person's behalf in the course of his business and that its content was false to the knowledge of the person carrying on the business.
>   My Lords, I accept the appellant's construction as correct. First, it advances

[80] [1984] 1 All E.R. 1046.
[81] [1984] 3 All E.R. 577 at 591.
[82] *ibid.* at p. 590.
[83] *ibid.* at p. 589.

the legislative purpose embodied in the Act, in that it strikes directly against the false statement irrespective of the reason for, or explanation of, its falsity. It involves, of course, construing the offence as one of strict liability to the extent that the offence can be committed unknowingly, that is, without knowledge of the act of statement; but this is consistent with the social purpose of a statute in the class to which the Act belongs."

Lord Scarman's reference to "strict liability" needs to be read carefully; earlier he describes it as an offence of "semi-strict liability".[84] The court decided that there is no need for the prosecution to prove fraud, intent or *mens rea* and "to that extent" the offence is one of strict liability. This contrasts with section 1 where an offence may be committed by a person who does not even know that his description is false.[85] It is clear from comments in all the judgments that the respondents might have been better advised to admit the offence and then to put forward their efforts to correct the erroneous information as a defence under section 24.[86]

When is a statement made?

13.40   A second question to be answered in *Wings Ltd v. Ellis* was what was meant by the word "make" in section 14(1). The question is particularly important in relation to brochures issued by tour operators and others where millions may be published and read by different members of the public over a period of many months. Are the statements in the brochures "made" when the brochure is published, when read by members of the public or in other circumstances? In *R. v. Thomson Holidays Ltd*[87] the Court of Appeal had decided that a statement is made only when communicated to someone, *e.g.* by reading. Although approving the decision in *Thomson* as correct, the House of Lords has not accepted the Court of Appeal's reasoning. A statement may be made although not communicated to anyone. Lord Hailsham explained the breadth of the meaning of the word in his judgment[88]:

"When, in the course of a trade or business, a brochure containing a false statement is issued in large numbers through a chain of distribution involving several stages, and intended to be read and used at all or some of the stages, it does not follow that it is only 'made' at its ultimate destination. It may be 'made' when it is posted in bulk, when the information is passed on by telephone or in smaller batches by post, and when it is read by the ultimate recipient, provided that at each stage what happens is in accordance with the original intention of the issuing house."

---

[84] *ibid.* at p. 585.
[85] Above, para. 13.13.
[86] Below, para. 13.45. See also *Yugotours v. Wadsley* [1988] Crim.L.R. 623, DC.
[87] [1974] Q.B. 592. The facts are given in para. 13.60.
[88] [1984] 3 All E.R. 577 at 582.

Future services

A decision showing that promises about the provision of services in the   **13.41**
future are not caught by section 14 is *Beckett v. Cohen*[89]:

> The defendant agreed to build a garage like the neighbours' within 10 days but
> did not do so. The Divisional Court held that section 14 did not apply to state-
> ments unrelated to existing facts which amounted to a promise as to the future,
> because these could not be true or false when made. (The court was prepared to
> accept for the purpose of the case that building a garage was within section 14.)

This interpretation of the section erodes very substantially the protection
afforded to consumers. Even so, as has been seen, if accommodation is advertised which at the time of publication of the holiday brochure does not exist,
then an offence can be committed. This is well illustrated by *R. v. Clarksons
Holidays Ltd*[90] where the brochures stated that Clarksons' hotels were chosen
for their cleanliness, good food and efficiency of service, and included a picture of a large modern hotel with a swimming pool. This turned out to be an
artist's impression: the hotel, which was still in the course of construction,
was not finished by the time the holidaymakers arrived and was never
intended to be ready by then.

Similarly in *British Airways Board v. Taylor*[91] the appellants would have
been liable for a statement as to the future, had the statement been made by
the Board and not by their predecessors BOAC. The facts were as follows:

> The case arose out of the common airline practice of overbooking to take account
> of "no show" passengers who fail to take up reservations; occasionally this
> results in passengers being transferred or "bumped" to another flight. Here a
> passenger received a letter confirming his reservation but in the event no seat was
> available on the flight. The House of Lords held that the statement in the letter
> was false, as at that time BOAC fully intended to off-load passengers if too many
> arrived for the flight.

Facilities and prices

Section 11 (now repealed) was concerned only with prices of *goods*. This   **13.42**
gap has now been filled by section 20 of the Consumer Protection Act 1987
which covers "goods, services, accommodation or facilities".[92] However in
the intervening 20 years ingenious, but mostly unsuccessful, attempts were
made to squeeze the price of services into section 14 by a broad interpretation
of the word "facilities" in section 14(1). A number of decisions of the Divisional Court show that the provision is to be construed strictly.[93]

---

[89] [1972] 1 W.L.R. 1593.
[90] [1972] Crim.L.R. 653.
[91] [1976] 1 All E.R. 65.
[92] See below, para. 14.08.
[93] *e.g. Westminster City Council v. Ray Alan Manshops* [1982] 1 W.L.R. 383, DC: permanent
"closing down" sale; no offence.

Thus in *Newell v. Hicks*[94] Robert Goff L.J. pointed out, "Although the word 'facility' is used widely in commercial circles to describe almost anything available commercially, when the word appears in a criminal statute it is wrong to stretch its meaning in that way."

> Motor dealers advertised a video cassette recorder "Absolutely free with every X-registration Renault" ordered within a specified period. The trade-in allowance of old vehicles, however, was reduced where customers wished to take up the offer.

The Divisional Court held that the statement fell outside section 14 because (1) the offer of a free recorder was a statement about the supply of goods, and (2) section 14(1) did not cover a false statement about the price at which services or facilities were provided.

Yet this case is not authority for the proposition that section 14 has no application merely because the supplier's statement relates to and is ancillary to goods. Thus the section has been held to cover a three months' guarantee of a second-hand car,[95] a statement that the purchaser of a moped would receive a year's insurance[96] and a 90-day money back guarantee on a book containing a fixed-odds gambling system.[96a]

In the event, as stated above, many of these problems have been solved by the Consumer Protection Act 1987, Pt. III.

4. PROPERTY

13.43   We have seen that section 14 of the 1968 Act includes statements about "accommodation", such as holiday hotels, and that "services" cover services relating to building, *e.g.* by an architect or builder. However, although some aspects of building and sale are covered, it seems clear that the 1968 Act does not apply to general statements about properties for sale such as their location or characteristics.

The Review recommended (para. 90) that it should become an offence to make false statements about property—houses, flats, shops, factories, building and agricultural land. Fifteen years later legislation was passed to fill the gap: a Private Member's Bill advocated by the Consumers' Association.

The Property Misdescriptions Act 1991, s.1(1), provides:

> Where a false or misleading statement about a prescribed matter is made in the course of an estate agency business or a property development business, otherwise than in providing conveyancing services, the person by whom the business is carried on shall be guilty of an offence under this section.

---

[94] [1984] R.T.R. 135.
[95] *Bambury v. Hounslow LBC* [1971] R.T.R. 1.
[96] *Kinchin v. Ashton Park Scooters* (1984) 148 J.P.N. 459. But statements about the provision of clothing were not within s.14.
[96a] *Ashley v. Sutton LBC* [1995] Crim.L.R. 657, DC.

The main impact is upon estate agents. It is intended to dissuade them from indulging in their previous practice of giving extravagant descriptions which often at best were half-truths—"the pretty cottage adjoining farmland" which turns out to be a one-up, one-down terraced house with open country at the front, but a noisy car exhaust and tyre fitting centre overlooking the back garden.

Its ambit also extends to a "property development business". Section 1(5) (f) provides that a statement is caught in this case only if the business is concerned with "the development of land" *and* the statement is made "with a view to disposing of an interest in a building or part of a building, constructed or renovated in the course of a business".

An offence is committed where the statement relates to "a prescribed matter", *i.e.* prescribed in an order made by the Secretary of State (s.1(5)(d)).

The defences, enforcement and penalties are similar to those relating to the 1968 Act discussed below. Thus the familiar "due diligence" defence is available (s.2). However, on conviction the defendant may be fined, but not imprisoned (s.1(3)).

5. DEFENCES

As has been seen, liability for offences under section 1 is strict, whereas the **13.44** offence under section 14 is committed only if the trader knows the statement to be false or makes it recklessly. However, certain defences are available. Section 24(1) applies to both types of offence. Section 24(3) assists only in the case of prosecution under section 1(1)(b). Section 25 is confined to the publication of advertisements.

The general defence

The defence provided by section 24(1) may be used by a defendant when **13.45** charged with an offence under section 14 in relation to services or under section 1(1)(b) for supplying goods with a false trade description. However, the Court of Appeal decided in *R. v. Southwood*[97] that it is not available in respect of a charge under section 1(1)(a) where the defendant *applied* the description himself. Lord Lane C.J. pointed out in this clocking case (at p. 1370): "By his initial actions in falsifying the instrument he has not taken any precautions, let alone all reasonable precautions." Section 24(1) reads as follows:

> In any proceedings for an offence under this Act it shall, subject to subsection (2) of this section, be a defence for the person charged to prove—
> (a) that the commission of the offence was due to a mistake or to reliance on information supplied to him or to the act or default of another person, an accident or some other cause beyond his control; and

[97] [1987] 1 W.L.R. 1361. Nor is a disclaimer effective: above, para. 13.22.

(b) that he took all reasonable precautions and exercised all due diligence to avoid the commission of such an offence by himself or any person under his control.

It may be split into five defences. The defendant must prove that the commission of the offence was due to any one of the following causes:

(i) a mistake;
(ii) reliance on information supplied to him;
(iii) the act or default of another person;
(iv) an accident;
(v) some other cause beyond his control.

As Lord Templeman pointed out in *Wings Ltd v. Ellis*,[98] where the company failed to invoke section 24, "Good intentions and mistake do not by themselves constitute a defence. The accused must plead and prove the circumstances specified in section 24."

Mistake

13.46   As far as mistake is concerned this is available only where the mistake is of the defendant himself; it cannot be used where someone else's mistake is involved (*e.g.* an employer pleading the mistake of an employee).[99]

Act or default of another person

13.47   The defence most frequently relied upon is that the offence was due to the "act or default of another person", for example, an odometer run back by a previous owner. When an employer is charged, he may rely on the default of an employee. When the Act first came into force, there were those who thought that the defence could be used only where the employee was in a junior position but it appeared to have been quickly settled that even where the "person" was a branch manager, the defence was still available.[1]

However, when the employer is a company, it is necessary to distinguish between those employees who are the *alter ego* of the company, when their defaults are the company's defaults, and those employees who are not thus identified with the company which can then claim that the defaults are those of "another person". The difficulty was fully discussed by the House of Lords in *Tesco Supermarkets v. Nattrass*,[2] a case involving section 11 (now repealed):

> Soap powder was advertised in a supermarket "Radiant 1 shilling off giant size 2/11d". This was intended to apply only to "flash packs" which were marked "1

---

[98] [1984] 3 All E.R. 577 at 594. See above, para. 13.39, for the facts.
[99] *Birkenhead & District Co-operative Society Ltd v. Roberts* [1970] 1 W.L.R. 1497.
[1] *Beckett v. Kingston Bros. (Butchers)*, above, para. 13.22.
[2] [1972] A.C. 153.

shilling off recommended price". As the supermarket had run out of these packs, ordinary packs were on display. A customer was charged the full price of 3/11d for one of these.

Their Lordships held that where the person charged is a limited company, the only persons who can be identified with the controlling mind and will of the company are the board of directors, the managing director and any other superior officer[3] to whom the board has delegated full discretion to act independently from the board. Thus, though a general manager may be the company's *alter ego*, the supermarket manager was not. Accordingly, since the offence was caused by his failure to ensure that sufficient flash-packs were available, Tesco were able to rely on his default.

To establish this defence the defendants must not merely produce the list of staff who might have been at fault; they must at least try to identify the actual person responsible by carefully investigating the circumstances to discover how the offences occurred.[4] Further, to rely on this defence section 24(2) requires the defendants at least seven clear days before the hearing to serve on the prosecutor a written notice giving such information as they have to identify the other person.[5] The reason for this provision is to enable the prosecution to consider whether to proceed directly against the other person either for one of the main offences or under the by-pass provision in section 23.[6]

Due diligence defence

It is not enough for the defendant to prove one of the five defences in section 24(1)(a). He must also prove that he falls within what is now popularly known as the "due diligence defence", a defence frequently found in consumer protection legislation, namely "that he took all reasonable precautions and exercised all due diligence to avoid the commission of such an offence by himself or any person under his control."[7] These factors have generally been considered by the courts in relation to the default defence, particularly with regard to its application in the areas of vicarious liability, odometers and sampling.   **13.48**

Vicarious liability

Where an employer is charged with an offence because of the conduct of an employee and endeavours to rid himself of this vicarious liability by showing that the offence was due to the act or default of the employee, broadly the employer will be acquitted if he can show that he is personally   **13.49**

---

[3] By s.20 such officers may be prosecuted too, where the offence has been committed with their consent or connivance.
[4] *McGuire v. Sittingbourne Co-operative Society Ltd* [1976] Crim.L.R. 268.
[5] See *Birkenhead & District Co-operative Society Ltd v. Roberts*, above, n. 99.
[6] See para. 13.53.
[7] s.24(1)(b).

blameless. Obviously, when this defence is used somebody is to blame. The question is whether the offence occurred in spite of the precautions and diligence of the employer. In the *Tesco* case the House of Lords rejected the argument that the employer has to show that he and all the persons to whom he has delegated responsibility are blameless: the company was held to have satisfied the requirements of section 24(1)(b) by having a chain of command with a careful system of control and supervision, even though one of the cogs in this machine, the supermarket manager, had failed to carry out his responsibilities properly.

Odometers

13.50   The second area where due diligence is of special significance relates to false odometer readings. Sometimes a car dealer honestly—not all car dealers are rogues—supplies a vehicle with an odometer which unknown to him has been tampered with by an earlier owner. Assuming that he can prove that the offence was due to reliance on information supplied, or the default of another person, the question arises whether he can also prove that he took precautions and was diligent. This normally involves checking with the person from whom he bought the vehicle and, if he has the registration document, with previous owners to verify the mileage.[8] However, in *Naish v. Gore*[9] the Divisional Court said that it was impossible to lay down as a general principle that a dealer selling second-hand cars must have the log book and check with previous owners. In that case the defence was available to a dealer who bought from somebody with whom he had been doing business for years and resold the car before receiving the log book from his seller. Nevertheless, Lord Widgery C.J. warned that justices "should be very quick and alert to consider whether there are further proper precautions which might have been taken".

Sampling

13.51   The last dictum should be borne in mind by suppliers dealing with large quantities of goods and relying on sampling to show that they have been taking reasonable precautions and been duly diligent. In *Rotherham Metropolitan B.C. v. Raysun (U.K.) Ltd*[10]:

> The defendants, large-scale importers of Far East products, imported once a year about 100,000 packets of children's wax crayons from Hong Kong. Their agents there had samples analysed and had to send back only adverse reports: none were received. The defendants tested in England a single packet. They sold the crayons as "poisonless". The black crayons contained excessive amounts of toxic material.

---

[8] *Richmond upon Thames LBC v. Motor Sales (Hounslow) Ltd* [1971] R.T.R. 116. See also *Wandsworth LBC v. Bentley* [1980] R.T.R. 429, DC.

[9] [1971] 3 All E.R. 737. See also *Crook v. Howells Garages* [1980] R.T.R. 434, DC.

[10] *The Times*, April 27, 1988. See also *Amos v. Melcon (Frozen Foods)* (1985) 149 J.P. 712, DC: "rump steak" was really silverside of beef; insufficient evidence of sampling; no defence.

The Divisional Court rejected their defence under section 24(1). They had not checked that the Hong Kong analyses were in fact taking place and their sample in England was "very moderate". "By itself", said Woolf L.J., "it did not indicate the taking of a standard of care required by the statutory provisions".

Supplier's defence

In *Naish v. Gore* the dealer also relied on the defence in section 24(3). This is confined to the offence of supplying goods with a false trade description under section 1(1)(b). The defence is:

> In any proceedings for an offence under this Act of supplying or offering to supply goods to which a false trade description is applied it shall be a defence for the person charged to prove that he did not know, and could not with reasonable diligence have ascertained, that the goods did not conform to the description or that the description had been applied to the goods.

The comments made above with regard to "diligence" in section 24(1) appear to be relevant here also, as the use of the adjective "reasonable" rather than "due" is not intended to affect or reduce the standard of diligence.[11] For example, in *Simmons v. Ravenhill*,[12] another "clocked car" case, the defence failed because in view of the vehicle's low mileage (19,000) the dealer should have made inquiries with the previous owner. The Divisional Court stated, however, that generally it would be unreasonable to expect a dealer to check the whole pedigree back through all its owners.

The by-pass provision

Although the so-called "by-pass provision" in section 23 is not a defence, it is appropriate to deal with it at this point in view of its close interaction with the defence in section 24(1). Section 23 states:

> Where the commission by any person of an offence under this Act is due to the act or default of some other person that other person shall be guilty of the offence, and a person may be charged with and convicted of the offence by virtue of this section whether or not proceedings are taken against the first-mentioned person.

Thus where A commits an offence, but the real culprit is B, B may be prosecuted for the offence committed by A. It is irrelevant whether or not proceedings have been taken against A. The corollary is that if no offence is committed by A, B cannot be prosecuted under section 23.[13]

13.52

13.53

---

[11] This interpretation, suggested in earlier editions of this book, was given by the Divisional Court in *Texas Homecare v. Stockport M.B.C.* [1987] Crim.L.R. 709.
[12] [1983] Crim.L.R. 749, DC. See also *Richmond upon Thames L.B.C. v. Motor Sales (Hounslow) Ltd*, above, para. 13.50.
[13] *Cottee v. Douglas Seaton (Used Cars) Ltd* [1972] 1 W.L.R. 1408.

Example

> B, a car dealer, runs an odometer back. He sells the car to another dealer A. A sells the car to a customer. On the assumption that A has committed an offence under section 1(1)(b), B can be prosecuted under section 23 because A's offence is due to the "act or default" of B.

In this example it can be seen that the prosecution need not resort to section 23 in order to charge B; for B has committed an offence under section 1(1)(a) by applying a false trade description. The example is not unrealistic. Quite frequently local authorities have taken themselves into unnecessarily deep water by using the by-pass provision instead of prosecuting directly for one of the main offences.[14] However, section 23 is not entirely superfluous. It can result in an offence being committed by a private person who cannot otherwise be charged, because he is not acting "in the course of a trade or business". Thus even if B were a private seller, he could be charged under section 23.[15]

Interaction with default defence

13.54   Earlier, the interaction between section 23 and section 24(1) was mentioned. In the example if A is charged under section 1(1)(b) he may plead the section 24(1) defence, *i.e.* that the offence was due to the "act or default of another person", namely B. This creates an apparently unbreakable circle. B is liable under section 23 only if A has committed the offence. So if A when prosecuted under section 1 successfully relies on section 24 due to B's default, B when prosecuted under section 23 can apparently argue that he has committed no offence in the absence of an offence by A. It would seem perverse that the real culprit B should escape with impunity merely because his guilt provides the innocent A with a defence.

This iniquitous circle was broken by the robust interpretation given to section 23 by the Divisional Court in *Coupe v. Guyett*.[16] The court stated that where A's sole defence is the section 24 defence, A can be regarded as having "committed" the offence for the purposes of section 23, *i.e.* for the purposes of a prosecution against B. Thus B (the real culprit) can be convicted under section 23 even though A is acquitted as a result of the section 24 defence. If, however, A has some other defence (*e.g.* absence of knowledge in a section 14 case) the prosecution will *not* be able to charge B under section 23, although they might well be able to charge him under one of the principal charging sections.

Review recommendation

13.55   We have already seen that the by-pass provision can result in a successful

---

[14] *ibid.* The facts appear on para. 13.13.
[15] *Olgeirsson v. Kitching* [1986] 1 W.L.R. 304, DC.
[16] [1973] 1 W.L.R. 669.

prosecution against a private person. The Review recommends that, while the possibility of such proceedings should be retained, it should be possible only where the private individual has deliberately falsified a trade description.[17]

Advertisements

Section 25 affords a special defence in the case of advertisements. In any proceedings for an offence relating to the publication of an advertisement the defendant is free from liability if he can prove that (a) the advertisement was received and published in the course of a business involving such publication, and (b) he did not know and had no reason to know that the publication would amount to an offence under the Act. The defence protects not only the publishers themselves, *e.g.* of newspapers and magazines, but also those who arrange for the publication of advertisements, *e.g.* advertising agencies.

13.56

6. ENFORCEMENT

One of the major defects of the Merchandise Marks Acts was the absence of anybody with a duty to enforce their provisions. Section 26(1) clearly places the obligation of prosecution on trading standards officers in the following unequivocal terms: "It shall be the duty of every local weights and measures authority to enforce within their area the provisions of this Act." The Minister may require such authorities to report to him and, if a complaint is received that any authority is not properly discharging its duties, may institute a local inquiry whose report must be published.[18]

13.57

To assist the inspectors in carrying out their duties the Act gives them the power to check compliance with the Act by purchasing goods or securing the provision of services, accommodation or facilities.[19] One can picture the more zealous inspectors as a matter of duty reluctantly sunning themselves on the beaches of Barbados in order to check that the amenities and location of hotels in travel brochures are not falsely described!

Section 28 of the Act enables them to enter premises to make spot checks and, if reasonable cause for suspicion of an offence exists, to require production[20] of the books and documents of the business.

Before instituting proceedings the local authority must give notice to the Department of Trade and Industry. Such liaison helps to prevent numerous prosecutions in different areas for the same offence, for example, for goods or services advertised and supplied nationally. However, multiple prosecutions do sometimes occur.[21]

---

[17] Para. 38.

[18] s.26.

[19] s.27.

[20] "Produce" does not mean "hand over and allow to take away": *Barge v. British Gas Corp.* (1983) 81 L.G.R. 53, DC.

[21] *e.g.* the travel brochures in *R. v. Thomson Holidays Ltd*, below, para. 13.60.

A prosecution must be brought within three years of the commission of an offence or one year from its discovery, whichever is the earlier.[22]

Finally, it should be observed that, although generally prosecutions are brought by local authorities, it is open to a member of the public to bring a private prosecution for an offence.

7. PENALTIES

13.58   The only sanctions under the Act for its contravention are of a criminal nature—fines or imprisonment. The Act affords the aggrieved consumer no separate civil remedy at all[23] (but see Chap. 16 where compensation orders are discussed). Yet clearly the threat of criminal proceedings brought at public expense is a much greater deterrent to the dishonest trader than the possibility of a civil action by a private individual at his own expense.

If proceedings are brought summarily, a fine not exceeding £5,000[24] may be levied in respect of each offence. If the defendant is convicted on indictment, not only may the fine be unlimited but imprisonment of up to two years may be imposed—both penalties may be meted out.[25] In a number of cases defendants have been fined substantial sums of £1,000 or more.[26] Occasionally prison sentences are imposed but the Divisional Court stated in *R. v. Haesler*[27] that imprisonment is normally reserved for cases involving dishonesty. Generally heavy fines and prison sentences seem to be a privilege of car dealers.[28]

Statistics

13.59   The scale of activity of trading standards officers in this area can be seen from the statistics set out in the Annual Reports of the Director General of Fair Trading. For example, his latest Report reveals that, for the year ending September 30, 1998, 929 prosecutions were brought for false descriptions of goods. The leading categories of criminals were suppliers of secondhand cars and clothing (349 and 142 prosecutions respectively). False statements about services resulted in 240 prosecutions, first place going to double glazing suppliers with 92 prosecutions.

Fines exceeded £800,000. In addition 44 defendants received prison sen-

---

[22] s.19(1). But see also s.19(2) and (4).
[23] See below, para. 13.61.
[24] Originally £400 (s.18). Increased by the Criminal Justice Act 1991, s.17.
[25] s.18.
[26] See *R. v. Hammertons Cars Ltd* [1976] 1 W.L.R. 1243.
[27] [1973] Crim.L.R. 586.
[28] See *R. v. Hewitt*, [1991] R.T.R. 357, CA: two months' imprisonment and fine of £500 on each of eight counts of "clocking".

tences, 54 had to undertake community service and three were put on probation.

Multiple prosecutions

It will be appreciated that multiple prosecutions may be brought in differ-   **13.60** ent areas in respect of the same false trade description with a new fine on each conviction. In *R. v. Thomson Holidays Ltd*[29]:

> Tour operators published a brochure containing a false statement. They were convicted in one area of an offence under section 14. When prosecuted by a different local authority in respect of the same false statement the defendants pleaded *autrefois convict* in respect of the previous conviction.[30] The Court of Appeal held that every time someone read one of the brochures a false statement was made, for it was made when communicated to the reader.[31] Accordingly, a new offence was committed on each occasion and the plea was unsuccessful. Theoretically millions of prosecutions could be brought in respect of a single error in the printed brochures.

The advantage of multiple prosecutions from the point of view of the consumer is that, if he wishes to seek compensation under the Powers of Criminal Courts Acts 1973, he will require the defendant to be convicted. Thus different consumers seeking compensation in different areas would each look for separate convictions.[32]

8. CIVIL REMEDIES

We have seen that the Act is essentially one which creates criminal offences   **13.61** to protect consumers, but gives no right to bring a civil action. Consumers are left to pursue their civil remedies in the ordinary way, for example, for breach of contract or misrepresentation where appropriate. It will be appreciated that not every set of facts giving rise to an offence under the Act will necessarily result in a civil remedy being available. Conversely a consumer may well have a civil remedy even where no offence has been committed (as, for example, where the trader lacks the necessary knowledge in s.14 cases or where a defence is available under s.24).

A separate but related question is whether, assuming there to be a contractual right available to the consumer, the contract is vitiated or the right of action lost because of the statutory contravention. As far as the supply of goods is concerned this question is answered by section 35 which states, "A contract for the supply of any goods shall not be void or unenforceable by reason only of a contravention of any provision of this Act." Clearly when the

---

[29] [1974] Q.B. 592.
[30] This is a rule that a defendant cannot be charged more than once for the same offence.
[31] Although the House of Lords approved this decision in *Wings Ltd v. Ellis*, they gave a wider meaning to "make a statement": see above, para. 13.40.
[32] See para. 16.03.

contract involves the supply of goods whether by way of sale, hire-purchase, rental or in any other way, the rights of both the supplier and the consumer are unaffected. Strangely, section 35 is not wide enough to cover contracts for the supply of services (the Review recommends in para. 256 that s.35 should be amended to cover such contracts). However, it seems unlikely that such contracts are invalidated by the commission of an offence under the Act. This is an example of what is usually described as "incidental illegality", *i.e.* illegality which has no effect on the contract. In any case the consumer's rights would not be affected, as he would not be *in pari delicto* with the guilty supplier.

As regards civil remedies the consumer is slightly worse off as a result of the 1968 Act. The Act repealed section 17 of the Merchandise Marks Acts 1887, whereby a seller was deemed to warrant the accuracy of any trade description, but in practice this warranty was very seldom used.

Finally, two points need to be made with regard to civil remedies and compensation for the consumer. First, a conviction under the Act may be used as evidence in a later civil action by virtue of the Civil Evidence Act 1968. Secondly, compensation may be claimed under the Powers of Criminal Courts Act 1973 as a consequence of the conviction.[33]

---

[33] Below, para. 16.02.

CHAPTER FOURTEEN

"THE PRICE WAS WRONG"

1. TRADE DESCRIPTIONS ACT 1968

"Recommended price £210, our price £170"
"Normal price £78, sale price £52"
"£8 off recommended price"
"Elsewhere £50, our price £28"

The public and consumer bodies have for many years been concerned at **14.01** the difficulty in distinguishing between genuine reductions and false comparative price claims. The Molony Committee recommended[1] that the problem should be tackled by including in the definition of trade description "the former or usual price of any goods". However, instead of following this approach the Trade Descriptions Act 1968 endeavoured to deal with the mischief with separate price provisions contained in section 11. It created three offences: (1) false comparisons with a recommended price; (2) false comparisons with the trader's own previous price; (3) an indication that the price is less than that actually being charged.

Recommended prices[2]

The first offence caused little difficulty inasmuch as it was obvious and **14.02** easy to prove from manufacturers' lists whether or not an offence had been committed. However, the Act had no deterrent effect on the practice—indeed it probably led to its expansion—of manufacturers setting unrealistically high recommended prices (so-called "sky prices") to enable retailers to offer an apparent bargain to their customers by discounting. The Review discusses the difficulties and some possible solutions, including the prohibition of recommended retail prices, but in the end the Director General of Fair Trading throws up his hands in despair stating that he "can put forward no suggestions for controlling this practice within the framework of the 1968 Act".[3]

At the same time, the Office of Fair Trading was considering the control of this and other price problems under the Fair Trading Act 1973. Its proposals were published in 1975 in *Bargain Offer Claims—A Consultative Document.*

---

[1] Para. 636.
[2] The Resale Prices Act 1976 makes it unlawful to impose *minimum* resale prices (resale price maintenance or RPM) on distributors; pharmaceuticals are exceptions.
[3] Para. 210.

Although ultimately an attack was made on some forms of bargain offers by the Price Marking (Bargain Offers) Order 1979, recommended prices were not generally prohibited.

Previous prices

14.03   The second offence was similar to the first offence except that the false indication related to the price at which the supplier previously offered the goods. The purpose of this provision was to attack the practice of buying in goods specially for sales and pretending that those goods were previously offered at a higher price.

Overcharging

14.04   The third offence was expressed in very wide terms and covered situations where the customer was charged a higher price than he would have expected to pay in view of the indications as to price given to him by the supplier.[4]

2. PRICE MARKING (BARGAIN OFFERS) ORDER 1979

14.05   Section 11 of the 1968 Act proved inadequate for its task and many loopholes were enthusiastically used by suppliers. For some years the OFT had been examining bargain offer claims and their effects on consumers. The Director General's original intention was to refer the matter to the Consumer Protection Advisory Committee under Part II of the Fair Trading Act 1973,[5] but it appeared that it might be difficult to provide evidence that the practice adversely affects the economic interests of consumers. Comparatively few complaints are made about bargain offers either because consumers do not realise that they have been misled or because they are chary of revealing that they have been duped and that the bargain which they obtained was not such a good deal after all.

Accordingly, early in 1978 the Director General made his first recommendations to the Secretary of State under section 2(3) of the 1973 Act which covers "any action which in the opinion of the Director it would be expedient for the Secretary of State or any other Minister to take in relation to any of the matters in respect of which the Director has any such duties", *e.g.* his duties under section 2(1). The Secretary of State used a regulation-making power under the Prices Act 1974 to introduce the Price Marking (Bargain Offers) Order 1979.[6]

The Order was complex and not a model of clarity. It well illustrates the difficult task of attempting by detailed regulations to block up numerous, distinct business malpractices. Such a specific approach was a challenge to

---

[4] See the *Tesco* case, above, para. 13.47.
[5] Below, para. 17.06.
[6] S.I. 1979 No. 364, as amended by S.I. 1979 No. 633.

entrepreneurs and their legal advisers to invent new practices and slogans which technically did not fall foul of the Order—hardly a valuable use of commercial time and ingenuity. In the event the severe criticism of the Order from both sides of the fence—business suppliers and trading standards departments—resulted in the replacement of both the Order and section 11 of the 1968 Act with primary legislation.

3. Services

Apart from the complexity of the law, which even so failed to control the **14.06** malpractices adequately, there was one major gap in the regulatory regime, namely services. Section 11 of the 1968 Act affected only the price of goods. For that reason enforcement authorities tried to control misleading prices relating to services by using section 14, but, as we have seen, the courts were unwilling to interpret the meaning of "facilities" to embrace prices.[7]

Although the Bargain Offers Order covered services too, it was limited in its scope. In his Review of the Order published in 1981[8] the Director General of Fair Trading proposed as one of the options for reform a general prohibition against false or misleading statements about the price of goods or services. After considerable delay this was the route chosen by the Government.

4. Consumer Protection Act 1987, Pt. III

Scheme of the Act

The purpose of Part III of the Consumer Protection Act 1987 is to adopt a **14.07** much more flexible approach than the previous legislation in the hope that this will cope with the constantly changing commercial practices and marketing techniques of the modern world. This more general approach can be found in the main offence created by section 20(1) of giving a misleading price indication. The offence covers "any goods, services, accommodation or facilities". This broad approach is not unique in the field of consumer protection. Indeed, it can be found elsewhere in the 1987 Act in that section 10 introduced the "general safety requirement" as an umbrella to cover areas not dealt with in specific regulations.[9] Similarly Part III contains a general umbrella offence. This is complemented by section 26 giving power to make regulations which will be activated when particular practices require specific provisions.

A major criticism of the Bargain Offers Order was that traders alleged that it was incomprehensible so that they did not know how to comply with it. Whether or not that was true, clearly it is desirable that legislation should be

---

[7] Above, para. 13.42.
[8] *Review of the Price Marking (Bargain Offers) Order 1979*, OFT, 1981.
[9] Below, para. 15.04.

easily understandable both by those in business and by the enforcement authorities. A fashionable theory at the time was that the regulation of detailed business practices is best left to codes of practice, which can be readily altered without the need for time-consuming legislation. With this in mind, section 25 enables a code of practice to be approved by the Secretary of State. This code is now in place and is discussed later in this chapter (para. 14.18).

The two offences

14.08   Section 20 contains two offences:

> (1) Subject to the following provisions of this Part, a person shall be guilty of an offence if, in the course of any business of his, he gives (by any means whatever) to any consumers an indication which is misleading as to the price at which any goods, services, accommodation or facilities are available (whether generally or from particular persons).
> (2) Subject as aforesaid, a person shall be guilty of an offence if—
> (a) in the course of any business of his, he has given an indication to any consumers which, after it was given, has become misleading as mentioned in subsection (1) above; and
> (b) some or all of those consumers might reasonably be expected to rely on the indication at a time after it has become misleading; and
> (c) he fails to take all such steps as are reasonable to prevent those consumers from relying on the indication.

The first offence appears in section 20(1); this is the main offence on which we shall concentrate our discussion. The second offence in section 20(2) is concerned with a price indication which is correct when given, but *later* becomes misleading. This is aimed at the sort of problems that have arisen in the package holiday industry which we discussed earlier in relation to section 14 of the 1968 Act.[10] In those cases the misdescription related to the facilities or accommodation themselves; section 20(2) covers misleading prices in those areas as well as in relation to goods.

Business "of his"

14.09   There is a similarity between these two offences and the offences under sections 1 and 14 of the 1968 Act[11] in that none of them can be committed by a private person. However, both the new offences require the misleading price indication to be given "in the course of any business of his". Thus, there is an important distinction between these new offences and those under the 1968 Act because the additional words "of his" have the effect of taking employees outside the ambit of the 1987 Act.[12] (In practice it has been unusual for junior employees to be prosecuted even under the 1968 Act.)

---

[10] Above, para. 13.38.
[11] Above, paras 13.06 and 13.37.
[12] *R. v. Warwickshire County Council, ex p., Johnson* [1993] A.C. 583. We correctly suggested this interpretation in the Third Edition of this book.

However, section 40(2) creates a danger for "any director, manager, secretary or other similar officer" of a body corporate, since proceedings may be brought against them personally where the company is guilty of an offence which was committed with their consent or connivance or is attributable to their neglect.[13]

Consumer

No offence is committed unless the indication is given "to any consumers". Again, this can be contrasted with the 1968 Act where it is irrelevant whether the recipient of the misleading information is a private consumer or a trader. Indeed, trading standards officers frequently put the view that the 1968 Act is intended mainly to protect the honest trader against the rogue trader rather than to protect consumers at large. The new price provisions are obviously aimed at consumer protection.

    14.10

"Consumer" is defined by section 20(6) as follows:

(a) in relation to any goods, means any person who might wish to be supplied with the goods for his own private use or consumption;
(b) in relation to any services or facilities, means any person who might wish to be provided with the services or facilities otherwise than for the purposes of any business of his; and
(c) in relation to any accommodation, means any person who might wish to occupy the accommodation otherwise than for the purposes of any business of his.

The subsection clearly brings out the scope of Part III in that it separately mentions (a) goods, (b) services or facilities, and (c) accommodation. In any of these cases a consumer is someone who "might wish" to be supplied, etc.; an offence may be committed even though no actual supply takes place. Thus, if in a supermarket the prices on the goods themselves and on the shelf edge differ, a prosecution may be brought.

Price

Prices are also defined in section 20(6) to mean:

    14.11

(a) the aggregate of sums required to be paid by a consumer for or otherwise in respect of the supply of the goods or the provision of the services, accommodation or facilities; or
(b) except in section 21 below, any method which will be or has been applied for the purpose of determining that aggregate.

It follows that if a trader merely gives an estimate as a rough guide to the likely charge to be made, he does not give an indication as to price; for at that stage no one can tell what the consumer will be *required* to pay when the

---

[13] *cf.* 1968 Act, s.20, above, para. 13.47.

work has been done. In contrast, a firm quotation by which the supplier makes an offer for the supply of goods, etc., will be caught.

Indication

14.12   Both offences require the supplier to "give an indication". It does not matter how the indication is given, as section 20(1) expressly states "by any means whatever". It obviously covers prices on goods, on shelf edges, in holiday brochures and on estate agents' photographs and also indications by word of mouth.

Presumably it also covers bar-coding. An increasingly common problem is that goods are not priced individually, so that the consumer relies on the price on the shelf and then assumes that the laser at the checkout reads out the same price from the bar-code. A number of supermarkets, some with famous names, have been prosecuted successfully under the old prices legislation because of discrepancies between the shelf price and the checkout price, usually because the computers at head office feeding the information to the tills have been altered without staff at the local supermarket altering the shelf prices too.

The word "indication" was also used in section 11 of the 1968 Act and was considered by the Divisional Court in *Doble v. David Greig Limited*.[14]

> Bottles of Ribena in a self-service store were priced at 5s. 9d. and bore a manufacturer's label "the deposit on this bottle is 4d. refundable on return". At the checkout was a notice reading "In the interests of hygiene we do not accept the return of any empty bottles. No deposit is charged by us at the time of purchase." Customers paid 5s. 9d. a bottle but were refused 4d. refund. This was held to be an offence under section 11(2).

The Divisional Court took the view that the word "indication" was designedly wider than some such word as "representation" and was chosen in order to protect customers. "Section 11(2) was looking at the customers and the effect on them of whatever was said, done or displayed" (Ashworth J.) and "was intended to extend over conduct or signs of many different kinds" (Melford Stevenson J.). On the facts there was an indication likely to be taken as an indication that the purchaser who paid 5s. 9d. would be given 4d. on returning the bottle. The store had argued that the counter-indication displayed at the check-out point had the effect of disabusing the customer of a false impression which he might have obtained at the shelves. The court decided that the offence was committed when the Ribena was placed on the shelf with the false indication.

Misleading

14.13   Having looked at two elements of misleading price indications ("price"

---

[14] [1972] 1 W.L.R. 703.

and "indication") we now turn to the meaning of "misleading". This is widely defined by the Act. Section 21(1) gives the main part of the definition:

> For the purposes of section 20 above an indication given to any consumers is misleading as to a price if what is conveyed by the indication, or what those consumers might reasonably be expected to infer from the indication or any omission from it, includes any of the following, that is to say—
> (a) that the price is less than in fact it is;
> (b) that the applicability of the price does not depend on facts or circumstances on which its applicability does in fact depend;
> (c) that the price covers matters in respect of which an additional charge is in fact made;
> (d) that a person who in fact has no such expectation—
>   (i) expects the price to be increased or reduced (whether or not at a particular time or by a particular amount); or
>   (ii) expects the price, or the price as increased or reduced, to be maintained (whether or not for a particular period); or
> (e) that the facts or circumstances by reference to which the consumers might reasonably be expected to judge the validity of any relevant comparison made or implied by the indication are not what in fact they are.

Similar provisions appear in section 20(2) where the misleading indication is as to the *method* of determining a price.

It is important to observe that the list of factors (a) to (e) is an exhaustive list in that an indication is misleading "if what is conveyed . . . includes any of the following"; so although the offences at first sight seem very wide, they are limited by this list of factors. If the list had been worded so as to make it clear that it was illustrative only and through marketing ingenuity a supplier were able to invent a scheme falling outside section 21, the courts could have turned to the all-embracing words of section 20. This is not the case.

A further point is that the test to be applied on the effect on consumers is not entirely objective. Although the first factor for the court to consider is "what is conveyed by the indication", the subsection goes on to ask "what those consumers might reasonably be expected to infer from the indication". So presumably the court should take into account the effect of the indication on the particular consumers—*those consumers* who receive the indication.

Examples

The following are examples of the five factors set out in section 21(1):

(a) shelf price £1.40, price charged at checkout £1.48;
(b) a discount on goods, apparently generally available, given only to cash customers, not to those paying by credit card;
(c) additional charges for delivery, postage and packing or fitting, when these appear to be included in the stated price;
(d) a sale stating that the price of goods will be increased after the sale, when there is no such intention to increase prices; a similar problem arises with introductory offers;

(e) flat pack book shelves at £60 compared with ready-assembled book shelves at £95, when the latter are not available or do not sell at the stated price.

Price comparisons

14.14   Two final points should be noted. First, the practices expected to be followed by traders, particularly in respect of the price comparisons mentioned in (e),[14a] are set out in the Code of Practice discussed below.[15] Secondly, section 21(3) deals specifically with price comparisons.

Services and facilities

14.15   We have already mentioned[16] that because section 11 of the 1968 Act applied only to goods, trading standards officers tried to fit misstatements about prices into section 14 of that Act, but achieved only limited success. Such verbal gymnastics will no longer be necessary as Part III covers these areas too. Section 21(1) shows the breadth of meaning of the words "services or facilities" by explaining, perhaps unnecessarily, that references to these words are "references to any services or facilities whatever". More helpfully the subsection contains a non-exhaustive list of some areas covered by these words to put their inclusion beyond doubt. They are:

(a) credit, banking or insurance services;
(b) the purchase or sale of foreign currency;
(c) the supply of electricity;
(d) the provision of off-street car parks;
(e) arrangements for keeping caravans on land unless occupied as the person's main residence.

Accommodation

14.16   Section 23 deals with the provision of "accommodation or facilities". It seems that facilities are mentioned both in section 22 in conjunction with services and in section 23 in conjunction with accommodation to make it clear that they are included in both contexts. It should be remembered that the words "services, accommodation or facilities" appear in section 14 of the 1968 Act and presumably the meaning given to those words in that legislation will be followed in interpreting the same words in this context. Package holidays offered by tour operators have provided a fruitful source of prosecution under the 1968 Act and will doubtless provide frequent causes for investigation by trading standards officers under the 1987 Act too.

[14a] *MGN Ltd v. Ritters, The Times*, July 30, 1997 (£50 watch offered for £4.99—not available on open market at higher price—offence).
[15] Below, para. 14.18.
[16] Above, para. 13.42.

Sales of new homes

A relatively new problem encountered by consumers in the early 1990s **14.17**
was the effect of falling house prices resulting from high interest rates, the
recession and the general absence of a "feel good" factor. This resulted in
property developers cutting the prices of their new houses and flats. There
had been a suspicion that these advertised reductions were not always genuine. The Government was shrewd enough to cater for these circumstances
when drafting section 23. Although section 23(1) excludes from the Act "the
creation or disposal of an interest in land", such a transaction is caught where:

    (a) the person who is to create or dispose of the interest will do so in the course of
        any business of his; and
    (b) the interest to be created or disposed of is a relevant interest in a new dwelling
        and is to be created or disposed of for the purpose of enabling that dwelling to
        be occupied as a residence, or one of the residences, of the person acquiring
        the interest.

It can be seen from this wording that the Act does not affect the sale by an
ordinary house-owner, or a sale by a property developer or other businessman of a shop, office, factory or other business premises. This provision is
aimed at the problem mentioned above—the sale by a builder or developer of
a new house or flat to be occupied by the buyer as his residence. The definition of "new dwelling" in section 23(3) makes it clear that both new con-
structions and the conversion of old buildings into flats are covered unless the
individual unit has previously been occupied as a residence. Section 23(3)
also defines "relevant interest" to take outside the Act leases which were
originally granted for 21 years or less or have such a short period left to run. If
evidence were needed that alleged price reductions on new houses was a
problem for consumers, such evidence can be provided by the fact that one of
the first prosecutions under Part III related to this area.

> Taylors Estate Agents, part of Hambro Countrywide, placed a newspaper adver-
> tisement stating that the price of a four-bedroom house in Oxfordshire had drop-
> ped from £194,950 to £164,950. The property had never been offered at the
> higher price. Its highest asking price had been £185,000. The defendants were
> fined £800.[17]

Not surprisingly the Act applies even where, as part of the land transaction,
goods or services are also provided, *e.g.* carpets or kitchen equipment.[18]
Finally, the Code of Practice needs to be borne in mind by builders as Part 4 is
devoted to the sale of new homes.

Code of Practice

We have referred already on a number of occasions to the Code of Practice.   **14.18**

---

[17] New L.J., January 18, 1991.
[18] s.23(2).

Its full title is *Code of Practice for Traders on Price Indications*.[18a] It was introduced under powers given to the Secretary of State under section 25(1) to approve a code for two purposes:

(a) to give practical guidance on the requirements of section 20; and
(b) to promote desirable practices as to the way in which price indications should be given.

It came into force on March 1, 1989.

There was considerable debate during the passage of the Bill of the effect on traders of compliance or non-compliance with the Code. Some argued that where the trader complied with the Code, he should have a complete defence. Arguments were also put forward for the reverse side of the coin, namely, that failure to comply with the Code would of itself be an offence. Such proposals were heavily criticised by the so-called "Concordat" comprising consumer bodies, trading standards representatives and the Retail Consortium. As a result, the proposals were amended and the position now is as stated in section 25(2).

> A contravention of a code of practice approved under this section shall not of itself give rise to any criminal or civil liability, but in any proceedings against any person for an offence under section 20(1) or (2) above—
> (a) any contravention by that person of such a code may be relied on in relation to any matter for the purpose of establishing that that person committed the offence or of negativing any defence; and
> (b) compliance by that person with such a code may be relied on in relation to any matter for the purpose of showing that the commission of the offence by that person has not been established or that that person has a defence.

The Code turns out to be rather like the Highway Code in that if a trader contravenes it, the prosecution can rely on that fact to establish the commission of an offence, whereas if the trader complies with the Code he can use that fact as a defence. It is very detailed with pictorial illustrations and other examples showing traders what to do and what not to do. It falls into four parts:

Part 1. Price comparisons
Part 2. Actual price to the consumer
Part 3. Price indications which become misleading after they have been given
Part 4. Sale of new homes.

Regulations

14.19   The power to make regulations is given to the Secretary of State by section 26. Two sets have been made so far.

[18a] S.I. 1988 No. 2078.

Payment by credit card

The first to be made were the Price Indications (Method of Payment) **14.20**
Regulations 1991.[19] They are concerned with differential pricing whereby
traders may charge different prices for goods or services depending on the
method of payment used by the customer. For example, they may wish to
charge more where payment is made by credit card compared with payment
by cheque or cash. Such discrimination between credit card customers and
others had often been prohibited by agreements made between the credit card
companies and their associated merchants, but any such agreements became
unlawful in 1991 thus permitting discrimination.[20]

The purpose of the 1991 Order is to ensure that customers are made aware
of any difference in price depending on the method of payment, which in
practice means the extra which they will have to pay if they use a credit card.
The main thrust of the Regulations can be seen in article 3. This provides that
where an indication of a price at which goods, services, accommodation or
facilities are available is given to consumers, but the supplier is not prepared
to do business at that price irrespective of the method of payment, then the
supplier must state the difference between the various prices. Generally that
statement must appear (a) at each public entrance to the premises, and (b) at
each point in the premises where consumers make payment.

Bureaux de Change

The only other regulations to be made are the Price Indications (Bureaux **14.21**
de Change) Regulations 1992.[21] Their purpose is obvious from their title and,
like the other regulations, they are concerned with transparency and information for consumers. Any traveller will have seen the effect of these regulations when obtaining foreign currency. For example, the selling, buying
and commission rates must be stated. If the rates for travellers' cheques and
notes are different, that must be shown. This information must be given
"clearly and prominently" and must be visible to consumers as they either
approach or enter the bureau de change.

Ticket agents

It had been originally anticipated that regulations would be made to cover **14.22**
the resale by landlords of electricity and gas, but this plan has been dropped.
However, regulations are expected soon to deal with the problem of the resale
of entertainment tickets; presumably the regulations will make clear to customers the face value of the tickets and the additional commission payable to
the ticket agency.

[19] S.I. 1991 No. 199.
[20] Credit Cards (Price Discrimination) Order 1990 (S.I. 1990 No. 2159).
[21] S.I. 1992 No. 737.

Defences

14.23   There are a number of defences in the Act. Part III contains some defences specific to section 20. Section 39 contains a more general defence relating to offences prosecuted under both Parts II[22] and III of the Act.

Specific defences

14.24   Four defences of limited scope are provided by the four subsections of section 24. The first three apply to offences under both subsections of section 20. The fourth defence relates to section 20(1) only. A brief comment will be made on each subsection.

(1) Here the defendant must show that his acts or omissions were authorised by section 26 regulations.

(2) This defence is to protect the media in respect of editorial comments. Where the price indication is in a book, newspaper, film or broadcast, there is no offence if the indication was not in an advertisement.

(3) This subsection provides a defence for publishers and advertising agents who have no reason to suspect that advertisements passing through their hands are illegal.

(4) This relates to recommended prices. It protects the business which recommends the price if the goods, services, etc., are provided by a third party and the offence results from the unexpected failure by the third party to follow the recommendation.

Due diligence defence

14.25   The defence provided by section 39, which relates to offences committed under Parts II and III of the 1987 Act, is like the familiar "due diligence" defence found in other consumer protection statutes. However, they are not exactly the same. Section 39(1) reads as follows:

> Subject to the following provisions of this section, in proceedings against any person for an offence to which this section applies it shall be a defence for that person to show that he took all reasonable steps and exercised all due diligence to avoid committing the offence.

This is very similar to section 24(1) of the Trade Descriptions Act 1968[23] in that it requires the defendant to show that he took all reasonable "steps"—a wider word than "precautions" in the 1968 Act—and exercised all due diligence[23a] to avoid the commission of an offence. However, there is no equivalent to section 24(1)(a), *i.e.* here the defendant does not also have to show that the offence was due to one of a number of specific reasons, *e.g.* "the act or

[22] Pt. II is concerned with product safety: below, para. 15.04.
[23] Above, para. 13.45.
[23a] See *Balding v. Lew-Ways Ltd* [1995] Crim.L.R. 878, below, para. 15.19.

default of another person". Nevertheless in practice it is likely that the defendant will produce evidence to similar effect.

If he does point the finger of blame in another direction by alleging that the offence was due to the act or default of or information given by another, he must give information to the prosecution to identify that other person at least seven days before the hearing to preserve the defence.[24] Further, in the case of information given by another, he must also show that it was reasonable for him to rely on and believe the information bearing in mind any steps he could take to verify it.[25]

The by-pass provision

Another similarity with the 1968 Act is the inclusion of a by-pass pro-   **14.26**
vision comparable with section 23 of the 1968 Act.[26] It appears in section 40(1):

> Where the commission by any person of an offence to which section 39 above applies is due to an act or default committed by some other person in the course of any business of his, the other person shall be guilty of the offence and may be proceeded against and punished by virtue of this subsection whether or not proceedings are taken against the first-mentioned person.

However, there is one major difference—a private person cannot be prosecuted under section 40. This is because the words "in the course of any business of his"[27] have been added.

This was a change we noted earlier when discussing section 20 which also has the effect of preventing a prosecution of employees. For this reason it is anticipated that employers may be more ready to blame employees knowing that the employees themselves are not thereby endangered.

Enforcement and penalties

We have already discussed these topics in relation to trade descriptions.[28]   **14.27**
The provisions in the 1987 Act are very similar with regard to enforcement which is once again the duty of trading standards departments. In view of the similarity, we think that no further comment is necessary except to direct attention to Part IV of the Act where the relevant provisions may be found.

However, there is one major difference with regard to penalties—the sanction of imprisonment is not available to the courts.[29]

---

[24] s.39(2) and (3).
[25] s.39(4).
[26] Above, para. 13.53.
[27] See the same wording in s.20(1) and (2): above, para. 14.09.
[28] Above, paras 13.57 and 13.58.
[29] See s.20(4). *Cf.* Pt. II, below, para. 15.19.

CHAPTER FIFTEEN

"THE GOODS AREN'T SAFE"

1. INTRODUCTION

In Chapter 5 we considered Part I of the Consumer Protection Act 1987 **15.01**
which imposes *civil* liability on *producers* of unsafe goods. In this chapter we
turn to Part II of the 1987 Act and the General Product Safety Regulations
1994[1] which impose *criminal* sanctions on *producers and suppliers* of unsafe
consumer goods. First this recent legislation will be placed in its historical
context by briefly reviewing its legislative predecessors.

We have seen in earlier chapters that some consumer protection legislation
is concerned as much with shoddy goods as with dangerous goods; no distinction is drawn. This is true of both civil and criminal statutes, *e.g.* the Sale
of Goods Act 1979 and the Trade Descriptions Act 1968.

However, in many statutes a different approach is adopted where death or
personal injury is concerned: provisions are likely to be more stringent or
restrictive than in cases where only financial or economic loss results. Thus,
under the Unfair Contract Terms Act 1977, s.2, a clause excluding liability
for negligence is void in the case of death or personal injury, but valid if
reasonable in the case of other loss or damage, *e.g.* damage to property.[2] In
other areas the same emphasis is placed on ensuring that the individual is
protected against death or injury. For example, the Health and Safety at
Work, etc. Act 1974, s.6, restricts its control with regard to articles for use at
work to ensuring that they are safe and without risk to health and safety when
properly used.

Concern for safety at home should be as serious as concern for safety in the
work place. The Foreword to *Consumer Safety. A Consultative Document*[3]
provides ample evidence.

> About 7,000 people in Great Britain die each year from accidents in the home,
> over a tenth of them from fires. This is comparable to the number killed on the
> roads. In addition over 100,000 receive hospital in-patient treatment for home
> accident injuries. No central statistics are kept for those not admitted to hospital,
> but it is estimated that in England and Wales 650,000 receive out-patient care in
> hospitals and 500,000 attend their general practitioner for treatment.
>   Apart from the toll of human suffering which these figures represent, there are

---

[1] S.I. 1994 No. 2328.
[2] Above, para. 8.23.
[3] Cmnd. 6398, (1976).

substantial economic costs, both direct—through damage to property, as in the case of the 50,000 or so fires in the home each year—and indirect—*e.g.* the cost of medical treatment and hours lost from work.

This Consultative Document is concerned with ways of reducing the cost and suffering caused by home accidents. It considers how information, publicity and education on causes of home accidents and means of avoiding them can be improved; and in particular it discusses how the law can best ensure that goods which reach consumers are as safe to use as the public may reasonably expect.

As the last paragraph states, the Green Paper paid particular attention to the way in which the law could be improved with a view to ensuring that goods used by the consumer are safe. At that time this branch of the law was regulated by the Consumer Protection Acts 1961 and 1971. Several of the proposals contained in the paper for improving the legal protective framework were incorporated in the Consumer Safety Act 1978.

Consumer Safety Act 1978

15.02 Its main purpose was to prevent dangerous goods reaching the market or, if they had done so, to prohibit their further sale. The most important changes effected by the Act were these:

(1) It gave any Secretary of State much more flexible powers to make regulations to ensure that goods are safe and to prohibit the supply of unsafe goods.[4]
(2) It enabled quick action to be taken to ban the supply of dangerous goods by the use of "prohibition orders"[5] and "prohibition notices".
(3) It provided power by the service of a "notice to warn" to require manufacturers and distributors of goods, which were found to be dangerous only after they had been sold, to publish notices warning the public of the danger.[6]
(4) It imposed an enforcement duty on local authorities.[7]

These improvements are retained in the 1987 Act.

Consumer Safety (Amendment) Act 1986

15.03 Less than six years after the 1978 Act came into force the Government published a White Paper, *The Safety of Goods*,[8] setting out the Government's conclusions with regard to the effectiveness of the consumer products safety legislation. It contained proposals for amending the 1978 Act with a view to strengthening its provisions. One example mentioned in the White Paper

---

[4] s.1.
[5] s.3(1). Prohibition orders are no longer available: below, para. 15.10.
[6] *ibid.*
[7] s.5(1).
[8] Cmnd. 9302, (1984).

illustrated the difficulties. In 1981 over a hundred types of electrical hair-curling brushes were imported in large numbers, mostly from the Far East. They failed to satisfy the regulations on matters such as insulation, but this hazard did not become apparent until they had reached the shops and market stalls, been sold and were in use. It proved to be an expensive, time-consuming exercise to track down the unsafe appliances and have them removed from sale. In the interval, a death or serious injury could easily have occurred.

The purpose of the recommendations was to introduce preventative measures to assist in identifying and halting the supply of unsafe goods before they reached the shops; to enable enforcement officers to suspend the supply of apparently unsafe goods; and to introduce a general safety duty on all suppliers.

The 1986 Act added the first two of those new weapons to the armoury of the enforcement authorities. They both reappear in the 1987 Act:

(1) Customs officers were given power to detain imported goods for two days and to pass on information to trading standards officers, who would thus be given time to activate their other procedures.

(2) Trading standards officers were empowered to serve suspension notices to prohibit supplies of goods for up to six months, and to apply to the court for an order that goods be forfeited and destroyed. Related compensation provisions were also enacted.

2. CONSUMER PROTECTION ACT 1987, PT. II

The proposal that there should be a general statutory duty on suppliers to supply safe consumer goods was first put forward in the consultative document *Consumer Safety*.[9] The absence of this duty on suppliers of consumer goods contrasted with the duty on suppliers of articles for use at work imposed by section 6 of the Health and Safety at Work, etc. Act 1974. The Government's policy remained consistent and was reiterated in paragraph 34 of the White Paper[10]:   **15.04**

> The Government accepts that there is a case for widening the scope of the Act to place a general obligation on the suppliers of consumer goods to achieve an acceptable standard of safety where it is reasonable to expect them to anticipate and reduce risks arising from those goods. This would induce a greater sense of responsibility on the part of those suppliers who currently regard themselves as unaffected by legislation (and who may not be adequately deterred by the common law duty of care). At the same time it would provide wider scope for swift remedial action by enforcement authorities in the case of newly identified dangerous products.

[9] Above, n. 3.
[10] Above, n. 8.

This "general safety requirement" (GSR) was the novel feature of the 1987 Act but it has been all but repealed and replaced by the GSR contained in the General Product Safety Regulations 1994.[11] Otherwise the 1987 Act is in the main a consolidating statute bringing together in Part II the provisions of the 1978 and 1986 Acts.

The regulatory regime now consists of the following measures which we shall consider below.

(1) Safety regulations impose specific requirements in relation to a particular type of product.
(2) Prohibition notices, notices to warn and suspension notices provide back-up powers to control particular traders dealing in unsafe goods.
(3) The GSR in the 1987 Act creates a general offence of supplying consumer goods which are not reasonably safe.
(4) The GSR in the 1994 Regulations prohibits producers from placing unsafe consumer products on the market and imposes on distributors a duty of care in this respect. These Regulations are considered in a separate section at the end of this chapter.

As a preliminary it is necessary to look at some key words defined in the Act.

Key definitions

15.05   The definitions are found in various places. Those definitions relating to the Act as a whole are found in sections 45 and 46 (some of these have already been discussed in Chap. 5 in relation to Pt. I); those relating only to Part II appear in section 19; and a few of more limited importance are given in the relevant section itself.

Safe

15.06   This is the core of Part II—it is essentially concerned with dangerous, unsafe goods, not with shoddy goods of poor quality (this is true of Pt. I too). Section 19(1) gives this meaning to the word "safe":

> "safe", in relation to any goods, means such that there is no risk, or no risk apart from one reduced to a minimum, that any of the following will (whether immediately or after a definite or indefinite period) cause the death of, or any personal injury to, any person whatsoever, that is to say—
>> (a) the goods;
>> (b) the keeping, use or consumption of the goods[12];
>> (c) the assembly of any of the goods which are, or are to be, supplied unassembled;

[11] Above, n. 1.
[12] s.19(2) amplifies this aspect.

(d) any emission or leakage from the goods or, as a result of the keeping, use or consumption of the goods, from anything else; or

(e) reliance on the accuracy of any measurement, calculation or other reading made by or by means of the goods,

and "safer and "unsafe" shall be construed accordingly.

It can be seen that goods do not have to be absolutely safe, but the risk at worst must be "reduced to a minimum". This is a commonsense approach, since otherwise some products would be outlawed, *e.g.* motor vehicles, lawn mowers.

It is enough to refer to some of the regulations made under the 1961 and 1978 Acts[13] to find examples of unsafe goods: unstable carry-cot stands or prams; anorak hoods causing strangulation; explosive oil heaters or lamps; babies' dummies which choke; toys with sharp edges or spikes or loose doll's eyes; flammable nightdresses and foam furniture.

Electrical appliances provide frequent examples; here faulty insulation brings with it the hazard of electrocution—electric blankets, hair-curling brushes, vacuum cleaners, electric razors, and illuminated, gold novelty gondolas (presumably even people with such appalling taste should not reap the penalty of death).

The importance of (b) lies in making regulations relating to the effectiveness of safety equipment, *e.g.* life jackets, buoyancy rafts, fire extinguishers; for the risk arises not from the product itself but from the fact that, when circumstances occur in which the equipment is in "use", it is found at that late, critical stage to be unsuitable and thus to expose the user to risk. The significance of the word "keeping" can be seen in relation to labelling requirements on goods which create a hazard if not safely stored, *e.g.* garden pesticides.

Examples of the other factors in the list may be helpful:

(c) flat pack furniture;

(d) household cleaning fluids, pressure cookers, hot water bottles, gas cylinders;

(e) tyre pressure gauges, speedometers.

Goods

The definition of "goods" in section 45(1) is very wide: **15.07**

"goods" includes substances, growing crops and things comprised in land by virtue of being attached to it and any ship, aircraft or vehicle.

---

[13] These regulations continue in force until replaced by new regulations. s.50(5) permits regulations made under the 1961 Act to be treated as if made under the 1987 Act, if the Minister so orders.

However, safety regulations may not be made in respect of crops, water, food, feeding stuff, fertilisers, mains gas, drugs and medicines.[14]

Supply

15.08   A supply is caught only if made "in the course of carrying on a business (whether or not a business of dealing in the goods in question[15]) and either as principal or agent."[16] Thus, the business supply is covered; the private supply is not.

What types of transaction are "supplies"? The definition provides a detailed answer.

> (i)   Sale.
> (ii) Hire or loan.
> (iii) Hire-purchase.

Section 45(2) provides that in the case of hire, hire-purchase, credit sale or conditional sale agreements, "the supplier" is not the provider of the credit (the "ostensible supplier") but "the effective supplier" who is enabled to provide the goods by virtue of such financial facility.

Example

> D wishes to acquire on credit terms a car owned by a dealer S. S sells the car to a finance house C. C lets the goods on hire-purchase to D. S is "the supplier" under the 1987 Act. (To use Consumer Credit Act jargon, the credit-broker S (not the creditor C) is the supplier.)

> (iv) Work and materials.
> (v)   Exchange, *e.g.* for trading stamps.
> (vi) Provision under a statutory function, *e.g.* the NHS.
> (vii) Gift, *e.g.* a prize.

Safety regulations

15.09   Safety regulations are an old feature of this area of consumer protection. Indeed, regulations under the Acts of 1961 to 1978 continue in force. The current offences for contravention of safety regulations are to be found in section 12, *e.g.* supplying goods prohibited by regulations. It is section 11 which contains the regulation-making power:

---

[14] s.11(7).
[15] s.46(5). These clarifying words do not appear in the equivalent provision of the 1961 Act. But in *Southwark LBC v. Charlesworth* [1983] C.L.Y. 3311 the Divisional Court reached the same conclusion: a shoe repairer who sold an unsafe electric fire through his shop breached the Electrical Equipment (Safety) Regulations 1975 (S.I. 1975 No. 1366).
[16] s.46(1).

(1) The Secretary of State may by regulations under this section ("safety regulations") make such provision as he considers appropriate for the purposes of section 10(3) above and for the purpose of securing—
   (a) that goods to which this section applies are safe;
   (b) that goods to which this section applies which are unsafe, or would be unsafe in the hands of persons of a particular description, are not made available to persons generally or, as the case may be, to persons of that description; and
   (c) that appropriate information is, and inappropriate information is not, provided in relation to goods to which this section applies.

Thus regulations may cover not only the goods, but also information about them. Further, section 11(1)(b) makes it clear that they may relate to the supply of goods to certain groups only, a doubtful point in earlier legislation, *e.g.* fireworks not to be sold to children.

The possible contents of regulations are illustrated by a list set out in section 11(2). They include provisions relating to:

   (i) composition or contents, design, construction, finish or packing;
   (ii) standards to be approved, *e.g.* British Standards;
   (iii) testing or inspection, *e.g.* manufacturers' quality control procedures to prevent faulty batches of aerosol cans from reaching the market;
   (iv) marks, warnings, instructions or other information on goods, *e.g.* warning symbols, first-aid instructions, lists of ingredients in cosmetics; or prohibiting the giving of "inappropriate information", *e.g.* misleading marks or insignia.

The regulations may also prohibit the supply of goods or components which are unsafe or do not satisfy the requirements of the regulations. Thus a permanent ban may be imposed on dangerous products which the Secretary of State considers to be inherently unsafe irrespective of design or construction.

Emergency procedures

Extensive consultation is required by section 11(5) before the making of **15.10** regulations. As many months may elapse in this way, the 1978 Act contained power for the Minister to make prohibition orders to by-pass the normal regulation-making procedures as a temporary measure in an emergency.[17]

Prohibition orders have now disappeared and been replaced by the expedited procedure set out in section 11(5). The Secretary of State may make regulations without consultation for a 12 months maximum where "the need to protect the public requires that regulations should be made without delay".

[17] See 2nd ed. of this book, pp. 238–240, for an explanation of this procedure.

Notices

15.11   The Act contains various powers to stop the distribution, or further distribution, of unsafe goods.

Suspension notice[18]

15.12   If an enforcement authority reasonably suspects that a trader is supplying goods in contravention of a safety provision, it may serve a "suspension notice" on him. This will prevent him disposing of his stock for a maximum of six months. The authority may have to pay compensation, if there was no contravention after all.[19] A separate, but sometimes related, route is to apply to the court for forfeiture of the goods, which usually involves their destruction.[20] In neither of these cases is a conviction of the trader a prerequisite; only a "contravention" is needed.

Prohibition notice[21]

15.13   Like the suspension notice, the "prohibition notice" is aimed at a particular trader. It is served by the Secretary of State and prohibits the supply of unsafe goods. This is a useful follow-up to the local authority's suspension notice.

Notice to warn[22]

15.14   Prohibition notices are appropriate where goods are still in the hands of the suppliers. What can be done if the goods have already reached the public and are in daily use? Prior to the Act the most that the Department of Trade and Industry could do was to ask manufacturers to publish a warning or itself to issue a press notice. Responsible manufacturers and importers readily do so. The motor industry is a good example; as soon as any apparent defect reveals itself as a danger, *e.g.* brakes, the producer gives it widespread publicity and advises owners to take in their vehicles to be checked.

Now it is possible for the Secretary of State to serve a "notice to warn" on any trader requiring him to publish a specified warning about unsafe goods at his own expense.

Recall

15.15   A major defect in the legislation is that no one has the power to order manufacturers to recall dangerous products, although in practice they do recall such goods to avoid being sued under Part I of the Act or for negligence.[23] However, the General Product Safety Regulations oblige producers to monitor their products to facilitate their recall.[24]

---

[18] s.14(1).
[19] s.14(7).
[20] s.16.
[21] s.13(1)(a).
[22] s.13(1)(b).
[23] See Chap. 5.
[24] Reg. 8, below, para. 15.30.

General safety requirement (GSR)

The wide-ranging GSR imposed on suppliers by the 1987 Act was the **15.16** linch-pin of United Kingdom safety legislation until its virtual replacement by the GSR imposed by the 1994 Regulations. Accordingly our discussion of the 1987 Act GSR will be brief.[25] No longer is it necessary to bring in regulations piecemeal when particular products prove to be dangerous. This was the difficulty faced by the enforcement authorities before the 1987 Act, when the closing of various specific loopholes by regulations was no help when tackling another type of unsafe product when it appeared on the market.

The offence

Section 10(1) contains the GSR offence: **15.17**

> A person shall be guilty of an offence if he—
> (a) supplies any consumer goods which fail to comply with the general safety requirement;
> (b) offers or agrees to supply any such goods; or
> (c) exposes or possesses any such goods for supply.

Unlike the safety regulations and the product liability provisions of Part I, it is confined to *consumer* goods, *i.e.* "ordinarily intended for private use or consumption".[26] This is followed by a non-exhaustive list of factors to be taken into account, *e.g.* instructions, warnings, published safety standards.

Defences

There are other general defences elsewhere in the Act,[27] but two groups of **15.18** provisions in section 10 itself should be discussed here. The first group in section 10(3) are not strictly defences: they provide, in a somewhat roundabout way, that goods do comply with the GSR when they meet certain requirements:

> For the purposes of this section consumer goods shall not be regarded as failing to comply with the general safety requirement in respect of—
> (a) anything which is shown to be attributable to compliance with any requirement imposed by or under any enactment or with any Community obligation;
> (b) any failure to do more in relation to any matter than is required by—
>   (i) any safety regulations imposing requirements with respect to that matter;
>   (ii) ...
>   (iii) any provision of any enactment or subordinate legislation imposing such requirements with respect to that matter as are designated for the purposes of this subsection by any such regulations.[27a]

---

[25] See the 3rd ed. of this book, pp. 249–251, for a more detailed analysis.
[26] s.10(7).
[27] Below, para. 15.19.
[27a] s.10(3)(b)(ii) was repealed by the 1994 Regulations, reg. 6(1).

"Requirement" is an important word which runs right through this subsection. The question is whether it is *compulsory* for the goods to meet the standards, etc.—not merely desirable because they were recommended, *e.g.* British Standards (BSI).

The second group of defences is found in section 10(4). They comprise three narrow defences confined to exporters, retailers and second-hand goods.

Defences and penalties

15.19   In addition to the special defences set out in section 10(4) in respect of the GSR, the familiar defence is available that the accused "took all reasonable steps and exercised all due diligence[27b] to avoid committing the offence", with the usual duty to notify the prosecutor of the identity of any one else who is being blamed.[28] These provisions are discussed elsewhere in relation to Part III.[29]

The penalty for any of the offences is the same—on summary conviction a maximum fine of £5,000 and up to six months' imprisonment.[30]

Enforcement

15.20   Although the 1961 Act merely gave a discretionary power to trading standards inspectors, section 27(1) makes it their duty to enforce the provisions creating the offences explained above. Whether with the depleted resources available to them local authorities are managing to cope with their ever-increasing responsibilities—the Consumer Credit Act 1974 is also their problem—is a matter of doubt. Nevertheless this duty is one which they must do their best to fulfil, unless the Secretary of State exercises the power given to him by section 27(2) to transfer the duty elsewhere. Sections 28 and 29 give the authorities the usual related powers of purchase, entry and seizure, testing, etc., and section 30 enables a customs officer to detain imported goods for two days.

Civil remedy

15.21   In the following chapter breach of statutory duty is examined. The Acts of 1961 to 1987 stand alone among the criminal statutes concerned with consumer protection in expressly affording the victim a civil remedy. Section 41(1) offers the remedy and section 41(4) prevents it being snatched away by invalidating any exclusion clause. Further, any contractual rights of the vic-

---

[27b] *Balding v. Lew-Ways Ltd* [1995] Crim.L.R. 878: non-compliance with Toys (Safety) Regulations 1989 (S.I. 1989 No. 1275); not "due diligence" to rely on analyst's report that toy complied with British Standard.
[28] s.39(1) and (2). See *Riley v. Webb* [1987] Crim.L.R. 477.
[29] Above, para. 14.25.
[30] *e.g.* s.12(5).

tim remain untouched.[31] However, this civil remedy applies only to breach of the safety regulations, not of the GSR. In practice, it is rarely, if ever, used.

3. General Product Safety Regulations 1994

E.C. Directive

We have just seen that the policy of ensuring that the consumer is protected   **15.22** from dangerous goods has been implemented in the United Kingdom by taking two complementary routes, First, legislation was introduced enabling regulations to be passed to regulate particular kinds of products which were inherently hazardous, *e.g.* paraffin heaters or foam furniture.[32] Such "vertical legislation" copes only with narrow sectoral problems which are attacked piecemeal, leaving the holes in the dyke to be plugged as and when they appear. So the second route was taken of introducing "horizontal legislation" with the imposition of a general safety requirement (GSR) by the Consumer Protection Act 1987.[33]

Of course, such problems exist at the European level too and can be met with similar solutions. The importance of safety was emphasised in point 72 of the 1985 E.C. White Paper *Completing the Internal Market* which stated that the health and safety of workers and consumers were interests which should be taken into account in the 1992 programme. This very same point was referred to in July 1985 when the European Commission submitted to the European Council a Communication concerning a *New Impetus for a Consumer Protection Policy*. This Communication gave a special priority to consumer safety and was followed in May 1987 by another Communication on *Safety of Consumers in Relation to Consumer Products*, which ended with the promise: "The Commission shortly intends to submit to the Council a proposal for a general Directive on consumer safety in relation to consumer products."

This ambition was not realised until June 1989 when the E.C. Commission submitted its proposal for a Directive on General Product Safety. Horizontal legislation already existed in such other influential countries as France and Germany. Indeed, in this area as in others there was a marked distinction between the approach adopted by the northern Member States and the southern or Mediterranean Member States whose legislation on product safety was much less stringent. These anomalies are highlighted in the Preamble to the Directive:

> Whereas some Member States have adopted horizontal legislation on product safety, imposing, in particular, a general obligation on economic operators to market only safe products; whereas those legislations differ in the level of pro-

---

[31] s.41(3).
[32] Above, para. 15.06.
[33] Above, para. 15.16.

tection afforded to persons; whereas such disparities and the absence of horizontal legislation in other Member States are liable to create barriers to trade and distortions of competition within the internal market.

One difficulty was how to dovetail specific Community or national rules relating to particular products or product sectors into the general safety duty at the core of the Directive. Should the specific and general duties be mutually exclusive or should they overlap? The Directive comes down firmly on the former solution—no overlap.

Another hotly debated issue was whether the Directive should cover all products or only consumer products. The original plan was to include only consumer products, but as the debate continued the scope of the draft directive was widened to encompass all products (whether manufactured or agricultural, new or used). However, the Directive in its final form applies only to consumer goods and excludes some second-hand goods.

The Directive on General Product Safety was finally adopted on June 29, 1992 and was supposed to come into force within two years. In the event the Government's consultation process was rather protracted and the implementation of the Directive within the United Kingdom was delayed until October 3, 1994. This was the date when the General Product Safety Regulations 1994 took effect.[34]

Relationship to 1987 Act

15.23   We saw in the previous section that the United Kingdom already had in place a "general safety requirement" (GSR) introduced by Part II of the Consumer Protection Act 1987. Its effective existence was limited to seven years as the main effect of the 1994 Regulations was to make the GSR in section 10 of the 1987 Act redundant. However, it has not been repealed as such. Regulation 5 provides as follows:

> For the purposes of these Regulations the provisions of section 10 of the 1987 Act to the extent that they impose general safety requirements which must be complied with if products are to be—
> (i) placed on the market, offered or agreed to be placed on the market or exposed or possessed to be placed on the market by producers; or
> (ii) supplied, offered or agreed to be supplied or exposed or possessed to be supplied by distributors,
> are hereby disapplied.

Thus where the 1994 Regulations do apply, section 10 of the 1987 Act does not apply, *i.e.* there is no overlap between the two GSRs.

One example where section 10 will continue to bite is the following. Suppose Community rules are put in place relating to the safety of a particular product. The Regulations cannot apply, as regulation 3(c) excludes from its ambit "any product where there are specific provisions in rules of Com-

---

[34] S.I. 1994 No. 2328.

munity law governing all aspects of the safety of the product". Suppose that those "specific provisions" impose obligations only on those businesses which first place the product on the market such as manufacturers, but not on distributors such as wholesalers and retailers. This "gap" in the Regulations is covered by section 10, for this catches all "suppliers", including wholesalers and retailers.[35]

GSR

The essence of the Regulations appears in regulation 7:   **15.24**

> No producer shall place a product on the market unless the product is a safe product.

Unlike the GSR in the 1987 Act this is limited to a "producer". However, it is backed up by a complementary provision in regulation 9 aimed at distributors:

> A distributor shall act with due care in order to help ensure compliance with the requirements of regulation 7 above and, in particular, without limiting the generality of the foregoing—
> (a) a distributor shall not supply products to any person which he knows, or should have presumed, on the basis of the information in his possession and as a professional, are dangerous products; and
> (b) within the limits of his activities, a distributor shall participate in monitoring the safety of products placed on the market, in particular by passing on information on the product risks and cooperating in the action taken to avoid those risks.

Contravention of regulation 7 or 9(a) is an offence. It can be seen that the producer is more in peril in that regulation 7 creates an offence of strict liability, whereas the distributor's offence depends on his actual or presumed knowledge that the products are dangerous.

Both offences involve the supply of dangerous products to consumers. To discover the precise meaning of these words we need to look closely at some key definitions in regulation 2(1).

Key definitions

Product

"Product" is defined as follows: **15.25**

> "product" means any product intended for consumers or likely to be used by consumers, supplied whether for consideration or not in the course of a commer-

---

[35] An example is the Personal Protective Equipment (EEC Directive) Regulations 1992 (S.I. 1992 No. 3139) (as amended by S.I. 1993 No. 3074). For the meaning of "supply", see above, para. 15.08.

cial activity and whether new, used or reconditioned; provided, however, a product which is used exclusively in the context of a commercial activity even if it is used for or by a consumer shall not be regarded as a product for the purposes of these Regulations provided always and for the avoidance of doubt this exception shall not extend to the supply of such a product to a consumer.

(1) Although the wording does not state so expressly, clearly the Regulations are concerned only with goods and not with services, like the Product Liability Directive.[36]

(2) The supply must be in the course of a "commercial activity" which is itself defined by regulation 2(1) as including "a business and a trade". Thus a private sale by a consumer is not caught.

(3) Only consumer goods fall within the Regulations. A product will be caught if it is "intended for consumers"; presumably it is the producer's intention which matters here. For example, if a producer makes a chain saw intending it to be sold to and used only by trained foresters, this would fall outside the definition even if occasionally one of his saws was sold on by a trade customer to a member of the public, perhaps in a garden centre, or was lent by a forester to a friend.

More problematical are the words "likely to be used by consumers". Suppose that in the above case the producer discovered that his chain saws were frequently being sold on to consumers, perhaps in contravention of his terms of sale to the trade. Arguably once the producer discovers this, it can be said that his products are "likely to be used" by a "consumer".[37] Such difficulties will clearly arise in the case of building or gardening equipment hired out by the day. The same is true of vans; large numbers of these are hired to consumers on a short-term basis to move house, etc., although the proportion of vans sold by producers to van and car rental companies is quite small compared to the sales to businesses which use the vans for their own transport purposes.

One further comment needs to be made on the definition by looking at the words after the semi-colon. This gloss has been added in the Regulations: no such wording appears in the Directive. Its purpose is to take outside the Regulations products which are actually being used by a trade or business even though such a product might equally be available for purchase by consumers. For example, if a bottle of shampoo is used by a hairdresser in his salon, the DTI considers that this product will fall outside the Regulations, whereas if the customer were to buy a bottle of the same type of shampoo from the hairdresser, it would be covered.

(4) It does not matter whether the product has been sold or given away in view of the words "whether for consideration or not".

(5) Unlike the GSR in the 1987 Act, second-hand goods are not excluded.

---

[36] Above, para. 5.15.
[37] reg. 2(1). See below.

Indeed, the definition expressly states that a "product may be new, used or reconditioned". However, two related exceptions appear in regulation 3:

> These Regulations do not apply to—
> (a) second-hand products which are antiques;
> (b) products supplied for repair or reconditioning before use, provided the supplier clearly informs the person to whom he supplies the product to that effect.

Antiques are not defined. Presumably a judge would take into account whether the price reflected merely its utilitarian value or whether it took account of the age and perhaps rarity of the artefact. The relevant offence here is doubtless the distributor's offence in regulation 9 since, fraud apart, there is an inherent contradiction in the manufacture of antiques.

Exception (b) will apply only where the supplier "informs" the consumer that the product is to be repaired or reconditioned before use. From the point of view of the supplier it will provide valuable evidence, if the sale note states this specifically.

Consumer

The definition in regulation 2(1) is somewhat circular: **15.26**

> "Consumer" means a consumer acting otherwise than in the course of a commercial activity.

The meaning, though, is obvious: a product intended for a commercial, business or trade customer is free from regulation.

Producer

The definition is as follows: **15.27**

> "producer" means
> (a) the manufacturer of the product, when he is established in the Community, and includes any person presenting himself as the manufacturer by affixing to the product his name, trade mark or other distinctive mark, or the person who reconditions the product;
> (b) when the manufacturer is not established in the Community—
>   (i) if the manufacturer does not have a representative established in the Community, the importer of the product;
>   (ii) in all other cases, the manufacturer's representative; and
> (c) other professionals in the supply chain, insofar as their activities may affect the safety properties of a product placed on the market;

This definition bears a close resemblance to the definition of producer given in the Product Liability Directive.[38] The definition includes businesses which are not "producers" in the ordinary sense of the word.

---

[38] Above, para. 5.18.

(1) The manufacturer himself is obviously included, but only if his business operates within the Community.

(2) Even though the producer may not be the actual manufacturer, if he gives the impression that he is the manufacturer ("presenting himself") by the way in which the goods are marked, he is treated as the producer.

(3) A business which reconditions its products is a producer, for example, a retailer taking goods in part-exchange and reselling after putting them in working order.

(4) Where there is no E.C. manufacturer, his representative carries the responsibility instead—presumably that means his agent. If there is no agent, the importer of the product into the Community is treated as the producer.

(5) Other businesses are also caught, even though they are merely distributors, if their "activities" may affect the product's safety. Examples would include a motor dealer conducting a pre-delivery inspection or a tyre distributor fitting replacement tyres.

Distributor

15.28   Distributor means:

> Any professional in the supply chain whose activity does not affect the safety properties of a product.

A "distributor" is someone whose activities do *not* affect the product's safety; if they do so, he will fall within the meaning of "producer" (see (5) above). Such a business may also be a producer because of "own labelling", reconditioning or being the E.C. importer (see (2), (3) and (4) above).

Dangerous and safe products

15.29   A "dangerous product" is "any product other than a safe product". The latter is defined in the following way:

> "safe product" means any product which, under normal or reasonably foreseeable conditions of use, including duration, does not present any risk or only the minimum risks compatible with the product's use, considered as acceptable and consistent with a high level of protection for the safety and health of persons, taking into account in particular—
> (a) the characteristics of the product, including its composition, packaging, instructions for assembly and maintenance;
> (b) the effect on other products, where it is reasonably foreseeable that it will be used with other products;
> (c) the presentation of the product, the labelling, any instructions for its use and disposal and any other indication or information provided by the producer; and
> (d) the categories of consumers at serious risk when using the product, in particular children,
> and the fact that higher levels of safety may be obtained or other products presenting a lesser degree of risk may be available shall not of itself cause the product to be considered other than a safe product.

Although the wording is not exactly the same, many of the factors appearing in this definition are reminiscent of the factors mentioned in the definition of "defect" in the Product Liability Directive and also in section 3 of the 1987 Act.[39] Again, instructions are important and here they are spelt out to include assembly, maintenance, use and disposal. One important feature is (d), highlighting particular categories such as children who might be at serious risk.

Another apparent similarity appears in the provision at the end about other products being safer. In the 1987 Act, s.3, the words are aimed at later products being safer than the product in question, whereas in these Regulations the comparison is between other products currently available. The Regulations also acknowledge that "higher levels of safety may be obtained".

Clearly the definition is not imposing on producers a duty to place on the market only perfectly safe goods. No product can be absolutely safe, so that the broad test is whether the risk has been reduced to an acceptable level. The beginning of the definition indicates as much by stating that a safe product is one which "does not present any risk or only the minimum risks compatible with the product's use, considered as acceptable and consistent with a high level of protection for the safety and health of persons". However, although a product may be safe in spite of their being "minimum risks", the emphasis on "a high level" of safety shows that producers should not be chary of spending a few pounds on introducing new safety features which will not price the goods out of the reach of the average consumer.

It should be noted, and we have made this point elsewhere, that the Regulations are not concerned at all with products which are shoddy and of poor quality. Their aim is simply to ensure that goods are not dangerous.

Information and monitoring

The GSR imposed on producers by regulation 7 and the lower duty on distributors by regulation 9(a) are intended to fulfil that aim, *i.e.* to prevent dangerous goods being supplied to consumers. However, even manufacturers with high standards and excellent quality control may make mistakes and place a product on the market which has unexpected and dangerous features. As a matter of self-interest manufacturers usually monitor the use of their products and react quickly, if the products turn out to be unsafe; otherwise they might be sued in tort or prosecuted. That self-interest is bolstered by the statutory requirements in regulations 8 and 9.

Regulation 8 is addressed to producers:

15.30

(1) Within the limits of his activity, a producer shall—

    (a) provide consumers with the relevant information to enable them to assess

---

[39] Above, para. 5.17.

the risks inherent in a product throughout the normal or reasonably foreseeable period of its use, where such risks are not immediately obvious without adequate warnings, and to take precautions against those risks; and

(b) adopt measures commensurate with the characteristics of the products which he supplies, to enable him to be informed of the risks which these products might present and to take appropriate action, including, if necessary, withdrawing the product in question from the market to avoid those risks.

(2) The measures referred to in sub-paragraph (b) of paragraph (1) above may include, whenever appropriate—

(i) marking of the products or product batches in such a way that they can be identified;

(ii) sample testing of marketed products;

(iii) investigating complaints; and

(iv) keeping distributors informed of such monitoring.

Regulation 9(b) is addressed to distributors:

Within the limits of his activities, a distributor shall participate in monitoring the safety of products placed on the market, in particular by passing on information on the product risks and cooperating in the action taken to avoid those risks.

Regulation 8(1)(a) and most of regulation 9(b) are concerned with ensuring that the consumer is informed of potential risks and dangers and so can take precautions to prevent being harmed. The second aspect of the information provisions is concerned with monitoring the products while in use, so that the producer can withdraw the product from the market, if necessary. These monitoring provisions appear in regulation 8(1)(b), backed up the possible measures listed in regulation 8(2) and coupled with the distributor's duties specified in regulation 9(b).

Compliance with E.C. rules

15.31   The policy adopted by the Directive and so by the Regulations, where there might be an overlap between the GSR and specific European Community or United Kingdom rules, is to disapply the GSR in such cases. In deciding whether a product is covered by the Regulations or not the following sequence is suggested.

(1) First, consider regulation 3(c) which provides that the Regulations do not apply to—

(c) any product where there are specific provisions in rules of Community law governing all aspects of the safety of the product.

Thus if *all* aspects of safety fall within specific E.C. Rules, the Regulations do not apply at all.

(2) In contrast where such specific rules deal with only *some* aspects of

safety, the GSR will apply to all other aspects. Regulation 4 deals with this possibility:

> The requirements of these Regulations apply to a product where the product is the subject of provisions of Community law other than the GPS Directive insofar as those provisions do not make specific provision governing an aspect of the safety of the product.

(3) Where there are no E.C. rules, one turns to regulation 10(1). This follows the policy set out in Article 4.1 of the Directive which states:

> Where there are no specific Community provisions governing the safety of the products in question, the product shall be deemed safe when it conforms to the specific rules of national law of the Member State in whose territory the product is in circulation.

Regulation 10(1) provides that where a "product conforms to the specific rules of the law of the United Kingdom ... there shall be a presumption that, until the contrary is proved, the product is a safe product." This is self-explanatory.

(4) In the absence of the above rules the GSR applies. Regulation 10(2) gives a list of factors to be taken into account in assessing whether the product conforms to the GSR:

> Where no specific rules as are mentioned or referred to in paragraph (1) exist, the conformity of a product to the general safety requirement shall be assessed taking into account—
> (i) voluntary national standards of the United Kingdom giving effect to a European standard; or
> (ii) Community technical specifications; or
> (iii) if there are no such voluntary national standards of the United Kingdom or Community technical specifications—
> (aa) standards drawn up in the United Kingdom; or
> (bb) the codes of good practice in respect of health and safety in the product sector concerned; or
> (cc) the state of the art and technology
> and the safety which consumers may reasonably expect.

Offences

The offences are listed in regulations 12 and 13. Regulation 12 succinctly states that "any person who contravenes regulation 7 or 9(a) shall be guilty of an offence".   **15.32**

Regulation 13 contains additional offences which are aimed at what are called "preparatory acts", so it is an offence to agree to supply or place on the market a dangerous product.

Defences

The familiar "due diligence" defence is contained in regulation 14.   **15.33**

Enforcement and penalties

15.34   Enforcement as usual is placed in the hands of trading standards officers.[40]
The penalties for contravention are a fine of up to £5,000 and imprisonment for up to three months. The maximum prison sentence contrasts with the six months available for contravention of safety regulations.

Civil liability

15.35   The Regulations (unlike the Consumer Protection Act 1987 as to which see above, para. 15.21) do not expressly confer a civil right or action. We shall see in the next chapter that the English courts adopt a somewhat negative attitude in allowing actions for breach of statutory duty. It must not be forgotten, however, that this is Euro-based legislation and the European Court of Justice has adopted a much more positive approach. It has, for example, held that certain Articles in the Treaty of Rome imposing duties on Member States (and public law sanctions) were enforceable by individuals in local courts and tribunals; this was necessary in order to give the provisions "teeth".[40a]

4. E.C. Directive

15.36   In the previous section we discussed the transposition into the law of the United Kingdom of those Articles of the Directive which are concerned with the responsibilities of producers and distributors. The 1994 Regulations are confined to those matters. However, the Directive has a broader scope and deals, in the rest of the Articles and the Annex, with the duty of public authorities to monitor compliance with its provisions and to ensure that, if dangerous products reach the market, action is taken by the appropriate Member State to have them withdrawn from the market.[41] This last obligation will be a novel one in the United Kingdom, where there has hitherto been no power for any public authority to order the recall of unsafe products.

The onus lies on the Member States to make appropriate monitoring arrangements and to establish or nominate appropriate authorities to effect compliance by suppliers with the GSR.[42] Presumably this time-consuming and expensive task will be added to the already onerous responsibilities of trading standards departments in the United Kingdom.

Emergency procedures are specially built into the Directive. Where there is a "serious and immediate risk", the Member State must ensure that there is a "rapid exchange of information" between its own authorities. If the grave risk is not merely local, it must immediately inform the E.C. Commission.[43]

---

[40] reg. 11.
[40a] The first and leading case was *Van Gend en Loos* [1963] C.M.L.R. 105.
[41] Art. 6.
[42] Arts. 5 and 6.
[43] Art. 8 and Annex.

In limited circumstances the Commission may take the initiative[44]—there was some anxiety in a number of countries that the Brussels bureaucracy, as they saw it, would be too keen to interfere. Such a "rapid exchange system" is a cornerstone of the structure in that nothing can be more important than the prompt recall of a product once it is discovered to be unsafe. The Commission will be assisted by a new Committee on Product Safety Emergencies.[45]

---

[44] Art. 9.
[45] Arts. 10–11.

CHAPTER SIXTEEN

CRIME AND COMPENSATION

1. Introduction

(1) Jane buys a used car described as "Immaculate. A really nice little **16.01** bus." It is clapped out and incapable of self-propulsion. The car dealer repudiates his liability with a few unequivocal words.

(2) James reads a holiday brochure. The tour operator confirms that the hotel facilities are exactly as described, whereupon James books a holiday. When he reaches his destination, he discovers that the hotel bears little resemblance except in name to that shown in the brochure. The tour operator refuses to give compensation.

A commonly held view of the consumer protection lobby is that it is a waste of effort for Parliament and the courts to amend and improve upon the long-standing rights of consumers, *e.g.* under the Sale of Goods Act 1979, and to launch new assaults across a broad front on attempts to rob the consumer of those rights, *e.g.* under the Unfair Contract Terms Act 1977. Thus in both the above examples the consumers clearly have a right of action for breach of contract, but of what benefit are their rights unless machinery exists to enable them to be enforced without difficulty? The immediate need is for reform to be concentrated upon the enforcement of existing rights rather than the creation of new ones.

We discussed in Chapter 10 enforcement under the civil law. We saw that frequently the consumer has no alternative to suing the recalcitrant trader in the county court; for there is often no ombudsman scheme in the particular sector nor even a trade association able or prepared to bring about a settlement of the complaint by conciliation or to discipline the trader for falling below the standards set out in a code of practice. In such circumstances there are clearly considerable advantages to consumers if they can reap some benefit from the fact that the trader has committed a criminal offence in addition to having broken one of its civil obligations. However, it should be borne in mind that criminal offences are not created for the purpose of providing consumers with compensation, as is pointed out in the Review of the Trade Descriptions Act 1968, para. 281:

> We believe that compensation is primarily a matter for the civil law, and that an award of compensation under the Powers of the Criminal Courts Act should be

regarded as a windfall rather than a right which itself justified prosecution under the Act.

It is proposed in this chapter to deal with two aspects of recovery arising out of the criminal law. First, we shall look at the power of the courts on conviction to award compensation under the Powers of Criminal Courts Act 1973. Secondly, we shall consider the circumstances in which it is possible to sue for breach of statutory duty.

2. POWERS OF CRIMINAL COURTS ACT 1973

16.02 The recommendations of the 1970 Widgery Report with regard to the remedies available under the criminal law for compensating victims of crime were broadly carried into effect by the Criminal Justice Act 1972. The particular provision which now concerns us was replaced by section 35(1) of the Powers of Criminal Courts Act 1973.

In essence it enables the court to order a convicted person to pay compensation for any damage resulting from the offence. The section states:

> A court by or before which a person is convicted of an offence, instead of or in addition to dealing with him in any other way, may, on application or otherwise, make an order (in this Act referred to as "a compensation order") requiring him to pay compensation for any personal injury, loss or damage resulting from that offence or any other offence which is taken into consideration by the court in determining sentence.[1]

This discretionary power is available whenever there has been a conviction in any court, including a magistrates' court. It is especially valuable in cases brought under the Trade Descriptions Act 1968,[2] where the loss may be too small to justify the cost of civil litigation.

Maximum

16.03 The amount of compensation where the conviction is on indictment in the Crown Court is unlimited. In the magistrates' court it is limited to £5,000.[3] This limit relates to each offence of which the accused is convicted; so if a supplier is convicted of four offences, the order may reach £20,000.

Special care must be taken when the accused asks for other offences to be taken into consideration for which he has not been prosecuted. No additional sums may be awarded in respect of such t.i.c. offences.[4]

---

[1] As amended by Criminal Justice Act 1982, s.67.
[2] The 1998 Annual Report of the DGFT shows that in the year ending September 30, 1998 £129,735 compensation related to convictions under the 1968 Act—nearly two-thirds of the total compensation in consumer protection cases.
[3] Magistrates' Courts Act 1980, s.40. Increased by the Criminal Justice Act 1991, s.17.
[4] See H. Street, "Compensation Orders and the Trade Descriptions Act" [1974] Crim.L.R. 345.

Example

> A tour operator publishes a brochure containing false statements in contra-
> vention of section 14 of the Trade Descriptions Act 1968. Forty people from
> different parts of the United Kingdom book holidays in reliance on the brochure.
> The tour operator, when prosecuted in one area, asks for the 39 other offences to
> be taken into consideration. The magistrates' order for the 40 offences cannot
> exceed £5,000 in total.

From the point of view of the victims in this example it would be preferable
for separate charges to be brought in each area, so that altogether the orders
would have a ceiling of £200,000.[5]

Type of loss

The compensation may relate to "any personal injury, loss or damage".   **16.04**
Thus claims for breach of contract (as in Examples (1) and (2), above) or for
negligence are covered. Further, the Act is wide enough for an order to be
made in respect of loss for which no civil remedy is available: in such a case
in the absence of a successful prosecution the victim would be remediless.[6]

This is most important in the case of misleading advertising, where usually
the advertisement will not be a term of the contract nor a misrepresentation
but mere puff. However, it may result in the commission of a criminal
offence, *e.g.* under the Trade Descriptions Act, when compensation for the
consumer's loss can be ordered.

Let us consider Example (2) given at the beginning of this chapter. There
the statements about the hotel facilities are terms of the contract in view of the
express confirmation prior to booking.[7] In the absence of that confirmation it
would be more difficult, but not impossible, for James to show that the wording in the brochure[8] was by itself a term or misrepresentation; nevertheless if
a conviction were obtained under the Trade Descriptions Act, compensation
could be claimed.

Assessment

As the assessment of compensation will commonly be made by lay magis-   **16.05**
trates, it is inappropriate for the power to be exercised in complicated cases,
e.g. where the principles of remoteness of damage need to be understood and
applied. An order will be made only in straightforward cases. Lawton L.J.
explained the court's approach in *R. v. Thomson Holidays Ltd*[9-10]:

> "Parliament, we are sure, never intended to introduce into the criminal law the
> concepts of causation which apply to the assessment of damages under the law of

---

[5] Multiple prosecutions are discussed in the chapter on Trade Descriptions: see para. 13.60.
[6] See *R. v. Chappel* [1984] Crim.L.R. 574.
[7] See *Jackson v. Horizon Holidays Ltd* [1975] 1 W.L.R. 1468, CA, above, para. 7.39.
[8] *Jarvis v. Swans Tours* [1973] 1 Q.B. 233 CA, above, para. 7.37.
[9-10] [1974] Q.B. 592 at 599.

contract or tort. . . . [The court] must do what it can to make a just order on such information as it has. Whenever the making of an order for compensation is appropriate, the court must ask itself whether loss or damage can fairly be said to have resulted to anyone from the offence for which the accused has been convicted."[11]

The defendants were convicted under section 14 of the Trade Descriptions Act 1968 for making a false statement in their brochure that a hotel had a night club and swimming and paddling pools. Compensation of £50 was awarded to the complainant.

A separate point to bear in mind is that the victim must show that the defendant is liable for the amount claimed. In *R. v. Vivian*[12] the Court of Appeal quashed an order in respect of damage to a car alleged to have been done by a thief in a collision, as there was no proof that he was responsible for all the damage: further, the appellant claimed that the sole estimate given for the repairs was excessive. Talbot J. said[13] that the view of the court was that "no order for compensation should be made unless the sum claimed by way of compensation is either agreed or has been proved." This appears to leave a large loophole for defendants and certainly makes it necessary in this type of case for victims to be less perfunctory in preparing claims, *e.g.* by obtaining more than one estimate.

Situations where it would be appropriate to make an order include misdescribed goods, *e.g.* clocked or misdescribed cars (Example (1)),[14] where the reduction in value or cost of repair can be easily proved, and holiday cases where part of the cost can be refunded to take account of inconvenience and loss of enjoyment (Example (2)).

In determining whether to make an order and, if so, for what amount, the court must take into account the defendant's means[15] and generally limits the award to a sum which he can manage to pay over two or three years. Thus in *R. v. McIntosh*[16] the Court of Appeal revoked a £90 order against a burglar on the grounds that he had no means and would find it hard to obtain employment on his release from prison because of his wooden leg—surprisingly not an impediment to the nefarious activities of this Long John McSilver in a trade where one would expect agility to be a *sine qua non*! Similarly it is not generally appropriate to make an order where the defendant is sentenced to a significant period of imprisonment, unless he has assets in hand to pay the compensation.[17]

---

[11] See also *R. v. Daly* [1974] 1 All E.R. 290; *R. v. Kneeshaw* [1974] 1 All E.R. 896: the machinery is intended "for clear and simple cases" (*per* Lord Widgery C.J.).
[12] [1979] 1 All E.R. 48.
[13] *ibid.* at p. 50.
[14] Above, para. 16.01.
[15] s.35(4).
[16] [1973] Crim.L.R. 378.
[17] *R. v. McCullough* (1982) 4 Cr.App.R.(S.) 98 CA; *R. v. Morgan* (1982) 4 Cr.App.R.(S.) 358, CA.

How to apply

No procedure is laid down for making the application for compensation. **16.06**
Generally it is enough for the victim to forewarn the clerk or prosecutor
before the trial commences, so that the application may be brought to the
notice of the court after conviction and the victim then heard. Alternatively
the court may act of its initiative without an application. Although it is cus-
tomary for the prosecution to pass on a request for compensation, they are not
under a duty to conduct an inquiry into the defendant's means.[18]

An order is enforceable in the same ways as a fine.[19] Thus the court may
impose a term of imprisonment in default.

Interrelation with civil claims

Generally the trial of the criminal charge will be held some time before any **16.07**
civil proceedings reach that stage. In the subsequent civil proceedings two
points must be borne in mind. First, the conviction may be used in evidence.[20]
Secondly, when awarding damages the court must take into account sums
paid under the order.[21]

If exceptionally the civil proceedings have already come to an end,
whether by judgment or settlement, no order can be made even though the
victim can still show loss. In *Hammertons Cars Ltd v. London Borough of
Redbridge*[22]:

> The complainant bought a car described as "in perfect condition". It was not. He
> settled an action against the sellers on the basis that he paid his own legal costs of
> £170 and expert's fee of £25. When the sellers were convicted under the Trade
> Descriptions Act he was awarded £195 compensation by the justices. The dealer
> successfully appealed against the order to the Divisional Court.

Lord Widgery C.J., doubting whether in any case the section would cover
such legal costs, said:

> "It seems to me to be abundantly clear that if the victim brings civil proceedings,
> and those civil proceedings are brought to an end, then they should be regarded
> as quite independent of the criminal proceedings and no compensation order
> should be made in respect of liabilities which arose, or might have arisen, in the
> civil proceedings."

3. BREACH OF STATUTORY DUTY

As has been seen earlier, frequently a consumer who has suffered loss will **16.08**

---

[18] *R. v. Johnstone* (1982) 4 Cr.App.R.(S.) 141.
[19] Magistrates' Courts Act 1980, s.76.
[20] Civil Evidence Act 1968, s.11.
[21] 1973 Act, s.38(2).
[22] [1974] 2 All E.R. 216.

have a remedy flowing directly or indirectly from the civil or criminal law. As far as the civil law is concerned, the remedy may be for breach of contract, *e.g.* against a supplier of goods or services who has not fulfilled obligations imposed upon him by statute or the common law, or in tort for negligence or under the Consumer Protection Act 1987, *e.g.* against a manufacturer. Alternatively or additionally, where the supplier's activities involve a criminal offence resulting in a successful prosecution, the consumer may seek compensation under the Powers of Criminal Courts Act.

However, a hiatus exists where the supplier has not broken a contract with the consumer, maybe because they are not in a contractual relationship; nor has he been negligent; nor does the Consumer Protection Act apply, perhaps because his damage is too small; nor has the consumer recovered compensation, even though the supplier has committed a criminal offence, *e.g.* because no prosecution was brought. In such circumstances the consumer's last resort is to try to show that the supplier is liable in tort for breach of statutory duty.[23]

If it were possible for such an action to be brought in every case where a supplier has failed to comply with his statutory duties, the consumer's position would be much more straightforward. In the absence of an award of compensation under the 1973 Act, he would be able to institute civil proceedings on this basis without concerning himself with such questions as privity of contract with the supplier.

However, the courts when construing statutes have been reluctant to imply into them civil rights for the victim. The rationale seems to be that the legislation is for the protection of the public generally and is not intended to afford a civil remedy to individual members of the public. The reasoning is unconvincing. To draw an analogy from the contractual principles of offer and acceptance, where an offer is made to the world at large, contracts are formed only with those individuals who accept the offer; similarly where a duty is imposed on suppliers for the benefit of the public at large, it should be possible for those particular members of the public who suffer loss as a result of a breach of that duty to come forward and claim damages in a civil action founded upon that statutory duty.

Yet generally the courts are content to leave consumers to their separate civil rights. Thus in *Square v. Model Farm Dairies (Bournemouth) Ltd*,[24] where the plaintiff alleged that contaminated milk sold in breach of the food legislation had made his family ill with typhoid fever, the Court of Appeal rejected his claim because he had a remedy under the Sale of Goods Act. A comparable case is *Buckley v. La Réserve*[25] where an action failed against a restaurant which, in contravention of the Food and Drugs Act 1955, sold food unfit for human consumption (the food was snails: legal symmetry would

---

[23] For a more general treatment of this topic, see the leading works on tort.
[24] [1939] 2 K.B. 365.
[25] [1959] Crim.L.R. 451.

have been attained had the contamination resulted from ginger beer). It is important to note that on the particular facts the plaintiff's civil rights would not have given him a remedy unless he could prove negligence, as he was taken to the restaurant as a guest, and had no contractual claim against the restaurant: nevertheless the court adopted the same stance as in the *Square* case.

Two cases involving defective cars also illustrate the courts' unhelpful attitude to consumers. In *Phillips v. Britannia Hygienic Laundry Co.*[26] the plaintiff failed to recover for injuries resulting from the defendants' breach of duties imposed by the antecedents to the present Motor Vehicles (Construction and Use) Regulations.[26a] Similarly a seller was not liable to a victim injured by a vehicle which the seller delivered in such a condition that its use on the road was unlawful, although he thereby committed an offence under what is now section 75 of the Road Traffic Act 1988.[27]

16.09

The courts' restrictive interpretation leads to this principle in the consumer field: an action for breach of statutory duty has a chance of success only if the statute *expressly* states that a breach of the duty is actionable, *e.g.* the Consumer Protection Act 1987, s.41(1)[28]:

> An obligation imposed by safety regulations shall be a duty owed to any person who may be affected by a contravention of the obligation and, subject to any provision to the contrary in the regulations and to the defences and other incidents applying to actions for breach of statutory duty, a contravention of any such obligation shall be actionable accordingly.

Where a statute states the opposite, the position is equally clear. Where a statute is silent on the point, the presumption is that it gives no civil remedy. Such a presumption is strengthened where the statute expressly preserves other civil remedies, following the reasoning in *Square v. Model Farm Dairies (Bournemouth) Ltd,*[29] for then Parliament is implicitly leaving the public to their general civil rights.

It is on these grounds that we take the view that no action will lie for breach of statutory duty arising out of the Trade Descriptions Act 1968, section 35[30] of which saves civil rights by stating, "A contract for the supply of goods shall not be void or unenforceable by reason only of a contravention of any provision of the Act." That view is fortified by observing that the 1968 Act does not include any provision equivalent to section 17 of the repealed Merchandise Marks Act 1887 whereby a seller was deemed to warrant the

[26] [1923] 2 K.B. 832.
[26a] S.I. 1986 No. 1078.
[27] *Badham v. Lambs Ltd* [1946] K.B. 45.
[28] Above, para. 15.21. For another example, see Consumer Credit Act 1974, s.92(3): entry to premises to recover possession of goods or land, below, para. 25.03.
[29] Above, para. 16.08.
[30] Above, para. 13.61.

accuracy of any trade description. The omission is deliberate and contrary to the recommendation in the Final Report of the Committee on Consumer Protection (Cmnd. 1781)[31] that the provision should remain and "contracting-out" be prohibited. We think it fitting to end with a plea that further consideration be given by parliamentary reformers to the view expressed in paragraph 459 of the Report.

> We cannot avoid the conclusion that Section 17 reflects a sound principle, namely that persons trading in goods to which false trade descriptions have been applied should be liable, not merely under the criminal law, but also to meet any civil claim in favour of a purchaser arising from the same circumstances.

[31] See above, para. 13.02.

Part III

ADMINISTRATIVE CONTROL

CHAPTER SEVENTEEN

FAIR TRADING

1. INTRODUCTION

The civil and criminal sanctions discussed earlier in this book do a great deal **17.01** to protect the consumer, but by themselves they are not enough. In particular:

(1) Industry is never static for long and the enterprising trader is likely to come up with new business practices. Some of these, while within the law, may be harmful to consumers and swift action may be needed to curtail them.

(2) There may be a number of dishonest or inefficient traders who may make large profits, *e.g.* by the delivery of shoddy goods or by practices which infringe the Trade Descriptions Act 1968. They may not be deterred by the occasional fine or award of compensation. What the consumer really needs is a system whereby such traders can be restrained from trading altogether unless they mend their ways.

(3) The standards set by the law are minimum standards and the consumer can benefit if traders can be persuaded to undertake additional voluntary obligations.

(4) Neither the civil nor the criminal law achieve one of the most important aims of consumer protection—making the consumer aware of his rights.

It is at this point that we meet the third weapon of consumer protection—administrative control. This involves a public body charged with the task of keeping the consumer scene under permanent review. The principal weapons of administrative control are to be found in the Fair Trading Act 1973 and the Consumer Credit Act 1974. The former (which also deals with monopolies, mergers and restrictive practices) is examined in this chapter and the Consumer Credit Act will be dealt with in Chapters 18 to 27.

2. THE FAIR TRADING ACT 1973

Unlike the Consumer Credit Act 1974, which was substantially based upon **17.02** the recommendations of the Crowther Committee's Report on Consumer Credit, the Fair Trading Act 1973 appeared out of the blue with no warning or consultation in the form of Green or White Papers.

Most of the Act does not break new ground inasmuch as broadly it consolidates, with some changes and improvements, the pre-existing law relating to competition, *i.e.* monopolies, mergers and restrictive practices. However, it contains five innovations. First, it created the post of Director General of Fair

Trading (Pt. I). Secondly, it gives to the Director General power to initiate subordinate legislation to protect the consumer by banning undesirable trade practices as and when they appear (Pt. II). Thirdly, it enables the Director General to bring into line individual rogue traders who regularly flout their legal obligations (Pt. III). Fourthly, the Director General is under a duty to encourage trade associations to prepare, and to disseminate to their members, voluntary codes of practice (s.124(3)). Finally, the Director General can arrange for publication of information and advice to consumers (s.124(1)). The last two topics have already been considered in Chapter 10[1] and accordingly this chapter will examine the other novel features of the Act mentioned above.

It is true that the Act gives to the consumer no right of action or opportunity to claim compensation, but he can lodge a complaint with the Office of Fair Trading directly or via a trading standards officer or CAB. This gives the consumer two benefits: the satisfaction of knowing that his complaint has added to the information kept by the OFT and may have helped to identify and ultimately to outlaw an undesirable trade practice within Part II; and the exhilaration of hoping that a note of his grievance on the file of the particular trader may tip the balance and provide the evidence to show that the trader is persistent in his improper activities and should be brought to book under Part III.[2] (One should not underestimate the importance to the consumer of a chance to vent his feelings to a public official in the expectation, sometimes vain, that some action will ensue whether or not he is able to recover financial redress.)

The Director General

17.03   The Director General is appointed by the Secretary of State for Trade and Industry for a term of office not exceeding five years although he may be re-appointed (s.1). The longest-serving DGFT was Lord Borrie, a barrister and formerly Professor of Law at Birmingham University[3] who remained at the helm for a remarkably long and successful period of 16 years. John Bridgeman, with a background in industry, currently fills this post.

The Director General has two general functions relating to consumer protection, which are set out in section 2(1). These duties must be carried out "so far as appears to him to be practicable from time to time". One is active, the other passive. His active role is to keep under review the carrying on of commercial activities which relate to the supply of goods or services to consumers and to collect information with respect to such activities and the persons by whom they are carried on. He is to do this with a view to becoming

---

[1] Above, paras 10.01 and 10.10 and see also Appendix One.
[2] Or, in appropriate cases, deprived of his licence under the Consumer Credit Act (below, para. 20.02).
[3] For a résumé of the functions of the Director General given by Sir Gordon Borrie, see the transcript of his lecture to the Bar Association for Commerce, Finance and Industry (1977) 74 L.S.Gaz. 70.

aware of and ascertaining the circumstances relating to practices which may adversely affect the economic interests of consumers—only the economic interests, nothing else.

His other role, his passive function, is to receive and collate evidence becoming available to him with respect to such activities. The purpose of this is to build up dossiers of evidence on practices which may adversely affect consumer interests, but in this case the interests may be not only economic but also interests with respect to health, safety or other matters. An example given in the debates on the Act was unsafe child "safety" harnesses. So unless economic interests are affected, the Director General is obliged to do nothing except to wait to see what information comes in to him.

In addition the Director General must assist the Secretary of State when required to do so and can make recommendations to him (s.2(3)), as happened in the case of the Price Marking (Bargain Offers) Order 1979.

The Office of Fair Trading

The OFT is not specifically created by or mentioned in the Act. Section **17.04** 1(5) enables the Director General to appoint such staff as he thinks fit—there are over 400 now. The OFT is the Director General and his staff in aggregate. It is a Government department but not all of the staff are civil servants. Its address is Field House, Breams Buildings, London, EC4A 1PR.

Perhaps it might be useful at this point to mention one function which the OFT does not have; *it does not deal with individual complaints* (although it will keep a record of the complaint which may become relevant in a future investigation) except in relation to unfair terms.[4]

The Consumer Protection Advisory Committee

The CPAC, established under section 3, has between 10 and 15 members **17.05** appointed by the Secretary of State. It has merely an advisory role. It cannot take any initiative by making proposals and exists to consider references to it under section 14 and any proposals for action too. The controlling and directing power lies with the Secretary of State under section 12.

It has been moribund since 1982 when the Minister for Consumer Affairs announced that he had "decided for the present not to reappoint existing members ... as their appointments expire or to appoint new members."[5] The last reference to the CPAC was made in 1977 in respect of VAT-exclusive prices.

3. Part II—Adverse Consumer Trade Practices[6]

The essential difference between Parts II and III of the Fair Trading Act is **17.06**

---

[4] See para. 9.11.
[5] Department of Trade Press Notice, September 24, 1982.
[6] See previous editions of this book for a more detailed analysis of Part II.

that Part II is concerned with undesirable *practices*, whereas Part III is concerned with undesirable *traders*. Thus under Part II it is possible for a statutory order to be made banning certain undesirable trade practices, whereas under Part III the attack is not upon a general practice but upon an individual trader who persistently acts in a way which is unfair to consumers.

The point of Part II is to refer consumer trade practices to the CPAC so that the CPAC may consider whether they adversely affect the economic interests of consumers and then report. More importantly it is possible to couple with that reference proposals for action, so that the CPAC when reporting may give its view on those proposals.

Consumer trade practice

17.07   There is no complete freedom of choice as to what practices may be referred; the term "consumer trade practice" is exhaustively defined in section 13, *i.e.* any practice carried on in connection with the supply of goods or services to consumers and which relates to one of the six matters specified in paragraphs (a) to (f) of the section:

(a) the terms or conditions of supply, *e.g.* the continued use of void exemption clauses, VAT-exclusive prices;
(b) the manner in which those terms are communicated, *e.g.* the size of print;
(c) promotion, *e.g.* advertisements, labels;
(d) methods of salesmanship, *e.g.* doorstep selling, traders masquerading as private sellers in small ads;
(e) packaging, *e.g.* large containers only half filled but accurately marked with the amount of their contents;
(f) methods of demanding or securing payment, *e.g.* requiring a deposit when an order is placed.

The procedure

17.08   A reference under section 14 can be made by the Director General or any Minister. The CPAC considers "whether a consumer trade practice specified in the reference adversely affects the economic interest of consumers" and reports back. Unless the reference falls within section 17 and includes proposals, that is the end of the matter.[7]

The real punch in Part II lies in section 17, which provides that references by the Director General may include proposals for action by the Secretary of State. The scope of section 17 is narrower than section 14 in that, although the reference must again relate to a consumer trade practice as defined in section 13, the practice must also fall within one of the four paragraphs of section 17(2).

---

[7] There are some exclusions from s.14: see ss.15 and 16 and Scheds. 4 and 5.

The common flavour of these paragraphs is of misleading or confusing consumers or pressurising them to enter into unfair transactions. Schedule 6 to the Act gives half a dozen illustrations of matters falling within the scope of section 17 proposals. The third one is "prohibition of the inclusion in specified consumer transactions of terms or conditions purporting to exclude or limit the liability of a party to such a transaction in respect of specified matters"; this proved to be the substance of the first order under Part II.[8]

The sequence of a section 17 reference is as follows. The reference is made by the Director General who may include proposals for recommending to the Secretary of State that he exercises his powers under the Act. The CPAC considers the reference and proposals and reports within three months, unless that period is extended by the Secretary of State.[9] In fact all four of the reports to date took six months or more to be published. In its report the CPAC states whether the practice is adverse and, if so, for which of the reasons mentioned in section 17. Unless the CPAC disagrees with the proposals, the Secretary of State may make an order by statutory instrument giving effect to the proposals as set out in the reference or as modified by the CPAC in its report.[10] This order will not be effective until it has been approved by a resolution of each House of Parliament.

Penalties and enforcement

Orders under section 22 are enforced by criminal sanctions only. There is a marked similarity between Part II of this Act and the Trade Descriptions Act 1968 as regards penalties, defences and enforcement. Accordingly, it is not proposed to discuss such provisions in detail in this chapter: readers are referred to Chapter 13.   **17.09**

Briefly, the maximum penalties for contravention of a prohibition are a £5,000 fine on summary conviction; an unlimited fine or two years' imprisonment or both if convicted on indictment.

Section 25 provides the same five defences, *e.g.* mistake, act or default of another person, etc. Again the defendant must prove the two factors of "reasonable precautions" and "due diligence".

Speedy procedure?

The intention and expectation was that it would be possible to identify new abuses at an early stage, to recommend and quickly to put into effect prohibitive measures and thus to squash the practice before it mushroomed. Indeed, in April 1974 the Director General stated, when announcing the first reference to the CPAC, that he hoped that in six months a statutory order would be made: it actually appeared two-and-a-half years later. The first two Director Generals both expressed disappointment with the slow working of Part II. It   **17.10**

[8] Below, para. 17.11.
[9] s.20.
[10] s.22.

may be significant that, in relation to bargain offers, the Director General chose to sidestep the CPAC completely by using his power to present the Secretary of State with a recommendation for action.[11] As the last reference was made in 1977, it seems that the Part II machinery has been moth-balled, if not placed in a museum.

Restrictions on statements

"No refunds"
"Money will not be refunded. Credit notes only"
"Sale goods may not be returned"

17.11   The first reference to the CPAC in April 1974 was described in the Director General's Dossier 17/1 as "The Purported Exclusion of Inalienable Rights of Consumers and Failure to Explain their Existence". The reference, the report and the Order embraced the supply of goods by way of sale, hire-purchase and trading stamps. It covers three practices.

CPAC reference

17.12   (1) The first practice is the continuing use of void exemption clauses. The Supply of Goods (Implied Terms) Act 1973 contained provisions which invalidated exemption clauses relating to the statutory implied terms in consumer sale and hire-purchase agreements.[12] However, such clauses, though void, were not illegal. So the practice continued of exhibiting shop notices like the above examples which purport to take away the buyer's right of rejection and money back for breach of condition. (Of course, if the customer has merely changed his mind though there is nothing wrong with the goods, he has *no remedy* at all as there has been no breach of contract, so the suppliers may refuse to do anything or impose whatever terms they think fit.[13])

Similarly, there was nothing to prevent a car dealer or other seller from incorporating a void exclusion clause in his printed sales agreement.

(2) The second practice is concerned with written statements furnished by suppliers of goods which purport to set out the rights and obligations of the parties but fail to advise consumers of their inalienable rights, *e.g.* under sections 13 and 14 of the Sale of Goods Act 1979. Thus a car dealer might give a three-month guarantee on a second-hand car, covering parts but not labour, without revealing to the buyer that, irrespective of the guarantee, the buyer has the benefit of the implied condition of satisfactory quality under the 1979 Act.

---

[11] s.2(3), above, para. 17.03.
[12] The relevant provisions are now ss.6 and 12 of the Unfair Contract Terms Act 1977. See Chap. 8, above, para. 8.27.
[13] A clause giving the trader a right to forfeit a consumer's deposit if he changes his mind could now be "unfair" under the Unfair Terms in Consumer Contracts Regulations 1994: see above, para. 9.16.

(3) The third practice is similar to the second practice except that the written statements relate to the consumer's rights against *third parties* such as manufacturers. Thus, a shopkeeper may pass on to his customer a manufacturer's guarantee giving the impression that the customer's rights in respect of defects lie only against the manufacturer under the terms of the guarantee without explaining the buyer's statutory rights against the shopkeeper *qua* seller.[14]

The CPAC published its Report[15] in December 1974. It found that all three practices fell within section 13(a) and adversely affected the economic interests of consumers by having the effects specified in section 17(2), namely, of misleading consumers as to their rights under relevant consumer transactions or otherwise confusing them as to the terms of the transaction. They agreed with the Director General's proposals subject to certain modifications narrowing their scope. Those modified proposals were put into effect by the Consumer Transactions (Restrictions on Statements) Order 1976.[16]

The Order

(1) Article 3 banned the first practice. It makes it an offence to display at **17.13** any place where consumer transactions are effected, *e.g.* a shop or car showroom, a notice containing a term invalidated by what is now section 6 of the Unfair Contract Terms Act 1977 (Art. 3(a)). A ban was also imposed on the following items in so far as they relate to consumer transactions and include similar void terms—advertisements, including catalogues and circulars; goods or their containers; and documents (Art. 3(b), (c) and (d)). However, *oral* statements are not illegal, even though void; this explains why shop assistants adopt the practice of telling customers, particularly at sale time, that they cannot bring goods back if dissatisfied.

Two Divisional Court cases have shed some darkness on the meaning of Article 3(d). Article 3 provides that "A person shall not, in the course of a business—

    (d) furnish to a consumer in connection with the carrying out of a consumer transaction or to a person likely, as a consumer, to enter into such a transaction, a document which includes a statement which is a term of that transaction and is void. . . .

In the first of the two cases, *Hughes v. Hall*,[17] the court considered the expression "sold as seen and inspected" in a document furnished to a private customer by a motor dealer. The court decided that an offence had been committed. The court agreed that the clause would not necessarily remove all the

---

[14] See Chap. 5, above, para. 5.03, for a discussion of guarantees.
[15] H.C. 6 Session 1974/75.
[16] S.I. 1976 No. 1813, as amended by S.I. 1978 No. 127 in consequence of the repeal by the 1977 Act of s.55(3) to (11) of the 1893 Act: no substantive changes result.
[17] [1981] R.T.R. 430.

consumer's rights and in particular that express obligations might remain. "But in my judgment he would lose some of his rights, even if he might still have other rights. This to my mind is quite sufficient to create an offence under this Act, because anything which has that effect would be voided by section 6(2) of the Unfair Contract Terms Act 1977."[18] The court was of the view that the clause excluded the condition as to description implied by section 13 of the 1979 Act.

The court reached the opposite conclusion when considering a very similar phrase—"bought as seen"—in the later decision of *Cavendish-Woodhouse Ltd v. Marley*.[19] The court distinguished the earlier decision on a number of questionable grounds. The first related to the fact that the expression appeared in an invoice relating to a suite sold by a furniture store, not to a car. Ackner L.J. distinguished *Hughes v. Hall*, "a puzzling decision", on the grounds that the court was dealing with a "somewhat different phrase in a different trade. I consider that we are entitled to treat it as a decision on its particular facts which we are not obliged to follow." This facile distinction is in our view a distinction without a difference.

An unfortunate aspect of the case was that both parties agreed that the sale was not a sale by description within section 13. "The respondent went into a shop during a sale and he chose the goods which he decided to purchase. They were specific goods which he inspected" (Ackner L.J.). Yet it is well settled that a sale may still be governed by section 13 even though the buyer buys specific goods inspected prior to purchase.[20] The authority of earlier decisions on the point is strengthened by section 13(3), the effect of which is that goods on display may describe themselves. It can hardly be correct that a buyer will have no redress under section 13 if, for example, a suite described on a label as "covered in leather" proves to be plastic. On the assumption that generally such sales are sales by description, what difference should it make whether the goods are a suite, a shirt or a second-hand car, or whether the words used are "bought" or "sold" as seen?

The crucial question, therefore, was whether the words purported to exclude the implied conditions of merchantable quality and fitness for a particular purpose. On this question of construction, as Ackner L.J. pointed out, "it was well-established that if the statutorily implied terms were to be excluded, very clear language had to be used."[21] Certainly applying the *contra proferentem* rule the phrase "bought as seen" is not an apt expression to exclude the conditions in section 14(2) and (3). The court's decision on the meaning was explained by Ackner L.J.:

> "In my judgment all this phrase does is to confirm that the purchaser has seen the goods which he has bought. Accordingly, if thereafter there is a dispute as to the

[18] *per* Donaldson L.J. *ibid.* at p. 437.
[19] (1984) 148 J.P. 299.
[20] Above, para. 3.09.
[21] Above, para. 8.14.

condition of the goods when he purchased them, a factor which can be used as part of the material to resolve that dispute is the fact that it was not a purchase by description. It was a sale of specific goods which he in fact did see and purchased as a result of seeing them."

Thus if the goods had an obvious defect, the seller could use the invoice as evidence of a pre-contractual examination by the buyer and call in aid the proviso in section 14(2C)(b).[22] As the phrase is not an exemption clause, it is not invalidated by section 6(2)(a) of the 1977 Act and so does not give rise to a criminal offence.

(2) The second practice was outlawed by Article 4. It makes it an offence to **17.14** supply goods, their container or a document to a consumer with a statement about his rights against the supplier with regard to defects, fitness for purpose or correspondence with description unless there is, "in close proximity" to that statement, another "clear and conspicuous" statement to the effect that the statutory rights of the consumer are not affected. Like Article 3 this applies only where the goods or documents are supplied in a consumer transaction where there is a *contractual relationship* between the supplier and the consumer.

(3) The third practice is prohibited by Article 5. Its requirement is similar to that in Article 4, *i.e.* an obligation on the supplier to give information by drawing the consumer's attention to his statutory rights where the goods, their packaging or a document contain statements setting out the obligations accepted by the supplier. The difference between the two is that Article 5 applies where, although there is no direct consumer transaction between the supplier and the consumer, the supplier intended or might reasonably have expected his goods to become the subject of a *subsequent* consumer transaction.

The provision applies to a manufacturer's guarantee where the manufacturer realises that the goods will reach a consumer indirectly via a retailer. It is unfortunate that the Order does not lay down any precise form of wording to be adopted by suppliers. A common formula in guarantees is "This does not affect your statutory rights". It is doubtful whether this cryptic message disabuses the shopper in Balham of the misapprehension that an express guarantee replaces the statutory implied terms, however self-explanatory it may be to readers of this book.

No exchange

One practice which is still legal and unaffected by the Order is that of **17.15** displaying notices stating "Goods may not be *exchanged*". The reason is simply that there is in law no right to claim a replacement, however defective goods may be—the remedies for breach are rejection with a refund and damages. Such a term is not, therefore, invalidated by the 1977 Act and so falls

---

[22] Above, paras 4.17 and 4.18.

outside the Order. Yet notices of this sort tend to mislead members of the public who are unlikely to see the distinction between refunds and exchanges and may well think that a notice denying one implicitly denies the other. Indeed the Director General proposed that such statements should fall within the Order but the CPAC decided that the Order should be limited to void terms and should not make it illegal to make an accurate statement of law.

Void but legal

17.16   Since the reference to the CPAC was made, the wider statutory attack on exemption clauses made by the Unfair Contract Terms Act 1977 has invalidated further contractual terms and notices, *e.g.* certain exemption clauses in contracts for the hire of goods or in work and materials contracts, and also clauses and notices excluding liability for death or personal injury resulting from negligence.[23] Statements relating to such matters, though void, are not illegal as they are not within the ambit of the 1976 Order. They may also be unfair under the Unfair Terms in Consumer Contracts Regulations 1994.[24]

Mail order transactions

"Send c.w.o."
"Payment with order POST FREE"
"Send now only £1 per pair including postage"

17.17   The second reference made in May 1974 related to "Prepayment in Mail Order Transactions and in Shops". It concerns the practice whereby suppliers require prepayments in full, or a deposit, when goods are ordered without specifying a delivery period or specifying a delivery date which is not met. Such problems are most frequent in mail order businesses where a wide range of goods is available either direct from the manufacturers or from the postal bargain trade, *e.g.* records, binoculars, beds, greenhouses, garages. Difficulties are more likely to arise when ordering from traders advertising in newspapers, magazines and colour supplements, than from the established catalogue firms whose business is conducted mainly on credit. However, the practice is not confined to mail order business. Frequently shops require deposits when taking orders for goods not in stock, *e.g.* furniture. Of course, the civil remedy available to the buyer if goods are not delivered within the specified time or, if none, within a reasonable time is to treat the contract as repudiated and to demand his money back, but if the deposit is not repaid he must resort to civil proceedings.[25]

The Director General's proposals were that mail order catalogues and advertisements should state a delivery period by prescribed wording, *e.g.*

---

[23] See Chap. 8, above, para. 8.23 *et seq.*
[24] Above, para. 9.12.
[25] See above, para. 7.14.

"Despatch within ... days of order or refund"; if the trader did not supply the goods on time, he would have to send a refund to the customer within seven days of receiving a request. However, the Secretary of State made a minor reform contained in the Mail Order Transactions (Information) Order 1976.[26] It merely requires the name and address of the business to be given where an advertisement, circular or catalogue (other than an advertisement by radio, television or film) invites orders for goods by post where payment is to be made before the goods are despatched.

The effect of this damp squib was slight. Complaints from consumers who had paid in advance continued at a high level, split about equally between mail order and other transactions. In 1979 the OFT published a consultative paper containing proposals for a further reference to the CPAC in relation to non-mail order transactions, but nothing came of it.[27] The current policy appears to be to leave the problem to be resolved piecemeal by codes of practice[28] and by the power to control individual rogue traders under Part III of the 1973 Act.[29]

Business advertisements

"ELECTRIC FIRE, £4.95. 2-bar coal effect, new—Tel. Whitehaven   **17.18**
0000"
"GOLF CLUBS, half set, new, £23.50—Tel. Whitehaven 0000"

These are two of 10 advertisements placed by one trader in one newspaper on one day. It is not obvious to a reader when seeing them scattered amongst the other small ads that he will be dealing with a trader. There are three obvious disadvantages to a consumer who deals with a trader masquerading as a private person. First, if the goods prove to be defective, the buyer will be advised that the implied conditions of satisfactory quality and fitness for purpose do not apply. Secondly, if any of the descriptions used is false, a trading standards officer will be reluctant to take action as the Trade Descriptions Act 1968 catches only descriptions applied in the course of a trade or business. Lastly, because he thinks that he is dealing with a private seller, he may think that he is getting a better bargain than if he were dealing with a trader.

The Director General's third reference to the CPAC in 1975 covered this consumer trade practice. The CPAC Report *Disguised Business Sales* was published in May 1976.[30] It showed the practice to be particularly widespread in relation to second-hand cars, furniture and electrical appliances.

The Director General's proposals were put into effect by the Business Advertisements (Disclosure) Order 1977.[31] The Order requires business sell-

---

[26] S.I. 1976 No. 1812.
[27] Prepayment in Non-Mail Order Transactions.
[28] See the direct marketing codes, above, para. 10.21.
[29] Below, p. 17.20.
[30] H.C. 355 Session 1975/1976.
[31] S.I. 1977 No. 1918.

ers of goods to make it clear in their advertisements directed at consumers that they are traders. The fact may be made apparent by "the contents of the advertisement, its format or size, the place or manner of its publication or otherwise."[32] This can be achieved in a number of ways: by using an obvious business name or company name; by placing an advertisement of a business size or format; or by adding the word "dealer", "trader" or "trade" at the end of the advertisement.

VAT-exclusive prices

17.19   "£15.24 VAT extra"
               "Recommended retail price £58.50 excluding VAT"

Since the introduction of VAT consumers frequently have been asked to pay more than they anticipated for goods or services. Sometimes, *e.g.* in DIY shops or builders' merchants, goods on display are priced but when the consumer reaches the cash desk VAT is added, although the price shown appeared to be VAT-inclusive. On other occasions as in the above examples an indication is given that VAT is payable in addition to the specified price but neither the amount nor rate of VAT is mentioned. These practices were referred to the CPAC in 1977 and they duly published their report *VAT-Exclusive Prices. A Report on Practices relating to Advertising, Displaying or otherwise Quoting VAT-Exclusive Prices or Charges.*[33]

The Director General identified two practices which he considered should be banned. The first, illustrated by the first of the above examples, is the practice of advertising, displaying or quoting to consumers as the price of goods or services an amount which excludes a sum to be added on account of VAT. The second practice, illustrated by the second of the examples, is that of advertising recommended retail prices which take no account of the VAT amount which the retailer is likely to add when selling to a consumer.

The CPAC in its report concluded that the first practice, but not the second, adversely affected the economic interests of consumers and went on to consider the Director General's proposals only in respect of the first practice. The main economic detriment to the consumer is the extra amount which he will be called upon to pay. In some cases it will be too late to withdraw from the transaction, *e.g.* when he has eaten a meal in a restaurant. In other cases where withdrawal is possible he may be too embarrassed to argue about the price at the cash desk or unwilling to start his search again in other shops. Broadly, the CPAC agreed with the Director General's proposal that only VAT-inclusive charges should be shown, but in the event no order was forthcoming.[34]

---

[32] Art. 2(1).
[33] H.C. 416 Session 1976/1977.
[34] The Code of Practice under Pt. III of the Consumer Protection Act 1987 provides that price indications to private consumers "should include VAT". Pt. III is discussed above, para. 14.18.

4. PART III—PERSISTENTLY UNFAIR TRADERS

I, Robert James Pickersgill, of Import House, Northallerton Road, Croft on Tees, **17.20**
Nr. Darlington trading as Solaire Electric, hereby give to the Director General of
Fair Trading written assurances sought by him pursuant to section 34(1) of the
Fair Trading Act 1973:

"That I will use all reasonable precautions and exercise all due diligence to avoid
continuing the following courses of conduct or any similar course of conduct in
the course of my business, namely—

(1) Committing offences under section 1 of the Trade Descriptions Act 1968
    by applying false trade descriptions to goods or by supplying or offering
    to supply goods to which a false trade description is applied.
(2) Committing offences under section 11(2) of the Trade Descriptions Act
    1968 by giving indications likely to be taken as indications that goods
    offered by me are being offered at a price less than that at which they are in
    fact being offered.
(3) Committing breaches of contract with consumers by supplying goods:
    (a) which do not correspond with any description by which they are
        sold as required by subsection (1) of the amended section 13 of the
        Sale of Goods Act 1893, or
    (b) which are not fit for a particular purpose for which they are being
        bought as required by subsection (3) of the amended section 14 of
        that Act.
(4) Failing to return to consumers money to which they are legally entitled,
    that has been received from them in the course of mail order transactions."

For the purpose of these assurances the word "goods" means lamps intended to
emit ultra violet rays and/or to emit infra red rays and any accessory supplied or
offered for supply with such a lamp.

This is the historic first assurance given in October 1974 to the Director
General under Part III of the 1973 Act. Since then hundreds of assurances
have been obtained covering diverse activities. Used car dealers, home
improvement firms, sellers of electrical goods and mail order businesses figure most prominently, but the club membership also includes a wide range of
other commercial activities, *e.g.* a correspondence school for freelance writers, a chain of 74 restaurants, a door-to-door salesman of goods said to be
made by the blind, and a major computer company.

The first assurance is typical in so far as it covers three improper practices
which frequently result in assurances being sought, namely, Trade Descriptions Act offences, breaches of the Sale of Goods Act implied conditions and
the non-delivery of goods paid for in advance.

Section 34(1) requires the Director General to try to obtain an assurance
where a person has "persisted in a course of conduct" which

(a) is detrimental to the interests of consumers in the United Kingdom, whether
    those interests are economic interests or interests in respect of health, safety
    or other matters, and[35]

---

[35] These criteria are similar to those laid down in section 2(1)(b): above, para. 17.03.

(b) in accordance with the following provisions of this section is to be regarded as unfair to consumers.

Business

17.21   The section applies only to a person carrying on a business where the conduct occurs in the course of that business. "Business" includes a professional practice and any undertaking which supplies goods or services otherwise than free of charge.[36] Thus private sellers are not caught, whereas charitable institutions are.[37]

Persistent

17.22   Part III is aimed at the trader who is a rogue in the sense that he repeatedly breaks his civil or criminal obligations and thumbs his nose at dissatisfied customers and trading standards officers alike. Only if he has "persisted" in such a course of conduct may the Director General take action. Evidence is built up from many sources: direct complaints from consumers; complaints passed on by trading standards departments, CAB, consumer advice centres, etc.; convictions and civil judgments notified by the courts. The Director General must have regard to all such complaints and information in determining the question of persistence.[38]

No criteria are laid down by the Act. Clearly what may amount to persistent conduct in the case of a small trader with one outlet may not be sufficient in the case of a retail chain with dozens of branches: the number of breaches must be weighed against the overall turnover and number of outlets of the business. It seems likely that successful prosecutions and civil actions carry more weight than complaints, however justified, and that a small trader with a half-dozen or so judgments and a score of complaints against him may well find himself being required to give an assurance.

Successive Director Generals have stressed the difficulty of proving persistence. In the consultation paper, *Reform of Part III of the Fair Trading Act 1973*,[39] it is suggested that the words "persisted in" should be replaced by "carried on" to ease the task of the OFT. The National Consumer Council made the same recommendation in its 1997 report *Unfair Trading*: "proving persistence should not be necessary".

Unfair

17.23   Conduct is not to be regarded as unfair unless it is one of the two types specified in the Act; there is no general concept of unfairness to which to resort. First, it may be contravention of an enactment imposing duties, prohibitions or restrictions enforceable by *criminal* proceedings.[40] It seems that

---

[36] s.137(2).
[37] *cf.* the definition in the Unfair Contract Terms Act 1977, s.12, above, para. 8.25.
[38] s.34(4).
[39] DTI, 1994.
[40] s.34(2).

some traders are still prepared to flout the provisions of the Trade Descriptions Act 1968 or the Food Safety Act 1990 on the basis that if they are prosecuted, the fines imposed are outweighed by the profitability of their unfair trading. Another example is offences under Part II Orders.

Secondly, the unfair conduct may consist of breaches of contract or other wrongs enforceable by *civil* proceedings.[41] For example, a trader may be content to sell defective goods confident in the knowledge that very few buyers are likely to go to the trouble and expense of suing him for the few pounds required to repair the goods; even if he is sued, his profits from this form of trading may far exceed the occasional damages awarded against him. In addition to such breaches of section 14(2) and (3) of the Sale of Goods Act 1979, other common courses of conduct are the supply of goods not corresponding with their description in accordance with section 13 of the 1979 Act; the failure to carry out contracts for work and materials with reasonable care and skill; the failure to deliver goods; and the failure to return money for goods or services not supplied.

It is important to notice that there is no need to show that the trader has in fact been prosecuted or sued, as section 34 states that it does not matter whether or not the person has been convicted or the subject of civil proceedings.

Finally, it should be remembered that for years proposals have been under discussion for the possible expansion of section 34 to include non-compliance with a code of practice or even with a general duty to trade fairly.[42] Proposals for reform were set out in the OFT Report *Trading Malpractices* published in July 1990. The essential change was to broaden the meaning of "unfair" to include "deceptive or misleading practices" or "unconscionable practices". Both of these general provisions would be supported by an illustrative "black list" of particular malpractices.

The DTI proposals appear in its 1994 consultation paper.[43] The definition of "unfair" may be extended to include "deceptive, misleading or oppressive" conduct. The Government has dropped the inclusion of "unconscionable practices" on the grounds that this concept is "too wide and too subjective to be readily enforced" (para. 6.3) and has abandoned the statutory, illustrative list of unacceptable practices. When will the saga end and legislation be bought forward?

Assurances and court proceedings

The Director General's first step is to "use his best endeavours" to obtain a satisfactory written assurance from the trader that he will discontinue the course of conduct and will not carry on any similar course of conduct.[44] If the

17.24

---

[41] s.34(3).
[42] See above, para. 10.06.
[43] Above, para. 17.22.
[44] s.34(1).

trader gives an assurance, it is given wide publicity and included in the Annual Report. If the trader abides by his assurance the matter rests there.

If the trader fails to observe his assurance or refuses to give one, the Director General may bring proceedings against him before the Restrictive Practices Court.[45] Alternatively, the county court (or sheriff court in Scotland) has jurisdiction except in the case of a company with share capital exceeding £10,000 or except where a question of general application is involved.[46] The court may accept an undertaking or, if it considers that the respondent is likely to continue as before in the absence of an order, may make an order to restrain the continuation of the malpractice.[47] The trader is then faced with the prospect of a fine or imprisonment for contempt of court if he does not comply with the order or undertaking. Thus the end of this long road for a trader who fails to honour his civil responsibilities can be imprisonment—this is the ultimate sword of Damocles to deter him under Part III. This happened for the first time in August 1984 when a double glazing supplier was committed to prison for 14 days for breach of an undertaking given to the court during earlier contempt proceedings.[48]

It is because the procedure is so long and complex that the 1994 DTI consultation paper proposes that the DGFT should be empowered to issue "warning notices" requiring rogue traders to discontinue their malpractices at once. The OFT too in its 1996 consultation paper *Consumer Affairs Strategy* states that it has "long argued for reform" of Part III because its effectiveness is "widely recognised to be limited, as a result of both the time which it may take to conclude cases, and of the relatively weak sanctions available" (para. 7.15).

It is seldom necessary for the Director General to have recourse to court proceedings. He regards them as a last resort and only a handful of cases occurs each year. For example, in 1978 legal proceedings were instituted against three businesses for refusal to give assurances. In one case the assurances were obtained at the door of the court; in another an undertaking was given by a trader whose place in the history of consumer protection is probably unchallenged with a record 800 complaints about him notified to the OFT. Lastly, in the first case of this kind to come before the Restrictive Practices Court, *Director General of Fair Trading v. Smiths Bakeries (Westfield) Ltd*,[49] undertakings were accepted from the company and its director as accessory who had refused to give assurances following 46 convictions under the Food and Drugs Act 1955 over a period of three years.

Accessories

17.25   An obvious loop-hole would be for a rogue trader to trade as a company

[45] s.35.
[46] s.41.
[47] s.37.
[48] 1983 Annual Report of the DGFT, pp. 21 and 57.
[49] *The Times*, May 11, 1978.

and, when cornered into giving an assurance on behalf of X Ltd, to set up in business with a different identity as Z Ltd. Sections 38 and 39 make this device ineffective by giving the Director General power to seek an assurance, order or undertaking from an "accessory" who has consented to or connived at the company's conduct. An accessory is defined as a director, manager, secretary or other similar officer, or someone with a controlling interest in that he can determine the way in which one-half of the votes can be cast at a general meeting.[50] Thus the above trader, who doubtless will be an accessory of X Ltd, can be required to give a personal assurance which will limit his activities when he puts X Ltd into liquidation and starts up in the guise of Z Ltd. The power is used frequently as in the *Smiths Bakeries* case mentioned above.

There are also provisions enabling the court to make an order binding members of a group of "interconnected bodies corporate", *i.e.* broadly a holding company and its subsidiaries.[51]

5. MISLEADING ADVERTISEMENTS

We now turn to a recent power given to the Director General in the consumer   **17.26**
protection area—the power to apply to the court for an injunction to prevent the publication of misleading advertisements. It emanates from the Control of Misleading Advertisement Regulations 1988.[52] The Regulations were passed in order to implement the 1984 E.C. Misleading Advertising Directive.[53]

The E.C. Directive

In 1978 the E.C. Commission presented to the Council a draft directive on   **17.27**
Misleading and Unfair Advertising. The Preamble expresses the Commission's view that:

> the laws against misleading and unfair advertising now in force in the Member States differ widely; whereas, since advertising reaches beyond the frontiers of individual Member States, it has a direct effect on the establishment and the functioning of the common market.

The draft directive[54] encountered considerable opposition in view of its extension beyond misleading advertising to unfair advertising, a concept unfamiliar in English law, and its legitimation of comparative advertising

---

[50] s.38(2) and (7).
[51] ss.40 and 137(5).
[52] S.I. 1988 No. 915, made under European Communities Act 1972, s.2(2).
[53] 84/450. O.J. 1984 L250/17.
[54] For a discussion of the background to the draft directive and of its provisions, see Freedman, "Proposed EEC Directive on Misleading and Unfair Advertising" in Woodroffe (ed.), *Consumer Law in the EEC*, Chap. III. See also 2nd ed. of this book, pp. 362–364.

("knocking copy") which is illegal in some Member States. In an effort to reach agreement the Council decided to omit unfair and comparative advertisements. This compromise achieved success in 1984 when the Council adopted the Misleading Advertising Directive.

The Directive was amended in 1997[55] so as to permit comparative advertising and was retrospectively given a new title: Directive concerning Misleading and Comparative Advertising. Its impact in the United Kingdom is slight in that comparative advertising was already legal here.

Member States were supposed to bring forward legislation to comply with the 1984 Directive by October 1986. However, the consultations between the DTI and commercial and consumer organisations were protracted. The major area of debate was the relationship between the self-regulatory bodies or "established means of dealing with complaints", as the Directive expresses it, and the courts or "administrative authorities" to which the Government had to give the power to control misleading advertising.

The Government's proposals set out in the consultative paper suggested that the powers should be given to the Director General of Fair Trading rather than to a multiplicity of other public authorities, e.g. local authorities. Its attitude to the existing self-regulatory system can be gleaned from the consultative document which stated that the Director General's power was seen "as a reinforcement to the self-regulatory system of control rather than a substitute for it". Commenting in particular on the areas of advertising where the Advertising Standards Authority provide the main control, the paper stated that "The Government sees the new powers which the Directive require to be introduced essentially as a 'long-stop.' The Government hope that the effect will be to strengthen rather than diminish the authority of the self-regulatory system." It will be seen that this policy was followed when the regulations were made.

Self-regulation

17.28   A brief note on the United Kingdom system of self-regulation may help to put in perspective the scope and purpose of the 1988 Regulations.

The Advertising Standards Authority (ASA) was established in 1962 to provide independent supervision of the industry's self-regulatory arrangements through a monitoring programme and investigation of complaints. The main instruments of control are the British Codes of Advertising and Sales Promotion.[56] The first Code was published in 1961 and modelled on the 1937 International Code of Advertising Practice. They are kept under continuous review and amendment by the Committee of Advertising Practice (CAP). The Code applies to advertisements in newspapers, magazines, posters, brochures, leaflets and other printed publications, for the public, cinema commercials and viewdata services.

---

[55] Directive 97/55/EC.
[56] In January 1995 a revised and consolidated version of the two codes was published.

A separate system operates in relation to broadcasting. The Broadcasting Act 1990 imposes a duty on the Independent Television Commission (ITC) and the Radio Authority to draw up and enforce codes governing standards and practice in advertising and programme sponsorship. These codes are the ITC Code of Advertising Standards and Practice[57] and the Radio Authority Code of Advertising Standards and Practice and Programme Sponsorship. Regulations 8 and 9 are relevant here, although the Independent Broadcasting Authority has been replaced by the ITC.

Other legislation

It should be remembered that legislative control of misleading advertise- **17.29** ments is not exercised only, or even mainly, under powers given by the 1988 Regulations. The Trade Descriptions Act 1968 covers advertisements relating to the supply of goods and services.[58] Misleading price indications are covered by the Consumer Protection Act, Pt. III.[59] Finally, credit advertisements are caught by the detailed regulations under the Consumer Credit Act 1974.[60]

1988 Regulations

The purpose of the Regulations is to enable the Director General to take **17.30** action in the courts to obtain an injunction to prevent the publication of a misleading advertisement. He cannot obtain compensation or other redress for a complainant. Before considering a complaint the Director General will normally require the complainant to show that "established means" of dealing with such a complaint have already been tried, *e.g.* the ASA.[61] This implements the Government's policy that the Director General should be a "long-stop".

Advertisement

Article 2 contains a number of definitions. "Advertisement" means: **17.31**

> any form of representation which is made in connection with a trade, business, craft or profession in order to promote the supply or transfer of goods or services, immovable property, rights or obligations.

The definition is wide enough to cover advertisements relating to land and houses as well as goods and services. In common with most legislation protecting consumers, it does not apply to an advertisement by a private person—it must be in connection with a trade, business, craft or profession.

---

[57] Revised 1998.
[58] See Chap. 13.
[59] See Chap. 14.
[60] See Chap. 20.
[61] reg. 4(3).

Misleading

17.32   A wide definition of misleading is given in Article 2(2). The question is whether it "deceives or is likely to deceive" the people whom it reaches. Further, it must be likely "to affect their economic behaviour or . . . to injure a competitor".

Injunctions

17.33   When considering an advertisement, the Director General must have regard not only to the public interest, but also "the desirability of encouraging the control, by self-regulatory bodies, of advertisements".[62] If he thinks it appropriate, he may bring proceedings for an injunction (including an interlocutory injunction).[63]

Article 6 deals with the functions of the court. It requires a court before granting an injunction to have regard "to all the interests involved and in particular the public interest". An injunction may be limited to the particular advertisement complained of or may extend to "any advertisement in similar terms or likely to convey a similar expression".[64]

In an important and instructive decision on these Regulations Hoffmann J. made some valuable comments on the meaning of "misleading" and on the court's functions under regulation 6. In *Director General of Fair Trading v. Tobyward Ltd*[65]:

> T advertised a product called "SpeedSlim" claiming (1) it could result in permanent weight loss; (2) success was guaranteed; (3) it contained an ingredient representing a medical or scientific breakthrough; (4) it prevented fats entering the blood stream; (5) the user could lose a specific amount of weight in a specified time; and (6) it was 100 per cent safe. The ASA received complaints and found the advertisements to be contrary to BCAP in that the six claims were misleading. The ASA advised T on how to comply with the code but T took no notice. The ASA referred the breaches to the Director General, who applied for a interlocutory injunction to restrain publication of the misleading advertisements and "any advertisement in similar terms or likely to convey a similar impression".

Hoffmann J. discussing the meaning of "misleading" in regulation 2(2) said that the requirement that the advertisement is likely to affect the economic behaviour of the persons to whom it is addressed "means in this context no more than that it must make it likely that they will buy the product". Turning to regulation 6 and the exercise of his discretion he thought there were two reasons why he should grant the injunction[66]:

> "First, the regulations contemplate that there will only be intervention by the

---

[62] reg. 4(4).
[63] reg. 5.
[64] reg. 6(2).
[65] [1989] 2 All E.R. 266.
[66] *ibid.* at pp. 270, 271.

director when the voluntary system has failed. It is in my judgment desirable and in accordance with the public interest to which I must have regard that the courts should support the principle of self-regulation. I think that advertisers would be more inclined to accept the rulings of their self-regulatory bodies if it were generally known that in cases in which their procedures had been exhausted and the advertiser was still publishing an advertisement which appeared to the court to be prima facie misleading an injunction would ordinarily be granted....

Second, in my view the interests of consumers require the protection of an injunction pending trial of the action. It does not seem to me that the respondents could complain of any legitimate interference with their business if they were restrained from making claims of the kind to which the director is here taking objection."

The respondents' main objection to the application for an injunction was the wording of the injunction. They claimed that it was too vague so that it would not be clear to them what they could lawfully do. In granting the injunction in the terms of the Director General's application Hoffmann J. said[67]:

"In a case like this the formulation of the injunction must avoid extremes on either side. On the one hand it must not be so specific that by a small variation in the terms of the advertisement the advertiser can escape its effect and publish an advertisement which is nevertheless misleading in the same kind of way. On the other hand, it must not be in terms so general that the advertiser does not have a clear idea of what he is not allowed to do."

It is no surprise that the form of the wording was approved, as it followed precisely the words in regulation 6(2). In due course on July 21, 1989, the High Court granted a permanent injunction in the same terms.[68]

---

[67] *ibid.* at p. 271.
[68] 1989 Annual Report of DGFT, p. 53. See also *DGFT v. Blinkhorn*, November 7, 1989: *ibid.*

Part IV

SPECIAL PROTECTION IN CREDIT TRANSACTIONS

CHAPTER EIGHTEEN

THE BACKGROUND TO CONSUMER CREDIT

1. INTRODUCTION

There has been a dramatic increase in consumer credit in the present cen- **18.01**
tury—both in this country and in other Western industrialised countries. By
far the greatest area is house purchase but there are many others including
furniture, electrical appliances, clothing, vehicles, holidays and home repairs
and improvements. The scale of consumer credit can be seen from figures
published in the Crowther Report on Consumer Credit. In the year 1966 the
amount of medium and long-term credit extended totalled £3,692,000,000
(house purchase credit accounted for approximately 45 per cent of this figure). At the end of the year the total outstanding was £9,684,000,000, of
which some 80 per cent was attributable to houses and flats. The members of
the Council of Mortgage Lenders held 10,821,000 mortgages at the end of
1998.

The Crowther Committee clearly realised that:

> The use of consumer credit . . . enables individuals to enjoy the services of con-
> sumer durable goods sooner than they otherwise would and in a period of
> inflation offers them a real prospect of acquiring them more cheaply. Consumers
> in general are able to obtain a more satisfying "basket" of goods and services
> with the same income. Thus consumer credit may be said to enhance consumer
> satisfaction. Furthermore, some individuals, who lack the self-discipline to save
> up for the purchase of a durable consumer good but are nevertheless unlikely to
> break their contract with a creditor, are able to buy a durable consumer good
> which might otherwise never be theirs.[1]

One need only add that this reason applies, *a fortiori*, to house purchase.

The situation described above has its corresponding dangers and these are
two-fold. First, borrowers may be tempted to overstretch their resources—
either through bad economic planning or because they do not appreciate the
full extent of their obligations. Secondly, some lenders might be tempted to
"cash in" on the attractions of consumer credit by inducing borrowers (some
of whom may already be under severe financial stress) to sign agreements
which are one-sided and impose unduly onerous obligations.

Until the passing of the Consumer Credit Act 1974 the law developed in a
fragmentary and piecemeal fashion—following rather than leading, check-

---

[1] Cmnd. 4596, p. 118.

ing abuses *after* they had come to light rather than laying down ground rules in advance. Thus:

(1) The Bills of Sale Acts 1878 to 1882 were passed to deal with (*inter alia*) mortgages of personal property where the borrower retained possession.

(2) The Moneylenders Acts 1900 to 1927 were passed to regulate the activities of certain moneylenders (but not, *e.g.* banks).

(3) The Pawnbrokers Acts 1872 to 1960 regulated the activities of pawnbrokers.

(4) The Hire-Purchase Act 1965 regulated hire-purchase agreements where the hire-purchase price did not exceed £2,000 and where the hirer was not a body corporate. (This limit was increased to £5,000 in 1978 and increased again to £7,500 in 1983.)

The unsatisfactory nature of this fragmentary approach can be seen by looking at moneylending. If the lender happened to be a bank, the Moneylenders Acts did not apply at all, even though the borrower may have been an inexperienced private individual and the contract may have been a harsh one on the particular facts. On the other hand, if the lender was within the provisions of the Act the full rigours of the Act were applied, even though the borrower was a large public company well able to look after itself. Again, as new forms of credit developed (*e.g.* credit cards) the absence of any regulatory machinery meant that there was virtually no effective control at all. All this was changed by the Consumer Credit Act 1974 which is almost certainly the most comprehensive and sophisticated Act of its kind in the Western world.

The Act is designed to sweep away the piecemeal controls listed above and to replace them with a single code governing all forms of lending. The only pieces of legislation which remain unrepealed are the Bills of Sale Acts 1878 to 1882—the reason is that the Consumer Credit Act does not regulate mortgages of personal property. A suggestion made by the Crowther Committee that the Government should introduce a Lending and Security Act has not so far been implemented.

2. CONSUMER CREDIT ACT 1974—TEN PRELIMINARY POINTS

18.02   The scope and effect of the Consumer Credit Act will be examined in detail in the next eight chapters. In the remainder of this chapter it is proposed to deal with ten preliminary matters.

(1) The Act contains no definition of the word "consumer". We have already seen that under the Unfair Contract Terms Act 1977 the term "consumer" means a "private consumer" as opposed to a business consumer, and the Fair Trading Act 1973 adopts a similar approach. *The Consumer Credit Act 1974 is not limited in this way*. In the two major types of agreement—consumer credit and consumer hire—the Act provides control where the debtor or hirer is an "individual" but the definition of this term is not what one might expect. By section 189:

"individual" includes a partnership or other unincorporated body of persons not consisting entirely of bodies corporate.

So then, the unincorporated trader is protected just as much as the private individual, *e.g.* a firm of solicitors. Conversely, the Act regulates (at least in part) agreements where the creditor or owner is *not* acting in the course of a business.[2] Indeed, in one section of the Act, the term "consumer" refers only to partnership and other unincorporated bodies (section 158 (as amended) post para. 26.03).

(2) The Act received the Royal Assent on July 31, 1974, but it took nearly 11 years to bring it fully into force. The Act was brought into force in stages and for many of its provisions the commencement date was May 19, 1985. There were a number of difficult problems as to whether or not a particular provision was retrospective (in the light of the general presumption against this) and these problems had to be solved by considering Schedule 3 and the relevant commencement order.

(3) Section 189 adopts the very helpful practice of drawing together all the definitions which appear throughout the Act. Section 189(1) contains no less than 177 definitions. Some are defined in the section itself (*e.g.* the term "individual"[3]). In other cases section 189 refers to the section where the definition is to be found, *e.g.*:

"exempt agreement" means an agreement specified in or under section 16.

It is vitally important to refer constantly to section 189 because words are often used in unexpected ways. Thus, for example, the definition of the word "surety" is wide enough to include the principal debtor (unless the context otherwise requires).

(4) Another helpful innovation (not so far copied by the draftsman of the annual Finance Act) is Schedule 2 which contains 24 worked examples showing the use of the new terminology. Section 188(3), however, provides that:

In the case of conflict between Schedule 2 and any other provision of this Act that other provision shall prevail.

A learned writer[4] has expressed the view that Example 18 (which relates to multiple agreements) is wrong.

(5) Although the Act is a long one, a very large part of the detail is contained in regulations. They cover such matters as the total charge for credit, regulated and exempt agreements, advertising, documentation and rebates for early settlements.

---

[2] See below, para. 19.08.
[3] See above.
[4] Goode, *Consumer Credit Law*, p. 156. The Government has recently introduced a new and helpful practice under which all Government Bills are accompanied by explanatory notes.

18.03   (6) The control provided by the Act is twofold:

(a) Control of business activity—notably through the licensing system administered by the Director General of Fair Trading.[5]

(b) Control of individual agreements.

(7) The Act provides various civil and criminal sanctions, as well as the administrative sanctions in sections 29 and 32 (non-renewal, suspension and revocation of a licence). The criminal sanctions are usefully collected together in Schedule 1. Section 170(1) provides that:

> A breach of any requirement made (otherwise than by any court) by or under this Act shall incur no civil or criminal sanction as being such a breach except to the extent (if any) expressly provided for under this Act.

Thus section 48 makes it an offence to canvass certain types of agreement (*e.g.* personal loans) off trade premises. If a person borrows money in a case where the lender has contravened section 48, he cannot avoid liability under that contract by pleading that it is illegal. Nor could he bring an action for breach of statutory duty. Such claims or defences are shut out by section 170(1). Presumably the criminal court would still be able to award compensation under section 35 of the Powers of Criminal Courts Act 1973.[6] The section does not affect the power of the court to grant an injunction (s.170(3)).

(8) As one might expect, the statutory rights enjoyed by the debtor, the hirer, a surety or a relative[7] cannot in any way be cut down or fettered by the agreement.[8]

(9) One of the features of the Act is that certain steps can only be taken if the court or the Director General makes an order to that effect. An example of the former is the enforcement of an agreement which has not been properly executed.[9] An example of the latter is the enforcement of an agreement made by a creditor or owner while he was unlicensed. In either case section 173(3) provides that consent of the debtor or hirer "given at that time" shall be as effective as an order. The words "given at that time" presumably refer to the time of enforcement so that a provision for consent in the contract would not be effective. Clearly the court would examine the facts very carefully to ensure that there was a true consent.

(10) It may be useful to end this chapter by setting out a few important definitions which will be met from time to time in the next eight chapters.

---

[5] See Chap. Twenty, below, para. 20.02.
[6] Above, para. 16.02.
[7] As to which see below, para. 18.06.
[8] See s.173(1) and (2).
[9] Below, para. 21.02.

(a) *Hire-purchase agreement*

This is defined as an agreement under which goods are bailed[10] in return for **18.04** periodical payments by the bailee and the property in the goods will pass to the bailee if the terms of the agreement are complied with and one or more of the following occur:

(i) the exercise of an option to purchase by the bailee or
(ii) the doing of any other specified act by any party to the agreement or
(iii) the happening of any other specified event.

(b) *Conditional and credit sale agreements*

A *conditional sale* agreement is an agreement for the sale of goods or land **18.05** under which the purchase price or part of it is payable by instalments and the property in the goods or land is to remain in the seller (notwithstanding that the buyer is to be in possession of the goods or land) until such conditions as to the payment of instalments or likewise as may be specified in the agreement are fulfilled.

If, however, there is a straight sale of goods on credit terms the property will usually pass to the buyer immediately (Sale of Goods Act 1979, s.18, r. 1[11]) and the agreement will be a *credit sale* agreement, *not* a conditional sale agreement.

Thus the crucial difference is whether the property passes to the buyer when the contract is made (credit sale) or at a later stage (conditional sale).

(c) *Relative*

Relative means husband, wife, brother, sister, uncle, aunt, nephew, niece, **18.06** lineal ancestor or lineal descendant. Relationship by marriage is also included and the reference to "husband or wife" includes a former or a reputed spouse.

(d) *Associate*

The associate of an individual means (i) a relative, and (ii) a partner, or the **18.07** relative of a partner, of that individual.

(e) *"Restricted-use" and "unrestricted-use"*

These terms are defined in section 11 and are largely self-explanatory. If the debtor can physically use the credit in any way he wishes the agreement will be an "unrestricted-use" agreement, even though certain uses would constitute a breach of contract. Thus a loan paid by the lender to the borrower

---

[10] Goods are "bailed" if one person ("the bailor") transfers possession to another ("the bailee") for a specific purpose.
[11] Above, para. 6.19.

would be an unrestricted-use agreement. On the other hand, a hire-purchase agreement, or a sale on deferred terms, or a loan where the money goes straight from the lender to a third party (*e.g.* the supplier of goods or services) would be a restricted-use agreement. We shall meet the distinction at several points in the following chapters.

3. The E.C. Dimension

18.08   There are two Directives—the Consumer Credit Directive (87/102/EEC) and the APR Directive (90/88/EEC). The United Kingdom authorities take the view that no legislation is required because the 1974 Act already covers the ground adequately.

4. Proposals for Reform

18.09   This topic is briefly considered in Chapter Twenty Seven.

CHAPTER NINETEEN

"WHAT AGREEMENTS ARE CAUGHT BY THE ACT?"

In this chapter and in Chapters 20 to 27 a reference to "the Act" is a reference **19.01** to the Consumer Credit Act 1974 (unless otherwise stated) and a reference to a section is to that section in the Act.

We have already seen that the scope of the Act is very wide. In this chapter it is proposed to work through the very intricate provisions of the Act and Regulations to find out the precise extent of control. The scheme of this chapter is as follows:

1. Regulated agreements
2. Partially regulated agreements
3. Exempt agreements
4. Linked transactions

1. REGULATED AGREEMENTS

Most of the statutory controls only apply to a "regulated agreement". In order **19.02** to find out whether an agreement is regulated it is necessary to proceed in two stages:

(1) Does the agreement come within the definition of "consumer credit agreement" in section 8 or "consumer hire agreement" in section 15? If the answer is "no", the agreement cannot be a regulated agreement.

(2) If the answer to (1) above is "yes", then by sections 8(3) and 15(2) any such agreement *is* a regulated agreement unless it is an exempt agreement. The concept of "exempt agreement", which depends on section 16 and the Regulations, is dealt with later in this chapter.[1]

Consumer credit agreement

Let us start by listing the many types of agreement which can come within **19.03** this term. They include:

(a) Hire-Purchase
(b) Conditional Sale
(c) Credit sale

---

[1] Below, para. 19.10.

    (d) Personal loan

    (e) Overdraft

    (f) Loan secured by land mortgage

    (g) Credit card

    (h) Pledges

    (i) Budget accounts in shops

Section 8(2) (as amended) defines a consumer credit agreement as an agreement whereby one person (the creditor) provides an individual (the debtor) with credit not exceeding £25,000. Four points are worthy of note:

(i) There must be an "agreement". Thus where a sale is for cash and on delivery of the goods the buyer asks for time to pay, the granting of "credit" would not amount to an "agreement" unless it formed part of a separate bargain—as, for example, where the borrower agrees to pay interest on the outstanding amount.

(ii) The creditor can be an "individual" or a body corporate, but the debtor must be an "individual".[2]

(iii) The Act draws a sharp distinction between the "credit" and the "total charge for credit." The term *"credit"* includes a cash loan and any form of financial accommodation[3] and clearly refers to the loan, etc., itself. The term "total charge for credit" refers to interest and other charges.[4] Section 9(4) provides that:

> An item entering into the total charge for credit shall not be treated as credit even though time is allowed for payment.

(iv) As an illustration of the above principles section 9(3) defines the "credit" in a hire-purchase agreement as the total price of the goods less (a) the deposit (if any), and (b) the total charge for credit.

Example

> A finance house C agrees to let a Porsche car on hire-purchase to D (an individual). The total price is £23,000; this includes a down payment of £5,000 and a total charge for credit of £3,000. When these two items are deducted from the price (£23,000–£8,000) one is left with credit of £15,000. This is, therefore, a consumer credit agreement within section 8(2).[5]

The provisions may be contrasted with the provisions of the Hire-Purchase

---

[2] See above, para. 18.02.

[3] s.9(3). For a recent example see *Dimond v. Lovell* at para. 7.36 above.

[4] Below, para. 19.11.

[5] For a recent case on s.9(4) see *Humberside Finance v. Thompson* [1997] C.C.L.R. 23 where the debtor paid a "payment waiver premium" under a clause extinguishing his liability if he died. The finance company claimed that this payment brought the "credit" above the statutory ceiling. The claim was rejected; the premium formed part of the "total charge for credit" and was not part of the "credit".

Act 1965. Under that Act protection was limited to cases where the hire-purchase *price* did not exceed £7,500. Under the 1974 Act the *price* may be far higher; what matters is the amount of the *credit*.

Fixed and running-account credit

The term "consumer credit agreement" is subdivided into "fixed-sum **19.04** credit" and "running-account credit"—the distinction is important in deciding whether an agreement is regulated or exempt[6] and for certain other purposes. Section 10(1)(a) tells us that:

> running-account credit is a facility under a personal credit agreement whereby the debtor is enabled to receive from time to time (whether in his own person or by another person) from the creditor or a third party cash, goods and services (or any of them) to an amount or value such that, taking into account payments made by or to the credit of the debtor, the credit limit (if any) is not at any time exceeded.

Perhaps the two most common examples are bank overdrafts and budget accounts in shops. It would clearly be possible to take the agreement outside the definition of "consumer credit agreement"[7] by fixing a credit limit in excess of the statutory ceiling or by fixing no credit limit at all. Section 10(3) is designed to block attempts to oust the Act in this way. It provides, in effect, that a running-account will still qualify as a consumer credit agreement if:

(i) the debtor cannot draw more than the "specified amount" (£25,000) at any one time; or

(ii) a term unfavourable to the debtor (*e.g.* raising of the rate of interest) will become operative if the debit balance rises above the "specified amount" or a lower figure; or

(iii) at the time of the agreement it it unlikely that the debit balance will rise above the "specified amount". An example of this provision (Sched. 2, Example 7) is where X agrees to provide Y with short-term finance to enable Y to acquire trading stock from time to time; at the time of the contract Y has trading stock worth £1,000 and it is therefore unlikely that he will require credit in excess of £25,000.

Debtor-creditor-supplier (D-C-S) agreements and debtor-creditor (D-C) agreements

These terms are defined in sections 12 and 13. It is necessary to mention **19.05** them at this point because a knowledge of them is vital when considering the all important question of whether the agreement is *regulated* or *exempt*.[8] The distinction between D-C-S and D-C turns on the relationship between the

---

[6] See below, para. 19.10, subpara. (6).
[7] Above, para. 19.03.
[8] Below, para. 19.10.

supplier of the credit and the supplier of the land, goods or services. The effect of sections 12 and 13 can be summarised as follows:

(i) If the supplier of the credit and the supplier of the goods, etc., is *the same person*, then it is D-C-S. Examples would include hire-purchase, credit sale, and sale of land where the seller agrees to leave the price outstanding. This can be referred to as "two-party D-C-S".

(ii) If the supplier of credit and the supplier of the goods, etc., are *different* but work together under "*arrangements*", then again it is D-C-S. Thus, a credit card company has "arrangements" with its approved suppliers and a finance company might have "arrangements" with a car dealer whereby they would provide loans to finance sales made by him to customers. In both these cases the credit contract would be a D-C-S agreement. This can be referred to as "three-party D-C-S".

(iii) If there are no such arrangements, the agreement is a D-C agreement. Thus if a customer borrows £2,000 from his bank to pay for central heating or for a holiday or to finance his business, this is a D-C agreement.

(iv) If an agreement is made to refinance an existing indebtedness, whether to the creditor or any other person, then again it is D-C.

As already stated the distinction is critical on the "regulated or exempt" point—we shall see that under a D-C-S agreement the critical factor is the number of instalments, whereas under a D-C agreement the critical factor is the annual percentage rate of charge for credit. The distinction is also important for other purposes, including joint responsibility of supplier and creditor in cancellation cases[9] and under section 75.[10]

Consumer hire agreement

19.06   The second type of agreement to which the Act applies is the consumer hire agreement. Clearly, this type of agreement is less important than the consumer credit agreement, but it is worth remembering that it covers not only the domestic hiring of, *e.g.* a television set but also the commercial hiring of, *e.g.* equipment. Section 15 makes it clear that there are six elements:

(a) a bailment of goods
(b) by one person (the owner)
(c) to an individual (the hirer), provided that
(d) it is not hire-purchase, and
(e) it is capable of lasting for more than three months and
(f) it does not require the hirer to make payments[11] in excess of £25,000.

Only the last point calls for comment. In deciding on how much the hirer is

---

[9] Below, para. 22.09.
[10] Below, para. 23.05. This is a vital provision in relation to credit cards.
[11] Inclusive of VAT: *Apollo Leasing Ltd v. Scott* [1986] C.C.L.R. 1.

required to pay one must look at his minimum contractual liability, having regard to any contractual right to terminate. Thus, if a three-year hiring (with no break clause) required the hirer to pay a rental of £9,000 per annum, this would bring the total to £27,000 and it would *not* be a consumer hire agreement (see Sched. 2, Example 20). The position would be different if, for example, the hirer had a right to terminate, without further payment, at the end of the second year.

2. PARTIALLY REGULATED AGREEMENTS

As already stated, the all important distinction is between *regulated* and **19.07** *exempt* agreements. Before considering the nature of exempt agreements it might be useful to mention two types of agreement which are regulated in part only.

Non-commercial agreements

By section 189 a non-commercial agreement is an agreement not made by **19.08** the creditor or owner in the course of a business carried on by him. It is important to notice the words "*a* business." If, for example, a manufacturer made loans to his employees to enable them to buy season tickets or houses, the loans *would* be made in the course of *a* business (even though it was not a consumer credit or consumer hire business) and accordingly it would not be "non-commercial." If, however, the agreement is non-commercial then a number of specific provisions do not apply. The most important area is formalities and cancellation.[12]

Small agreements

A small agreement is defined in section 17 as either;   **19.09**

(a) a regulated consumer credit agreement for credit not exceeding £50,[13] other than a hire-purchase or conditional sale agreement[14]; or
(b) a regulated consumer hire agreement which does not require the hirer to make payments exceeding £50.

There is a further condition, namely, that the agreement is unsecured or secured by a guarantee or indemnity only. Not surprisingly, section 17(3)

---

[12] See s.74(1)(a) and ss.77–79.
[13] The figure is reduced to £35 if it comes within the Consumer Protection (Cancellation of Contracts Concluded away from Business Premises) Regulations 1987, reg. 9. See above, para. 6.05.
[14] See above, paras 18.04–18.05.

blocks attempts to split up a transaction into a series of small agreements (at one time encyclopaedia salesmen were notorious for this) by providing that in such a case each small agreement shall be treated as a regulated non-small agreement.

Small debtor-creditor-supplier agreements for restricted-use credit are exempt from most of the provisions relating to formalities and cancellation.[15]

3. Exempt Agreements

19.10   Having decided that an agreement is a consumer credit or consumer hire agreement, we must now decide whether it is taken out of control by one of the exemptions. These are to be found in section 16 and in the Consumer Credit (Exempt Agreements) Order 1989 (as amended). The first four of them relate to land.

(1) A debtor-creditor-supplier agreement is exempt if (a) the creditor is a local authority or a body named in the regulations, and (b) the agreement finances (i) the purchase of land, or (ii) the provision of dwellings on any land, and in either case is secured by a mortgage of *that* land.[16]

(2) A debtor-creditor agreement is exempt if (a) the lender is a local authority, and (b) the agreement is secured by a mortgage of land. It will be apparent that in this case the purpose of the loan is immaterial.[17]

(3) A debtor-creditor agreement is exempt if (a) the lender is a body named in the regulations, (b) the agreement is secured by a mortgage of land, and (c) the agreement is to finance the purchase of land, the provision of dwellings or business premises on land and certain ancillary purposes.[18]

The bodies named in the Regulations include a large number of insurance companies, friendly societies and charities. Also included are certain public bodies (*e.g.* development corporations), but there the exemption only applies to a more limited class of purpose which is set out opposite to their names in Part II of the Schedule to the Regulations.

Building Societies originally enjoyed blanket exemption but with the widening of their powers under the Building Societies Act 1986 this was abolished. Instead, any Building Society authorised under that Act will enjoy exemption if and only if the relevant agreement is exempt under the Order. For example, a Building Society loan of £25,000 or less not linked to house purchase, etc., would be regulated. Quite apart from section 16, the £25,000 ceiling will take many land mortgages outside the definition of "regulated arrgement." There is growing pressure for mortgages to be regulated under the Financial Services and Markets Bill now before Parliament and this (or some other form of regulation) could well happen.

---

[15] See below, paras 21.05 and 22.04.
[16] s.16(2)(a).
[17] *ibid.*
[18] *ibid.*

(4) Even if an agreement to finance the purchase of land is not exempt under (1) to (3) above (*e.g.* because the lender is not one of the specified bodies) a further exemption is to be found in article 3(1)(b) which exempts a debtor-creditor-supplier agreement to finance the purchase of land, if the number of payments to be made by the debtor does not exceed four. There are further exemptions covering agreements to finance a premium under a contract of insurance relating to land.

(5) A debtor-creditor-supplier agreement is exempt under article 3(1)(a)(i) if (a) it is not hire-purchase or conditional sale, (b) it is for fixed-sum credit, (c) the number of payments to be made by the debtor *in respect of the credit* does not exceed four, and (d) they must be paid within 12 months of the date of the agreement. This exempts (*inter alia*) normal trade credit (*e.g.* payment within 30 days of invoice).

(6) A debtor-creditor-supplier agreement is exempt under article 3(1)(a)(ii) if (a) it is not hire-purchase or conditional sale, (b) it is for running-account credit, and (c) the whole of the credit for a period is repayable by a single payment. This will exempt many budget accounts in shops and certain charge card agreements, *e.g.* American Express and Diners Club.

(7) A further important exemption is to be found in article 4 and relates to debtor-creditor agreements where (a) it is offered to a class or classes of person (*e.g.* employees) and not to the public generally and (b) the only item in the "total charge for credit" is interest which cannot exceed 1 per cent above the highest of any base rates published by the English and Scottish Clearing Banks, being the latest rates in force 28 days before the making of the agreement.

In practice, many agreements seek to protect the creditor by including a term in the agreement whereby the debtor's liability fluctuates according to a specified formula (*e.g.* the retail price index or changes in Bank of England minimum lending rate). In deciding whether the "low interest exemption" applies to such a case it is necessary to distinguish sharply between *credit* and *the total charge for credit*. If the *credit* can fluctuate then exemption under regulation 4 is destroyed. On the other hand the fluctuation of the annual *rate* of charge is permissible and this will not destroy the exemption—provided that *at the date of the agreement* the rate did not exceed the statutory ceiling set out above.

> Thus if the agreement provided for interest to be paid annually at "1 per cent above Lloyds Bank base rate for the time being" the agreement will be exempt if at the date of the agreement the base rate did not exceed the highest rate prevailing 28 days before the making of the agreement. An increase in the rate after the date of the agreement will not destroy the exemption.[19]

The total charge for credit

We have already met this term on several occasions and it is now necessary   **19.11**

---

[19] See below, para. 19.14.

to examine it more closely. It is vitally important for a number of reasons, including the following:

(a) Any sum forming part of the total charge for credit does not form part of the credit[20] and must, therefore, be ignored in deciding whether or not the credit exceeds £25,000.

(b) Under article 4[21] a debtor-creditor agreement is exempt if the annual percentage rate of charge (below, para. 19.14) does not exceed the statutory maximum.

(c) One of the cardinal principles of the Act is to give the debtor information on various matters and one such matter is the "true cost of borrowing".[22] In the United States this is known as "truth in lending". One of the objects of the legislation is to give the debtor an opportunity of "shopping around" and comparing the cost of credit offered by different lenders. It is certainly debatable whether many debtors are likely to take advantage of this facility and it could well be that the effect of this requirement could be counter-productive, in that the extra cost involved will doubtless increase the cost of borrowing and may put the credit beyond the reach of some prospective borrowers.

The total charge for credit is dealt with in the Consumer Credit (Total Charge for Credit) Regulations 1980. The object of these regulations is three-fold, namely (a) to specify what items are to be included, (b) to specify what items are to be excluded, and (c) to require the charge to be calculated as an annual percentage rate.

Items included

19.12   Regulation 4 provides that there shall be included (a) the total of the interest payments, and (b) other charges at any time payable under the transaction by or on behalf of the debtor or a relative of his, whether to the creditor or to any other person. This would clearly cover the general costs incurred in setting up the agreement—survey fees, legal fees and stamp duty are obvious examples.

Items excluded

19.13   The generality of regulation 4 is cut down by regulation 5. Among items excluded are the following: (a) sums payable on default, (b) sums which would be payable in any event even if it were a cash transaction (*e.g.* installation charges), (c) sums paid under a maintenance or insurance contract where the debtor had a free choice in the matter and could have made substantially the same arrangements elsewhere, and (d) a life insurance premium in a case where the policy monies are to be used to repay the credit.

[20] s.9(3) above, para. 19.03.
[21] Above, para. 19.10 subpara. (7).
[22] See s.20.

Annual percentage rate (APR)

To enable comparisons to be made, regulation 7 requires the total charge to **19.14** be stated as an annual percentage rate reflecting (a) annual compounding, and (b) the continuing repayment of credit. If a prospective borrower is told by a finance house that the rate of interest is 12 per cent this is seriously misleading, because it does not acknowledge that the *outstanding capital is reducing* all the time: the true rate of interest (APR) is about double the flat rate of 12 per cent.

As part of the policy of providing an annual percentage rate, regulation 7 provides a formula for converting a period rate (*e.g.* 10 per cent per six months) into an annual rate. Conversely, regulation 8 provides a formula whereby the annual rate can be extracted where the whole indebtedness (credit and total charge) is repayable in a single lump sum.

This leaves the question—how can the annual rate be calculated in the case of a land mortgage or hire-purchase agreement where capital and interest are being repaid over several years? The calculation can be a nightmare but fortunately the Government has produced Consumer Credit Tables in 15 volumes. These tables (complete with amendment slips!) can produce the annual percentage rate, provided that the instalments and the repayment periods are equal. Thus, for example, the tables cannot be used if the final hire-purchase instalment is larger than the others because it contains a small extra amount (*e.g.* £1) for the option to purchase.

If the tables cannot be used, the annual rate must be calculated (by trial and error) in accordance with regulation 9. This provides (in effect) that the annual rate is the rate at which the present value of all future repayments equals the amount of the credit.

The above explanation presupposes that all the items are constant and known at the date of the agreement. In practice this may not be so and the regulations recognise this by making certain assumptions. For example, a provision giving the creditor the right to increase the charges (very common in mortgage contracts) must be disregarded.[23] Similarly, there may be a clause for the index linking of the total charge for credit; here again it is to be assumed that changes will not occur (reg. 15). If, however, the amount of a particular item is unknown at the date of the agreement and is not covered by the assumptions, then it seems that the exemption for low cost credit[24] cannot be claimed. This could arise where, for example, the creditor's insurance company require the debtor to pay for the installation of a burglar alarm and the cost of this is not known at the date of the agreement.

---

[23] reg. 2(1)(d). For a recent case on variation of the initial rate see *National Westminster Bank v. Devon C.C.* [1993] C.C.L.R. 69, DC.
[24] See above, para. 19.10 subpara. (7).

4. Linked Transactions

19.15   Having examined the crucial distinction between regulated and exempt agreements, it is necessary to end this chapter with a brief mention of linked transactions, *i.e.* transactions which are linked to an actual or prospective regulated agreement. The term "linked transaction" is important for a variety of reasons, including withdrawal, cancellation, early settlement and extortionate credit bargains. It is clear from section 19 that an agreement for security will not be a linked agreement but, subject to this, the following are included:

(1) A transaction entered into in compliance with a term of the principal agreement, *e.g.* "the debtor shall insure his life with XYZ insurance company and shall enter into a maintenance contract with Eezikleen Ltd".

(2) A transaction to be financed by a debtor-creditor-supplier agreement; thus where the supplier of a car and the supplier of the credit have "arrangements", the sale of the car is "linked" to the loan contract, so that cancellation of the latter will also cancel the former.[25]

(3) A transaction entered into by the debtor, hirer or a relative at the suggestion of the creditor, owner, an associate of his[26] or a person negotiating the principal agreement. Thus a dealer might say to a prospective borrower "you would have a better chance of getting a loan from the finance company if you took out a life policy". Such tie-ins are now rendered unlawful by the Courts and Legal Services Act 1990, but many building societies offer discounted rates of interest—but with "strings" such as a house or contents insurance.

Regulations have been made[27] whereby certain types of linked agreement are excluded from the provisions of the Act relating to effectiveness,[28] cancellation and early settlement. The excepted classes are:

(1) Contracts of insurance
(2) Guarantees of goods
(3) Agreements for the operation of a deposit and/or current account.

---

[25] s.69(1), below, para. 22.09.
[26] Above, para. 18.07.
[27] Consumer Credit (Linked Transactions) (Exemptions) Regulations 1983 (S.I. 1983 No. 1560).
[28] In general a linked agreement is ineffective until the main agreement is made (s.19(3)).

CHAPTER TWENTY

CONTROL OF BUSINESS ACTIVITIES

We have already seen that the Consumer Credit Act controls business activities as well as individual agreements. It is clear that business control is of very great benefit to the consumer. It should help to ensure that the other party to the transaction is a reputable trader and that the consumer is not pressurised into a transaction by misleading advertising or other undesirable business practice. In this chapter it is proposed to consider this aspect of consumer protection under three main headings, namely: **20.01**

1. Licensing
2. Advertising
3. Canvassing

1. LICENSING

The licensing system set out in sections 22 to 24 and 147 to 150 can be described as the linch-pin of the whole Act. For the first time a centrally administered licensing system enables the entire credit industry to be kept under close scrutiny. There is little doubt that the threat of the refusal or revocation of a licence (*i.e.* loss of livelihood) is by far the strongest sanction provided by the Act. It is a perfect example of the administrative control mentioned earlier in this book.[1] **20.02**

Who needs a licence?

The Act lists seven types of business for which a licence is required, namely: **20.03**

(a) consumer credit
(b) consumer hire
(c) credit brokerage
(d) debt-counselling
(e) debt-adjusting
(f) debt-collecting
(g) credit reference agency

---

[1] Above, para. 17.01.

A number of problems arise. The first one is "what is a business?" The Act merely tells us that it includes a profession or trade; presumably cases from other branches of the law (*e.g.* income tax) can offer some guidance. The key factors include (i) the frequency of the transactions, (ii) the manner of operation, and (iii) profit motive. The word "frequency" leads on naturally to section 189(2) which provides that:

> A person is not to be treated as carrying on a particular type of business merely because *occasionally* he enters into transactions belonging to a business of that type [italics supplied].

There will clearly be borderline cases. Thus section 189 defines "consumer credit business" by reference to the crucial phrase "regulated agreement" which was considered in Chapter 18. It provides that:

> "consumer credit business" means any business so far as it comprises or relates to the provision of credit under regulated consumer credit agreements.

Let us take an example. Suppose that John sells television sets. Most of his customers pay cash but from time to time he sells a set on credit. Such a sale will be a debtor-creditor-supplier agreement and will be regulated, unless the credit is repayable by four or fewer instalments. Whether John needs a licence will depend on whether the credit sales take place more than "occasionally". If they only took place at very long intervals, and if they formed a very small part of John's turnover, then no licence would be required.[2]

Even if there is a business, a licence will only be required if the trader makes *regulated* agreements. Thus, if a creditor only makes exempt agreements, or if the credit always exceeds £25,000 or the debtors are all companies, no licence will be required.

The above remarks also apply, *mutatis mutandis*, to a consumer hire business, but when we turn to the five other types of business defined in section 145 (the Act uses the term "*ancillary credit business*") we find that there is one significant difference—the concept of "regulated agreement" is not critical. Thus, for example, an estate agent who introduces clients to an insurance company will require a licence as a credit-broker, even though his clients make (a) agreements which are not consumer credit agreements at all (because the credit exceeds the statutory ceiling), or (b) agreements which are exempt under section 16.[3]

A local authority does not require a licence[4] even though the agreements which it makes may be regulated by the Act.

---

[2] See *Hare v. Shurek* [1993] C.C.L.R. 47, CA. Even if a licence is not required, the agreement may still be a "regulated agreement" and subject to control (*e.g.* the formality rules, below, paras 21.02–21.07).
[3] Above, para. 19.10.
[4] See s.21.

Nature and duration of licences

A licence is personal and non-assignable.[5] The licence period was reduced **20.04**
from 15 years to five years from June 1, 1991. The first licences started to
come up for renewal in August 1991, as licensing began in 1976. Since then
over 300,000 applications have been made.[6]

The criteria and the wide powers of the Director General

The onus is on the applicant to prove to the Director General that he is a fit **20.05**
person to engage in activities covered by the licence.[7] In considering the
application the Director General must consider any circumstances appearing
to him to be relevant.[8] Section 25 sets out a non-exhaustive list of relevant
matters including offences involving dishonesty or violence, contravention
of the Act or certain other legislation, sex and race discrimination and undesirable business practices. In all these cases the section refers not merely to
the trader himself but also to his employees, agents and associates (past or
present). It is important to appreciate that the conduct in question need not
involve any breach of the law, *e.g.* certain types of high-pressure salesmanship. As an alternative to refusing a licence the Director General may limit
the licence to specified activities.[9]

If the Director General is "minded to refuse" an application[10] he must
invite the applicant to make written representations and to give notice, if he
thinks fit, that he wishes to make representations orally. Appeal against
refusal lies to the Secretary of State who delegates his powers to certain
appointed persons.[11] Further appeal lies to the High Court on a point of law.
The above procedure is also followed in cases involving variation, suspension and revocation.[12] It will be seen that these provisions provide a potent
weapon for the consumer. If a licensed trader is guilty of breaches of the Sale
of Goods Act or of the Trade Descriptions Act, or continues to exhibit void
exemption clauses, these matters may come to the attention of the Director
General via trading standards inspectors or via the courts.[13] Even a letter from
an individual consumer will be relevant in building up evidence against the
trader and such evidence can, in appropriate cases, lead to refusal, suspension
or revocation of the licence.[14] The very existence of these provisions can have

---

[5] See s.22(2).
[6] OFT Press release, April 10, 1991.
[7] s.25(1)(a).
[8] s.25(2).
[9] See s.23(2).
[10] This has happened in 1,530 cases from 1977–1993: 1993 Annual Report of the DGFT.
[11] See s.41 and S.I. 1998 No. 1203.
[12] See ss.31–33. See *Credit Default Register and Homes v. Secretary of State* [1993] C.C.L.R. 59
(revocation for intimidatory conduct).
[13] See s.166.
[14] In 1990 the licences of 26 motor traders were revoked and 25 refused, usually because of
clocking: OFT Press release, April 16, 1991.

a salutary effect; thus they may induce the trader to alter his business practices before he applies for a licence.

Contracts by or through unlicensed traders

20.06   An unlicensed trader who engages in any activity for which a licence is
required commits an offence for which the maximum fine on summary
conviction is £2,000. If he is convicted on indictment the maximum penalty
is two years' imprisonment or a fine or both.[15] It may well be, however,
that the most effective sanction is the unenforceability of agreements.
Thus by section 40 a regulated agreement made by an unlicensed trader
is only enforceable if the Director General makes a validating order.
The Director General must consider (*inter alia*) the extent to which
debtors and hirers have been prejudiced, the degree of culpability and
whether or not he would have granted a licence to the trader if he had applied
for it. He can limit the order to specific agreements and he can impose
conditions.

These sanctions are a powerful deterrent against unlicensed trading.
Section 149 goes one step further; in effect it places the creditor or
owner under a duty to ensure that the credit-brokers with whom they do
business are themselves licensed. The creditor or owner has a strong
incentive to check on this; the section provides that a regulated agreement
made by a debtor or hirer who, for the purpose of making that agreement, was
introduced to the creditor or owner by an unlicensed credit-broker is only
enforceable against the debtor or hirer if the Director General makes a
validating order. Thus a finance company might be unable to enforce a hire-
purchase agreement if the debtor was introduced to them by an unlicensed
dealer.

Section 148 contains a similar "unenforceability" provision where an
agreement is made for the services of an unlicensed person carrying on an
ancillary credit business. Such a person can only enforce the agreement if the
Director General makes a validating order. The wording of the section is not
entirely clear. If we take the case of an estate agent whose business includes
that of being a "credit-broker", does the unenforceability apply solely to an
introduction fee payable to him by the borrower, or does it mean that he
cannot sue the seller for his commission? On principle the former view
should prevail—the sanctions imposed by the Act should be confined to his
activities *qua* credit-broker and the words "agreement for the services of a
person carrying on an ancillary credit business" should be construed
accordingly.

In considering these provisions it must be borne in mind that consent by
the debtor or hirer is as effective as a validating order (see s.173(3)).

---

[15] See Sched. 1.

2. Advertisements and Quotations

We have already seen that the very nature of credit carries the danger that the **20.07** consumer may overcommit himself. The likelihood of this is greatly increased if the creditor is allowed to exhibit a misleading advertisement with words like "five years to pay" in bold type and a very high interest charge tucked away in the small print.

Advertisements and the consumer

Before embarking on a brief examination of the scope and content of **20.08** advertisement regulation it may be relevant to consider what rights accrue to the consumer as a result of a defective advertisement. There are three over-lapping possibilities:

(1) If he is induced by a misleading advertisement to make a contract with the advertiser, he may have a civil claim under the general law for misrepresentation or for negligence. (See Chaps. 3 and 7.)
(2) If an advertisement contravenes the Act, the regulations or other legislation (*e.g.* the Trade Descriptions Act 1968[16] or the Control of Misleading Advertisement Regulations 1988 which were discussed in Chap. 16), the criminal court can exercise its general power to award compensation under the Powers of Criminal Courts Act 1973. (See Chap. 15.)
(3) There is the ever-present possibility of a complaint to the Office of Fair Trading which could, in the last resort, lead to the suspension or revocation of a licence.

Scope of advertisement control

The advertising provisions stand apart from the rest of the Act; in some **20.09** respects the controls are wider and in some narrower. Thus:

(1) The controls are not restricted to "regulated agreements" (above, para. 19.02). If, for example, a credit agreement is to be secured on land, the statutory advertising controls will apply even where the credit exceeds the statutory ceiling of £25,000. On the other hand, the controls will not apply if the advertisement indicates that the credit is only available to a body corporate (see s.43(3)(b)).
(2) The effect of the Consumer Credit (Exempt Advertisements) Order (S.I. 1985 No. 621 (as amended)) is to take many—but not all—types of exempt agreements outside the advertising controls.
(3) When we turn to the Advertisement Regulations themselves (S.I.

[16] Above, para. 13.20.

1989 No. 1125) we find one of the few distinctions between private and business transactions. These regulations will not apply to an advertisement which (1) expressly or by implication states that the credit or hire facilities are available for the purposes of a person's business, and (2) does not indicate that the facilities are available for non-business purposes (see reg. 9).

The definitions

20.10   It is clear from section 189 that the concept of "advertisement" is extremely wide and is not confined to visual forms. It can therefore include anything from a catalogue or brochure to films, radio and television commercials and even sales patter. It is also important to note that "the advertiser" is not necessarily the person who causes the advertisement to be inserted; it is the person who is indicated in the advertisement as willing to provide the credit, hire or credit brokerage facilities.

False advertisements

20.11   By section 46 an offence is committed if an advertisement is false or misleading in a material respect. Thus an "APR nil" advertisement has been held to be false where the trader made a hidden charge by giving a lower part-exchange allowance to instalment buyers than to cash buyers.[17] Similarly, the Rover company was convicted when, in large print, they gave £595 as the price of a new Metro while adding (in very small print at the bottom) that an extra £480 was payable for twelve months' road tax, number plates and delivery to the dealer.[17a]

The advertising regulations

20.12   These deal in some detail with the form and content of advertisements falling within their scope. Thus (a) the statutory information must be clear and easily legible; (b) (subject to exceptions) it must be presented together as a whole; (c) due prominence must be given to the APR (above, para. 19.14) where this is stated; and (d) the advertisement must contain a prescribed form of "health warning" in cases involving foreign currency mortgages or mortgages over a borrower's home. As regards content the regulations divide controlled advertisements into three types—simple, intermediate and full.[18] The advertiser must study the regulations carefully and then make sure that the advertisement does not contain either too little information or too much. For example, an advertisement "A. Smith—Moneylender" is a simple advertisement and must not indicate any price or any other willingness to enter into

---

[17] *Metsoja v. H. Norman Pitt & Co. Ltd* (1989) 153 J.P.N. 630.

[17a] *Rover Group Ltd v. Sumner* [1995] C.C.L.R. 1, Chester Crown Court.

[18] Full advertisements are subdivided into those aimed at *new* customers and those offering variations of existing agreements.

credit agreements. The Office of Fair Trading has published some helpful booklets (complete with cartoons!) to illustrate what the advertiser can and cannot do.

Quotations

As part of the policy of giving customers pre-contractual information the **20.13** Act enables quotation regulations to be made (see sections 52 and 152) Regulations came into force on February 1, 1990 (S.I. 1989 No. 1126) but following a recommendation by the Director General of Fair Trading[19] they have been revoked (S.I. 1997 No. 211).

3. CANVASSING

Section 49 follows the precedent set by the Moneylenders Acts by prohibit- **20.14** ing the canvassing of debtor-creditor agreements, *e.g.* personal loans, off-trade premises.

When is an offence committed?

The canvasser must be an individual and must solicit the debtor into the **20.15** making of a regulated agreement by making oral representations to the debtor, or to any other individual, during a visit by the canvasser to non-trade premises. The visit must have been for the purpose of making such oral representations, so that a crime is not committed if one individual makes representations to another individual while they are both guests at a party. On the other hand, a social visit can be caught if the underlying intention was to make representations leading to the debtor-creditor agreement.

Previous request

No offence is committed if the visit was in response to a request made on a **20.16** previous occasion, provided that the request was in writing signed by or on behalf of the person making it.[20] Presumably the person making the request need not be the debtor.

Trade premises

For *this* purpose the term trade premises is defined[21] as any premises where **20.17** a business is carried on (whether on a permanent or temporary basis) by (a)

---

[19] The recommendation was included in a Report, *Consumer Credit Deregulation* which was published in June 1994. He felt that the Regulations were not particularly helpful to consumers and that the direct and indirect cost outweighed the benefit.
[20] s.48(1)(b) and 49(2).
[21] *cf.* cancellation, below, para. 22.05.

the creditor or owner, (b) the supplier, (c) the canvasser's employer, or (d) the debtor.

Overdrafts

20.18   The Director General has made a determination[22] which exempts the soliciting of an agreement enabling the debtor to overdraw on specified types of current account, provided that the debtor already keeps an account with the creditor. This could be relevant where a bank manager invites his customer, ostensibly for a meal or a game of golf, but in reality to offer him overdraft facilities.

Circulars to minors

20.19   Minors (persons under 18) are particularly vulnerable to blandishments of "easy credit" and accordingly section 50(1) makes it an offence for a person, with a view to financial gain, to send to a minor any document inviting him or her to (a) borrow money, (b) obtain goods on credit or hire, (c) obtain services on credit, or (d) apply for information or advice on borrowing money or otherwise obtaining credit or hiring goods.[23] A defence is available where the person sending the circular did not know and had no reasonable cause to suspect that the addressee was a minor (s.50(2)) but the following subsection makes this defence somewhat difficult to raise if the document is sent to a school! Any such offence will not invalidate any resulting agreement[24] and such an agreement will be governed by a combination of common law rules, the Minors Contracts Act 1987, section 3 of the Sale of Goods Act 1979 and the Act.

---

[22] On June 1, 1977.

[23] For a recent unsuccessful prosecution, see *Alliance & Leicester Building Society v. Babbs* [1993] C.C.L.R. 77, DC.

[24] s.170(1), above, para. 18.03.

CHAPTER TWENTY-ONE

"I CAN'T REMEMBER WHAT I SIGNED"

In the previous chapter we examined vitally important provisions relating to **21.01**
the control of business activities.

We now turn to the other main form of control—the regulation of individual agreements. The law is to be found in Parts V to IX of the Act and much of it is modelled on the previous hire-purchase legislation. This chapter is concerned with formalities and copies.[1] The object of the legislation is to make sure that the debtor or hirer is made aware of his rights and obligations and that he can obtain further information if, for example, he has failed to keep a record of his payments. Once again a large amount of the detail is contained in regulations.

Sanctions for non-compliance

The sanctions are potentially severe. If the creditor or owner fails to com- **21.02**
ply with the various formalities, the agreement is said to be "*not properly executed*". By section 65 the creditor or owner cannot enforce such an agreement against the debtor or hirer unless (a) the court makes an enforcement order,[2] or (b) the debtor or hirer consents to enforcement (s.173(3)).[3] What happens if the creditor or owner, in defiance of section 65, enforces the agreement by retaking the goods? If the repossession amounts to the tort of trespass or conversion, the creditor or owner will be liable for this. If, however, the repossession is only unlawful because it contravenes section 65, it seems that the only remedy of the debtor or hirer is to apply for a mandatory injunction to restore the status quo.[4] That leaves merely the administrative sanction of taking action which can put the licence of the creditor or owner in jeopardy.

The purpose of the sanctions is to put the creditor or owner at a disadvantage if they do not comply with the rules designed for the protection of the consumer. The agreement is not invalidated[5]: it becomes *unenforceable by the creditor or owner* without an order of the court.[6] From the point of

---

[1] ss.58–65 and 77–80.
[2] Below, para. 25.01. Sometimes no such order can be made at all (para. 25.03).
[3] Above, para. 18.03.
[4] *ibid.*
[5] *R. v. Modupe* [1991] C.C.L.R. 29, CA (total price omitted; liability to repay continued, though unenforceable). See also the county court case of *Barclays Bank v. Lee* (1993) C.L.Y. 474 where the debtor unsuccessfully tried to recover sums paid under an unenforceable credit card agreement.
[6] The court has a wide discretion—see s.127, para. 25.01 below.

view of the debtor or hirer it is still valid and fully enforceable. For example, if goods held under a hire-purchase agreement are defective, the debtor can bring a claim under the Supply of Goods (Implied Terms) Act 1973 even though the agreement is "improperly executed". Further, a dishonest hirer can be prosecuted for seeking to evade an "existing liability", even though the "liability" is unenforceable without a court order under section 65.[7]

If the creditor applies for summary judgment under Part 24 of the Civil Procedure Rules the debtor may say "this agreement is unenforceable because I never received a copy" (or words to that effect!). There is no need for him to *prove* this fact; he can defeat the claim for summary judgment by showing that there is a real prospect of the defence succeeding.[7a]

Pre-contractual information

21.03   As part of the policy outlined above, section 55 enables regulations to be made whereby specified information must be disclosed to the prospective debtor or hirer before a regulated agreement is made. No regulations have so far been made.

Special pre-contract formalities in land mortgage cases

21.04   We have already seen that many land mortgage cases are outside the main control provisions because (i) the credit exceeds the statutory ceiling[8] or (ii) the agreements are exempted under section 16 or by regulations.[9] If, however, the agreement is a regulated agreement (*e.g.* a loan not exceeding the statutory ceiling granted by a non-exempt lender) section 58 lays down a special pre-contractual period of reflection and isolation; the reason for this is that the post-contractual cancellation provisions do not apply to any agreement secured on land.[10]

In two cases, however, the special reflection rules do not apply, namely (a) a restricted-use agreement to finance the purchase of the mortgaged land, and (b) an agreement for a bridging loan in connection with the purchase of the mortgaged land or other land. In these two cases the debtor will have neither reflection rights nor cancellation rights.

Let us suppose that John, a moneylender, is prepared to lend George £4,000 on the security of George's house. The reflection and isolation rules can be summarised as follows:

(1) At least seven days before sending the agreement for signature, John must give to George a copy of the agreement (and of any document referred

---

[7] *R. v. Modupe*, above, n. 5.
[7a] *Anglo Leasing Plc v. Pascoe* [1997] C.C.L.R. 69. The wording of rule 24.2 strengthens the creditor's chances of success by weeding out weak defences.
[8] £25,000 for agreements made on or after May 1, 1998.
[9] See above, para. 19.10.
[10] s.67, below, para. 22.05.

to therein) containing a notice in the prescribed form indicating George's right to withdraw from the transaction.[11]

(2) When seven days have elapsed, John can post the agreement for signature unless he has received a notice of withdrawal.[12]

(3) John must not approach George in any way during the "*consideration period*" except at George's specific request. The consideration period begins when the "reflection copy" is sent[13] and ends seven days after the sending of the agreement for signature[14] or, if earlier, its return by George duly signed.

Regulations have now been made relating to the wording of the "reflection copy". Thus the heading of a prospective credit agreement must be as follows:

> Copy of proposed credit agreement containing notice of your right to withdraw DO NOT sign or return this copy.

The document must also contain an explanatory box containing the following words:

YOUR RIGHT TO WITHDRAW

This is a copy of your proposed Credit agreement which is to be secured on land. It has been given to you now so that you may have at least a week to consider its terms before the actual agreement is sent to you for signature. You should read it carefully. If you do not understand it you may need to seek professional advice. If you do not wish to go ahead with it you need not do so.

If you decide NOT to go ahead with the agreement you should inform   or, if you prefer, any supplier or broker involved in the negotiations. You can do this in writing or orally for example by telephone. If the agreement arrives for signature and you have decided NOT to go ahead DO NOT SIGN IT. Then you will not be legally bound by the agreement.

Finally the agreement itself must contain the following box:

YOUR RIGHTS

Under the Consumer Credit Act 1974 the creditor should have given you a copy of this agreement at least seven days ago to allow you time to consider whether to go ahead. If he did not, the agreement cannot be enforced without a court order.

---

[11] s.58(1) and 61(2). Thus a copy of the proposed mortgage would have to accompany the reflection copy which refers to it.
[12] s.61(2) and (4).
[13] See (1) above.
[14] See (2) above.

The above requirements also apply to a regulated consumer hire agreement secured by land mortgage.

Formalities of the agreement itself

21.05   Sections 60 and 61 enable regulations to be made to ensure that the debtor or hirer is made aware of his rights and duties, the amount and rate of the total charge for credit and the protection and remedies available to him under the Act. The detail is to be found in the Consumer Credit (Agreements) Regulations 1983 which specify the information which must be included, having regard to the particular type of agreement.[15] Thus the debtor under a hire-purchase agreement must be made aware of (*inter alia*) his right of termination,[16] and the restriction on the creditor's right to repossess protected goods.[17] The regulations (not surprisingly) require that the information should be easily legible and of a colour which is easily distinguishable from the colour of the paper.[18] They also specify the prominence to be given to particular parts of the agreement, and the place where the debtor or hirer must sign and the words to be contained in the signature box. The financial and related particulars (description of goods, deposit, credit, cash price, APR, total charges, repayments, etc.) must be shown together as a whole and not interspersed with other information.

The Act itself lays down three broad requirements in section 61:

(a) a document in the prescribed form itself containing all the prescribed terms[19] and conforming to regulations under section 60(1) is signed in the prescribed manner both by the debtor or hirer and by or on behalf of the creditor or owner, and

(b) the document embodies all the terms of the agreement, other than implied terms, and

(c) the document is, when presented or sent to the debtor or hirer for signature, in such a state that all its terms are readily legible.

The wording of paragraph (a) makes it clear that the debtor or hirer must sign *personally*. It is also clear that a signature on a blank form, with the details filled in later, would not be sufficient.[20]

Copies

21.06   Sections 62 to 63 contain copy provisions which are similar, but not identical, to the provisions in the Hire-Purchase Act 1965. The basic rule is that the debtor or hirer is always entitled to at least one copy of the agreement; in many cases he is entitled to two copies.

---

[15] See S.I. 1983 No. 1553, regs. 2–5.
[16] Below, para. 22.13.
[17] Below, para. 25.10.
[18] reg. 6(2).
[19] See reg. 6 of and Sched. 6 to the Agreements Regulations for the meaning of this term.
[20] Consider *Eastern Distributors v. Goldring* [1957] Q.B. 600, a decision on a slightly different provision in the Hire-Purchase Act 1938.

The provisions are complex but they can be conveniently divided into (a) cases where the agreement is presented to the debtor or hirer for signature, (b) cases where it is sent to him for signature and (c) cases where it is neither presented nor sent.

(a) *Agreement presented to debtor or hirer*

In the vast majority of cases in practice the document which he signs will be "*an unexecuted agreement*", *i.e.* a document embodying the terms of a prospective regulated agreement. In other words, the document is an offer by the debtor or hirer and there will be no concluded agreement until the document is signed by the creditor or owner thus accepting the offer. In this situation one copy must be given to the debtor or hirer immediately after he has signed[21] and, in addition, a copy of the executed agreement must be delivered or sent to him within seven days after the making of the agreement.[22]   **21.07**

In the less likely situation where the creditor or owner has already signed, signature by the debtor or hirer will convert the document into an "*executed agreement*", *i.e.* a contract; in that situation a copy of that agreement must be given to him there and then. In this situation no further copy is required.[23]

(b) *Agreement sent to the debtor or hirer for signature*

Here again the position is somewhat similar to that mentioned above. In all cases the agreement which is sent to the debtor or hirer for signature must be accompanied by a copy.[24] If the document becomes an "executed agreement" when he signs, no further copy need be sent to him.[25] Usually, however, the document which the debtor or hirer signs is an offer to the creditor or owner and will not become an "executed agreement" until a later date—*i.e.* until it is signed by the creditor or owner. In that situation a copy of the executed agreement must be delivered or sent to the debtor or hirer within seven days of the making of the agreement.   **21.08**

(c) *Cases where the prospective agreement is neither delivered nor sent*

The situations contemplated here are those where the debtor completes an application form which he sees in a newspaper or which he picks up from a dispenser. In this situation the creditor or owner must deliver or send a copy of the executed agreement within seven days of the date on which it is made.[26]   **21.09**

(d) *Cancellation cases*

Special provisions apply in cancellation cases.[27]   **21.10**

[21] s.62(1).
[22] s.63(2).
[23] s.63(1) and (2)(a).
[24] s.62(2).
[25] s.63(2)(b).
[26] s.63(2).
[27] Below, para. 22.06.

(e) *Form and contents of copies*

21.11   This matter is dealt with in considerable detail in the Consumer Credit (Cancellation Notices and Copies of Documents) Regulations 1983.[28] A failure to comply with these formalities will mean that the agreement is "not properly executed" (see ss.62–65 read with s.182(2)) and the consequences for the creditor or owner can be very serious.[29]

(f) *Other documents*

21.12   The duty to supply a copy includes a duty to supply a copy of every other document referred to in the agreement. Read literally this would require the creditor or owner to supply a copy of the Consumer Credit Act merely because the agreement referred to it. Fortunately the regulations make it clear that this is not necessary.[30]

Post-contractual information

Additional information on request

21.13   The copy provisions are supplemented by sections 77 to 79 which, as already stated, are designed to assist the debtor or hirer who has failed to keep a record of his payments (alternatively, he may have mislaid either or both of the copies referred to above). In each of these cases the debtor or hirer must make a written request and send the sum of 50 pence. To ensure that the creditor or owner is not put to unreasonable trouble, the sections require him to send to the debtor or hirer, within the prescribed period,[31] a copy of the executed agreement and a signed statement containing certain particulars (*e.g.* as to sums paid, due and payable) "according to the information to which it is practicable for him to refer". Further, to prevent the creditor or owner from being inundated with such requests, the information need not be given at all if the request was made within one month of a previous request having been complied with.

The sanctions for non-compliance are two-fold. Thus, (a) while the default continues the creditor or owner cannot enforce the agreement, and (b) if the default continues for one month he commits an offence.

Additional information without request

21.14   In the case of a running-account credit agreement, other than a small agreement,[32] the creditor must send to the debtor periodic statements containing the information required by regulations.[33]

---

[28] S.I. 1983 No. 1557.
[29] See above, para. 21.02 and below, para. 25.03.
[30] S.I. 1983 No. 1557, reg. 11(e).
[31] Twelve working days (S.I. 1983 No. 1569, reg. 2).
[32] Above, para. 19.04.
[33] s.78(4) and S.I. 1983 No. 1570 which deal with form, contents and time-limits.

Information as to the whereabouts of the goods

So far all the provisions have required information to be given *by* the credi-   **21.15**
tor or owner, but section 80 is concerned with the reverse situation. It provides that where a regulated agreement requires the debtor or hirer to keep
goods in his possession or control, he must, within seven working days after
receiving a written request from the creditor or owner, tell the creditor or
owner where the goods are. If the information is not given within 21 days of
receiving the request the debtor or hirer commits an offence.

Transitional matters

The various sections discussed in this chapter came into force on May 19,   **21.16**
1985 and sections 77 to 79 are retrospective—they apply to agreements made
before that date which would have been regulated if made on that date.[34]

Guarantees

Formality and copy provisions also apply to guarantees of regulated   **21.17**
agreements.[35]

---

[34] See Sched. 3, para. 17(2), read with the Eighth Commencement Order.
[35] See ss.105–110 and S.I. 1983 No. 1556.

CHAPTER TWENTY-TWO

"CAN I GET OUT OF THE AGREEMENT?"

We have seen that a debtor or hirer may commit himself too heavily (perhaps **22.01** aided by an over-enthusiastic salesman). In this chapter we shall consider his right to resile from a regulated agreement and the financial consequences of his doing so. The subject will be considered under four headings, namely:

1. Withdrawal
2. Rescission and Repudiation
3. Cancellation
4. Termination

The above topics must be distinguished from the problem which arises where the consumer wants to perform the agreement ahead of time. This matter is considered in Chapter Twenty-Five—below, para. 25.04.

1. WITHDRAWAL

On general contractual principles a prospective debtor or hirer can withdraw **22.02** from the transaction at any time before his offer has been accepted by revoking his offer. In the case of a regulated agreement his position is strengthened by section 59(1) which provides that an agreement is void if it binds a person to enter, as prospective debtor or hirer, into a prospective regulated agreement. This provision may, however, be cut down by regulations but the only regulations so far made are confined to certain types of business credit.[1]

Section 57, which deals with withdrawal, provides that no special form of wording is required[2] and the notice of withdrawal can be written or oral. Two important points should be noted:

(1) The list of persons to whom notice of withdrawal can be given is surprisingly wide. It includes not only the credit-broker or supplier but also "any person who, in the course of a business carried on by him, acts on behalf of the debtor or hirer in any negotiations for the agreement."[3] Thus if, for example, the prospective debtor had instructed a solicitor to negotiate on his behalf, a notice given by him to that solicitor would be sufficient. Such a

---

[1] See S.I. 1983 No. 1552.
[2] s.57(2).
[3] s.57(3).

deemed agent is under a deemed contractual duty to transmit the notice to his deemed principal (the creditor or owner) forthwith.[4]

(2) Withdrawal has the same effect as cancellation. Thus, (a) the prospective debtor or hirer can recover all payments made by him to the creditor or owner (*e.g.* a pre-contract deposit, or a payment made for a survey of the house); (b) the withdrawal will also terminate any linked transaction[5] and sums paid under it become repayable; (c) under a three-party D-C-S agreement[6] the creditor and the supplier are jointly liable to repay the sums paid by the debtor; and (d) the prospective debtor or hirer will have a lien over the goods until sums repayable to him have been repaid.[7]

One final point: the Act does not cut down the general rule that the revocation of an offer must be communicated to the offeree before acceptance. Thus if the consumer uses the post he runs the risk that his letter of withdrawal will be lost in the post or will only reach the creditor or owner after acceptance. In either of these cases the withdrawal is ineffective.[8]

2. Rescission and Repudiation

22.03   Again on general contractual principles a debtor or hirer may have a right to rescind an agreement for misrepresentation or to treat it as repudiated by a breach by the creditor or owner. One example of this is considered in the next chapter. The deemed agency provisions referred to above also apply to rescission.[9] The principal distinction between rescission and accepting a repudiation is that the former is retrospective and the innocent party is treated as if the agreement had never been made. In the latter case obligations arising before the acceptance of repudiation remain enforceable, although they can usually be reduced or extinguished by a claim for damages.

3. Cancellation

22.04   We have already seen that a "consumer" will have cancellation rights in cases covered by the Consumer Protection (Cancellation of Contracts Concluded away from Business Premises) Regulations 1987—above, para. 6.06. A somewhat similar cancellation right is available under sections 67 to 73 of the Act (for a somewhat wider class of "consumer") and this is considered below. Although the 1987 Regulations do not expressly exclude overlap between the two rights, this is the effect of regulation 4; in other words the cancellation

---

[4] s.175.
[5] For the meaning of this term see above, para. 19.15.
[6] Above, para. 19.05.
[7] The consequences of cancellation are considered in more detail in paras 22.09–22.12.
[8] See Goode, *Consumer Credit Legislation*, Vol. I, para. 575, where a similar view is taken.
[9] See s.102.

rights under the regulations will not apply if the consumer has cancellation
rights under the rules discussed below.

The cancellation provisions in sections 67 to 73 are modelled on those in
the Hire-Purchase Act 1965, although there are significant differences
between them. The object of the legislation is clear enough—to give the debt-
or or hirer a chance for second thoughts (*i.e.* a "cooling-off period") in a case
where he may have been pressurised by a doorstep salesman into signing an
agreement. The matter can be considered under the following headings:

(1) What agreements are cancellable?
(2) The copy provisions
(3) The time for cancellation
(4) How is cancellation effected?
(5) Effect of cancellation
(6) Duty to return goods
(7) The part-exchange allowance

(1) **What agreements are cancellable?**

A regulated consumer credit or hire agreement is cancellable if two con-   **22.05**
ditions are satisfied, namely, (a) oral representations were made by or on
behalf of the negotiator in the presence of the debtor or hirer[9a]; *and* (b) the
unexecuted agreement was not signed by the debtor or hirer at premises
where a business was carried on by (i) the creditor or owner, (ii) any party to a
linked transaction (other than the debtor or hirer or a relative of his), or (iii)
the negotiator in any antecedent negotiations.

Let us suppose that John, a trader, goes to a car dealer to buy a new car. The
transaction is financed by a loan from a finance company who require John to
take out a life policy with an insurance company. The car dealer (the negotiator) makes oral representations in John's presence. If John signs the agreement at the office of the dealer, finance company or insurance company, he
will have no right of cancellation. On the other hand, if he signs at his own
home, or at his own business premises, then cancellation is available. Thus,
the definition of business premises does *not* include the business premises of
the debtor or hirer.[10] The place where the representations were made is immaterial. They must, however, have been made in the *presence* of the debtor or
hirer. Representations made on the telephone would not give cancellation
rights. If no oral representations were made at all (*e.g.* a mail-order purchase)
there is no right of cancellation.

In the case of land transactions the concept of post-contractual cancellation can result in considerable administrative problems. Accordingly, the
cancellation provisions do not apply to (a) an agreement secured on land, (b)

[9a] *See Moorgate Services Ltd v. Kabir, The Times,* April 25, 1995, CA.
[10] Contrast the canvassing rules, above, paras 20.07.

a restricted-use agreement to finance the purchase of land, or (c) a bridging loan in connection with the purchase of land. It will be recalled that in case (a) above the prospective debtor or hirer will have a pre-contractual period of reflection and isolation.[11]

Two other types of agreement are not cancellable. They are (a) a non-commercial agreement,[12] and (b) a "small" debtor-creditor-supplier agreement for restricted-use credit.[13]

> Let us suppose that a doorstep salesman induces Mrs Smith to buy a children's encyclopedia at a price of £45 payable by nine instalments of £5. Nothing is said about the passing of property. (i) This is a "small" agreement[14]; (ii) since the supplier of the goods and the supplier of the credit are the same person it is "debtor-creditor-supplier"; (iii) since Mrs Smith cannot get her hands on the credit it is "restricted-use"; (iv) therefore no cancellation is possible.

(2) The copy provisions

22.06   The basic rules in sections 62 and 63[15] are modified in three respects by section 64. Thus:

(a) each copy must contain a notice in the prescribed form indicating the right of cancellation, how and when it is exercisable and the name and address of a person to whom notice of cancellation may be given[16];
(b) in cases where a second copy is required it must be sent *by post*[17];
(c) in cases where a second copy is not required a notice, containing the information mentioned in (a) above, must be posted to the debtor or hirer within seven days of the making of the agreement.[18]

We shall see that the usual "unenforceability" sanction can be particularly severe in these cases.[19]

Exemptions

The Director General can grant exemption from the duty to send a cancellation notice in certain specified cases if he is satisfied that this requirement can be dispensed with without prejudicing the interests of debtors or hirers (see s.64(4) and the Consumer Credit (Notice of Cancellation Rights) (Exemptions) Regulations 1983 No. 1558).

---

[11] Above, para. 21.04.
[12] Above, para. 19.08.
[13] s.74(2).
[14] Above, para. 19.09.
[15] Above, para. 21.06.
[16] s.64(1)(a) read with the Consumer Credit (Cancellation Notices and Copies of Documents) Regulations 1983 (S.I. 1983 No. 1557).
[17] s.63(3).
[18] s.64(1)(b).
[19] See below, para. 22.02.

(3) The time for cancellation

The cancellation period starts when the debtor or hirer signs the **22.07** unexecuted agreement and ends five days after the debtor or hirer *receives* the statutory second copy or notice.[20] Thus, if the second copy is received on a Friday the cancellation period runs out at midnight on the following Wednesday. If the second copy is delayed in the post the cancellation period will, to that extent, be prolonged since the period only starts to melt away when the debtor or hirer *receives* the second copy.

What happens if the second copy is not received at all and the creditor or owner then sends a further copy? Alternatively, what happens if the second copy or notice is sent off more than seven days after the making of the agreement? The wording of the Act is ambiguous. If the third copy or the late copy could be regarded as given "under" section 63, then it would start the five-day period running. On the other hand it could be argued that a notice is only given "under" section 63 if it is posted within seven days; if this is correct then the effect of delay or non-receipt would be that the right of cancellation would remain permanently available. This seems so absurd that the court is likely to prefer the former view.

(4) How is cancellation effected?

By section 69 the agreement can be cancelled if the debtor or hirer serves a **22.08** notice of cancellation on (a) the creditor or owner, (b) the person specified in the copy or notice or (c) the agent of the creditor or owner (including his deemed agent).[21] No special form of wording is required but it is clear from the definition of "notice"[22] that it must be in writing. If it is posted it takes effect as from the date of posting and the mere fact that it is not received by the creditor or owner is immaterial (this is in marked contrast to the second copy or notice which only triggers off the count-down of the cancellation period when it is received).[23] The regulations require that the second copy or the notice (see (2) above) must include a cancellation form which the debtor or hirer can use to cancel the agreement.[24]

(5) Effect of cancellation

Subject to two exceptions the general effect of cancellation is to treat the **22.09** agreement, and most linked transactions,[25] as if it had never been made.[26]

---

[20] s.68.
[21] See above, para. 25.03.
[22] s.189.
[23] Notice of cancellation (effective when posted) can also be contrasted with notice of withdrawal—see above, para. 22.02.
[24] S.I. 1983 No. 1557, regs. 5 and 6 and Sched., Pts. IV and VI.
[25] By S.I. 1983 No. 1560 certain linked transactions (insurance, guarantee of goods, deposit accounts and current accounts) will survive the cancellation of the main agreement.
[26] s.69(4).

Thus the debtor or hirer can recover his payments and is discharged from liability to make further payments. In the case of a three-party D-C-S agreement[27] for restricted-use credit the creditor and supplier are jointly and severally liable to repay sums paid by the debtor or a relative. The debtor, hirer or relative has a lien over the goods until repayable sums are repaid to him. Thus, if Albert paid a £200 deposit to buy a £2,000 car and the remaining £1,800 was paid by a creditor who had "arrangements" with the seller, the effect of a cancellation of the loan agreement would be that (a) the sale contract, as a linked transaction, would also be cancelled, (b) the seller and creditor would be jointly and severally liable to repay the £200 to Albert, and (c) if the £1,800 were paid direct to the supplier he would have to repay it to the creditor.[28]

Two exceptions

22.10   (1) The first exception is in section 70(2) and deals with a debtor-creditor-supplier agreement for restricted-use credit to finance (a) the doing of work or supply of goods to meet an emergency, or (b) the supply of goods which have become incorporated in any land or thing before service of the notice of cancellation. Since the debtor is unable to return the goods, it would clearly be wrong to allow him to avoid payment simply by serving a notice of cancellation. Accordingly, in this type of case the cancellation will wipe out the credit part of the agreement but the debtor will remain liable to pay the cash price for the goods or work.

(2) The second exception is to be found in section 71 and it deals with a case where the credit has already been advanced by the creditor before the expiry of the cancellation period. Here the strict application of the cancellation provisions would cause hardship. On the one hand, since the agreement is treated as never having been made, the creditor might be able to bring an action to recover money lent. On the other hand the debtor might try to avoid all liability in reliance on section 70(1)(b) which provides that any sum payable by the debtor or his relative shall cease to be payable. To deal with these problems section 71 starts by providing that cancellation of a regulated consumer credit agreement (other than a debtor-creditor-supplier agreement for restricted-use credit) shall not destroy the obligation to repay the credit and interest. The words in brackets are inserted because, as we have seen, this type of transaction does not raise the type of problem at which section 71 is aimed—the supplier merely repays the credit to the creditor. The section then goes on to provide a complex formula. First of all it provides that if the whole or part of the credit is repaid within one month of cancellation, or not later than the first instalment repayment date, no interest is chargeable on the amount repaid. In other words, the consumer will have had the use of the

---

[27] Above, para. 19.05.
[28] s.70(1)(c).

money interest-free. It then goes on to deal with credit which is repayable by instalments where any part of the credit is still outstanding after the first repayment date. In such a case the creditor must serve a notice[29] recalculating the instalments over a period starting when this notice is served and ending with the final contractual repayment date. This shortening of the repayment period will often mean larger instalments.

(6) Duty to return goods

Let us remind ourselves at this point of the distinction between debtor-creditor-supplier agreements and debtor-creditor agreements: **22.11**

(a) Where the debtor under a debtor-creditor agreement uses the credit to buy goods, the sale contract is *not* a linked transaction and is not affected by cancellation of the credit agreement.
(b) In the case of a debtor-creditor-supplier agreement the supply of the goods is either an integral part of the credit agreement itself (*e.g.* hire-purchase) or it is a linked transaction under section 19 which is cancelled along with the credit agreement. In either case the debtor will have to restore the goods to the other party under the rules set out below.

Section 72 deals with a case where a debtor-creditor-supplier agreement for restricted-use credit, a consumer hire agreement or a linked transaction (to which the debtor, hirer or a relative is a party) is cancelled after the debtor, hirer or relative has obtained possession. In such a case the possessor is under a duty to restore the goods to the person from whom he got them and in the meantime to retain possession and to take reasonable care. The duty to restore the goods is merely a duty to redeliver them at *his own* premises on receiving a written request from the other party. The duty is also discharged if the possessor delivers the goods (whether at his own premises or elsewhere) to any person to whom a notice of cancellation could have been sent other than the "deemed agent".[30] Alternatively, he can send the goods to such a person, but in this case he must take reasonable care to see that they are received by the other party and are not damaged in transit. The duty to take reasonable care comes to an end 21 days from cancellation unless within that time the possessor has received a written request for redelivery and has unreasonably failed to comply with it.

There is, however, a sting in the tail. The duty to restore does not apply to emergency or incorporation cases where, as we have seen, the debtor remains liable to pay the price.[31] Nor does it apply to perishable goods, nor to goods which by their nature are consumed by use and were so consumed before

---

[29] See S.I. 1983 No. 1559 which sets out the form of the request.
[30] See above, para. 22.08.
[31] s.69(2)(b), above, para. 22.10.

cancellation—a classic case of having one's cake and not having to pay for it![32]

Any breach of section 72 is actionable as a breach of statutory duty.

(7) The part-exchange allowance

22.12   Section 73 deals with a case where, as part of a cancelled agreement, the negotiator agreed to take goods in part exchange and those goods have been delivered to him. The effect of section 73(2) is to give the debtor or hirer a right to recover the part-exchange allowance from the negotiator unless within 10 days of cancellation the goods were returned to the debtor or hirer in substantially the same condition. If the negotiator was the supplier in a three-party debtor-creditor-supplier agreement, the negotiator and the creditor are jointly and severally liable to repay the allowance, and the lien of the debtor or hirer[33] extends to cover the return of the goods (during the 10-day period) or the part-exchange allowance.

4. TERMINATION

22.13   If there is no right of withdrawal, rescission or cancellation the final possibility (apart from any contractual right of termination) is a right of termination under sections 99 to 101. These are limited in scope; sections 99 and 100 only apply to regulated hire-purchase and conditional sale agreements while section 101 relates to regulated consumer hire agreements. In either case the statutory rights cannot be cut down by agreement; on the other hand if the agreement is *more* favourable to the debtor or hirer he can take advantage of it.

(1) Hire-purchase and conditional sale

22.14   The provisions of sections 99 and 100 are very closely modelled on the corresponding provisions in the Hire-Purchase Act 1965, although modifications have had to be made because the 1974 Act extends to land as well as goods. The right to terminate a hire-purchase or conditional sale agreement is available at any time before the last instalment falls due. It can be exercised by giving notice to any person who is entitled or authorised to receive payments. However, there are two cases in which the right to terminate is not available. The first is where, under a conditional sale agreement relating to land, title has passed to the buyer. The second is where, under a conditional sale of goods, the property has become vested in the buyer and has then been transferred to a third person, *e.g.* a sub-buyer.

Termination only operates for the future, so that sums which have *accrued*

---

[32] Thus the hirer of a motor vehicle would not have to pay for petrol consumed before cancellation.
[33] Above, para. 19.05.

due remain payable.[34] The effect of termination may well be to leave the creditor with heavily depreciated goods. In order to provide some measure of compensation, section 100(1) requires the debtor to pay such further sum (if any) as will bring the total payments up to *one-half* of the total price. If, however, in any action the court is satisfied that a smaller sum is adequate to cover the creditor's loss, the court may order such smaller sum to be paid. This could clearly be relevant if, for example, a hirer bought a car with a hire-purchase price of £3,000 and then wished to terminate the agreement after only a few weeks' use. He would presumably tender a sum falling far short of one-half, leaving it to the creditor to take court proceedings. The court has no discretion with regard to sums which have already accrued due.

The debtor may also have to pay damages if he is in breach of an obligation to take reasonable care of the goods[35] and he must allow the creditor to retake them.[36]

If the creditor agrees to carry out any installation and if the cost of the installation forms part of the total price, it is clearly reasonable that he should be paid for this in full. Accordingly, the reference to one-half is a reference to the installation charge in full and one-half of the balance.[37]

Example

A television set is let out on hire-purchase at a price of £300, including a £30 installation charge. The debtor pays a £50 deposit and one instalment of £10 is outstanding. He now wishes to terminate the agreement. He must first of all pay the £10. Then (unless otherwise ordered) he must bring his payments up to one-half of the total price:

$$\text{one half} = £30 + \frac{270}{2} = £165$$

$$\text{less sums paid and due} = 60$$

$$\text{further sum payable}[38] = £105$$

(2) Consumer hire

Section 101 gives the hirer a new and non-excludable right to terminate the agreement, but the earliest termination date is 18 months after the making of the agreement (unless the contract provides for an earlier termination date).[39] Once again termination only operates for the future and sums which have accrued due are not affected. The hirer must give a termination notice equal

22.15

[34] s.99(2).
[35] s.100(4).
[36] s.100(5).
[37] s.100(2).
[38] s.100(1).
[39] s.101(3).

to the shortest payment interval, or three months, whichever is less. Thus, if rentals are payable monthly, the hirer can end the agreement by giving one month's notice at the end of month 17.

The exercise of a right of termination can often cause financial problems to the owner, especially where the owner leases out commercial equipment. Accordingly, section 101(7) provides that in three cases the statutory right of termination is not available at all. These are:

(a) where the total payments (disregarding sums payable on breach) exceed £900 in any one year;
(b) where goods are let out for the hirer's business and were selected by the hirer and acquired by the owner, at the hirer's request, from a third party;
(c) any agreement where the hirer requires the goods to relet them in the course of a business.

Apart from these special cases the Director General has a general power to exclude the operation of section 101 from agreements made by a particular trader.[40]

The section does not mention damages for failure to take reasonable care but on principle the hirer owes a duty of reasonable care as a bailee at common law and will be liable to pay damages for breach of that duty.

[40] See s.101(8) as amended by the Consumer Credit (Increase of Monetary Amounts) Order 1983 (S.I. 1983 No. 1571).

Chapter Twenty-Three

"THE GOODS ARE DEFECTIVE"

In Part I of this book we considered the terms implied by sections 12 to 14 of **23.01** the Sale of Goods Act 1979, and we also dealt briefly with hire-purchase and hiring agreements. In this chapter we shall consider these problems again in the context of credit transactions. The basic point can be made very briefly at the outset—the differences between cash and credit transactions are very slight. It is proposed to consider this topic under five headings and for convenience the term "connected lender" will be used in preference to "creditor with whom the supplier had arrangements". The five headings are:

1. Cash sale—unconnected lender
2. Cash sale—connected lender
3. Credit sale and conditional sale
4. Hire-purchase
5. Hire

1. Cash Sale—Unconnected Lender

Let us suppose that Robert borrows money from his bank and uses it to buy a **23.02** car. The loan is a debtor-creditor agreement and, as we have seen, the purchase of the car is not a linked transaction. As between seller and buyer, the position is governed by the Sale of Goods Act 1979, and this is fully discussed in Chapters 3 and 4. Alternatively, if the seller was guilty of misrepresentation Robert may be entitled to rescind the contract or to claim damages.[1] As between Robert and his bank the bank are not affected by any breach of contract on the part of the seller. It follows that Robert will have to continue to repay the loan and his sole remedy is against the seller. If he cannot afford the repayments his sole right as against the bank is to wait for a notice of default[2] or for proceedings to enforce the loan agreement and then apply to the court for a time order.[3]

2. Cash Sale—Connected Lender

Let us now suppose that the seller introduces Robert to a finance company **23.03**

---

[1] Above, paras 7.02–7.09.
[2] Below, para. 25.04.
[3] *ibid.*

with whom the seller has arrangements. The finance company makes a loan to Robert to finance the sale. This is a three-party debtor-creditor-supplier agreement. As between Robert and the seller, the position is exactly the same as in the previous example. As regards the position between Robert and the finance company there are two overlapping provisions of considerable practical importance which may enable Robert to hold the finance company responsible for the seller's default.

Section 56

23.04   The first provision is section 56 of the Consumer Credit Act which applies (*inter alia*) to antecedent negotiations with the debtor conducted by the supplier in relation to a transaction financed by a debtor-creditor-supplier agreement.[4] The key provision is section 56(2) which reads as follows:

> Negotiations with the debtor ... shall be deemed to be conducted by the negotiator in the capacity of agent of the creditor as well as in his actual capacity.

In other words, if the seller made a misrepresentation (*e.g.* as to credit terms or the quality of the goods), he will have made it as *agent* for the finance company. Thus Robert could bring proceedings against the finance company, or he could merely discontinue his payments, wait to be sued and then counterclaim. It remains to add that section 56(3) makes void a clause (a) purporting to make the negotiator the agent of the dealer, or (b) relieving a person from liability for acts or omissions of any person acting as, or on behalf of, a negotiator. This raises a problem in relation to a clause in a contract between creditor and debtor excluding liability for all misrepresentations, including those made by the dealer. Would such a clause automatically be void under section 56(3) or would it still be subject to the reasonableness test under section 3 of the Misrepresentation Act 1967?[5] It is felt that a carefully drafted clause should be given the latter construction—it would seem strange that the creditor should be in a worse position merely because the misrepresentation was made by the dealer rather than by the creditor himself or by some other agent.

Section 56 can be regarded as an exception to the general rule that the dealer is not an agent of the creditor—even if he carries stock of the creditor's finance application forms.[5a] It should also be noted that section 56 is not limited to defects in the goods but applies to all negotiations. Suppose that H takes a car on hire-purchase from F1. Before completing his payments he takes it to a dealer D and agrees to "sell" it to D in part exchange for another car owned by D. D sells the new car to a linked finance company F2 who then

---

[4] s.56(1)(c).

[5] As redrafted by s.8 of the Unfair Contract Terms Act 1977, above, para. 8.33.

[5a] The leading case is *Branwhite v. Worcester Works Finance Co.* [1969] 1 A.C. 552. See also *Woodchester Equipment (Leasing) Ltd v. British Association of Canned and Preserved Food Importers and Distributors* [1995] C.C.L.R. 51, CA.

let it out to H. D promises H to pay off the balance owing to F1 but fails to do so and becomes insolvent. By section 56 the promise by D was made as agent of F2; accordingly if F1 sues he can claim an indemnity from F2.[5b]

Section 75

The second provision affecting three-party debtor-creditor-supplier agreements is section 75. In this situation it is provided that: **23.05**

> (1) if the debtor ... has ... any claim against the supplier in respect of a misrepresentation or breach of contract, he shall have a like claim against the creditor, who, with the supplier, shall accordingly be jointly and severally liable to the debtor.

Subsection (3)[6] lays down two limitations.

> Subsection (1) does not apply to a claim—
> (a) under a non-commercial agreement, or
> (b) so far as the claim relates to any single item to which the supplier has attached a cash price[7] not exceeding £100 or more than £30,000.

As already stated there is substantial overlap between sections 56 and 75. If the "negotiator" makes a misrepresentation, the buyer/borrower may well have a claim against the creditor under either section. In two respects, however, section 56 is wider; it is not limited to three-party D-C-S agreements and it is not subject to the section 75 upper and lower limits.[8]

The real importance of section 75(1) lies in the words "or breach of contract". It means that the creditor will be liable not merely for the misrepresentation or for breach of express terms but also for breach of the *implied* terms, *e.g.* under the Sale of Goods Act 1979.[9] This seems reasonable enough; finance companies who finance the transaction by letting the goods out on hire-purchase have been responsible for the quality of the goods ever since 1938. The effect of section 75 is to place them in basically the same position if they choose to finance the transaction by means of a loan. From the debtor's point of view the effect of section 75 can be very favourable. In an extreme case he might have a claim against a solvent finance company whereas a person buying with his own money, or with money borrowed from an unconnected lender, might only have had a claim against an insolvent seller. It will be appreciated that the amount of the claim can be far greater than the amount of the credit.

[5b] *Forthright Finance v. Ingate* [1997] C.C.L.R. 95, CA.
[6] As amended by the Consumer Credit (Increase of Monetary Limits) Order 1983 (S.I. 1983 No. 1878).
[7] This is the *cash* price of the item, *not* the credit advanced.
[8] See above.
[9] See above, Chaps. 3 and 4.

Unless the supplier is insolvent, the creditor will not be saddled with ultimate liability, for as between creditor and supplier the creditor is entitled to join the supplier as a party to the proceedings and to claim an indemnity from him.[10]

Credit cards

23.06   In the example above[11] we took the case of a car buyer, dealer and connected lender. Another situation where section 75 is highly relevant is in relation to buyer, credit card company and approved supplier. If goods bought with a credit card prove to be defective and cause enormous damage (*e.g.* death or personal injury), the buyer (or his personal representatives) will have a claim against the credit card company for the full amount of the damage.

The precise legal effect of a renewable credit card still remains to be decided—is it a standing offer or a single contract or a new contract at each renewal?[12] One further point has recently been decided: a credit card payment by the consumer gives him an absolute discharge and he cannot be made to pay again if the credit card company becomes insolvent before it has paid the retailer.[13]

As a modern example of section 75 in operation, many holiday-makers used Access and Barclaycard to book holidays with tour operators which went into liquidation before the holidays had been completed. The credit card companies have been resisting section 75 claims against them on the ground that the holiday-makers should look to the special fund set up by the tour operators. Similarly a buyer placing a deposit when ordering, say, furniture, curtains or domestic electrical equipment would be well advised to pay by credit card; then if the retailer goes bust, the buyer can recover the deposit from the credit card company. Problems may arise when booking a package holiday through a travel agent. The OFT takes the view in its paper *Connected Lender Liability* (March 1994) that section 75 will apply even though the payment is made directly to the travel agent, where he is acting as agent for the tour operator.[13a] While we support this view, we urge consumers to pay the tour operator itself; without doubt the tour operator will then be "the supplier" within the meaning of section 75(1).

As part of an aggressive sales campaign a creditor card company C2 may persuade a customer of C1 to surrender his and take a C2 card instead. This can raise a problem of timing. Consider the following scenario:

---

[10] s.75(2) and (5).
[11] Above, para. 23.03.
[12] We prefer the third view.
[13] *Re Charge Card Services* [1988] 3 W.L.R. 764.
[13a] He usually is: see above, para. 10.48.

January	consumer with card company X orders goods and pays by card
February	consumer switches to card company Y
March	the goods are delivered and are defective

On these facts, some companies in the position of X are refusing to pay a section 75 claim (see para. 23.05 above) on the ground that the card has been surrendered. We believe that this argument can be successfully attacked; the use of the X card in January crystallised a potential claim against that company.

A related matter is the use of a credit card abroad. Here again we agree with the OFT that section 75 applies to overseas transactions by a U.K.-based cardholder.[13b]

Some further points on section 75

Clearly section 75 is of great importance to consumers (even though in 1983 the lower cash limit in section 75(3) was raised from £30 to £100—thereby taking many credit transactions outside the section 75 protection). It must however be appreciated that section 75 can only be used by the consumer if the relevant credit agreement was a "regulated agreement" (above, para. 19.02). If, for example, he books a holiday and pays with his American Express or Diner's Club charge card, the credit agreement is within the "single repayment" exemption (above, para. 19(10) subpara. (6)); accordingly it is not a regulated agreement and section 75 will not help the consumer.   **23.07**

It is also important to note that a consumer who has a claim against the supplier has "a like claim" against the creditor. In a Scottish case[14] it was held that a breach of the sale contract gave the consumer a right to rescind not only that contract but also the connected loan contract. It is thought that this reasoning cannot be correct since the two claims are not identical. The court could have reached the same (and correct) result by a different route—namely to allow the consumer to sue the supplier and the creditor for the return of the price of the goods which he had rejected.

3. CREDIT SALE AND CONDITIONAL SALE

A dealer may sell goods and allow the customer to pay by instalments. If nothing is said about the passing of property, it will pass as soon as the con-   **23.08**

[13b] *Connected Lender Liability*, pp. 26–28. See also *Connected Lender Liability—A Second Report* (OFT, May 1995).
[14] *U.D.T. v. Taylor* (1980) S.L.T. 18.

tract is made[15] and the sale will be a credit sale. If, however, the passing of property is postponed it will be a conditional sale.[16] In either case the obligations of the seller with regard to the goods are to be found in the Sale of Goods Act 1979 (as amended). It will be recalled that a notification of purpose to a credit-broker will be as effective as if it had been notified to the seller (see above, para. 4.24).

There are just three further points. First, the relevant provisions of the Sale of Goods Act apply even though the agreement is outside the Consumer Credit Act (*e.g.* because it is a debtor-creditor-supplier agreement with four or fewer instalments). Secondly, a trader who buys goods on credit for his trade will not be "dealing as consumer" and therefore an exemption clause which satisfies the reasonableness test will be binding on him. Thirdly, section 11(4) of the Sale of Goods Act (above, para. 7.19) does not apply to a "consumer" conditional sale agreement.

4. Hire-Purchase

23.09 In the case of a hire-purchase agreement (*whether or not it is regulated* by the Consumer Credit Act) the implied obligations with regard to the goods are contained in sections 8 to 11 of the Supply of Goods (Implied Terms) Act 1973 as redrafted by the Consumer Credit Act 1974[17] and by the Sale and Supply of Goods Act 1994.[18] The terms are virtually identical to those for the sale of goods and they include notification of purpose to a credit-broker.[19]

In practice, the dealer will frequently sell the goods to the finance company, which will then let the goods out on hire-purchase. If the hire-purchase agreement is a regulated agreement the dealer will be a "credit-broker" or "negotiator" and section 56[20] will apply. In other words, any representations made by the dealer are treated as made as agent for the finance company as well as in his personal capacity. Thus, the debtor has two concurrent remedies; he can bring a claim against the finance company which is bound by the dealer's representations. He can also bring a claim against the dealer, either in negligence[21] or on the basis of a collateral contract.[22]

---

[15] Above, para. 6.19.
[16] Above, para. 18.05.
[17] Above, paras 2.14, 3.13 and 4.27.
[18] Above, para. 4.18.
[19] Above, para. 4.27.
[20] Above, para. 23.04.
[21] *Hedley Byrne & Co. Ltd v. Heller and Partners Ltd*, above, para. 3.15. There can also be liability without any statement under the general law of negligence which was discussed in Chap. 5.
[22] *Andrews v. Hopkinson* [1957] 1 Q.B. 229. The dealer was also liable in negligence. See above, n. 21.

5. HIRE

The statutory implied terms have already been considered[23] and the law is not **23.10** affected in any way by the Consumer Credit Act. Section 56[24] does not apply and there is no rule of law that the dealer is to be regarded as the agent of the finance company; in many cases this will not be so. If, however, the documentation used by the finance company misleads a consumer into thinking that he is dealing with the dealer, the finance company may be estopped from denying that the dealer's sales staff had authority to speak on its behalf. In such a case statements made by the sales staff will bind the finance company.[25]

[23] Above, para. 4.29. See also Law Commission Report No. 95.
[24] Above, para. 23.04.
[25] *Lease Management Services v. Purnell Secretarial Services, Canon (South West) Third Party, The Times*, April 1, 1994, CA.

CHAPTER TWENTY-FOUR

"I HAVE LOST MY CREDIT CARD"

The credit token, and especially the credit card, is of great importance as a **24.01** form of consumer credit and the 1974 Act brings them within the ambit of control.

The Act contains a number of provisions relating to "credit tokens" and "credit token agreements" and these provisions will be considered in this chapter.

What is a credit token?

The term is defined in section 14(1) as a card, check, voucher, coupon, **24.02** stamp, form, booklet or other document or thing given to an individual by a person carrying on a consumer credit business who undertakes:

(a) that on production of it (whether or not some other action is also required) he will supply cash, goods and services (or any of them) on credit, or

(b) that where, on the production of it to a third party (whether or not any other action is also required), the third party supplies cash, goods and services (or any of them), he will pay the third party for them (whether or not deducting any discount or commission) in return for payment to him by the individual.

Thus the term clearly includes credit cards and trading checks used in a form of credit known as "check trading". It does *not* include a cheque card, because the bank issuing a cheque card merely promises to honour cheques. Debit or switch cards fall outside the term, as the bank does not provide any credit. Nor does it cover trading stamps or free gift vouchers (*e.g.* on the back of a cereal packet), because the customer will not receive goods *on credit*.

Unsolicited credit tokens

The mass-mailing of Access cards provoked widespread criticism and **24.03** now section 51 makes it an offence to give a person a credit token if he has not asked for it. The request must be in writing and signed by the person making it, unless (a) the credit token agreement is a small debtor-creditor-supplier agreement, or (b) the card is renewed.

What is a credit token agreement?

By section 14(2) (read with section 189) it is a regulated consumer credit **24.04** agreement for the provision of credit in connection with the use of a credit token. Thus the term will not apply to an agreement where (a) the credit exceeds the statutory ceiling, (b) the debtor is a body corporate, or (c) the agreement is exempt. It will be recalled that agreements involving the use of Diner's Club or American Express cards are exempt agreements, because they are debtor-creditor-supplier agreements for running-account credit and the indebtedness over a period has to be discharged by a single payment.[1]

Modification of formalities

24.05   The formalities required for a regulated agreement were considered in Chapter 20. They are modified in two minor respects in the case of a credit token agreement. The first relates to the sending of the second copy; by section 63(4) it need not be given within seven days following the making of the agreement if it is given before or at the time when the credit token is given to the debtor. The second relates to the notice setting out cancellation rights; by section 64(2) it need not be posted within seven days following the making of the agreement if it is posted to the debtor before the credit token is given to him, or if it is sent by post with the credit token.

Additional copies

24.06   Where, under the credit token agreement, the creditor issues a new token to the debtor he must at the same time give the debtor a copy of the executed agreement (if any) and of any document referred to in it. Failure to do so has the usual consequences, *i.e.* the creditor cannot enforce the agreement while the default continues and, if it continues for one month, he commits an offence.[2] The section does not apply to a small agreement.[3]

Liability of debtor

24.07   We come now to the problem which is likely to be the most troublesome one in practice—the extent of the debtor's liability if the token is used by someone else without the debtor's authority. This matter is primarily governed by sections 66 and 84. By section 66 the debtor under a credit token agreement is not liable for use made of the token by another person unless (a) the debtor had previously accepted the token, or (b) its use constituted an acceptance by him. The debtor accepts a credit token when he or a person authorised by him to use it under the terms of the agreement:

(a) signs it, or
(b) signs a receipt for it, or
(c) uses it.

---

[1] Above, para. 19.10 subpara. (6).
[2] s.85.
[3] *ibid.*

If the token has been accepted under section 66 we can turn to section 84 to consider the debtor's liability for its misuse by someone else. The provisions of this section can be summarised as follows:

(1) The underlying principle is that the debtor should give notice of the loss or misuse as soon as possible. Accordingly, the credit token agreement must contain, in the prescribed manner,[4] particulars of the name, address and telephone number of a person to whom notice of loss, etc., can be given. If the agreement does not contain this information the debtor will not be liable for misuse at all.[5]

(2) The debtor is not liable for any loss arising after the creditor has been given written or oral notice that the token has been lost or stolen or is otherwise liable to misuse.[6] The notice takes effect when received, but if it is given orally the agreement may provide that it is not effective unless confirmed in writing within seven days.[7]

(3) Subject to (1) and (2) above, the debtor's liability depends on the person by whom the token was misused. If it was misused by a person who acquired possession of the token with the debtor's consent, he is liable *without limit*.[8] In other cases (*e.g.* loss or theft) his liability is limited to £50,[9] or the credit limit if lower, for misuse in a period beginning when the token ceased to be in the possession of an authorised person and ending when the token is once again in the possession of an authorised person.[10]

Thus the moral is clear: the onus is on the debtor to notify the loss to the creditor without delay.

Cancellation

If the debtor cancels a credit token agreement he can only recover a sum paid for the token, and he will only cease to be liable for such a sum, if the token has been returned to the creditor or surrendered to a supplier.[11]   **24.08**

Some further points on misuse

There has been massive publicity concerning the enormous losses sustained by credit card companies through credit card frauds—although   **24.09**

---

[4] *i.e.* prominently and so as to be easily legible (see Consumer Credit (Credit-Token Agreements) Regulations 1983 (S.I. 1983 No. 1555), reg. 2).
[5] s.84(4).
[6] s.84(3).
[7] s.84(5).
[8] s.84(2).
[9] See S.I. 1983 No. 1571; the limit was formerly £30.
[10] s.84(1).
[11] s.70(5).

the companies have largely themselves to blame by agreeing to honour transactions where goods are ordered over the telephone without a signature by the customer. Consumers are urged to be very wary in giving their card number over the telephone. In any event the consumer should always check his statement carefully and immediately report any unauthorised transactions.

CHAPTER TWENTY-FIVE

"I CAN'T AFFORD TO PAY"

In practice there are two main areas where a debtor is likely to seek legal **25.01** advice. The first is where he is dissatisfied with the goods. This has been considered in Part I of this book and in Chapter 22. The second is where, for one reason or another, he finds himself in difficulties with his payments. The legal adviser can approach the problem by asking a number of preliminary questions:

(1) Is there a contract at all?

If, for example, the document signed by the debtor was merely an offer, revocation is possible before it has been accepted.[1]

(2) Is the contract voidable for misrepresentation?

If so, it can be rescinded, and money recovered, if it is not too late.[2]

(3) Has the debtor a claim for breach of contract against the creditor?

If so, he may be able to treat the contract as repudiated, or he may have a claim for damages which he can set against the instalments.[3]

(4) Is the agreement cancellable?

If so, the debtor may be able to serve a notice of cancellation under provisions which have already been discussed.[4]

(5) Was the agreement "improperly executed"?

We have seen that if the creditor fails to comply with the statutory formalities as to contents, signature and copies (and pre-contractual reflection in certain land mortgage cases) the agreement can only be enforced against the debtor or hirer on an order of the court[5] or with the consent of the debtor or hirer given at the time.[6]

---

[1] See also s.57, above, para. 22.02.
[2] See above, paras 7.02–7.09.
[3] Above, paras 7.31–7.41 and 23.03–23.07.
[4] Above, para. 22.04.
[5] s.65.
[6] s.173(3).

One of the features of the legislation is the very wide power given to the court to rewrite the agreement or to postpone its enforcement. If the creditor or owner brings proceedings for an enforcement order, the court must consider the degree of culpability for the defect and the prejudice (if any) which it has caused to any person.[7] The court can then do any of the following things:

(a) it may make an enforcement order;
(b) it may make a "time order" under section 129[8];
(c) it may modify the agreement as set out below and then make an enforcement order relating to the agreement as modified; or
(d) it may dismiss the application—but only if it considers it just to do so having regard to the matters mentioned above.[9]

There are, however, three cases where an enforcement order *cannot* be made and these are considered below.

Power to modify agreement

25.02   Section 127(2) provides that:

> If it appears to the court just to do so, it may in an enforcement order reduce or discharge any sum payable by the debtor or hirer or any surety, so as to compensate him for prejudice suffered as a result of the contravention in question.

We must also consider sections 135 and 136 which are not confined to proceedings for an enforcement order but apply to any order made by the court in relation to a regulated agreement. By section 135(1) an order may include a provision:

(a) making the operation of any term of the order conditional on the doing of specified acts by any party to the proceedings;
(b) suspending the operation of any term of the order either—
     (i) until such time as the court subsequently directs, or
     (ii) until the occurrence of a specified act or omission.

Section 136 gives the Court a wide power to alter the agreement in consequence of a term of an order made under the Act. This can include a reduction in the rate of interest.[9a]

These very wide powers cannot be used to suspend an order requiring a person to deliver up goods unless the court is satisfied that they are in that person's possession or control.[10] In the case of a consumer hire agreement the section cannot be used to extend the period for which the hirer is entitled to possession.[11]

---

[7] s.127(1).
[8] Below, para. 25.04.
[9] s.127(1).
[9a] *Southern and District Finance Plc v. Barnes, The Times*, April 19, 1995, CA.
[10] s.135(2).
[11] s.135(3).

We must also mention certain special powers available to the court in the case of hire-purchase and conditional sale agreements. These are considered later.[12]

Finally, the court has a general power under section 136 to amend any agreement or security in consequence of a term of the order.

The cases show that, as forecast in the Third Edition of this book, these wide powers will only be exercised if the court feels that the debtor or hirer has been prejudiced by the failure to comply with the formalities. If the breach is only a technical one (*e.g.* the second copy sent a few days late) the court is likely to waive the breach entirely.[13]

Three special cases

There are, however, three cases where the court has *no* power to make an enforcement order at all. In these cases the fortunate debtor or hirer can retain possession and cannot be sued for any instalments or other payments. These three cases are dealt with in sections 127(3) and (4) and can be summarised as follows:

25.03

(a) If the agreement was not signed as required by section 61(1)(a) no enforcement order can be made, unless some other document, containing all the prescribed terms (above, para. 21.05), was signed by the debtor or hirer (whether or not in the prescribed manner).

(b) In a cancellation case the court cannot make an enforcement order if sections 62 or 63 (copy provisions) are not complied with, and if the creditor or owner did not give a copy of the executed agreement (and of any other document referred to in it) to the debtor or hirer before the commencement of the proceedings.

(c) The court cannot make an enforcement order in a cancellation case if the provisions of section 64(1) were not complied with. It will be recalled that section 64(1) deals with the duty to include cancellation information in the copies, and also in certain cases requires a notice to be posted to the debtor or hirer within seven days of the making of the agreement.[13a]

In the case of contravention the debtor or hirer may sometimes have a double right—the agreement cannot be enforced against him and (if the defect relates to the second copy or notice) it may well be that the right of cancellation remains open.

---

[12] Below, paras 25.08 and 25.10.
[13] See *Nissan Finance U.K. v. Lockhart* [1993] C.C.L.R. 39, CA, and contrast *National Guardian Mortgage Corporation v. Wilkes* [1993] C.C.L.R. 1: failure to supply the section 58 pre-contract copy (above, para. 21.04); prejudice to borrower; court reduced interest by 40 per cent.
[13a] For a recent case where an agreement was unenforceable for this reason see *Moorgate Services Ltd v. Kabir, The Times*, April 25, 1995, CA.

What happens if the creditor or owner purports to terminate the agreement and repossesses the goods? If it involves entry on premises without the consent of the debtor or hirer there may be liability for breach of statutory duty.[14] Apart from this there may be very little that the debtor or hirer can do about it, because of the "no sanctions" rule in section 170.[15] The section does not however prevent the grant of an injunction[16] and it is just possible that a mandatory injunction could require the goods to be returned to the debtor or hirer. Apart from this, the only sanction is the ever-present administrative sanction of reporting the matter to the Director General of Fair Trading.

Despite the unenforceability of the agreement for defective formalities (see above) there is no doubt that the creditor or owner can sue the debtor or hirer in tort if, for example, the debtor or hirer wrongly disposes of the goods.[17] Similarly the sanction of not allowing enforcement of "the agreement" would not apply where, for example, the agreement has expired by effluxion of time so that the creditor or owner has a common law right to repossess which he can, it is thought, enforce by action.

In this Chapter and elsewhere in Part IV of this book there are numerous references to "the court". By section 141 any action by the creditor to enforce a regulated agreement must be brought in the County Court. An attempt to gain an advantage by starting in the High Court may be struck out as an abuse of process.[17a]

(6) Can the debtor terminate the agreement?

25.04   This has already been considered. See above, para. 22.13.

(7) Can the debtor pay off early and obtain a rebate?

The debtor may be able to find another source of credit which is less expensive to him. In the case of hire-purchase the debtor may be better advised to settle early, become the owner of the goods and re-sell them.[18] Section 94 gives the debtor a non-excludable right to complete the agreement ahead of time on service of a notice on the creditor and on payment of all sums due, less any statutory rebate of the charge for credit.[19]

In calculating the total charge for credit the critical factor is the time during which the creditor will be kept out of his money. Accordingly, it is clearly reasonable to allow for a rebate where the debtor pays off early, because the

---

[14] s.92(3), below, para. 25.09.
[15] Above, para. 18.03.
[16] s.170(3).
[17] See *Eastern Distributors Ltd v. Goldring* [1957] 2 Q.B. 600.
[17a] *Barclays Bank v. Brooks* [1997] C.C.L.R. 60, QBD.
[18] If the finance company gives an incorrect settlement figure, it may be estopped from claiming the true amount due if their mistake has caused the hirer to alter his position: *Lombard North Central v. Stobart* [1990] Consumer Credit Law Reports 53, CA.
[19] Where sums are due from a debtor who has made only a partial early payment, the creditor can get judgment for the (unrebated) sum due; but the debtor can claim the rebate when satisfying the judgment: *Forward Trust Ltd v. Whymark* [1990] 2 Q.B. 670, CA.

creditor will be able to earn fresh interest on the repaid amount. Section 95 enables regulations to be made for the calculation of this rebate, which will apply in any case of early settlement—whether by reason of re-financing, breach or for any other reason. How then is the rebate to be calculated? Three points must be borne in mind:

(a) the total charge for credit should be spread actuarially over the repayment period and the debtor should get a rebate corresponding to the proportion of the total charge for credit which would have accrued after the settlement date;

(b) where capital is being constantly repaid (as in the case of mortgages and hire-purchase agreements) the proportion will reflect the fact that the interest payable at the beginning of the agreement is much greater than it is at a later stage when the outstanding capital is much lower;

(c) a completely even actuarial spread would be unfair to the creditor because certain expenses are incurred at the beginning of the transaction (legal fees, survey fees, stamp duty, etc.).

The Regulations (S.I. 1983 No. 1562) are exceedingly complex but they do reflect the principles set out above. Thus:

(1) The regulations seek to meet point (c) above by allowing the settlement date (on which the rebate calculation depends) to be notionally deferred. If the credit is repayable on, or at the end of, a period of more than five years the deferral is one month; if the period is five years or less the deferral is two months (see reg. 5 with reg. 6).

(2) The regulations also assist the creditor by allowing him to exclude from the rebate calculations (a) taxes and duties, and (b) sums payable or paid under a linked transaction.

The regulations contain no less than five formulae and the correct choice depends upon the contractual repayment provisions (lump sum repayment, repayment by equal instalments, repayment by unequal instalments, etc.) and upon the settlement arrangements. If, for example, the credit is repayable at equal intervals the amount of the deferred rebate (see above) is calculated by applying the so-called "rule of 78"; the name is derived from the fact that a loan for one year repayable with interest by equal monthly instalments can be said to represent a series of 12 (reducing) monthly loans and the total of the 12 months $(1 + 2 + 3 + 4 + 5 + 6 + 7 + 8 + 9 + 10 + 11 + 12)$ comes to 78.

Example (taken from the Regulations)

A loan of £1,000 is agreed to be repaid by 36 monthly instalments of £48 starting one month after the date of the loan. The consumer settles the loan at the end of the 30th month with 6 instalments still outstanding.

The statutory formula is $\dfrac{m\ (m\ +\ 1)}{n\ (n\ +\ 1)} \times k$

where m = the (deferred) number of future repayments,
  n = the total number of repayments, and
  k = the total charge for credit on which the rebate is to be allowed, *i.e.* (36 × £48) − £1000 = £728

The formula produces the following result:

$$\frac{4(4\ +\ 1)}{36(36\ +\ 1)} \times £728\ =\ £10.93\ \text{rebate}$$

If a debtor is contemplating making an early settlement, he can in writing ask the creditor to give him a statement containing the settlement figure.[20] If the creditor fails to comply within 12 working days the usual consequences will follow.[21]

The Office of Fair Trading is strongly critical of the Rule of 78 and has urged lenders to stop using it (Guidance Notes 1997 cited in the *Kidlance* case (para. 27.01 below)).

(8) Time orders

If the debtor or hirer is unable to withdraw, rescind, cancel, terminate or settle early, and if all the formalities have been complied with, the next possibility is to apply for a "time order". Apart from section 127[22] the debtor or hirer can apply for a time order (a) after he has been served with a notice of default,[23] or (b) where the creditor or owner brings proceedings to enforce a regulated agreement or any security or to recover possession of any goods or land to which a regulated agreement relates.[24]

In *Southern and District Finance v. Barnes*,[24a] which was reported as our previous edition went to press, the Court of Appeal laid down the following guidelines:

(1) The power to grant a time order only relates to "any sum owed"—but where a creditor brings a possession action the balance of the loan can be treated as "owed" and section 136 will apply to it.

(2) The court can only vary the terms of a regulated agreement under this section if:

---

[20] s.97. The contents of the statement and the calculation of the settlement date are contained in the Consumer Credit (Settlement Information) Regulations 1983 (S.I. 1983 No. 1564).
[21] See above, para. 21.02.
[22] Above, para. 25.01.
[23] See County Court (Amendment) Rules 1985 (S.I. 1985 No. 566), Ord. 49, r. 4(5).
[24] s.129. See *First National Bank v. Syed* [1991] C.C.L.R. 37, CA (debtor proposed instalments which would not even cover interest accruing; order refused).
[24a] [1995] C.C.L.R. 62, CA and see comment on p. 72.

(a) the proposed amendment is truly a consequence of the term of the order; and

(b) the making of the amendment is also just (see below).

(3) In any time order application the court must first consider whether it is just to make the order. This will involve a consideration of all the circumstances and the position of the creditor as well as that of the debtor.

(4) Any time order should normally be made for a stipulated period on account of temporary financial difficulty.

(5) The court must consider what instalments would be reasonable, both as regards amount and timing.

(6) If the rate of interest is altered, the court will bear in mind that (a) smaller instalments will result in a liability to pay interest on accumulated arrears and (b) the payment period will be extended.

(7) If the full amount is due, the order will clearly affect the term of the loan, or the rate of interest, or both.

(8) If justice requires the making of a time order, the court should suspend any possession order while the time order is complied with.

Notice of default

The agreement may provide that, on default by the debtor or hirer, the creditor or owner shall become entitled to take certain action, *e.g.* to terminate the agreement, or to demand early payment of any sum, or to recover possession of any goods or land, or to enforce any security, or to treat any right conferred on the debtor or hirer (*e.g.* an option to purchase in the case of a hire-purchase agreement) as terminated, restricted or deferred. The effect of section 87 is that such a provision will not be enforceable unless the creditor or owner first serves on the debtor or hirer a notice of default in the prescribed form.[25] The notice must contain the following information[26]:

25.05

(i) it must specify the breach;

(ii) if the breach is capable of remedy (*e.g.* default in payment) the notice must indicate what action has to be taken to remedy it and the date before which it must be done;

(iii) if the breach is incapable of remedy (*e.g.* causing permanent damage to the goods) what compensation (if any) is required and the date before which it is to be paid;

(iv) the consequences of non-compliance; and

(v) in appropriate cases the restrictions on the creditor's right to repossess "protected goods" (below, para. 25.10).

[25] See Consumer Credit (Enforcement Default and Termination Notices) Regulations 1983 (S.I. 1983 No. 1561). Note that if the notice claims a sum larger than the amount owed by the debtor or hirer the notice is invalid: *Woodchester Lease Management Services Ltd v. Swain & Co* [1999] 1 W.L.R. 263, CA.

[26] s.88.

The date in (ii) and (iii) above must be not earlier than seven days after the service of the notice of default. Presumably, if the notice is posted on February 1 it can specify February 8 as the date before which the act must be done.

Effect of notice

25.06   If, before the specified date the debtor or hirer takes the steps specified in the notice, the default is treated as never having taken place.[27] Alternatively, as already stated, the debtor or hirer can apply under section 129 for a "time order". Such an order may contain either or both of the following provisions:

   (a) a provision that any sum owed by the debtor or hirer or any surety shall be payable at such times as the court, having regard to the means of the debtor or hirer and any surety, considers reasonable;

   (b) a provision that a breach by the debtor or hirer (other than the non-payment of money) shall be remedied within such period as the court may specify.

Effect of repossession

25.07   The Act does not specify what remedies are available if the creditor or owner repossesses the goods or land without a default notice. The section provides that the creditor or owner is not *entitled* to repossess, etc., without serving a notice of default. It may well be, therefore, that non-compliance could be actionable as trespass to goods or conversion or there might be a breach of the implied warranty for quiet possession. There may also be liability for breach of statutory duty if there is unauthorised entry on premises[28] and the "snatch-back" of protected goods[29] will lead to the severe sanctions set out in section 91.[30]

(9) **Additional protection in hire-purchase and conditional sale cases**

The notice of default provisions are backed up by four other provisions aimed at what is known as "snatch-back"—the repossession of goods or land without an order of the court.

(a) *Entry on premises*

25.08   In the case of a regulated hire-purchase or conditional sale agreement the creditor or owner cannot enter any premises to repossess the goods without an order of the court.[31] Clearly, a contractual provision conferring such a right would be void[32] but a consent at the time of entry would be effective.[33]

---

[27] s.89.
[28] Below, para. 9(a).
[29] Below, para. 25.10.
[30] *ibid.*
[31] s.92(1).
[32] s.173(1).
[33] s.173(3).

(b) *Land*

If the debtor is in breach under a conditional sale agreement relating to land **25.09**
the creditor cannot recover possession of the land from the debtor, nor from
any person claiming under him, without an order of the court.[34] The point
relating to the debtor's consent will be equally relevant here.

In both (a) and (b) above section 92(3) does provide a sanction—any entry
in contravention of either of these provisions is actionable as a breach of
statutory duty.

(c) *Protected goods*

In the case of hire-purchase and conditional sale it is clearly inequitable **25.10**
that the debtor, having paid a substantial part of the price, should have the
goods snatched away (with no credit for his payments) merely because he
gets into arrears. Accordingly, section 90 gives him protection if (a) he is in
breach, (b) he has not terminated the agreement, (c) he has paid to the creditor
one-third or more of the total price and (d) the property in the goods remains
in the creditor. In such a case the goods are called "*protected goods*". The
creditor cannot recover possession of the goods from the debtor without an
order of the court.

These provisions are modelled upon the provisions in the Hire-Purchase
Act 1965 and both Acts impose serious sanctions for contravention. By section 91 if goods are recovered by the creditor in contravention of section 90
the agreement, if not already terminated, will terminate, the debtor is released
from all further liability and he can recover from the creditor all sums paid by
him under the agreement. A number of points arise under this very important
provision.

(i) Where the agreement requires the creditor to carry out any installation
work, and if the cost of this work forms part of the total price, then the fraction
of one-third is calculated by taking the installation charge in full and adding
one-third of the balance.[35] Thus, if the price of £300 includes an installation
charge of £30 the fraction of one-third will be:

$$£30 + \frac{270}{3} = £120$$

(ii) A dealer might be tempted to avoid the "protected goods" provisions in
one of two ways. First of all there might be an agreement for a television set
with a price of £150, of which £60 has been paid. If the customer then comes
in for a £300 music centre the dealer might say "let us cancel the original
agreement and make a new one for both items (£450) with a credit for sums
already paid (£60)." Secondly, if the original agreement (with payments
exceeding one-third) related to a tape recorder and a camera, he might sug-

---

[34] s.92(2).
[35] s.90(2). Similar to s.100(2), above, para. 22.14.

gest that the tape recorder should be treated as fully paid up and that a new agreement should be made relating solely to the camera. In either case the debtor starts inside section 90 and ends up outside it—because he has not paid one-third under the new agreement. To prevent such avoidance the effect of section 90(3) is to bring the new agreement within the section, even though one-third has not been paid.

Where the agreement provides that on default the hirer must pay default interest in addition to the hire-purchase price, the hire can appropriate any payment towards the price (so as to gain protection under section 90). If he fails to do so, the creditor can appropriate. In a recent case[35a] the creditor issued proceedings for possession and the summons showed that just over one-third of the price had been paid. He then sought to amend the summons by earmarking a small amount towards default interest. It was held that it was too late for him to do so.

(iii) Repossession of the goods from the debtor without a court order kills the agreement. Thus, on the one hand, the debtor cannot claim the return of the goods[36] while on the other hand the creditor cannot breathe any fresh life into the agreement by returning the goods to the debtor.[37]

(iv) Section 90 only prohibits recovery of possession "from the debtor". Thus, if the creditor seizes the goods which the debtor has abandoned the section is not infringed.[38] A similar principle would apply where the creditor seizes the goods from a third party to whom the debtor has purported to sell them.[39]

(v) A consent by the debtor given at the time is as effective as an order of the court[40] but the court is likely to examine the facts closely to make sure that there was a true and free consent.[41]

(vi) If the debtor chooses to terminate under section 99,[42] the goods are not protected.

(d) Relief against forfeiture

25.11   The court has a general power to grant relief against the forfeiture of a proprietary or possessory right (which could be relevant where, for example, the finance company sought to repossess after the debtor had paid most of the instalments). Such a power will only be exercised in exceptional circumstances.[43]

[35a] *Julian Hodge Bank Ltd v. Hall* [1998] C.C.L.R. 14.
[36] *Carr v. Broderick & Co. Ltd* [1942] 2 K.B. 275.
[37] *Capital Finance Co. Ltd v. Bray* [1964] 1 W.L.R. 323.
[38] *Bentinck Ltd v. Cromwell Engineering Co. Ltd* [1971] 1 Q.B. 324.
[39] Consider *Eastern Distributors Ltd v. Goldring* [1957] 2 Q.B. 600.
[40] s.173(3).
[41] The matter could be raised if the debtor took proceedings alleging a breach of section 90 and denying his consent to the repossession. See *Chartered Trust plc v. Pitcher* [1988] R.T.R. 72, CA.
[42] Above, para. 22.14.
[43] *Transag Haulage Ltd v. Leyland Daf* (1994) 13 Tr.L.R. 361.

(e) *Additional powers of the court*[44]

In any proceedings for an enforcement order, or for a time order, or in **25.12** proceedings by the creditor to recover possession, the court may (in addition to its other powers) make (i) a return order, or (ii) a transfer order.[45] A return order, as the name implies, requires the debtor to return the goods to the creditor. A transfer order is, in effect, a "split" order, in that it orders the debtor to return *some* of the goods to the creditor and it vests in the debtor the creditor's title in the remainder. This is subject to a ceiling set out in section 133(3), namely, that the maximum transferable to the debtor is found by deducting from the sum paid one-third of the unpaid balance. Thus, if the debtor had paid £80 out of a total price of £200, the court can vest in the debtor goods to the value of:

$$£80 - \left[\frac{200 - 80}{3} \right] = £40$$

In practice, the court frequently makes a return order and then exercises its powers under section 135 to suspend the operation of the order on condition that the debtor pays the balance by instalments fixed by the court.

(10) Additional protection in consumer hire cases

A number of provisions which are relevant to consumer hire have already been considered earlier in this chapter. They include section 65 (improperly executed agreements), section 87 (notice of default), section 92 (no entry on premises without court order) and section 129 (time orders). In addition section 132 provides that where the owner recovers possession otherwise than by action the hirer may apply to the court for an order (a) extinguishing any further liability to make payments in whole or in part, or (b) requiring the owner to repay sums paid by the hirer in whole or in part. The court can also include such a provision when it makes an order for delivery to the owner. Such a power could be exercised where, for example, the hirer has paid a year's rental in advance and then finds it necessary to terminate the hiring after only a few weeks or where the owner retakes the goods following the hirer's default.

A hirer can also argue, in appropriate cases, that the owner had no right to terminate at all. The right to terminate depends primarily on the terms of the contract; if the termination clause is very precise it may be construed as exhaustive and as excluding the general common law right to terminate if the hirer commits a repudiatory breach.[45a]

It will be recalled that the general power to make a "suspended" order

---

[44] The county court has exclusive jurisdiction over regulated agreements; see s.141 and *Sovereign Leasing v. Ali* [1992] C.C.L.R. 1 (transfer of action started in High Court).
[45] s.133.
[45a] *Eurocopy Rentals v. McCann Fordyce* [1995] C.C.L.R. 4.

under section 135 cannot extend the period for which the hirer is entitled to possession.[46]

(11) **Appropriation of payments**

A debtor or hirer may have two or more separate regulated agreements with the same creditor or owner. If he finds himself unable to pay a sum to cover all the sums due, he can send in a smaller amount and section 81 allows him, on making the payment, to appropriate it to one or more of the agreements in such proportions as he thinks fit. If he fails to appropriate at the time of payment, then section 81(2) may come into play. It provides that where one or more of the agreements is a hire-purchase, conditional sale, consumer hire or secured agreement, the payment shall be appropriated in the proportion which the sums *due* bear to each other.

Example

> £20 is due under a hire-purchase agreement relating to a dishwasher and £10 is due under a hire agreement relating to a television set. The debtor/hirer sends in a cheque for £12. If he fails to appropriate at the time of payment, £8 will go towards the dishwasher and £4 towards the television set.

Finally, if the debtor fails to appropriate in a case to which section 81(2) does *not* apply (*e.g.* if he has two debtor-creditor agreements with the same creditor) the general law will apply and the creditor will have the right of appropriation.

1. Extortionate Credit Bargains

25.13 The final weapon available to a debtor who finds himself unable to pay is to claim that the agreement is extortionate. The law is to be found in sections 137 to 140 of the Act.

Scope

25.14 These provisions are wider than most of the rest of the Act because they apply to a "credit bargain". This is defined as (a) an agreement whereby a creditor provides an individual (the debtor) with credit of *any amount*, plus (b) any other transactions which must be taken into account in computing the total charge for credit (*e.g.* a linked transaction). Thus these provisions will apply even though the credit exceeds the statutory ceiling and even though the agreement is an "exempt agreement". The only feature common to the whole Act is that the debtor must not be a body corporate.

What bargains are extortionate?

25.15 Section 138 provides that a bargain is extortionate if it requires the debtor

---

[46] Above, para. 25.02.

or a relative of his to make payments which are grossly exorbitant or otherwise grossly contravenes ordinary principles of fair dealing. The section then sets out a non-exhaustive list of relevant factors which include:

(a) prevailing interest rates at the time when the bargain was made[47];
(b) factors affecting the debtor such as age, health, business capacity and the extent to which he was under financial pressure;
(c) factors affecting the creditor, such as his relationship with the debtor and the degree of risk undertaken by him;
(d) the extent to which a linked transaction was reasonably required for the protection of the debtor or the creditor.

How and when can the matter be raised?

The debtor or a surety can take proceedings to have the bargain re-   **25.16**
opened[48]; in the case of a regulated agreement such proceedings must be brought in the county court.[49] Alternatively, the debtor or surety can raise the matter (a) in any proceedings to which the debtor and creditor are parties, being proceedings to enforce the agreement or any security or any linked transaction, or (b) in other proceedings where the amount paid or payable under the credit agreement is relevant. This could include bankruptcy proceedings, or proceedings where the debtor's wife brings a claim for financial provision, or where the judge investigates the means of the debtor as a preliminary to the enforcement of a judgment against him. Section 171(7) provides that if the debtor or surety alleges that the bargain is extortionate, the onus is on the creditor to prove that it is not. It is likely, however, that the court will require some evidence from the debtor or surety before putting the creditor to proof.

Powers of the court

The court has wide powers to (a) direct accounts to be taken, (b) set aside   **25.17**
obligations imposed on the debtor or a surety, (c) order sums to be repaid to the debtor or a surety, (d) order property given as security to be returned, and (e) re-write the terms of the agreement of any security instrument.[50]

Conclusion

A great deal will depend on how the courts will exercise these sweeping   **25.18**
new powers and how they will interpret the factors listed in section 138. What about the debtor who is old, ill, inexperienced and under great financial pressure from many sources? On the one hand the creditor must not take an unfair

---

[47] The court can rely on its own knowledge of prevailing interest rates even if no evidence is presented: *Castle Phillips Finance Co. Ltd v. Williams* [1986] C.C.L.R. 43.
[48] s.139(1).
[49] s.139(5).
[50] s.139(2).

advantage of such a person, and if he does so the courts may well treat the bargain as extortionate. On the other hand, the risk undertaken by the creditor in this type of case is unusually high and may well justify an interest rate which reflects this added risk.

Thus, in *Ketley v. Scott*[51] the lender agreed to lend £20,500 (with interest at a nominal rate of 48 per cent) to a prospective home buyer at a few hours' notice. Foster J. rejected the borrower's argument that the bargain was extortionate. A similar result was reached by the county court judge in another house-purchase case[52] involving APR of 29.5 and 31.25 per cent and material risk to the lender; the Court of Appeal refused to interfere. On the other hand in *Castle Phillips & Co. v. Wilkinson*[53] a lender who had ample security charged interest at more than three times the building society rate. The bargain was found to be extortionate and the interest rate was reduced.

[51] [1981] I.R.C. 241.
[52] *Leading Instrument Co. Ltd v. Parna*, unreported.
[53] [1992] C.C.L.R. 93.

Chapter Twenty-Six

"I WANT TO SEE MY CREDIT FILE"

At the beginning of Chapter 17 we drew attention to the explosion of credit **26.01** business. A credit transaction can, of course, cause problems at both ends. The consumer may overreach himself and may plunge into debt. The creditor may supply goods or services on credit terms and then suffer substantial financial loss if the consumer fails to pay the sums due.[1] To protect himself the creditor will frequently consult a credit reference agency[2] as to the financial standing of the prospective debtor. If the debtor then finds that his application for credit has been rejected, or has been granted on unfavourable terms, he may well suspect that the credit reference agency may have passed on unfavourable information. The Act, as originally drafted, contained provisions—which stand apart from the remaining provisions of the Act—giving the debtor a right:

(1) to ask for details of any credit reference agency consulted by the creditor or credit-broker;
(2) to obtain a copy of his file from the agency; and
(3) to have errors corrected.

The limited right to seek information from a credit reference agency (see (2) above) has been replaced by the much wider right of an individual to access personal data under the Data Protection Act 1998 which replaced, with substantial amendments, the Data Protection Act 1984. The 1998 Act (which was passed to give effect to an E.U. Directive) is not limited to computerised data; it also covers data which is "recorded as part of a relevant filing system"—a term which leaves considerable room for debate.

It is now proposed to conclude this Part of the book by looking briefly at the three matters listed above. It can be said at the outset that a company which keeps its own credit records of customers would not of itself be a credit reference agency; the reason is that the statutory controls only apply where the activities of the credit reference agency is carried on as a business (see s.145(8)).

---

[1] In many cases the creditor will take security from the debtor or from a third party and Pt. VIII of the Act contains provisions which regulate security arrangements. The term "security" includes a guarantee.
[2] Such an agency will require a licence under the Act—see s.145(1)(e).

Duty to disclose name and address of agency

26.02   The debtor or hirer can make a written request to the creditor, owner or negotiator asking for the name and address of any credit reference agency to which the creditor, owner or negotiator applied for information as to his financial standing at any time during the antecedent negotiations. The creditor, etc., must then give him notice containing this information within seven working days of receiving the request (see s.157(1) and the Consumer Credit (Credit Reference Agency) Regulations 1977, reg. 3).[3] The debtor or hirer must, however, act quickly because the duty to supply him with the information does not arise where his request is received more than 28 days after the end of the antecedent negotiations (whether on the making of the regulated agreement or otherwise).[4]

In practice the consumer will often be dealing with a credit-broker (as for example with a car dealer who arranges to finance the transaction through the creditor). Accordingly any request is likely to come from the consumer to the credit-broker. The regulations seek to ensure that the credit-broker will be able to pass on to the consumer the names of the agency or agencies consulted by the creditor as well as the agencies which he himself consulted. Accordingly, they provide that the creditor must give this information to the credit-broker not later than the date on which he informs him that he is not willing to make a regulated agreement.[5] The credit-broker must then include this information in the section 157 notice which he gives to the debtor or hirer.[6]

A creditor, owner or negotiator who fails to give the notice within the seven-day period commits an offence (see s.157(3)).

Duty on agency to disclose filed information

26.03   We have seen that the information rights of an individual are now to be found in the Data Protection Act 1998. Accordingly, section 158 now only applies to a "consumer" which is defined, for this purpose only, as a partnership or other unincorporated association. A consumer (see above) who suspects that a credit reference agency has information on him can make a written request for that information ("the file") together with a fee of £2. On receipt of the request and fee and such particulars as the agency may reasonably require to identify the file the agency must within seven days supply him with a copy of the file together with a statement in the prescribed form[7] informing him of his rights under section 159 (as to which see below). It may

---

[3] S.I. 1977 No. 329.
[4] See s.157(2).
[5] Consumer Credit (Conduct of Business) (Credit Reference Agencies) Regulations 1977 (S.I. 1977 No. 330), reg. 2.
[6] *ibid.* reg. 3.
[7] Consumer Credit (Credit Reference Agency) Regulations 1977 (S.I. 1977 No. 329), reg. 2 and Sched. 1.

well be that the file is not readily intelligible (perhaps because it is computerised). In any such case the consumer's right to a "copy of the file" is a right to a transcript reduced into plain English (see s.158(3)).

It may be of course that the agency has no file on the consumer; in that case they must give him notice of that fact but they need not return any fee paid (see s.158(3)).

An agency which contravenes any provision of section 158[8] commits an offence.

Rights of individual to obtain information

Under sections 7–9 of the 1998 Act an individual who makes a request in writing and pays the appropriate fee has the following rights: **26.04**

(1) The data controller must inform him or her whether any data relating to him or her is being processed.
(2) The data controller must also give a description of:
    (a) any relevant personal data;
    (b) the purposes for which it is being processed; and
    (c) the recipients or class of recipients to whom it is, or may be, disclosed.
(3) There must be communicated to him or her in intelligible form:
    (a) the information constituting the personal data; and
    (b) any information available to the data controller as to the source of that information.
(4) Where data is processed by automatic means to evaluate matters relating to him or her (*e.g.* reliability), and where this is the sole basis of any decision significantly affecting him or her (*e.g.* the grant or refusal of credit), the data controller must inform him or her as to the logic involved in that decision taking.

Where compliance with the request would involve information relating to a third party the controller can refuse to comply with that request unless (a) the third party consents or (b) it is reasonable to comply with that request even without such consent.

Where the data controller is a credit reference agency, section 9 provides that (a) the individual may limit the request to personal data relating to his or her financial standing (and the request is to be treated as limited in this way unless it shows a contrary intention) and (b) where the data controller is processing the data, the information must include a statement as to the rights available under section 159 (as to which see below).

Correction of wrong information

A consumer may realise that the information disclosed under section 158 **26.05**

[8] See also s.160 which lays down an alternative procedure for "business consumers".

(or under the 1998 Act) contains an entry which is incorrect—perhaps that he is an undischarged bankrupt or that he has an outstanding unsatisfied judgment against him. If the consumer considers that an entry is incorrect, and that he is likely to be prejudiced if it is not corrected, he may give notice to the agency requiring them to remove the offending entry or to amend it. The agency must then within 28 days send the consumer a notice stating that they have (a) removed the entry, (b) amended it, or (c) taken no action (see section 159(2)). In case (b) above the notice must include a copy of the amended entry (*ibid.*).

If the notice is given under (b) or (c) above (or is not given at all within the 28-day period) the consumer is given a further right under section 159(3). In any such case he can within 28 days serve a further notice on the agency requiring it (a) to add to the file an accompanying notice of correction, not exceeding 200 words, drawn up by himself, and (b) to include a copy of it when furnishing information included in or based on that entry. On receiving this further notice the agency has a choice. It can either (a) comply with it and inform the consumer that it has done so, or (b) it can apply to the Director General on the grounds that it would be improper for it to publish a notice of correction because it is incorrect or unjustly defames any person or is frivolous or scandalous or is for any other reason unsuitable (s.159(5)). Conversely, the consumer may apply to the Director General[9] on the ground that he has not received a correction notice within 28 days of requesting it (*ibid.*). The Director General after considering the relevant facts and the documentation[10] can make such order as he thinks fit.

The consumer may have one further problem; the correction of an erroneous entry may be all very well for the future but what about the past? What can be done to correct damage which he may already have suffered as the result of the erroneous information having been passed on to an enquirer? The regulations deal with this problem.[11] If the agency agrees to remove or amend an entry, or if it is ordered to do so by the Director General, the agency must notify each person to whom it furnished information relevant to the financial standing of the consumer at any time within six months before it received a section 158 request, particulars and fee (see above, para. 26.03). This must be done within 10 working days after the notice of removal or compliance or after the expiry of the compliance period specified by the Director General under section 159(5) (see above).

The section 159 rights summarized above are supplemented by further rights under the 1998 Act. Thus:

(1) Section 10 allows the individual to serve a notice on the data controller requiring him not to process (or to cease processing) any data on

---

[9] Form CC 314/77 must be used for such an application.
[10] See S.I. 1977 No. 329, reg. 4; the consumer must state why the information is false and why it is likely to prejudice him.
[11] S.I. 1977 No. 330, reg. 5.

the ground that it would cause him or her unwarranted damage or distress. The controller must then within 21 days give a written notice stating that (a) he has complied or intends to do so or (b) the extent to which he considers the request unjustified.

(2) By section 13 the individual can claim compensation for damage and distress (but not for distress on its own) if he or she suffers damage flowing from inaccuracy of the data or from unauthorised disclosure—subject in either case to a "reasonable care" defence.

(3) By section 14 the court can order rectification, erasure destruction and notification to third parties.

CHAPTER TWENTY-SEVEN

PROPOSALS FOR REFORM

In Chapter Twenty-Six of our fourth edition we dealt with an extensive report **27.01** from the Director-General of Fair Trading entitled Consumer Credit Deregulation which was published in June 1994. This contained a number of proposals for reform. The Report made 18 proposals for reform but, at the time of going to press with this fifth edition, only two have been implemented— abolishing the quotation regulations and raising the ceiling from £15,000 to £25,000. There are, however a number of further changes in the pipeline (many of them designed to assist consumers when they take out a mortgage).

The proposals include measures:

(1) requiring lenders to specify the way in which the APR for low start and discount mortgages is calculated, requiring it to refleot the interest and total charges throughout the entire life of the loan;

(2) implementing an E.U. Directive (98/7) which requires a single formula for calculating the APR across the European Union. This will enable consumers to easily compare the rates of United Kingdom lenders with those from countries such as France and Germany— (whether they will ever do this is more than doubtful);

(3) limiting the circumstances in which interest rates other than the APR can be shown in advertising and information material;

(4) requiring statutory warnings such as "your home is at risk if you do not keep up repayments on a mortgage or other loan secured on it" to be shown in all pre-contractual information on mortgage offers; and

(5) amending the Consumer Credit (Rebate on Early Settlement) Regulations by removing the so-called "rule of 78" method of calculation which has been described as unfair and oppressive as it can result in a borrower paying a disproportionately high sum to redeem a mortgage (this was one of the reasons why the redemption clause in *Kidlance Ltd v. Murphy* (para. 9.09 above) was held to be unfair).

In addition the DTI will consult on measures to (1) simplify the credit advertisement regulations and make them more sharply focused on requiring information and truthful advertising and (2) improving protection for vulnerable consumers who enter into extortionate credit agreements.

Chapter Twenty-Eight

THE EUROPEAN UNION DIMENSION

1. Introduction

In this chapter we shall deal only with the basis for European Union com-   **28.01**
petence in the field of consumer protection. Our discussion of particular
Directives that have already been implemented into United Kingdom law
appear in the relevant chapters elsewhere in the book.

For example, most of Chapter 5 is devoted to the Product Liability Directive and the related Consumer Protection Act 1987, Pt. I. Chapter 10 is dedi-
cated entirely to the Directive on Unfair Terms in Consumer Contracts and
the 1994 Regulations. Similarly the General Product Safety Directive and its
1994 Regulations are examined in Chapter 15.

Three important Directives, however, remain in the pipeline and must be
implemented and become part of United Kingdom law by January 1, 2002.
The Directive concerned with Distance Selling is dealt with earlier at
para. 10.22. An overview of the Directive concerned with Injunctions and the
Directive on Sale of Goods and Associated Guarantees is provided at the end
of this Chapter.

2. Treaties

To set the scene, the original EEC Treaty of Rome has been amended con-   **28.02**
siderably over the years, most importantly by the single European Act of
1987, the Maastricht Treaty on European Union of 1992 and, finally, by the
Treaty of Amsterdam of 1997.

As a result of the Treaty of Amsterdam, Articles for Treaty provisions
were re-numbered. The new numbering is referred to below but where appropriate reference is also made to the old number.

Article 2 of the Treaty sets out in very broad terms the objectives of the
Community—to treat the Member States as one single market and to promote
the development of economic activities subject to environmental
considerations:

> The Community shall have as its task, by establishing a common market and an
> economic and monetary union and by implementing common policies . . . to pro-

mote throughout the Community a harmonious and balanced and sustainable development of economic activities . . .

To achieve such objectives, Article 3 sets out various key activities of the Community. Article 3(h) specifies as one of these activities:

the approximation of the laws of Member States to the extent required for the proper functioning of the Common Market.

And a new Article 3(t) expressly refers to:

a contribution to the strengthening of consumer protection.

We see in Article 3(t) the first direct formal recognition of the importance of consumer protection. Before the Maastricht Treaty amendments, consumer protection initiatives were developed without a specific Treaty basis.

Institutional involvement

28.03   The original European Treaties established supra-national bodies to be involved in the workings of the European Community now referred to as the European Union. The following institutions are the most important ones from the viewpoint of consumer protection.

(i) *The Commission*

28.04   The Commission's role includes establishing E.U. wide policies and in that light to develop proposals for consideration by the legislative bodies of the E.U. Within the Commission, major subject areas for developing policy and proposals for legislation are allocated to separate units called Directorates-General. Consumer Policy and Consumer Health Protection was allocated its own Directorate-General (DGXXIV) in 1995 reflecting the increased importance of Consumer Affairs from the Commission perspective. The Commission consults widely before finalising proposals for legislation to present to the Council.[1]

(ii) *The Council (of Ministers)*

28.05   The Council is still the main legislative body, despite an increased role for the European Parliament. The Council usually acts on proposals from the Commission.[2] The Council issues Directives, instructions to Member States to legislate to achieve the parameters set out in the Directive. A time limit for

---

[1] For a full discussion of the role of the institutions, see Craig & de Burca, *E.U. Law* (1998), Chapters 2 and 3.
[2] See n. 1, above.

achieving the national legislation (either by means of primary or secondary legislation) is set out in the Directive.

Failure to comply fully by the due date may result in the Commission bringing an action against the defaulting Member State under Article 226 (formerly Article 169) before the European Court of Justice.

In future, compliance may also be achieved by the further development of *Francovich* damages.[3] Following the Francovich case and later case law, a Member State may be obliged to compensate any individual suffering loss as a result of a Member State's failure to implement or implement correctly a directive by the due date.

Treaty basis for Community action—Articles 94 and 308 (formerly Articles 100 and 235)

Articles 94 and 308 of the Treaty on European Union form the basis of   **28.06**
Community action in the area of consumer protection.

Article 94 reads:

> The Council shall, acting unanimously on a proposal from the Commission and after consulting the European Parliament and the Economic and Social Committee, issue directives for the approximation of such laws, regulations or administrative provisions of the Member States as directly affect the establishment or function of the common market.

Article 94 has been the mainstay of the Commission in its Treaty justification for intervention in the consumer protection area. It may seem strange that the Treaty did not contain a specific legal basis for consumer legislation, but it should be remembered that it was drafted at a time when the consumer movement in Europe was in its infancy. An example of Article 94 being used by way of justification is the Product Liability Directive mentioned above.

Article 308 can be brought into play where a proposal does not fit within the ambit of Article 94. Article 308 reads:

> If action by the Community should prove necessary to attain, in the course of the operation of the common market, one of the objectives of the Community and this Treaty has not provided the necessary powers, the Council shall, acting unanimously on a proposal from the Commission and after consulting the European Parliament, take the appropriate measures.

It can be seen that this wide-ranging provision gives the Council power to take measures to attain an objective where the Treaty does not contain the power elsewhere.[4] Article 308 was approved as an appropriate legal basis by

---

[3] See above, para. 9.03 and MacArthur & Wilson, "E.U. Law: Compensating Consumers" (1996) *Consumer Policy Review* Vol. 6, No. 4, pp. 145–148.

[4] See Close, "The Legal Basis for the Consumer Protection Programme of the EEC and Priorities for Action", in Woodroffe (ed.), *Consumer Law in the EEC* (1984), Chap. I, where Arts. 94 and 308 are discussed as bases for the Programme.

the Heads of State or of Government in 1972 when they gave the green light to the preparation of a consumer protection programme.

Article 94 provides the primary basis for the E.C. consumer protection policy, but has the drawback that directives must be adopted unanimously. (For this reason the Product Liability Directive took more than a decade to see the light of day.) A crucial change made by the Single European Act was to permit the adoption of a proposal by a "qualified majority". The amendment appears in Article 95 (formerly 100A).

Under the qualified majority procedure in the Council, the votes of Member States are weighted to reflect in part differences in their populations. The weighting ranges from 10 votes for each of the large Member States (Germany, France, Italy and the United Kingdom) to two votes for Luxembourg. The total number of votes is 87—a qualified majority in most cases will be achieved when 62 or more votes are obtained. This means that use of the qualified majority procedure can lead to the adoption of more controversial directives despite the opposition of one or more Member States. It should be noted that the Council is obliged, under Article 95, to consult the European Parliament and the Economic and Social Committee before adopting any proposal. Moreover, Article 95 contains an express reference to consumer protection and aims at "a high level of protection".

The importance of the qualified majority procedure can be gauged from the fact that the Directives on Unfair Terms in Consumer Contracts and on General Product Safety both relied on Article 95 as their justification.

The Consumer Protection Programmes and Action Plans

28.07   We have already commented upon the fact that in 1972 the Consumer Protection Programme was approved on the basis of Article 308. In the following year the Consumers' Consultative Committee was set up by a Commission Decision[5] which stated in its Preamble that close and continuous contact with consumer organisations at Community level could contribute to the achievement of the aims of the Treaty. In 1989 it was redefined and renamed the Consumers' Consultative Council[6] and in 1995 became the Consumer Committee.[7]

In 1975 the Commission drew up its first programme of measures for consumer protection and information.[8] In 1981 a second Consumer Protection Programme[9] was adopted which placed consumer interests in five basic groups of rights:

(1) the right of protection of consumers' health and safety;

---

[5] Dec. 73/306 [1973] O.J. L283/18.
[6] Dec. 90/55 O.J. 1990 L38/40.
[7] O.J. L162, July 3, 1995.
[8] [1975] O.J. C92/1.
[9] [1981] O.J. C133/1.

(2) the right of protection of their economic interests;
(3) the right of redress, help and assistance in judicial and para-judicial proceedings;
(4) the right to information and education;
(5) the right to be heard on matters affecting consumers' interests.[10]

A third programme, again resulting from a Council Resolution, followed in 1986. Although the 1975, 1981 and 1986 Resolutions on programmes for a consumer protection and information policy do not strictly form part of European law, as they fall outside the list of formal acts in Article 249 (formerly 189), they have been recognised by the European Court of Justice as part of the structure of European law and policy.[11]

The next steps were the publication by the Commission of "Three-Year Action Plans" of consumer policy in 1990 and 1993. The first[12] for 1990 to 1992 covered four main areas—consumer representation, information, safety and transactions. The second[13] for 1993 to 1995 focuses on distance selling, comparative advertising, time-shares, services,[14] implementation of the General Product Safety Directive,[15] labelling and an information system for home and leisure accidents (EHLASS).

Maastricht

The second Three-Year Action Plan states expressly that it "belongs in the **28.08** context of the Maastricht Treaty on European Union". The Treaty on European Union, signed at Maastricht in the Netherlands on February 7, 1992, inserted for the first time into the Treaty of Rome a separate Title XI, Consumer Protection. This was further amended by the Treaty of Amsterdam and now consists of Article 153 (formerly 129a):

(1) In order to promote the interests of consumers and to ensure a high level of consumer protection, the Community shall contribute to protecting the health, safety and economic interests of consumers, as well as to promoting their right to information, education and to organise themselves in order to safeguard their interests.
(2) Consumer protection requirements shall be taken into account in defining and implementing other Community policies and activities.

Article 153 also confirms the importance of Article 95 in the area of consumer protection.

[10] See Kraemer, "European Consumer Protection—A Progress Report," in Woodroffe, Chap. II (see n. 2).
[11] *GB-INNO v. CCL* Case C–362/88 [1990] E.C.R.I–667.
[12] COM(90)98.
[13] COM(93)378 final.
[14] This draft directive was dropped in 1994.
[15] Above, para. 15.22.

The Maastricht Treaty raises the status of consumer protection to that of an independent E.U. policy. In particular, Article 153 provides the basis for the development of consumer policies which do not have to be justified on the basis of harmonisation or market integration.

Post-Maastricht

28.09 Further Three-Year Action Plans have been published by the Commission since Maastricht came into force. The Plan[16] for 1996–8 outlined a broad range of priorities including enhanced consumer education, aspects of consumer financial services and better marketing and safety of foodstuffs. However, despite the long list of concerns, the Action Plan was notable for its lack of firm legislative initiatives.

The latest Action Plan[17] for 1999–2001 sets out three target objectives:— a more powerful voice for the consumer; a high level of health and safety for Europe's consumers; and full respect for the economic interests of E.U. consumers. Within these objectives, the Commission has committed itself, amongst other things, to update consumer credit legislation, to develop guidelines for food and product safety and to boost confidence in electronic means of payment.

General framework for E.U. activities in favour of consumers

28.10 Most recently, European consumer policy based on Article 153 was given a guaranteed long-term budget.[18] As a result, a financial allocation of ECU 114 million will be provided for the period 1999–2003. Four priority areas are singled out as eligible for financial support: consumer health and safety; protection of economic interests of consumers; education and information of consumers; and promotion and representation of their interests.

Legislative initiatives in the pipeline—an overview

(i) *Directive on Injunctions for the protection of the consumers' interests*

28.11 The Commission's determination to stamp out unlawful trading practices across the single market is reflected in the Directive on Injunctions which must be implemented by January 2001.

Essentially, the Directive requires Member States to ensure that means are available for an injunction to be sought within their national courts[19] to pre-

---

[16] COM(95)519.
[17] COM(98)696.
[18] O.J. L34 February 9, 1999.
[19] In some Member States this could be an administrative authority where such bodies are competent to grant injunctions.

vent an infringement of consumer protection laws harmonised under E.U. Directives.

Only qualified entities will be allowed to bring an action for an injunction. Under Article 3 this means any body or organisation with a legitimate interest in ensuring the consumer protection Directives are complied with. In the United Kingdom, the DTI is unlikely to take a narrow view and restrict this entitlement to the Director General of Fair Trading as has been the practice in the past.[20] A recent change of policy suggests that qualified entity status will be extended to a range of consumer bodies including private organisations such as the Consumers' Association.

Importantly, Article 4 provides that qualified entities from one Member State will have standing to bring an action for an injunction in another Member State. So if, for example English consumers were victims of unlawful timeshare practices in France, the Director General of Fair Trading (as a qualified entity) would be able to seek an injunction against the offending timeshare company in the French courts.

Under Article 2 the action for an injunction envisages an order requiring the infringement to stop and for appropriate publicity to be given to the decision. Moreover, the losing defendant is required to pay a penalty if the decision is not complied with within a time limit specified by the relevant court.

(ii) *Directive on the Sale of Consumer Goods and Associated Guarantees*

The main objective of the Directive on the Sale of Goods and Associated   **28.12** Guarantees is to introduce a minimum level of protection for consumers when something goes wrong with the goods they purchase in the E.U. This important harmonisation initiative must be implemented by January 1, 2002.

Article 2 provides that consumers should have the right to bring a claim against the seller if the goods supplied do not conform to the contract because they are not as described or not of satisfactory quality and fit for their purpose. These basic rights broadly mirror those which already exist under United Kingdom sale of goods law.[21]

Article 3 specifies, however, that the seller is responsible only for problems that come to light within two years of delivery (one year in the case of second-hand goods). In addition, a consumer with a claim must first ask for the goods to be repaired or replaced (remedies not formally known to United Kingdom consumer law). If this is impossible, or is disproportionate compared with other remedies, then a price reduction or a refund must be given.

In certain respects, the protection offered by the Directive is weaker than existing United Kingdom law. In particular, United Kingdom consumers have potentially six years (not two years as provided by the Directive) in

---

[20] See above, para. 9.03, for details of the DTI's approach to the enforcement of the Unfair Terms in Consumer Contracts Regulations.
[21] See above, paras 3.08–3.11, 4.18 and 4.20.

which to exercise their rights. Moreover, United Kingdom law provides for more extensive rights for consumers to reject the goods and claim a refund.[22] However, the Directive is intended as only a minimum harmonisation measure. Member States with higher levels of protection (such as the United Kingdom) are encouraged to maintain them in accordance with Article 7.

In other ways, though, the Directive improves legal rights for United Kingdom consumers. For example, if a fault arises during the first six months after purchase it is presumed to have existed at the time the goods were delivered. This effectively reverses the burden of proof and therefore makes it easier for consumers to prove their case against the seller. Also, any doubts that may have existed about the legal status of a manufacturer's guarantee[23] will be removed since Article 5 of the Directive requires that they become legally enforceable.

[22] See above, paras 7.12–7.30.
[23] See above, para. 5.03.

ADDRESSES OF TRADE ASSOCIATIONS SPONSORING CODES SUPPORTED BY THE OFT

Caravans   **A1.01**

British Holiday and Home Parks Association Ltd,
Chichester House,
Pullman Court,
Great Western Road,
Gloucester, GL1 3ND

National Caravan Council,
Catherine House,
Victoria Road,
Aldershot, GU11 1SS

Cars

Retail Motor Industry Federation Ltd,
201 Great Portland Street,
London, W1N 6AB

Society of Motor Manufacturers and Traders Limited,
Forbes House,
Halkin Street,
London, SW1X 7DS

Scottish Motor Trade Association Ltd,
3 Palmerston Place,
Edinburgh, EH12 5AF

The Vehicle Builders & Repairers Association,
Belmont House,
102 Finkle Lane,
Gildersome,
Leeds, LS27 7TW

British Vehicle Rental and Leasing Association,
River Lodge,
Badminton Court,
Amersham, HP7 0DD

Credit

Finance and Leasing Association,
Imperial House,
15–19 Kingsway,
London, WC2B 6UN

The Consumer Credit Trade Association,
Tennyson House,
159/163 Great Portland Street,
London, W1N 5FD

The Consumer Credit Association of the United Kingdom,
Queen's House,
Queen's Road,
Chester, CH1 3BQ

The National Consumer Credit Federation,
98/100 Holme Lane,
Sheffield, S6 4JW

London Personal Finance Association,
"Hill Top",
Berghers Hill,
Wooburn Common,
High Wycombe, HP10 0JP

Credit Services Association,
Ensign House,
56 Thorpe Road,
Norwich, NR1 1RY

Direct Marketing

Direct Marketing Association (UK) Ltd,
Haymarket House,
1 Oxendon Street,
London, SW1Y 4EE

Direct Selling

The Direct Selling Association Ltd,
29 Floral Street,
London, WC2E 9DB

Double Glazing

Glass and Glazing Federation,
44–48 Borough High Street,
London, SE1 1XB

Dry Cleaners and Laundries

Textile Services Association Ltd,
7 Churchill Court,
58 Station Road,
North Harrow, HA2 7SA

Electrical Goods

The Association of Manufacturers of Domestic Electrical Appliances,
40 Lambs Conduit Street,
London, WC1N 3NW

The Radio, Electrical and Television Retailers' Association
    (RETRA) Ltd,
RETRA House,
St John's Terrace,
1 Ampthill Street,
Bedford, MK42 9EY

British Retail Consortium,
5 Grafton Street,
London, W1X 3LB

Estate Agents

Incorporated Society of Valuers and Estate Agents,
3 Cadogan Gate,
London, SW1X 0AS

National Association of Estate Agents,
Arbon House,
21 Jury Street,
Warwick, CV34 4EB

Royal Institution of Chartered Surveyors,
12 Great George Street,
London, SW1P 3AD

Introduction Agencies

Association of British Introduction Agencies,
25 Abingdon Road,
London, W8 6AH

Mail Order

The Mail Order Traders' Association,
40 Waterloo Road,
Birkdale,
Southport, PR8 2NG

Motor Cycles

Motor Cycle Industry Association,
Starley House,
Eaton Road,
Coventry, CV1 2FH

Scottish Motor Trade Association Ltd,
3 Palmerston Place,
Edinburgh, EH12 5AF

Retail Motor Industry Federation Ltd,
201 Great Portland Street,
London, W1N 6AB

Photography

The National Pharmaceutical Association,
Mallinson House,
40–42 St Peter's Street,
St Albans,
Herts, AL1 3NP

Photo Marketing Association International (UK) Ltd,
Peel Place,
50 Carver Street,
Hockley,
Birmingham, B1 3AS

The British Institute of Professional Photography,
2 Amwell End,
Ware, SG12 9HN

Master Photographers Association (MPA),
Hallmark House,
2 Beaumont Street,
Darlington, DL1 5SZ

The Association of British Manufacturers of Photographic, Cine and
Audio-Visual Equipment,
1 West Ruislip Station,
West Ruislip, HA4 7DW

Professional Photographic Laboratories Association,
35 Chine Walk,
Ferndown, BH22 8PR

The British Photographic Association,
Ambassador House,
Brigstock Road,
Thornton Heath, CR7 7JG

The British Photographic Importers' Association,
Ambassador House,
Brigstock Road,
Thornton Heath, CR7 7JG

Shoes

The Footwear Distributor's Federation,
5 Grafton Street,
London, W1X 3LB

The Independent Footwear Retailers' Association
24 Fairburn Grove,
Chiswick,
London, W4 5EH

Instock Footwear Suppliers Association Ltd,
Marlone House,
Churchill Way,
Fleckney,
Leicester, LE8 0UD

The British Footwear Association,
5 Portland Place,
London, W1N 3AA

Tickets

The Society of Ticket Agents and Retailers,
PO Box 43,
London, WC2H 7LD

Travel

Association of British Travel Agents,
55–57 Newham Street,
London, W1P 4AH

Tyres

The National Tyre Distributors Association,
Elsinore House,
Buckingham Street,
Aylesbury, HP20 2NQ

THE FUNERAL OMBUDSMAN SCHEME

FUNERAL OMBUDSMAN'S TERMS OF REFERENCE

(1) The powers and duties of the Ombudsman shall be:
   (a) to receive complaints by or on behalf of any individual in relation to the provision of funerals, marketing, management and administration of funerals, funeral planning services or any other services incidental thereto;
   (b) subject to the following paragraphs, to investigate such complaints and facilitate their satisfaction, settlement or withdrawal by giving advice, conciliation, arbitration, adjudication or by any other means which may seem appropriate, including the making of recommendations and financial awards;
   (c) to establish satisfactory procedures for the investigation and resolution of complaints and to give advice on these procedures as appropriate; and
   (d) to produce an annual report to the Council.

(2) The Ombudsman shall have power to make an award against, or recommendation or representation to, any Member named in a complaint. In making a decision, the Ombudsman shall take into account the law, any relevant codes of practice and what would be fair and reasonable having regard to all the circumstances. Any decision of the Ombudsman shall bind both parties but only after it has been accepted in writing by the complainant.

(3) An award shall comprise a money sum of up to £50,000 which shall be binding on the Member once accepted by the complainant; (such awards may include compensation of up to £5,000 for aggravation, distress, inconvenience and expenses to the complainant where appropriate). Complaints involving sums in excess of £50,000 may be investigated by the Ombudsman, but any monetary sum in excess of the above limit shall not be binding on the Member, but shall constitute the Ombudsman's recommendation of a fair resolution of the complaint.

(4) Having made an award against a Member the Ombudsman may name or identify the Member and give details of the circumstances in which the award has been made in any publication provided consent for the Ombudsman to do so has been given in writing by the complainant.

(5) The Ombudsman has power to request the provision, within a reasonable period of time, of all information concerning the subject-matter of the complainant from the member and the complainant. If the member fails to reply to such request or admits possession of the information but refuses or fails to supply it within a reasonable period of time, the Ombudsman shall give particulars of such request and refusal to the Council, the Board, and any relevant trade or professional association.

(6) Subject to the supervision of the Council and to the extent that the Council shall determine, the Ombudsman shall be responsible for the day to day administration and conduct of the business of the Scheme.

(7) The Ombudsman shall have power to incur expenditure in accordance with the financial budget approved by the Board on a recommendation from the Council.

(8) In consultation with the Chairman of the Council and subject to his approval, the Ombudsman shall have the power to appoint and dismiss employees, consultants and independent advisers and to determine their duties, terms and conditions of employment or engagement.

(9) The Ombudsman shall not exercise any power which the Articles expressly assign to the Board, the Council or any other person.

(10) The Ombudsman shall endeavour to attend each meeting of the Council and shall give to the Council any information and assistance, including information about individual complaints and decisions, which it reasonably requests.

(11) Not less than 28 days before the annual meeting of the Council, the Ombudsman shall submit a report to the Council containing a general review of the performance of his functions during the year in question and such other information as the Council may reasonably direct. Once agreed, the Ombudsman shall supply copies of the annual report to each member of the Board.

(12) Subject to the approval of the Board and the Council, the Ombudsman shall have power to delegate to a deputy all or any of the powers and duties assigned to him and shall exercise such power if directed to do so by the Council with the approval of the Board.

Overlap with other schemes

(13) To the extent that a complaint relates to any matter other than the carrying on of a funeral business, where there exists another Scheme for the resolution of complaints in relation to such a matter (which, in the Ombudsman's opinion, provides protection for the complainant equivalent to that provided under the Scheme) the Ombudsman may refer, or advise the complainant to refer, to that other Scheme such part of the complaint as relates to such a matter provided always that

this shall not prevent the Ombudsman carrying out a joint investigation with another body where such procedure is considered expedient.

(14) To the extent that a complaint involving a Member relates to any matter other than the carrying out of a funeral business and there exists no equivalent system for resolving such complaints, the Ombudsman may investigate such part of the complaint as relates to the funeral business but only if the complainant and the Member agree.

(15) When a complaint, or part of a complaint, relates to any business in connection with which the Member is a member, or an appointed representative of a member, of a recognised self-regulatory organisation (as defined under the Financial Services Act 1986) or is otherwise authorised by the Securities and Investments Board, the Ombudsman shall refer the complaint, or advise the complainant to refer it, to the complaints body for the relevant self-regulatory organisation.

Conditions relating to the investigation

(16) The Ombudsman shall investigate any complaint by an individual against a funeral business which is a member of the Scheme provided the complaint falls within the scope of these Terms of Reference.

(17) The Ombudsman shall only consider, or continue to consider, a complaint if he is satisfied that:

(i) the complaint is made by, or on behalf of, an individual for whom the service was provided or intended to be provided, or the personal representatives of that individual;

(ii) the complaint has previously been considered by the director, named senior manager or internal complaints procedure of the Member and remains unresolved. If the complainant has not received and accepted any observations or offer of settlement within six weeks of reference to the Member, the Ombudsman may commence his investigation and

(iii) the complaint is made to the Ombudsman not later than six months after the later of (a) the date when the complainant received the final offer of settlement or observations from the Member or (b) the date on which the complainant received notification of his right to make a complaint to the Ombudsman provided such date falls within two years from the occurrence of the event giving rise to the complaint. The Ombudsman may at his discretion waive this requirement if it was not reasonably practical for the complaint to be made earlier and/or there are other extenuating circumstances and

(iv) the matter giving rise to the complaint first occurred after April 4, 1994 and

      (v) except where relevant new and substantial evidence is available, the subject matter of the complaint has not been previously considered by the Ombudsman and

     (vi) except where the Member consents in writing to the Ombudsman's investigation, the matter giving rise to the complaint has not been or become the subject of proceedings before any court, arbitrator or other independent conciliation body.

(18) The Ombudsman shall in his absolute discretion decide whether or not a complaint falls within Article III hereof and in reaching this decision he shall consider representations from the complainant and the member.

(19) The Ombudsman shall not be bound or in any way limited by any previous decision made by him or by any predecessor in his office.

Procedures

(20) Subject to the other provisions of these Terms of Reference, the Ombudsman shall in his absolute discretion decide the procedure to be adopted in considering complaints and may, without prejudice to the generality of the foregoing, conduct an investigation into a complaint entirely by means of an oral hearing. He shall act impartially and fairly in all circumstances.

(21) The Ombudsman shall require the complainant or Member to furnish to him, for the purpose of his investigation:

      (i) such information which is within his or its knowledge or reasonably ascertainable by him or it;

     (ii) such documents in his or its possession or under his or its possession or control

as is, are or may be relevant to the complaint. Where a Member refuses to supply such information within a reasonable period of time, the Ombudsman shall inform the Council, the Board and any other relevant organisation.

(22) In all cases investigated, the Ombudsman shall notify all parties of the decision and give the reasons in writing. Where a Member refuses to comply with the Ombudsman's decision, the Ombudsman shall notify the Board and the Council which shall have power to require publication of the non-compliance.

(23) The Ombudsman shall not be bound by any legal rule of evidence.

Exclusions

(24) The Ombudsman shall not:

     (a) investigate matters concerning funeral businesses which are not members of the Scheme.

     (b) investigate matters concerning amounts above £100,000.

(c) investigate a complaint or shall discontinue his investigation if:
  (i) the complaint relates to services provided to an individual by virtue of the fact that he (or his spouse) is an employee or former employee of a Member;
  (ii) at any time it appears to the Ombudsman that it is more appropriate for the complaint to be dealt with by a court, or under another independent complaints procedure, or an arbitration arrangement;
  (iii) the action is the subject of proceedings in a court of law or has been the subject of such proceedings in which a judgment on the merits has been given;
  (iv) the complaint relates to a matter or matters that took place before April 4, 1994;
  (v) the complaint has not been considered by the management of the Member, although this shall not prevent the Ombudsman considering complaints which have not been resolved to the satisfaction of the complainant within six weeks of the original complaint being lodged with the Member;
  (vi) the complaint is out of time.
(d) In all cases which the Ombudsman decides not to investigate, he will notify the decision to the complainant and state the reasons for it.

OMBUDSMEN

VOTING MEMBERS OF THE
BRITISH AND IRISH OMBUDSMEN ASSOCIATION*

Banking   A3.01

Banking Ombudsman,
70 Gray's Inn Road,
London, WC1X 8NB

Broadcasting

Broadcasting Standards Commission,
7 The Sanctuary,
London, SW1P 3JS

Building Societies

Building Societies Ombudsman,
Millbank Tower,
Millbank,
London, SW1P 4XS

Estate Agents

Ombudsman,
Ombudsman for Estate Agents,
Beckett House,
4 Bridge Street,
Salisbury,
Wiltshire, SP1 2LX

Funerals

The Funeral Ombudsman,
26 Bedford Row,
London, WC1R 4HE

* Irish members are excluded from this list because of the scope of this book.

Health Services

Health Service Ombudsman

England

Millbank Tower,
Millbank,
London, SW1P 4QP

Scotland

28 Thistle Street,
Edinburgh, EH2 1EN

Wales

Capital Tower,
Greyfriars Road,
Cardiff, CF1 3AG

Housing

Independent Housing Ombudsman,
Norman House,
105–109 The Strand,
London, WC2R 0AA

Insurance

Insurance Ombudsman,
City Gate One,
135 Park Street,
London, SE1 9EA

Investment

The Investment Ombudsman,
4th Floor,
6 Frederick's Place,
London, EC2R 8BT

Legal Services

Legal Services Ombudsman,
22 Oxford Court,
Oxford Street,
Manchester, M2 3WQ

Legal Services (Scotland)

Scottish Legal Services Ombudsman,
Mulberry House,
16 Picardy Place,
Edinburgh, EH1 3JT

Local Government (England)

Local Government Ombudsman,
21 Queen Anne's Gate,
London, SW1H 9BU

Local Government (Scotland)

Commissioner for Local Administration in Scotland,
23 Walker Street,
Edinburgh, EH3 7HX

Local Government (Wales)

Commissioner for Local Administration in Wales,
Derwen House,
Court Road,
Bridgend, CF31 1BN

Parliamentary Commissioner

Parliamentary Commissioner for Administration,
Millbank Tower,
Millbank,
London, SW1P 4QP

Parliamentary Commissioner (Northern Ireland)

Northern Ireland Parliamentary Commissioner for Administration and
Commissioner for Complaints,
33 Wellington Place,
Belfast, BT1 6HN

Pensions

Pensions Ombudsman,
11 Belgrave Road,
London, SW1V 1RB

Personal Investment

Personal Investment Authority Ombudsman,
Hertsmere House,
Hertsmere Road,
London, E14 4AB

Police Complaints

Police Complaints Authority,
10 Great George Street,
London, SW1P 3AE

Police Complaints (Northern Ireland)

Independent Commission for Police Complaints for Northern Ireland,
Chamber of Commerce House,
22 Great Victoria Street,
Belfast, BT2 7LP

COUNTY COURT PRECEDENTS

In the Bigtown County Court　　　　　　　　　　Case No.　　　**A4.01**

BETWEEN:

　　　　　　Robert Lowe　　　　　　　　Claimant

　　　　and

　　　　New Antiques Ltd　　　　　　　Defendants

PARTICULARS OF CLAIM

1. By an oral agreement made between the Claimant and the Defendant on December 1, 1998 the Defendant sold to the Claimant a pair of antique vases for £1,400 and the Claimant paid that sum to the Defendant. Attached to these particulars is a copy of the receipt for purchase.

2. It was an implied condition of the sale that the Defendant had a right to sell the vases.

3. The Defendant was in breach of this implied condition because he had no right to sell. On or about January 3, 1999 the police seized the vases on the ground that they belonged to a Mr Jones and that they were stolen from him by an unknown person who had sold them to the Defendant.

4. The Defendant has refused to refund the £1,400 (or any part of it) to the Claimant.

5. By reason of the matters set out above the Claimant is entitled to the return of £1,400 as money paid for a consideration which has wholly failed.

6. The Claimant is also entitled to interest under section 69 of the County Courts Act 1984 at the rate of 8 per cent per annum from December 1, 1998 until today's date (£56) and further interest at the rate of 0.31p per day until judgment or earlier payment.

And the Claimant claims
(a) £1,400 and interest as set out above.
(b) Costs

[I believe] [the claimant believes] that the facts stated in [this claim form] [these particulars of claim] are true.

In the Bigtown County Court   Case No.   **A4.02**

BETWEEN:

Robert Lowe   Claimant

and

Reliable Karsales Ltd   Defendant

PARTICULARS OF CLAIM

1. By an agreement made in writing dated November 1, 1998 the Defendant sold to the Claimant a second-hand Bonecrusher car registration
   number M123 ABC at a price of £5,000, a copy of the sales receipt being
   attached to these particlars.

2. During the negotiations for the sale the Claimant was informed by one
   Woodroffe, an employee of the Defendant, that the engine was "good as
   new" and had done only 3,000 miles. This statement was an express term
   of the contract. Alternatively it was a misrepresentation which induced
   the Claimant to enter into the contract.

3. It was an implied condition of the contract that the car was of satisfactory
   quality and reasonably fit for the Claimant's purpose.

4. On or about January 10, 1999 the Claimant took the car to a garage for
   repair and was then informed that the engine had done 30,000 miles and
   that it was worn out and that it would cost £1,000 to replace.

5. The Defendant is accordingly in breach of the representation in paragraph 2 above and the express and implied terms under paragraphs 2 and
   3 above.

6. The Claimant then wrote to the Defendant rejecting the car by reason of
   the misrepresentation and/or the breaches of contract and claiming the
   return of his £5,000 but the Defendant refused and has continued to
   refuse to accept the rejection.

7. On February 10, 1999 the Claimant hired an alternative Screecher
   vehicle from Carhire Ltd and has paid a weekly hire charge of £100 per
   week, a copy of the hire agreement being attached to these particulars.

8. The Claimant has not used the Bonecrusher car since giving notice of rejection and it has at all material times been available for collection by the Defendant.

9. The Claimant is entitled to rescind, and has rescinded, the contract by reason of the misrepresentation by the Defendant. Similarly the Claimant is entitled to treat, and has treated, the contract as discharged by the Defendant's breaches.

10. Alternatively, the Claimant is entitled to damages under section 2(1) of the Misrepresentation Act 1967 and/or under section 53 of the Sale of Goods Act 1979 in the sum of £3,000 (being the amount by which the price of £5,000 and the hire-charges of £2,000 exceed the current value of the car namely £4,000) plus further damages to cover additional hire charges of £100 per week until judgment or earlier payment.

11. Under section 69 of the County Courts Act 1984 the Claimant is also entitled to interest at such rate and for such period as the court thinks just.

And the claimant claims:

1. Under paragraph 9 £5,000;

2. Alternatively, under paragraph 10 damages for misrepresentation and/or for breach of contract;

3. Under paragraph 11 above interest under section 64 of the County Courts Act 1984.

4. Costs

[I believe] [the claimant believes] that the facts stated in [this claim form] [these particulars of claim] are true.

In the Bigtown County Court   Case No.   **A4.03**

BETWEEN:

JOHN LOWE   Claimant

(A child, by ROBERT LOWE, his
        litigation friend)

                        and

TOY IMPORTERS LTD   Defendants

PARTICULARS OF CLAIM

1. On January 4, 1998 Robert Lowe the father and litigation friend of the Claimant bought a catapult for the Claimant (then aged eight) from Rundown Stores Ltd a company now in liquidation.

2. The said Robert Lowe has been informed by the liquidator that Rundown Stores Ltd purchased all their catapults from the Defendants who imported them from Taiwan. Accordingly under section 2(2)(c) of the Consumer Protection Act 1987 the Defendants are liable for damage under the Act.

3. The catapult was defective within section 3 of the 1987 Act and when it was first used by the Claimant it broke and a piece entered his left eye.

PARTICULARS OF DEFECT

The moulded plastic which formed the catapult frame was too weak to withstand normal use by a child.

4. By reason of the defect the Claimant has suffered damage within section 5 of the 1987 Act.

PARTICULARS OF DAMAGE

The Claimant was born on November 1, 1991 and is now aged eight years. He suffered acute pain and suffering and underwent two operations in an unsuccessful attempt to save the sight of his left eye. Full particulars are set out in the medical report served with these Particulars of Claim.

PARTICULARS OF PAST AND FUTURE EXPENSES AND LOSSES

Full particulars are set out in the statement which is served with these Particulars of Claim.

5. The Claimant is also entitled to interest under section 69 of the County Courts Act 1984 for such periods and at such rate as the court thinks just.

And the claimant claims:

1. Under paragraphs 3 and 4—damages in excess of £15,000;

2. Under paragraph 5—interest under section 69 of the County Courts Act 1984.

3. Costs

[I believe] [the claimant believes] that the facts stated in [this claim form] [these particulars of claim] are true.

In the Bigtown County Court   Case No.   **A4.04**

BETWEEN:

                    Robert Lowe   Claimant

                and

            Ghastly Holidays Ltd (1)   Defendants
            Eesipay Ltd (2)

                    PARTICULARS OF CLAIM

1. By an agreement in writing ("the agreement") dated January 10, 1998
   the First Defendant agreed to provide a skiing holiday for the Claimant
   and his wife and son, a copy of the relevant page in the brochure being
   attached to these particulars of claim.

2. The Claimant paid the sum of £2,000 for the holiday by means of a credit
   card issued by the Second Defendant under arrangements made between
   the First and Second Defendants. The agreement between the Claimant
   and the Second Defendant was therefore a fixed sum restricted use
   debtor-creditor-supplier agreement falling within section 75 of the Consumer Credit Act 1974. A copy of the claimant's credit card account
   showing the payment made by the claimant through the second defendant to the first defendant is attached to these particulars of claim.

3. It was an express term of the contract between the Claimant and the First
   Defendant that the Claimant and his family would stay at the Ski Palace
   Hotel which was described in the First Defendant's brochure as a "first
   class luxury hotel".

4. In breach of the said term the Claimant and his family were unable to stay
   at the Ski Palace Hotel because it was still in the course of construction.
   They were compelled to accept accommodation at the Backstreet Mews
   Hotel which was not a first class luxury hotel.

                        PARTICULARS

   1. There was no bar.

   2. There was no lift.

3. The walls were peeling.

4. The Claimant and his family were unable to sleep because of the noise from a nearby discotheque.

5. In consequence of the said breach the Claimant's holiday was ruined and he and his family came home more tired than when the holiday started.

6. The Claimant is entitled to the return of the £2,000 as money paid on a total failure of consideration or alternatively as damages for loss of enjoyment and mental distress.

7. The Claimant is also entitled to interest under Section 69 of the County Courts Act 1994 at such rate and for such period as the court thinks fit.

And the Claimant claims against the First and Second Defendants jointly and severally:

1. Under paragraph 6 £2,000;

2. Under paragraph 7 interest under section 69 of the County Courts Act 1984.

3. Costs

[I believe] [the claimant believes] that the facts stated in [this claim form] [these particulars of claim] are true.

In the Bigtown County Court   Case No.   **A4.05**

BETWEEN:

Robert Lowe   Claimant

and

Furnishings Ltd   Defendant

PARTICULARS OF CLAIMS

1. By a hire-purchase agreement ("the Agreement") in writing made on November 1, 1997 between the Claimant and the Defendant and bearing number 12345, a copy of which is attached to these Particulars, the Defendant supplied to the Claimant a suite of furniture at a hire-purchase price of £1,500. The Claimant signed the Agreement at the Defendant's store.

2. Under the terms of the agreement the Claimant paid a deposit of £300 and he agreed to pay the balance by twelve monthly instalments of £100 on the first day of each month. The agreement was a regulated consumer credit agreement within the Consumer Credit Act 1974 ("the Act").

3. The Claimant paid the first seven instalments and the goods became "protected" goods within section 90 of the Act. The total paid up sum is £1,000.

4. On June 20, 1998 the Claimant was made redundant and he failed to pay the instalment due on July 1, 1998.

5. On or about September 10, 1998 a driver employed by the Defendant knocked at the door of the Claimant's home and when the door was opened by the Claimant's wife the said driver and another man forced their way into the house and removed the suite. In doing so the Defendant was in breach of section 92(1) of the Act.

6. Under the Act the Claimant is entitled to damages for trespass and to the return of all his payments.

7. Under Section 69 of the County Courts Act 1984 the Claimant is also entitled to interest at such rate and of such period as the court thinks just.

And the Claimant claims against the Defendant:

1. Under Paragraph 6 £1,000 and damages for trespass not exceeding £5,000;

2. Under Paragraph 7 interest under section 69 of the County Courts Act 1984.

3. Costs

[I believe] [the claimant believes] that the facts stated in [this claim form] [these particulars of claim] are true.

INDEX

(References are to paragraph numbers)